SMOKE and MIRRORS

The War on Drugs and the Politics of Failure

Dan Baum

LITTLE, BROWN AND COMPANY
BOSTON NEW YORK TORONTO LONDON

To the memory of my brother Michael

Originally published in hardcover by Little, Brown and Company, 1996
First Back Bay paperback edition, 1997

Library of Congress Cataloging-in-Publication Data

Baum, Dan.
Smoke and mirrors: the war on drugs and the politics of failure / Dan Baum.
1st ed.
p. cm.
Includes bibliographical references.
ISBN 0-316-08412-3 (hc) 0-316-08446-8 (pb)
1. Narcotics, Control of—United States. 2. Drug traffic—United States. I. Title.
HV5825.B37 1996 95-41051
363.4'5'0973—dc20

10 9 8 7 6 5 4 3 2

MV-NY

Published simultaneously in Canada
by Little, Brown & Company (Canada) Limited

Printed in the United States of America

Contents

Author's Note

THIS IS A WORK of journalism, the product of more than 200 interviews and many hours poring over documents. Every effort was made to portray the events herein as they occurred. There are no composite characters in these pages, no anonymous sources, and no pseudonyms. When sources wanted to "go off the record" to tell me something, I asked them instead not to tell me at all. When somebody wants to talk, I've found, they eventually will do so on the record.

Where there was a written record of conversations, or in cases where sources remembered conversation verbatim, dialogue is re-created in quotation marks. Where quotation marks are absent, sources remembered the gist of the conversation, but not its exact wording. Where possible, I asked sources to confirm each others' recollections of shared conversations.

All references to what characters thought, felt, and believed come either from interviews with that person or that person's memoirs.

Notes for each chapter, citing the sources of my information, appear at the back of the book.

Introduction

Mistrust those in whom the impulse to punish is strong.

— *Friedrich Nietzsche*

FOR MORE THAN A QUARTER CENTURY the United States has been on a rampage, kicking in doors and locking people up in the name of protecting its citizens from illegal drugs. Hundreds of billions of dollars into the Drug War, nobody claims victory. Yet we continue, devoted to a policy as expensive, ineffective, delusional, and destructive as government gets.

The country began using police to control the use of certain drugs in 1914. But the "War on Drugs," in name and in spirit, started during the 1968 presidential campaign, when the country discovered how "drugs" could stand in for a host of troubles too awkward to discuss plainly.

The war metaphor worked for Richard Nixon that year. It continues to work for politicians ranging from Jesse Jackson to Jesse Helms because nearly everyone has found a reason to enlist: parents appalled by their teens' behavior, police starved for revenue, conservative politicians pandering to their constituents' moral dudgeon, liberal politicians needing a chance to look "tough," presidents looking for distractions from scandal, whites — and blacks — striving to "explain" the ghetto, editors filling page one, spies and colonels needing an enemy to replace Communists. . . .

The War on Drugs is about a lot of things, but only rarely is it really about drugs.

To sustain this precious metaphor we spend wildly. Adding together local, state, and federal drug budgets, Americans spend more on the Drug War than on private health insurance: $120 *billion* during the Bush years alone. Even the mid-1990s passion to cut spending hasn't dented the drug budget. Under Bill Clinton, the War on Drugs continues to consume more federal dollars than the Commerce, Interior, and State Departments put together. While we argue about whether the country can afford foreign aid, the Environmental Protection Agency, public broadcasting, or the National Endowments for the Arts and the Humanities, the federal drug budget quietly exceeds all of them combined.

But money is only part of the price. At a time when the public debates whether gun laws and wetlands protection violate the Constitution, the War on Drugs concentrates unprecedented police power inside the Beltway, all but eliminating Fourth Amendment rights and turning the attorney general into a kind of urban viceroy who can mete out punishment without trial. The Drug War clogs the courts to the point of breakdown. It keeps more Americans in federal prison for drug crime than were in *for all crimes put together* in 1980. It criminalizes a generation of African-American men, being the main reason a third of all black males in their twenties are under correctional control — jail, prison, probation, or parole.

Moreover, the War on Drugs frequently makes drug problems worse. From scag in Da Nang to crack in the Bronx to superpotent hydroponic marijuana in the schoolyard, waves of enforcement have consistently inspired people to import, sell, and use ever-stronger drugs in ever more dangerous ways.

Costly, destructive, and failing in its stated mission, the War on Drugs is government lunacy beyond the wildest waste-fraud-and-abuse accusations of Rush Limbaugh and Ross Perot. Yet we soldier on, speaking the language of war, writing the budgets of war, carrying the weapons of war, and suffering the casualties of war. We've trapped ourselves in a classic self-fulfilling prophecy. That the merest contact with drugs now may cost you your job, your home, or your freedom only reinforces our belief that drugs radiate a supernatural evil, like Kryptonite. Call it collateral damage: among the things destroyed by the Drug War is our ability to debate our way toward a reasonable approach to drug abuse. As Joycelyn Elders learned, even the mildest questioning of severe prohibition is the closest thing this country has to forbidden speech. For the moment, all paths away from excess are boobytrapped. We're stuck.

~

When Richard Nixon declared his War on Drugs, the conventional wisdom about drugs and crime was that they reflect "more than the character of the pitiful few" who engage in them and instead reveal shortcomings of "the entire society." Three decades later, we believe the opposite. Congress debates a "Personal Responsibility Act" that exonerates society and blames everything from homicide to teenage pregnancy on "crises of individual values."

It's no coincidence that the leading guru of the mid-nineties "values" crusade is the most famous and aggressive drug czar of them all: William Bennett. He pins the country's drug problems — and, lately, crime, teenage pregnancy, and even poverty — simply on bad people with corrupt values. In step with Bennett, Americans each year redefine more and more of what used to be considered social ills as failings of personal character. Since Nixon's "law and order" campaign of 1968, the War on Drugs has walked point for a national retreat from handling crime and drug abuse as symptoms of larger problems — racism, exclusion, injustice, and poverty — for which all Americans bear some responsibility. The appeal is obvious.

As wars will do, the War on Drugs escalated piecemeal, a product of the hopes, fears, and ambitions of people with varying motives and disparate points of view. Some Drug War hawks have labored cynically, others with the best of intentions. *Smoke and Mirrors* is the story of how they kindled Drug War fever and led the country into the intractable mess we call the War on Drugs. A byproduct of that fever, the Drug War in Latin America — well covered by other reporters — is treated only tangentially here. This book isn't a bureaucratic scorecard, either, despite the incessant and wasteful turf wars among drug-fighting agencies. Nor is it a manifesto for legalization, though perhaps it will be useful to those plotting a more humane and cost-effective drug policy. *Smoke and Mirrors* is offered as a map of how we got here, in the hope of suggesting a way back.

Dramatis Personae

(in order of appearance)

DON SANTARELLI: Republican counsel to the House Judiciary Committee; later associate deputy attorney general and then administrator of the Law Enforcement Assistance Administration.

RAMSEY CLARK: President Johnson's attorney general.

EGIL KROGH: deputy to White House domestic policy adviser John Ehrlichman.

JOHN EHRLICHMAN: Richard Nixon's domestic policy adviser.

JOHN MITCHELL: Richard Nixon's attorney general.

WILLIAM REHNQUIST: director of the Justice Department's Office of Legal Counsel; later associate justice and then chief justice of the U.S. Supreme Court.

ROBERT DUPONT: psychiatrist who created the D.C. Narcotics Treatment Administration; later White House drug czar and then director of the National Institute on Drug Abuse.

NICK KOZEL: Robert DuPont's assistant in D.C.; later chief of epidemiology at the National Institute on Drug Abuse.

JEFFREY DONFELD: Egil Krogh's deputy in charge of drug-abuse policy.

GORDON BROWNELL: assistant to Nixon political adviser Harry S. Dent; later West Coast organizer for the National Organization for the Reform of Marijuana Laws.

LLOYD JOHNSTON: creator and administrator of the National High School Survey on Drug Abuse.

BOB HALDEMAN: Nixon's White House chief of staff.

KEITH STROUP: founder of the National Organization for the Reform of Marijuana Laws.

BOB BLAKEY: Notre Dame Law School professor who created the Racketeering Influenced and Corrupt Organizations Act, or RICO.

JEROME JAFFE: director of Illinois's methadone-treatment program, appointed the first drug czar by President Nixon.

JOHN INGERSOLL: director of the Bureau of Narcotics and Dangerous Drugs during the Nixon administration.

MICHAEL SONNENREICH: executive director of President Nixon's Marijuana Commission.

MYLES AMBROSE: President Nixon's commissioner of Customs; later director of the Office of Drug Abuse Law Enforcement, or ODALE.

PAUL GOLDSTEIN: researcher of the street culture of drug abusers and co-author of *Taking Care of Business*.

PETER BOURNE: British-born psychiatrist, drug policy adviser to both Governor and President Jimmy Carter.

BOB RANDALL: medical-marijuana activist; the first legal marijuana smoker in the United States.

KEITH SCHUCHARD: a founder of the antidrug parents' movement; under the name Marsha Mannatt authored *Parents, Peers & Pot*.

SUSAN RUSCHE: antiparaphernalia activist and founder of National Families in Action.

CARLTON TURNER: pharmacologist and director of the marijuana farm at the University of Mississippi; later President Reagan's drug czar.

LEE DOGOLOFF: Peter Bourne's assistant and then successor as drug czar.

BUDDY GLEATON: co-founder and president of PRIDE.

IAN MACDONALD: Florida pediatrician and parents' antidrug activist; later head of federal drug-abuse agency and Carlton Turner's successor as drug czar.

PETER BENSINGER: administrator of the Drug Enforcement Administration under Presidents Nixon, Ford, Carter, and Reagan.

PEGGY MANN: prominent and prolific antidrug journalist.

ANDY KOWL: founding editor of *High Times* magazine; later publisher of a drug-paraphernalia-industry newsletter.

H. ROSS PEROT: organizer of the Texans' War on Drugs and Carlton Turner's political sponsor.

DICK WILLIAMS: behind-the-scenes manager of the White House drug policy office under Presidents Nixon, Carter, and Reagan.

DAVID STOCKMAN: director of President Reagan's Office of Management and Budget.

WILLIAM FRENCH SMITH: President Reagan's first attorney general.

LOWELL JENSEN: William French Smith's number two deputy.

RUDOLPH GIULIANI: William French Smith's number three deputy.

PAT BURCH: wife of Republican National Committee chair Dean Burch and president of the National Federation of Parents for Drug-Free Youth.

WILLIAM VON RAAB: President Reagan's commissioner of Customs.

ED MEESE: President Reagan's senior adviser; later Reagan's attorney general.

JOSEPH RUSSONIELLO: U.S. attorney in San Francisco.

STEPHEN JACOBS: public relations consultant who created antidrug comic books.

KAREN NORTON: imprisoned by Straight Inc. for eighteen months.

REP. BILL HUGHES (D-NJ): chair of the House Subcommittee on Crime.

ERIC STERLING: member of Bill Hughes's staff.

JAMES REILLEY: defense attorney who argued both *Illinois v. Gates* and *Illinois v. Rodriguez* to the U.S. Supreme Court.

WILLIAM BENNETT: philosophy professor, chairman of the National Endowment for the Humanities; later, President Reagan's secretary of education and then George Bush's drug czar.

KURT SCHMOKE: prosecutor in Baltimore; later mayor of Baltimore.

CLAIRE COLES: neonatal researcher in Atlanta.

JOHN WALTERS: William Bennett's lieutenant at NEH, and Education; later ONDCP deputy director for supply reduction.

ARNOLD WASHTON: director of the 1-800-COCAINE hotline.

LEN BIAS: University of Maryland basketball star, signed by the Boston Celtics the day he died of cocaine poisoning.

DELBERT J. LACEFIELD: chief of the Federal Aviation Administration's forensic toxicology unit working under contract to the Federal Railroad Association on the Amtrak-Conrail crash.

ADMIRAL PAUL YOST: commandant of the U.S. Coast Guard.

BRUCE CARNES: a Bennett aide at NEH and the Department of Education; later budget director of ONDCP.

TERENCE PELL: Bennett's personal lawyer at the Department of Education; later chief counsel of ONDCP.

PAUL MCNULTY: director of communications at the Justice Department during the Bush administration.

JENNIFER JOHNSON: the first woman prosecuted for prenatal drug use.

JEFF DEEN: Jennifer Johnson's prosecutor and inventor of the cocaine-delivery-through-the-umbilical-cord principle.

DAVID TELL: Bennett's speechwriter at the Department of Education; later co-author of Bennett's National Drug Control Strategies.

DAN CASSE: another Bennett aide from the Department of Education; later co-author of Bennett's National Drug Control Strategies.

MICHAEL QUINLAN: director of the federal Bureau of Prisons during the Bush administration.

BRUCE LAVOIE: occasional marijuana user killed by police in Hudson, New Hampshire.

REGGIE WALTON: D.C. criminal courts judge appointed deputy director of state and local drug policy at Bennett's ONDCP.

BENJAMIN H. RENSHAW III: Justice Department statistician under the Reagan, Bush, and Clinton administrations.

RICHARD WEATHERBEE: drug-policy coordinator for Attorney General Richard Thornburgh.

RICHARD THORNBURGH: attorney general under President George Bush.

TOM FITZGERALD: presiding judge of Cook County Criminal Court, creator of Chicago's Night Drug Court.

MARK DAVIS: writer of President Bush's major speech on drugs.

CHRISS WINSTON: deputy director of White House communications under President Bush.

DAVID DEMEREST: White House communications director under President Bush.

JACK MILLFORD: second-in-command of the DEA's D.C. field office and instigator of the Lafayette Park drug buy for President Bush's speech.

SAM GAYE: the DEA agent who bought the crack for President Bush's speech prop.

KEITH JACKSON: eighteen-year-old lured to Lafayette Park to sell the DEA the crack for President Bush's speech.

MARION BARRY: mayor of Washington, D.C.

DONNY CLARK: Floridian sent to federal prison for marijuana crime for which he'd already served a state sentence.

WILLIAM BARR: deputy attorney general under Richard Thornburgh, and later attorney general for President Bush.

BOB MARTINEZ: William Bennett's successor at ONDCP under President Bush.

JAMES O. MASON: chief of the Public Health Service under President Bush who cancelled the program giving marijuana experimentally to the sick.

THOMAS KLINE: Idahoan arrested after writing pro-legalization letter to his local newspaper.

GARY SPENCER: Los Angeles County drug detective who searched the home of, and ultimately killed, Donald Scott.

DONALD SCOTT: Los Angeles millionaire killed by police in mistaken marijuana raid.

JAMES GRAY: Orange County superior court judge who became a legalization advocate.

JOE HICKS: director of the Los Angeles office of the Southern Christian Leadership Conference.

BEN BANTA: press secretary for ONDCP under President Bush.

ALLEN ST. PIERRE: assistant national director of NORML.

JOYCELYN ELDERS: President Clinton's first surgeon general.

Drug use — especially heavy drug use — destroys human character. It destroys dignity and autonomy, it burns away the sense of responsibility, it subverts productivity, it makes a mockery of virtue.

— *William Bennett to the Kennedy School of Government at Harvard, December 11, 1989*

Virtue itself turns vice, being misapplied;
And vice sometime's by action dignified.

— Romeo and Juliet, *II, iii*

SMOKE and MIRRORS

Prologue: Law and Order
1967–1968

We have been talking a long time about color, when in fact we should also be talking about conduct.

— *Republican Senate leader Everett Dirksen, 1967*

FOR A YOUNG REPUBLICAN on the make, 1967 was a gloomy time to be laboring in Washington.

Don Santarelli felt sidelined. Slim, dark, and elegant at thirty-one, he held both a law degree and a master's in rhetoric from the University of Virginia and had burned through two years as a prosecutor in the District of Columbia. Then, because young conservatives were rare in the late sixties and Santarelli was demonstrably brilliant, the Republicans in the House of Representatives reached down and plucked him up to be minority counsel to the House Judiciary Committee.

But the title was grander than the job; the entire committee had only three lawyers on staff.* Democrats had held the White House for the past six years, and LBJ seemed a shoo-in for a second full term. The GOP's last effort to win the presidency — Barry Goldwater's 1964 campaign — had been an agonizing joke. As for Congress, it had been Democratic for a generation and was likely to stay that way. Few in Dixie were likely to vote for the party of Abraham Lincoln, and the "labor/Negro coalition" kept a lock on the populous industrial Northeast. Lawyering for congressional Republicans was largely a game of obstruction and catch-up.

* In 1993 the committee would have thirty lawyers on staff.

All through the summer of 1967, Santarelli and his Republican mentors debated what issue the GOP could make its own. Anti-Communism wouldn't cut it; the president was escalating the anti-Communist war in Vietnam. The economy was thriving on the war. Inflation and unemployment were low. Landing a punch on the Democrats was going to be tough.

From where he sat at Judiciary, though, Santarelli thought the Democrats had set themselves up for a fall. Ever since JFK, the country had been trying to satisfy the demands of the civil rights movement by spending money. Ruddy with postwar wealth and convinced they could solve any problem through sound management and substantial investment, Americans at first applauded the massive social spending of the Democrats' "Great Society." As recently as 1964 most whites told pollsters the effort to end racial inequality was moving ahead either "just right" or "not fast enough."

Three years later, however, poverty hadn't succumbed to the quick fix Americans seemed to expect. Blacks were angrier than ever, their rhetoric evolving from Martin Luther King's tempered Christianity to the hot rage of Stokely Carmichael and the Panthers. The temperature could hardly go over eighty without another city going up in flames. Watts in '65, Cleveland and Chicago in '66, and 1967 was turning out to be the longest and hottest of them all, with blacks rioting in eleven cities at once. Night after night television offered grainy images from Newark and Milwaukee that looked more like the madness in Stanleyville or Algiers. White Americans were complaining to reporters that after putting up with sit-ins and marches, higher taxes and busing, they could hardly go downtown anymore because they never knew when the colored were going to "get whitey." Whenever Santarelli came across such quotes, he made a note of them.

At the same time the riots were erupting, street crime was on the rise. Social scientists invariably warned against making too much of the FBI's annual release of increasingly grim statistics; the baby boom was coming of age, and a growing population of young men naturally increases crime without indicating a societal slide toward lawlessness. But such academic mumbling was shoved aside by the 1967 numbers, which revealed that the number of blacks arrested for homicide had nearly doubled in seven years. Black murder was an image that stuck.

So did the image of the black junkie. Heroin deaths, arrests, and seizures all climbed during the sixties and, with them, the kinds of crime associated with addicts — burglary, petty theft, and mugging. Nobody knew exactly how many heroin addicts there were, but the usual estimates ranged from a quarter to half a million, mostly in New

York, Detroit, and Chicago. The profile of a 1967 addict was much like that of a 1947 addict or, for that matter, a 1987 addict: over thirty and male, usually but not always black. It was a manageable population epidemiologically, but heroin — combined with race riots and incendiary crime statistics — gave Americans one more reason to sour on their short-lived attempt to improve the lot of minorities. By 1967, a majority of whites told pollsters efforts to end racial inequality were "moving ahead too fast."

Santarelli kept that poll in his desk drawer. Finally, it seemed, the country was turning against the Democrats' big-government agenda of social spending. Crime — Santarelli's personal bailiwick — was the issue turning the tide.

To Santarelli's amazement, the Democrats didn't seem to be paying attention. LBJ convened a commission to study crime, and when Santarelli read the report, he could hardly believe his eyes. What did the Katzenbach Commission recommend? More handouts! "Warring on poverty, inadequate housing, and unemployment is warring on crime," the report read. "Medical, psychiatric, and family counseling services are services against crime. More broadly and importantly, every effort to improve life in America's inner cities is an effort against crime."

Katzenbach even recommended the government stop enforcing laws against drug abuse. "The application of these laws often tends to discriminate against the poor and subcultural groups in the population," the commission said, so that "poverty itself becomes a crime."

To the Republican members of the Judiciary Committee, the embodiment of the Democrats' outdated thinking was LBJ's attorney general, Ramsey Clark. The country's top law enforcement officer, Clark seemed to them more social worker than cop, preaching that it wasn't the criminals' fault they were robbing and looting and mugging, it was everybody else's fault. Republicans felt Clark had let the Justice Department's criminal division fall idle, and they deplored one of his biggest legislative achievements: he had strengthened the hand of *defendants*. Now prosecutors had to prove a suspect was dangerous before a judge could deny bail. "Crime reflects more than the character of the pitiful few who commit it," Clark wrote. "It reflects the character of the entire society. . . . What [criminals] are and what they experienced came largely from society — from its influence on them and on their forebears." There's no point in locking up individuals, Clark explained to the Judiciary Committee, until we get about examining the root causes of their criminality.

Root causes. That concept, lying at the heart of everything the

Great Society stood for, rankled Republicans. A black man snatches a white woman's purse and *she's* suppósed to feel guilty! Santarelli and his colleagues figured their best shot at the Democrats was to cast the Great Society as a soft-headed failure at preventing crime and the Republican platform as the path back to law and order. They began drafting a crime bill full of tough measures to catch and punish miscreants.

Nobody foresaw the War on Drugs in 1967. But the GOP strategy would lead directly to its invention barely a year later at the culmination of the presidential campaign. For the GOP to bury the Great Society, it would have to convince Americans that people are poor and violent not because of grand social pressures the mainstream can correct, but because they are bad individuals deserving only of discipline and punishment. In this context, drug use was the perfect crime on which to focus. While stealing to feed one's family might conceivably be excused, drug taking could be framed as purely escapist and pleasure driven. In the War on Drugs, users would come to provide a bottomless well of villains and scapegoats for administrations looking to unburden the electorate of taxes, shed federal responsibilities, and divert attention from their own failures.

Santarelli, working on the big new crime bill, unwittingly assembled prototype weapons for the coming War on Drugs. He first tinkered with an idea to get at the addicts and pushers LBJ's commission wanted to coddle. No longer should they be able to flush their heroin down the toilet while police waited politely at the front door, listening to the furtive gurgling of the plumbing. Santarelli's law would let police executing drug-related search warrants kick down doors without warning. Santarelli called this provision "no-knock."

He also had in his desk three recent newspaper clippings about suspects committing violence while on bail, and he began laying out a bill to reverse Clark's bail initiative: Santarelli would put the burden back on the defendant to prove he should be released pending trial. Santarelli called his provision "preventive detention."

Both no-knock and preventive detention would be fixtures of the War on Drugs by the mid-1980s, but in 1967 they were radical departures in criminal law. Santarelli had no illusions that either provision would pass the Democratic Congress. But he submitted them anyway. It would be fun to watch the Democrats argue during an election year *against* helping police bust drug pushers and *against* locking up dangerous criminals.

~

In October 1967, the *Reader's Digest* published an article that framed the crime question precisely the way Santarelli and his mentors wanted it. "Our opinion leaders have gone too far in promoting the doctrine that when a law is broken, society, not the criminal, is to blame," it argued. The country should stop looking for the "root causes" of crime and put its money instead into increasing the number of police. America's approach to crime must be "swift and sure" retribution. "Immediate and decisive force," the article concluded, "must be the first response."

Its author was former vice president Richard Nixon, on the eve of his campaign for the presidency.

~

The ghetto wasn't the only place disorder reigned in 1967. When Americans flipped the channel from the race riots, similar images beamed from the country's most prestigious college campuses — lines of helmeted police, clouds of tear gas, flailing nightsticks. The antiwar movement was dragging legions of perfectly nice kids into what many saw as a frightening "counterculture" of insubordination, poor grooming, and promiscuous sex. To the offensive blare of rock and roll, young people were burning the flag, tearing up draft cards, praising the enemy, ridiculing everything their parents represented. The whole country seemed to be coming unglued, with blacks tearing down one side and the kids tearing down another.

It was in the hands of rebellious hippies that most Americans first saw wrinkled little cigarettes of marijuana. In 1967, pot wasn't feared much as a health threat; it was the "soft" drug beside heroin and the hallucinogens. From the start, the country understood marijuana as a cultural symbol with political punch. Gallup got it: the polling company measured the connection between marijuana and politics and tabulated the results in two neat columns — demonstrators and nondemonstrators — showing vastly more demonstrators had tried pot. LBJ's commission on campus unrest got it: "If the rest of the society wears short hair, the member of this youth culture wears his hair long. If others are clean, he is dirty. If others drink alcohol and illegalize marijuana, he denounces alcohol and smokes pot . . . by all these means, he declares himself an alien in a large society with which he is fundamentally at odds." Yippie leader Jerry Rubin got it: "Smoking pot makes you a criminal and a revolutionary," he said. "As soon as you take your first puff, you are an enemy of society." And J. Edgar Hoover got it: "Since the use of marijuana and other narcotics is widespread among members of the New Left," he memoed his agents, "you should be alert to opportunities to have them arrested by local authorities on drug charges."

~

Marijuana and heroin had little in common. Both were imported psychoactives, but the drugs were as pharmacologically and culturally different as Tylenol and Prozac. Impoverished middle-aged inner-city addicts shot heroin for one set of reasons; affluent college kids smoked pot for another.

The media, however, combined the two drugs into a single story. Heroin addicts in New York City began appearing in the same news accounts as teenyboppers smoking reefer. It is "incontrovertibly clear," *Newsweek* reported in a dispatch typical of the day, that "the age of US drug users is dropping rapidly, sometimes reaching down into elementary schools." The article offered no data. Instead, on the same page as vivid photos of junkies overdosing in Harlem, the authors quoted principals saying they'd found young teenagers smoking pot in school bathrooms. *Life* magazine scrambled the stories further. "Drug abuse and marijuana, once confined to the shadowy underworld of junkie row, are now very much in the open," it wrote.

What the magazines called drug abuse was in 1967 almost entirely a matter of young people smoking pot; barely a hundredth as many Americans shot heroin. Conflating the two drugs, the media made the country's "drug problem" appear infinitely more threatening than it was; drugs became a bigger story.

Richard Nixon and congressional Republicans benefited directly from this blurring of the distinction between marijuana and heroin. Broadly defined, drugs were common to the cultures of both urban blacks and college hippies, and Republicans were eager to link race rioters with campus protesters. "Disturbances and demonstrations are lumped together" in the public mind, read a memo circulating through the Johnson White House, "and the blame for these civil disorders is placed on the Administration."

By the end of 1967 almost half of all Americans said they'd turn in their own kids to the police if they found them using drugs.

~

President Johnson recognized he was being painted as "soft on crime" and set out to stiffen the crime-fighting image of Ramsey Clark. In so doing, LBJ inadvertently began a trend that would come to define the War on Drugs: the concentration of more and more police power inside the Washington Beltway. Johnson chose to make Ramsey Clark look tough by turning him into a bona fide drug fighter.

Until 1967, the federal government had a tiny role in drug enforcement and the Justice Department no role at all. There was no War on Drugs. Customs seized what it could at the border, the Treasury Department's diminutive Federal Bureau of Narcotics made a feeble attempt at investigating heroin rings, and a wing of the Food and Drug Administration regulated pharmaceuticals. Johnson tried to get J. Edgar Hoover to add drug enforcement to the FBI's mission, which would have brought it under Clark. Hoover, though, refused. In sixty years of running the FBI Hoover was notorious among police for never allowing his agents to work undercover on narcotics. Protective of his agency's reputation, Hoover knew what legions of police chiefs had learned the hard way, that narcotics enforcement is the type of police work most likely to corrupt cops. There's so much cash involved, and so much opportunity for undercover officers to get cozy with the traffickers, that some amount of corruption is inevitable.

Unable to sway Hoover, Johnson took drug enforcement away from Treasury and yanked the regulatory powers from FDA. He combined them to create an agency in Clark's Justice Department called the Bureau of Narcotics and Dangerous Drugs, or BNDD — the predecessor of the Drug Enforcement Administration. Opposition to the move came from the left. Federal police and prosecutors had always answered to separate authorities — just as they do in state and local governments. The presence of the FBI in Justice was the only exception. Now Johnson wanted to put more enforcers — drug police — in the same department as the country's prosecutors.

Johnson had another idea to polish the federal government's crime-fighting image. He asked Congress to create a new agency to dole out massive assistance to local police departments. Johnson called it the Law Enforcement Assistance Administration, or LEAA. As a means of strengthening the bond between Washington and local police, LEAA was successful beyond LBJ's wildest dreams. At the height of the Drug War, municipal police would become as dependent on Washington as an addict on his pusher.

~

On January 30, 1968, Americans opened their newspapers to find they were in for a longer, bloodier Vietnam War than they'd thought. The reflected *only* the character of the few who commit it and *not at all* the character of society as a whole. While the Democrats wanted "billions more for federal jobs and federal housing and federal welfare," Nixon promised to lead his people out of that quagmire of social guilt and high taxes. His administration would restore "the peace forces as against the criminal forces" and ask little else of the "forgotten Americans" who "go to work and pay their taxes and support their schools and churches." Rather than argue with the critics of either racial discrimination or the Vietnam War, Nixon and the Republicans were learning to discredit them indirectly. Rather than debate policy, they denounced conduct.

As he slogged through the primaries in early 1968, Nixon discovered something about the age of television. People don't have to experience crime firsthand to feel threatened by it, he wrote to his old mentor, Dwight Eisenhower. "I have found great audience response to this [law and order] theme in all parts of the country, including areas like New Hampshire where there is virtually no race problem and relatively little crime."

~

Meanwhile, Nixon's Republican colleagues in Congress bulldozed their big crime bill toward a vote. The cities exploded again after Martin Luther King was murdered in April, boosting the country's appetite for ever-harsher treatment of criminals. By June, preventive detention and no-knock had been dropped, but the crime bill included other fixtures of the War on Drugs to come. It allowed police to use wiretaps in criminal investigations. It weakened the 1966 *Miranda* ruling that required police to read suspects their rights. Congress created LEAA for the lame-duck LBJ to funnel federal money to local police, but as a special slap to Ramsey Clark placed the new agency outside the control of the attorney general. Bobby Kennedy was assassinated the night of June 6. Although Kennedy was a vocal opponent of the proposed changes to *Miranda* and wiretap law, the bill's supporters, in speeches the next day, used the fact of his assassination to argue for its passage. The crime bill passed the Senate that afternoon with only seventeen nay votes.

~

Two months before the election, Nixon stood in the shadow of Disneyland's Matterhorn and put the capstone on his law-and-order campaign by conjuring up a War on Drugs. "As I look over the problems in this country, I see one that stands out particularly," he told a rally of Republican supporters. "The problem of narcotics."

Drugs, Nixon said, "are among the modern curse of the youth, just like the plagues and epidemics of former years. And they are decimating a generation of Americans." Half of all crime in New York, Nixon insisted, was committed by drug addicts. So his administration, he promised, would "accelerate the development of tools and weapons" to fight illegal drugs: a tripled Customs Service, more federal drug agents, massive assistance to local police, and antidrug operations abroad.

"I believe in civil rights," Nixon concluded. "But the first civil right of every American is to be free from violence, and we are going to have an administration that restores that right in the United States of America."

1

A Practical Matter
1969

> [President Nixon] emphasized that you have to face the fact that the whole problem is really the blacks. The key is to devise a system that recognizes this while not appearing to.
>
> — *H. R. Haldeman to his diary*

AS A PRACTICAL MATTER, there was only one problem with Nixon's law-and-order campaign: once he won, he had to deliver, and at that time the federal government had almost no role in keeping the streets safe. From the Founding until Nixon, people looked to their local police to keep order in the neighborhoods. The federal government prosecuted only interstate crime — the Mafia, white-collar fraud, national security, smuggling, civil rights, crimes that crossed state lines. Safe streets were a community matter. But having won the election on a law-and-order promise, Nixon had to create a federal role in policing street crime. This, in large part, would be the job of Egil Krogh Jr.

Then twenty-nine, Egil Krogh was — even by the standards of the Nixon crew — a square. At the age of eleven he'd made a deal with his father: if Dad would stop drinking alcohol and smoking tobacco — both of which he did heavily — "Bud," as junior was called, would never touch either. His father stopped drinking and smoking, and Bud embarked on a life of total abstinence from alcohol or drugs of any kind. Even more fateful for young Krogh was the family friendship with the Ehrlichmans from up the street, whose teenage son, John, took a liking to little Bud.

After a stint in the navy and law school, Krogh went to work in

John Ehrlichman's Seattle firm, one of the first to specialize in environmental law. It was 1968; Ehrlichman was away managing the travel arrangements of Richard Nixon's campaign, and when he was named White House domestic policy adviser he asked his young friend to be deputy. Krogh didn't even take the time to ask his wife; he agreed on the spot and within a week was living in transition headquarters, New York's Hotel Pierre, just down the hall from the president-elect himself.

Shortly before Christmas, Ehrlichman took Krogh aside for a chat. The president-elect wants some ideas on crime, Ehrlichman said, and some recommendations on how to handle the antiwar demonstrations. That's going to be your area, Bud. We're flying down to Washington tomorrow to talk with Roman Hruska.

Republican senator Roman Hruska of Nebraska, ranking minority member of the Senate Judiciary Committee, was the Republicans' Senate point man on crime. Krogh entered Hruska's office with a giddy sense of awe. Barely a month earlier Krogh had been a first-year associate fresh out of law school with no criminal law experience. Now he was at the right hand of the White House domestic policy adviser, shaping criminal law with one of the most powerful men in the United States Senate.

Hruska had a plan: the White House should create a big crime bill specifically for the District of Columbia. As you know, he said, the federal government administers the District directly. This is the one place we can have a hand in the kind of policing people care about. It's a disgrace you can't walk the streets of the nation's capital without worrying about getting mugged. This is the kind of issue that moves people. You send a D.C. crime bill over right after the inauguration and I'll get it passed, Hruska said. It will be good for the White House and good for me.

As Krogh scribbled notes on a legal pad, Hruska dictated what he wanted in the bill. He described the preventive detention and no-knock provisions Santarelli had failed to get into the big national crime bill a year earlier. Taking no chances, Hruska ordered Krogh to take a couple of trusted GOP staff members over to the Justice Department to write the bill. He introduced two dark-suited men no older than Krogh. One was Don Santarelli. The other was the chief Republican counsel in the House, John Dean III.

You take these fellows over to Justice, Hruska told Ehrlichman and Krogh. Have them write the bill and send it to me. I'll do the rest.

~

A couple of weeks after the inauguration, the new attorney general, John Mitchell, convened a meeting at the White House. Mitchell had run Nixon's campaign; he knew what promises had been made and their political importance. Ehrlichman was there, along with Krogh, and from Justice, Mitchell brought his new associate deputy, Don Santarelli.

This administration was elected on a law-and-order platform, Mitchell said. Let's have some ideas about how to deliver.

Krogh and Ehrlichman talked about the D.C. crime bill they were writing. That's fine, Mitchell said. What else?

Santarelli mentioned the new agency LBJ had created to provide federal assistance to local police departments. It's called the Law Enforcement Assistance Administration, or LEAA, Santarelli said, and Congress authorized only $75 million for it the first year. We should think about expanding that, Santarelli said. Shiny new police cars are the kind of thing people notice.

Good idea, Mitchell said.

Street robbery and burglary are the crimes most people fear, an aide chimed in; how about making those crimes federal, launching a big federal initiative on that?

No, no, no, Mitchell said, shaking his huge head and pulling the curved pipe from his mouth. Robbery and burglary are purely local. There is no conceivable federal jurisdiction. Can't you do better than that?

Well, somebody said, there's drugs.

Mitchell nodded approvingly. Drugs were almost entirely imported. Protecting borders was a federal responsibility, and drugs often moved across state lines. I like it, Mitchell said. Problem is, nobody ever hears anything about federal drug enforcement. We'll have to make BNDD more visible to the public. Work on that, would you?

~

The White House considered the *Washington Post* a sworn enemy of Richard Nixon: the paper never gave him a break. But John Ehrlichman had met the *Post*'s owner and publisher, Katherine Graham, at a dinner party and they'd enjoyed each other's wit. Now she was in his office, offering an olive branch.

Crime in this city is out of control, John, she said. My son, Donny, is a D.C. patrolman and you should hear the stories he tells. I've been talking to a few friends of mine, and we think the White House should do something. At a minimum, the District needs a thousand more police officers on patrol.

Ehrlichman was pleased: Graham would be happy when they announced the D.C. crime bill that Krogh was working on for Roman Hruska. Usually, the *Post*'s evening rival, the *Washington Star,* was the friendly paper in the capital. It would be nice to see one issue on which the *Post* could applaud the White House. We're working on something, Kay, Ehrlichman said, and I think you're going to like it.

~

A D.C. crime bill presented a perfect opportunity, Santarelli thought. Congress never fought much about D.C. Few legislators were willing to squander political capital on laws that affected only one city. But any law the administration could pass in D.C. would serve as a model for the rest of the country. The administration could point to D.C. and say, "See how well this worked on a small scale? Now let's pass it nationally." The District could serve as a kind of Spanish Civil War for the coming War on Drugs — a place to field-test new weapons and tactics. The first things he wrote into the new D.C. bill were the provisions that didn't make it into the 1968 crime bill: preventive detention and no-knock.

In addition, Santarelli created something called "loose search warrants" that let police search property not specifically named in the warrant. He proposed extending wiretaps and electronic surveillance to such traditionally privileged conversations as those with doctors, lawyers, and clergy. And he suggested a life sentence for a third felony conviction, although nobody in 1969 thought to call it "three strikes and you're out."

Some of these new provisions were pushing the Bill of Rights pretty hard, Santarelli knew. Nixon's White House and Justice Department were as ideologically conservative as Ramsey Clark had been ideologically liberal, and Santarelli sometimes worried about them doing real violence to the Constitution. The lawyer running the Office of Legal Counsel was a good example. He was young, like Santarelli, and from Arizona. He was smart enough, but doctrinaire, ponderous, and unimaginative. Nixon could never keep his name straight — kept calling him "Renchburg." Rehnquist was too unusual a name for Nixon. In any case, this was the guy who would be checking Santarelli's D.C. bill for constitutionality. Santarelli liked to think of himself as "conservative in a liberal tradition" and sometimes worried about giving people like Rehnquist too much ammunition.

Ultimately, though, Santarelli put his misgivings aside and sent his legislation up to the Hill in good conscience. The law provided checks and balances. Police couldn't get a no-knock warrant without presenting a pretty good stack of evidence to a judge. That was key. As conservative as the executive and legislative branches might become, Santarelli was certain the judiciary would remain liberal. It seemed to Santarelli a fixed truth, as dependable as the firmness of the earth, that the judiciary would always be the liberal branch of government. Judges, especially the justices of the United States Supreme Court, would forever counterbalance whatever the Don Santarellis and William Rehnquists could cook up.

Weeks after sending the preventive-detention portion of Santarelli's D.C. crime bill to Congress, the Justice Department decided to find out if it was good policy as well as good politics. It commissioned a study of people arrested for violent crimes and released on bond during a recent four-week period. While the premise of the bill was that such people are likely to commit another violent act while on bail, the study found that only one out of every twenty did so. As Senator Sam Ervin pointed out in an acid speech, this meant prosecutors could hold nineteen harmless people in order to detain one dangerous suspect. The bill, the inimitable Ervin said, was "as full of unconstitutional, unjust, and unwise provisions as a mangy hound dog is full of fleas." Still, Congress brushed aside both the Justice Department's study and Ervin's objections, passing the D.C. bill largely as Santarelli had written it. Against a hostile majority in both houses of Congress, Richard Nixon had his first big legislative victory and a blueprint for future success. Having lost the White House over the crime issue, Democrats finally were hip to its power and were eager to climb aboard.

Ignoring inconvenient studies like the Justice Department's was just a beginning; the White House was on the lookout for evidence to support the link between drugs and crime. Right in the White House's own backyard, a couple of obscure researchers were about to provide some.

~

This doesn't look like the office of a Harvard-trained psychiatrist, Bob DuPont mused, looking around his dingy green cubicle at the D.C.

Department of Corrections. But this is exactly where I want to be. Great things are coming. I can feel it.

Tall and gangly, DuPont emoted a gollygosh cheerfulness that infected those around him. He'd planned a private psychiatry practice after Harvard Medical School, but as part of his residency he worked at Norfolk Prison, the same Massachusetts lockup where Malcolm Little became Malcolm X. Inmates were fascinating, DuPont found. What drove them to crime? What effect did a prison stretch have on them?

Those questions gnawed at DuPont while he worked as a researcher at the National Institutes of Health in suburban Washington, and he jumped at the chance to take a second job — as an informal adviser and consultant — at the D.C. Department of Corrections. Though lower in prestige and pay than NIH, the Corrections work was a lot more interesting, and in July 1968 DuPont went there full-time as director of community services. "These people can't believe they have a psychiatrist from Harvard and the NIH willing to work fifty hours a week and make so little money," he'd tell people with a laugh. In D.C. he not only had a whole prison system to study and tinker with, it was a prison system at the center of power.

The District was under a microscope. Although D.C. had the lowest murder rate of any major U.S. city, mugging and robbery were high and the perception among D.C. residents was that crime was out of control. Because those residents included members of Congress, White House staff, and top dogs of the news media, District officials were eager to do something — anything — about crime. DuPont had a deskful of ideas for reform of the Corrections Department, including halfway houses and new types of drug treatment. He figured his work here would be noticed.

His plan in the spring of 1969 was to interview every inmate booked into the jail and urine-test as many as possible. Common sense told DuPont that addicts committed crimes to finance their habits. But researchers were barely beginning to study the possible links between drug use and crime. DuPont wanted his own data.

To get it, he hired a squat, energetic Philadelphian named Nick Kozel, who had just finished a Peace Corps stint in Ecuador. Kozel recruited a cadre of students from George Washington University to stand in the gloomy receiving area of the jail and interview newcomers. These were crazy times: some of the interviewers, self-styled revolutionaries, tried to foment rebellion inside the jail — getting nothing but cold stares from the inmates — while others swiped a pile of

"D.C. Dept. of Corrections" T-shirts and started a minor fad on campus. In August and September 1969 they interviewed 229 inmates and got urine samples from 129.

Forty-five percent of the inmates either told Kozel's interviewers they were addicted to heroin or yielded a positive urine sample.

Forty-five percent! DuPont was elated. This was the kind of news that would get his ideas for reform out of his desk and into play.

Wait a minute, Kozel said. Two hundred and twenty-nine men is a small sample, especially when only about half were urine-tested. And even if half the men arrested in D.C. are heroin addicts, that doesn't mean their addiction *caused* crime. We didn't ask them, for example, whether they had criminal records before they started using heroin. Maybe they were criminals first and addicts second.

DuPont wasn't interested in such quibbling. Here was the first scientific support of the conventional wisdom: addicts cause crime. Despite his own misgivings, Kozel helped DuPont write up the findings in a slim article for the *International Journal of the Addictions*. "What is worth noting . . . is the extent to which addiction and criminal activity are linked," they wrote. The article speculated only that addicts commit street crimes *as frequently* as nonaddicts. But the conclusion strayed ominously from the data: "The addict poses a very real threat to property as well as to persons in the community," they wrote.

At any other time, such a small, obscure, and imperfect study might have been quietly ignored. But not in Richard Nixon's Washington. And not with Bob DuPont promoting it.

~

Jeff Donfeld was Richard Nixon's idea of a fine young man. He had hewed to his buttoned-down Republican conservatism all through college, and at UCLA had been the only University of California student body president to speak out against the Free Speech Movement. Donfeld had been openly pleased when the DA in Oakland prosecuted Mario Savio and 772 other unruly protesters. The two assistant DAs on the case particularly impressed Donfeld. One was a tall, patrician lawyer named Lowell Jensen. The other was a bulldog named Ed Meese.

After law school, Donfeld clerked for the law firm of Nixon, Mudge in New York and dated Nixon's daughter Tricia. Like Krogh, Donfeld was a devout Christian who had never gotten high on any substance, even beer. When Krogh was putting together his staff in the new Nixon White House, Donfeld was a natural choice, and since nobody else particularly wanted responsibility for drug abuse, Donfeld took it. At age twenty-six he was now in charge of drug-abuse policy for the Nixon administration.

Though he had no personal experience with drugs or the drug culture, Donfeld understood drugs' political potential. They were showing up as the second or third most pressing concern in poll after poll, just after crime. The two were related, of course: Donfeld had just seen a study the D.C. jail had sent over that absolutely proved the connection between heroin and crime.

Donfeld had another motive for taking a hard line against drug use. He believed strenuously in the Puritan ethic, which demanded that a person be in command of himself at all times. Drugs were not only unhealthy but immoral. Knowing that his boss was equally religious, Donfeld expounded often to Krogh on the moral depravity of drugs. Finally, Krogh cut him off.

That's offensive to me, Krogh said coldly. This isn't a moral issue; the president wants us to bring down the crime rate, and we can do that by lowering the incidence of drug abuse. This is a matter of health and public safety.

Jeff Donfeld was ahead of his time.

∾

Fear and anger, Gordon Brownell thought. That's what got Richard Nixon elected and that's what will keep him in office.

A smooth-faced, heavyset politics junkie of twenty-four, Brownell had a dream job: administrative assistant to Nixon's political manager, Harry S. Dent. Dent had masterminded the so-called "southern strategy" that pried white southerners away from the Democratic Party during the last election by playing to their fear of black power and their anger at the civil rights movement. It had transformed the GOP's image from country-club golfer to defender of working whites fed up with expensive hand-wringing over Negroes and the cities. The strategy worked, but was poorly named. Nixon's win was national, and its most visible new adherents were manifestly northern — union-affiliated former Democrats known loosely as "hardhats."

The White House lived by the principles of the southern strategy, and Dent's office had its own lingo. There were issues that mattered to "our" people, and those that mattered to "their" people. "Their" people were what the White House called "the young, the poor, and the black." The phrase rolled off the tongue like one word: theyoungthepoorandtheblack. The young were the long-haired student antiwar types for whom the president had open and legendary contempt; the poor and the black were leftover concerns from the Great Society.

Brownell daily read a dozen newspapers from around the country and clipped stories that played on those themes. He looked for stories about badly managed social programs, watched for currents of localized resentment, combed the columns for colorful quotes and juicy anecdotes the presidential speechwriters might use. He particularly kept an eye out for drug stories. Drugs were one thing the young, the poor, and the black all seemed to have in common.

Despite Nixon's assertion to the preelection Disneyland crowd that drugs were "decimating a generation of Americans," drugs were so tiny a public health problem that they were statistically insignificant: far more Americans choked to death on food or died falling down stairs as died from illegal drugs.

So Brownell was delighted that the media were inflating the story by melding the tiny "hard drug" heroin threat with the widespread "soft drug" marijuana craze. Marijuana, Brownell knew, was a perfect focus for the anger against the antiwar counterculture that Nixon shared with "his people." Brownell dug out a recent clip from *Newsweek:* "Whether picketing on campus or parading barefoot in hippie regalia, the younger generation seems to be telling [the middle-class American] that his way of life is corrupt, his goals worthless and his treasured institutions doomed. Logically enough, a good many middle-class citizens tend to resent the message." In an article Brownell might have penned himself, *Newsweek* identified the targets of that middle-class resentment this way: "The incendiary black militant and the welfare mother, the hedonistic hippie and the campus revolutionary." *The young, the poor, and the black.* Nixon couldn't make it illegal to be young, poor, or black, but he could crack down hard on the illegal drug identified with the counterculture.

Brownell loved his job and — until he went wildly apostate and joined the opposition — he was good at it.

~

It figures May 19 would be a bad day for the Nixon administration — it was the birthday of both Malcolm X and Ho Chi Minh. It was also, in 1969, the day the Supreme Court sided with drug guru Timothy Leary.

Leary had been arrested four years earlier on a complicated

charge stemming from the 1937 Marihuana Tax Act,* a law that established federal control over marijuana not by banning it but by requiring possessors to pay a tax of $100 an ounce, a great deal of money in 1937. The thinking was that most people wouldn't pay it and could then be arrested for tax evasion.

Customs agents on the Tex-Mex border had found a joint on Leary and charged him with failing to pay the $100-an-ounce transfer tax. Three months later, a federal judge in Texas sentenced him to thirty years in prison and a $30,000 fine.

Leary argued in his appeal that had he paid the tax, he would have been admitting to marijuana possession, a crime in Texas. The tax requirement, therefore, constituted double jeopardy. Earl Warren's Supreme Court agreed, and suddenly, as Woodstock summer loomed, the federal government found itself with no control over the possession of marijuana.

By coincidence it was two days later that Nixon nominated the conservative Warren Burger to replace Earl Warren as chief justice of the United States Supreme Court. The transformation of the Court, which Don Santarelli had thought impossible when writing his get-tough laws, was beginning.

~

City Works was having a rough night at the Irma Hotel. Maybe these kids just didn't like rock and roll. The band pulled out the stops, even tried some well-worn comedy patter, but the San Fernando Valley crowd wasn't buying.

During a break, lead guitarist Tommy Chong asked his singer, Richard Marin, if he could think of some shtick they hadn't tried. Chong, a half-Chinese Canadian, had met Marin in Vancouver, where Marin was sitting out the Vietnam War as a lounge singer. Marin was pretty good at clowning.

"I got a character," Marin said. "But I don't like doing it."

"What is it?"

"It's a low-rider, man. You know, a stoned-out Chicano. But it's kinda demeaning." As a kid, Marin had created a down-and-out Mexican character for laughs; his dad was an LA cop who'd tried to boil any Hispanic identification out of the family. But now Marin was hip to his roots and wary of ethnic sensitivities.

* Until the early 1980s, the drug was referred to by its anglicized spelling in all official publications.

"Sounds great!" Chong said, shoving aside Marin's objections. "He got a name?"

"I used to use the nickname they gave me as a baby," Marin said. "They said I looked like a little pork rind, you know, a *cuchifrito*, so they called me 'Cheech.' "

With that, Cheech and Chong took the stage for the first time, launching the two most wasted potheads in showbiz. Van Nuys went wild. Getting stoned is not only mind-expanding and political, Cheech and Chong told America, it's *funny*.

~

On September 19 the California Medical Association held a press conference to announce its findings about the marijuana "epidemic" among California youth. "Subversive elements have found that drugs can be invaluable," said Dr. Edward Bloomquist, chair of the association's panel. Bloomquist himself had spoken with students who admitted their "inhibitions" were released through drugs supplied by "anarchists." Rebellion and contempt for elders make young people susceptible, Bloomquist said. Standing grimly beside the doctor as he delivered this news was California's governor, Ronald Reagan.*

~

Had the White House been willing to learn it, a tussle with the Mexican government in 1969 might have offered a lesson about how heavy-handed drug enforcement can make the problem worse.

The Mexican government wouldn't crack down on the marijuana trade the way Washington wanted it to. The marijuana problem is on your side of the border, the Mexicans kept telling the Nixon administration. If your people want to buy pot, there's not much we can do. A young Treasury official suggested the U.S. spray Mexican marijuana with herbicides whether the Mexicans approved or not. The U.S. decided not to go that far, but the suggestion would resurface explosively years later. In the meantime, the young official — a former prosecutor and FBI agent — was put to work on a plan to shock the Mexicans into compliance by slamming the border shut. The young official was G. Gordon Liddy. The plan was Operation Intercept.

* This is the same Dr. Bloomquist who, in Hunter Thompson's 1971 classic *Fear and Loathing in Las Vegas*, was keynote speaker at the National District Attorney's Conference on Narcotics and Dangerous Drugs. "In cannabis society," he told the assembled prosecutors to the amusement and disgust of Thompson and his 300-pound Samoan attorney, there are "four states of being: Cool, Groovy, Hip and Square."

On September 21, 1969, the border suddenly squeezed closed. Customs inspectors who usually waved almost everyone through began exhaustively searching every glove compartment, wheel well, backpack, and pocket. The result was predictable chaos, with lines of cars extending for miles. The Mexicans screamed blue murder, then pledged cooperation, and after twenty days the blockade was lifted.

While few arrests were made, Intercept yielded two noticeable effects. First, aerial drug smuggling began on a scale never seen before. "Recently positioned radar installations showed the blips of intruding aircraft from the south," the *New York Times* reported. Second, Intercept succeeded at drying up marijuana supplies temporarily. Whether this was good news, however, was questionable. "I know of four kids — and they're really kids, like under 16 — who've tried smack because they couldn't get grass," one Cambridge, Massachusetts, dealer told *Newsweek*. A doctor running the Haight Ashbury Free Clinic in San Francisco noticed a sudden increase in kids strung out on stronger drugs than pot and was furious. "The government line is that the use of marijuana leads to more dangerous drugs," David Smith told reporters. "The fact is that the *lack* of marijuana leads to more dangerous drugs."

~

As the first year of the Nixon presidency drifted into autumn, White House chief of staff Bob Haldeman asked Nixon's "house liberal," Daniel Patrick Moynihan, to draw up a list foretelling the administration's eight biggest achievements. Moynihan's response was more cheerleading than prophecy. He predicted an early end to a war that would last another four years. He forecast a downturn in prices on the eve of the worst inflation since World War II. And he promised an easing of tensions between blacks and whites that has yet to occur. But he did predict rightly that the rate of crime would slow and Nixon's high-profile drug policy would pay off.

"With respect to the drug traffic," Moynihan wrote, "[the president] will have impressed the nation with the fact that those in high office really know, and really care, about what is going on."

~

The same day Moynihan sent his forecasting memo, Gordon Brownell opened his first newspaper of the day and found a nugget of pure gold.

There in the *New York Daily News* was a report that Art Linkletter's daughter Diane had killed herself while tripping on LSD.

Perfect, thought Brownell. The drug issue occasionally threatened to slip from the attention of Nixon's middle-class constituency — they thought of it as either a ghetto or a campus problem. But Art Linkletter was one of the biggest celebrities in Middle America. If drugs could take his daughter, they could take anybody's.

What better way, also, to dispel the notion that drugs are the fault of murky "root causes"? Diane Linkletter seemed a picture-perfect young lady — rich, white, Christian, and loved. This one can't be laid at the feet of poverty or racism, Brownell thought.

He clipped the story and sent a memo to Harry Dent recommending Nixon pen a personal condolence note to the TV personality. "Hopefully this letter would be released to the press, and even better, it might be read on Linkletter's daily afternoon television program 'Art Linkletter's House Party' which millions of 'Middle America housewives' watch daily to absorb what Linkletter brings to them," Brownell wrote.

Two weeks later, Linkletter appeared at the White House for a hastily assembled bipartisan conference on the drug menace. His presence, Nixon said, "gives a lie to the idea that this is something that simply happens to the poor. It is moving to the upper middle-class and so forth." Linkletter agreed.

"Diane was not a hippie. She was not a drug addict," he said. Rather, she was "a well-educated, intelligent girl from a family that has traditionally been a Christian family and has been straight." Linkletter added categorically that Diane "had no personal problems." It was the drug, and the drug only, that wreaked this tragedy.

~

Health, Education and Welfare secretary Robert Finch was at the Linkletter conference too, to relinquish officially his department's primary role in drug control. Under the big drug bill Nixon was sending up to Congress, health officials and the surgeon general would no longer be responsible for ranking drugs according to their danger and potential for abuse. The job of "scheduling" drugs would fall to the attorney general and his chief narcotics officer. Cops, not doctors, would henceforth judge drugs' toxicity. The bill also did away with the complicated drug tax that Timothy Leary had challenged in his successful marijuana defense and banned drugs outright. This took Treasury out of drug enforcement and, as liberals had feared when Johnson put the BNDD under the Justice Department, culminated a trend. All federal drug-enforcement authority now lay with the Justice Department: prosecutors and narcs answered to the same authority.

It was John Mitchell's first big win. Even after Mitchell was indicted and forced to resign in 1974, the authority to "schedule" drugs remained with the office of attorney general. Although health officials since Finch have sought to reclaim it, none has succeeded.

~

Lloyd Johnston, a graduate student at the University of Michigan's Institute of Social Research, had for three years been sending questionnaires to the same group of 2,200 high school boys — of all races, incomes, and geographic locations — in the hope of learning something about the causes and effects of dropping out of high school. By 1969, when the boys were entering their senior year, he had learned two things: adding questions to established studies is relatively inexpensive, and researching hot topics is a ticket to generous funding. The "teenage drug epidemic" was a hot topic. Newspapers and magazines said "most" high school kids were drug users; estimates ran as high as 70 percent. But the news media's information was anecdotal; studies by academics, as well as by Gallup for *Reader's Digest* and *Newsweek,* had surveyed only adults and college students. Johnston saw an opportunity and tacked a few new questions onto his 1969 questionnaire.

What drugs have you used? Johnston's survey asked. Have you used them in the last year? The last month? The last week? How accessible are drugs? Johnston also included questions about alcohol and tobacco.

When the questionnaires were processed, it emerged, unsurprisingly, that tobacco was the most widely used drug among high school students and about a third of them smoked it every day. Alcohol was next, predictably, with about one-fifth of the students drinking once or twice a week and another fifth once or twice a month.

What surprised Johnston was that nearly 80 percent of the group had never smoked marijuana. Barely 1 percent smoked every day. Other drugs were hardly visible; neither heroin nor cocaine had ever been tried by nine-tenths of the sample. The kids were pretty clean: black, white, rich, poor, grind, and dropout.

This was news, Johnston thought. In the book he and his team rushed together, Johnston wrote that "there certainly was not a widespread 'epidemic' of illegal drug use among these high school students as the popular press had suggested." His interpretation: American youth are "less radical" and "more traditional" than their public image would indicate. "In fact, their continuing adherence to *traditional* practices — namely, the widespread use of alcohol and cigarettes — may ultimately be the most important fact about youthful drug practices to emerge from this study" (emphasis in the original).

~

The antidote to *Art Linkletter's House Party* was *The Dick Cavett Show,* a putative electronic salon for intellectuals. Each week, the urbane Dick Cavett bantered wittily with the nation's intelligentsia. Margaret Mead, for example, wasn't likely to show up on *House Party,* but she and Cavett conversed on October 27 and the subject of marijuana came up. It should be legal, the sixty-seven-year-old anthropologist said, for anyone over sixteen. Prohibition, she said, "is a new form of tyranny by the old over the young. You have the adult with a cocktail in one hand and a cigarette in the other saying 'you cannot' to the child. This is untenable."

The reaction was quick and hot. "Kids are taught patriotism and morality in the classroom," boomed one critic, Governor Claude Kirk of Florida, "but when they get home they see a television set with this dirty old lady on it."

~

Read this with an open mind, Jeff Donfeld urged Egil Krogh.

He handed his boss an article about a couple of researchers in New York, Vincent Dole and Marie Nyswander. They had been experimenting with heroin addicts, trying to get them to kick the habit. Nothing worked very well — counseling, detox, cold turkey — because as soon as the addict hit the street, temptation loomed.

Only one type of treatment showed promise. If addicts took a daily oral dose of a particular synthetic narcotic, they could control their craving for heroin without getting high. Eventually they might reduce the dose and be weaned from drugs. But even if weaning wasn't possible, "maintenance" kept addicts functioning.

Initially, Krogh was repulsed. It seemed too close to the British experiment in which addicts took controlled doses of heroin. The idea of giving addicts a drug, when the function of government should be to break their addiction, was repugnant to the teetotaling Krogh. As you can imagine, Donfeld told him, I had the same reaction.

But as you've said, Donfeld continued, the president was elected to bring down the crime rate, not guard the nation's morals. The addicts in the Dole-Nyswander study commit fewer crimes. Krogh flipped back to the beginning and read the study again. Donfeld was right. Methadone, the new drug the researchers used, was the first really positive news that anyone could remember on the addiction-treatment front.

- Number of Americans who died in 1969 falling down stairs: 1,824.
- Number who choked to death on food: 2,641.
- Number who died from cirrhosis of the liver: 29,866.
- Number who died from legal and illegal drugs: 1,601.

2

The Magic Bullet
1970

> Commercial traffic in deadly mind-soul-and-body-destroying drugs is beyond a doubt one of the greatest evils of our time. It cripples intellects, dwarfs bodies, paralyzes the progress of a substantial segment of our society, and frequently makes hopeless and sometimes violent and murderous criminals of persons of all ages who become its victims. Such consequences call for the most vigorous laws to suppress the traffic as well as the most powerful efforts to put these vigorous laws into effect.
>
> —*Justice Hugo Black, 1970*

THE WASHINGTON RUMOR MILL is like the children's game of telephone. Bob DuPont "had it on good authority": Katherine Graham had read John Ehrlichman the riot act. Personally. Stormed into his office, pounded the desk, and told him: either you bring the crime rate in D.C. down or the *Post* will run an editorial a week denouncing you for breaking your law-and-order promise.

If he had the words wrong, DuPont had the tone right. The White House was on the lookout for anything that held the promise of results. Nixon was still in his first hundred days and already asking Congress for more patrolmen and better street lighting in the capital. He was urging more police powers to search, wiretap, and arrest. And he was revamping the entire D.C. criminal court system to make it work more like a proper state superior court.

DuPont was eager and ready to grab a piece of the crime-control action.

He had a vision: a citywide network of heroin-addiction treatment centers owned and operated by the federal government. It would cost millions. But given the atmosphere in Congress and the White House, DuPont was optimistic that his idea for a D.C. Narcotics Treatment Administration would be eagerly signed into law by a president hot to do something about crime.

DuPont had no illusion that Richard Nixon would be an easy sell on treatment, especially treatment of an affliction largely befalling poor black men. He would have to sell his Narcotics Treatment Administration as crime control, not social service; junkies cause crime, and fewer junkies mean less crime. But first he had to figure out what kind of treatment to push.

The old way — cold turkey — was not promising. It depended entirely on psychological counseling, ignoring the physical aspects of chemical dependence. Also, because addicts tend to go back on the spike once released into their old heroin-sodden milieu, DuPont dismissed talk sessions with shrinks as mere Band-Aids.

Another treatment model was emerging in private experimental communities such as Synanon in California and Daytop Village in New York. This involved the addict moving into a residence with other reformed and reforming addicts and immersing himself in a drug-free culture. A new lifestyle; that was the buzzword. Surveillance at these treatment centers was intense. Opportunities to backslide were limited. In some cases, the recovering addicts' experience bordered on the religious. But such treatment was by nature small-scale. As an instrument of public policy in a land of half a million addicts, Synanon-style centers were impractical, DuPont felt.

At the other end of the treatment spectrum was a cudgel with the softened moniker "civil commitment." Little about it was civil; addicts were locked up in hospitals against their will until they dried out. For a public fed up with "crime by addicts," civil commitment had a clear, hard ring to it. It was preemptive, removing addicts from the streets before they had a chance to commit crimes. It was neither a Democratic nor a Republican notion, being the treatment of choice in New York, under Republican governor Nelson Rockefeller, and in California, under Democratic governor Pat Brown. The federal government, too, used hospital lockup, diverting addicts convicted on federal drug charges from prison to a huge federal hospital in Lexington, Kentucky. Civil commitment, though, was wildly expensive. Nobody pretended the country could afford to lock up half a million addicts even if the police could afford to catch them all.

The most controversial new way to treat addicts was with methadone. Addicts were compelled to appear daily at a center where they were questioned about their drug use and had their arms examined for needle marks. Then they drank a cup of Tang with the synthetic narcotic in it. Daily surveillance was a big part of what seemed to make methadone work — and this echoed the success of the Synanon-style centers. Daily appearances provided opportunities for counseling and also for monitoring health, which was important because addicts tend to pass around hepatitis and other infections.

The methadone itself didn't get addicts high, it just prevented them from getting sick from lack of heroin. So methadone worked only for addicts who wanted to get off heroin. In DuPont's eyes that was a big part of what made it successful. The addicts were motivated. From a civil-liberties standpoint, methadone was the happy flip side of civil commitment.

Methadone maintenance therapy was relatively inexpensive, too. It cost about $2,000 a year to keep an addict on methadone — way less than civil commitment. But the real bonus was that methadone patients didn't commit crimes the way untreated addicts did. They were, regrettably, addicted to a new drug, but they could function: working, holding marriages together, caring for children as competently as, say, a diabetic on insulin. As a treatment to use on a mass scale, methadone carried the most promise.

DuPont stalked Capitol Hill with his D.C. jail study under one arm and the Dole-Nyswander methadone studies under the other. Al From, a staff member on the Senate committee that oversaw the District of Columbia, was savvy enough to recognize the political potential in DuPont's proposal.* With DuPont's help, From arranged picture-perfect hearings, finding gainfully employed, clean-cut addicts to come and testify about the miracle of methadone. The D.C. press, in one of its periodic feeding frenzies on the crime issue, gave the hearings splashy coverage. Krogh signaled to Congress that if it wanted such a program for the District of Columbia, the president would not object.

Congress gave DuPont $7.5 million. By July, he had twenty centers open, with 2,500 addicts sipping methadone daily. For the first time, the federal government was handing out "maintenance" doses of narcotics to its addicted citizens.

~

Hip to the power of television, Ehrlichman and Krogh planned a White House gathering of television producers to enlist them in the antidrug

* From would later head the Democratic Leadership Council and launch Bill Clinton toward the presidency.

fight. It isn't enough, they thought, to put thirty-second antidrug commercials on TV; the cop shows and even the sitcoms should carry the message that drug abuse is dangerous and illegal. They invited the producers of the most popular TV shows of the day: *Mod Squad, Mission Impossible, My Three Sons, Hawaii Five-O, Andy Griffith, Room 222, Adam 12, The FBI, The Name of the Game,* and others. It was a delicate business; no White House had ever explicitly asked television executives to tailor scripts to a president's political measurement.

Clearly Ehrlichman and Krogh shared the eagerness of Gordon Brownell's political office to overstate the nation's "drug problem" and generate middle-class support for Nixon's burgeoning War on Drugs. In his opening address to the producers, Ehrlichman stressed that "it would not be accurate to portray the drug problem as a ghetto problem. It is a problem which touches all economic, social and racial stratas [sic] of America."

But Ehrlichman's address that day is remarkable in retrospect for its sobriety. He went out of his way to sharpen the distinction between marijuana and other drugs — a distinction the media, to Gordon Brownell's delight, was busy muddying. "I would caution you not to treat marijuana as you would heroin in your programs," he said. "That kind of treatment would produce a credibility gap for television." And in his interpretation of "the drug problem," Ehrlichman sounded more like Ramsey Clark than other members of his party. "The causes of drug abuse are numerous and complex," Ehrlichman said. "It is not just a child-parent communication gap, nor America's affluence, nor America's system of government, nor America's contradictions, nor the war — it is all of these and maybe none of these and probably much more."

Perhaps because he'd tailored his remarks to a sophisticated audience, Ehrlichman got his wish. By the summer of 1970, villainous pushers and drug-abusing teens were driving the plots of *General Hospital, Mannix, Mod Squad,* and *Love American Style*. Metromedia Corp. was marketing an antidrug series that promised to find drama in dusty bureaucratic corners. Each week, *Three Seals* would find protagonists in the Bureau of Narcotics and Dangerous Drugs or the Customs Service or the National Institute of Mental Health. By the time the producers of *The FBI* finally bought *Three Seals*, the mental-health angle was dropped. David Jansen ended up starring in a cop-style show called *O'Hara: US Treasury*.

~

William Randolph Hearst once said magazines sell best with a pretty girl, a dog, or a child on the cover. For the press, a drug epidemic was a pretty girl; a *childhood* drug epidemic was a pretty girl with a dog.

As the University of Michigan study demonstrated to anyone willing to read it, children of high school age and younger were hardly using drugs at all, and when they were, it was mostly marijuana. Children were not, as far as anyone knew, shooting heroin.

But in March 1970, *Time* magazine found a twelve-year-old heroin addict named Ralphie de Jesus and ran a photo essay about him under the headline "Kids and Heroin: The Adolescent Epidemic."

"The gathering tragedy is that Ralphie is not special," *Time* wrote. "Heroin, long considered the affliction of the criminal, the derelict, the debauched, is increasingly attacking America's children."

The magazine went on to suggest, quoting unnamed "experts," that the number of teenage addicts in New York "may mushroom fantastically to 100,000 this summer. . . . However imprecise the figures, there is no doubting the magnitude of the change or the certitude that something frightening is sweeping into the corridors of US schools and onto the pavements of America's playgrounds.

"It has not yet cropped up everywhere," *Time* warned, "but many experts believe that disaster looms large."

Time based this dire prediction on this assertion by another anonymous expert: "If a young person smokes marijuana on more than ten occasions, the chances are one in five that he will go on to more dangerous drugs." Here was a convenient new theory about drug abuse guaranteed to mobilize a public lackadaisical about the "soft" drug. Marijuana itself might be relatively harmless, but *it leads to* heroin. Your kid isn't just experimenting with a little grass, he's in the first stage of full-blown addiction. Marijuana, it was said, is the *gateway drug*.

~

Egil Krogh and Gordon Brownell weren't the only ones trying to raise marijuana as an issue for the middle class. They had able opponents, notably a young D.C. lawyer named Keith Stroup.

Stroup never went to Vietnam, and the way he avoided it shaped his career. By the time Stroup graduated Georgetown Law School in 1968, the people of his tiny hometown of Mt. Vernon, Illinois, had become so fed up with the number of native sons killed in the war that they'd shut down the local draft board and told the Pentagon to take a hike. Stroup was everlastingly grateful, and he made a mental note of how apolitical people like the farmers of Mt. Vernon could be riled to action.

He shunned private law after graduation and poured himself instead into a job at the National Commission on Product Safety, Congress's response to Ralph Nader. Part of Stroup's daily routine was to walk over to the office of Nader's Raiders and cull their mail, looking for issues for the commission to address. He hung out there a lot, watching.

Another part of Stroup's daily routine was to smoke a joint. He'd first tasted pot at an antiwar rally and liked it for both its high and its politics. Pot was everything to Stroup that alcohol wasn't — energizing, mind-expanding, and utterly free of corporate profit. To Stroup, the 600,000 people being arrested every year for simple possession was outrageous. Watching Nader, he formulated an idea: marijuana prohibition should be fought from the platform of consumers' rights. If automobile consumers were being given a voice in automobile policy, marijuana consumers had a right to a voice in marijuana policy. Even if only a fraction of the country's pot smokers were being arrested, millions and millions of Americans were potential members of a movement to legalize pot. After two years, Stroup quit his job in 1970 and declared the opening of the National Organization for the Repeal of Marijuana Laws.

A friend convinced him to soften "repeal" to "reform," and NORML was born.

It is a measure of how gentle the War on Drugs was in the early 1970s that NORML was considered a legitimate player in the drug policy debate. NORML was a place for reporters to call when they wanted a quote to balance the staunch prohibitionists. Reporters were always looking for a good pot story, and Stroup suddenly was everywhere: in the papers, on TV, speaking at pro-pot rallies and antiwar sit-ins. Boyish and nearsighted with a slight puckish lisp, he was also handsome, likable, and invariably dressed in an outsized velvet bow tie. He quickly became Mr. Marijuana, giving a face and address to the country's growing interest in marijuana legalization. Until the War on Drugs "went nuclear" in the 1980s, as Stroup describes it, NORML had the deliciously naughty legitimacy of an enemy embassy before the outbreak of hostilities.

~

Sooner or later, H. L. Mencken once said, a democracy tells the truth about itself. Such a moment came early in the summer of 1970, during the waning hours of a House committee hearing on drug abuse. When heroin was only in the ghetto, an official from the White House Office of Management and Budget told the committee, "it was a problem we could live with."

Black leaders were furious. Only a couple weeks earlier, Daniel Patrick Moynihan had written a memo to Nixon urging a toning down of racial rhetoric on all sides — a period of "benign neglect" of racial differences. The memo leaked and, when reported out of context, looked like a plan to ignore black concerns. Then Nixon came out against a holiday in honor of Martin Luther King Jr. Now a White House official was saying heroin was okay in the ghetto.

Blacks had been living with heroin addicts — among a long list of other woes — for generations, and the government had paid them little mind save to round them up now and then. Now, as many blacks saw it, one tiny portion of the ghetto's misery was making itself felt in the suburbs, and Mr. Charlie was acting like drugs were something new. "You know what people up here are saying?" a black policeman in Harlem asked *Life* magazine. "Now that white people's kids are involved, the politicians are worried."

"You know the best way to deal with the dope problem?" asked a Harlem mother in an *Ebony* article. "Get as many white kids on it as possible! The best news I've heard in a long time is that more [white] kids are getting hooked on heroin. If I had the money I'd buy it and give it to them free!"

∾

The CBS show 60 *Minutes* asked eleven hundred Americans how they felt about pieces of the Bill of Rights — *without* telling them where the questions came from.

A majority in 1970 believed the government should be allowed to suppress news stories it doesn't like and to ban even peaceful demonstrations. So much for the First Amendment. A majority thought prosecutors should be able to try an acquitted suspect a second time for the same crime. So much for the Fifth. And most people told CBS that police should be allowed to hold a suspect until enough evidence is gathered for a conviction. So much for the Eighth, which bars excessive bail.

As John Mitchell put it in a speech soon after the 60 *Minutes* show, "Americans don't like the Constitution."

∾

In such an atmosphere, Congress in July passed a revolutionary law that would in time become one of the War on Drugs's most fearsome weapons. It would evolve to let prosecutors confiscate the homes of marijuana smokers — and of the *parents* of marijuana smokers. It would help imprison for ten years college students who did nothing more than introduce two people later caught peddling drugs. It would allow a new double jeopardy: trying people in federal court for crimes of which they've already been acquitted in state court.

It started as a way to fight organized crime. Congress had been searching for a way to do this since a string of commissions in the 1950s and 1960s identified "the Mafia" and "La Cosa Nostra." Although the FBI would occasionally send one of the *capos* to jail, the overall problem of criminal families and syndicates never went away.

Bob Blakey thought he had figured out why. Blakey had been working on the problem of organized crime for most of a decade, first as a federal prosecutor under Attorney General Robert Kennedy and then as staff to various Republican members of Congress. In 1970, he was an instructor at Notre Dame Law School, brilliant and known for being obsessed with the mob. He was, at age thirty-four, an obvious choice to help the Senate Judiciary Committee write an organized crime bill.

The problem, as Blakey saw it, was that sending a crime boss to prison didn't hurt the organization. Prison was seen as a cost of doing business; you did your time and got on with it. To hurt a criminal organization, *you had to take away its money.*

The Fifth Amendment of the Constitution specifically bars the government from taking away a citizen's property — even a criminal's — "without due process" and "without just compensation." But one form of confiscation had been a comfortable fixture of American law since the earliest days of the republic. The first Continental Congress passed a law letting the navy seize slave ships even if the owner wasn't aboard or wasn't known. The principle was this: a slave ship is of itself offensive to the law and must be shut down. Ever since slave days, police have been allowed to seize obvious contraband — a robber's gun, say, or during Prohibition a barrel of whiskey. The technical term for government confiscation of illegal objects is "forfeiture." And because such seizures aren't necessarily connected to a criminal prosecution, they are called "civil." In a case of "civil forfeiture," prosecutors don't need to convict anyone to take away the property; they don't even have to know whose property it is. If the law calls it illegal, the government can take it. As much as anything, civil forfeiture was — until recently — a matter of public safety. Dangerous stuff was removed from circulation.

But civil forfeiture was of limited use against organized crime. Only illegal assets like bootleg liquor or illegal slot machines could be taken. The cash derived from them could not. And if the syndicate chose to invest its dirty liquor money in, say, a pizzeria, the place was untouchable. It galled Blakey that the pizzeria could then go on to make the crime bosses rich, a pizzeria they wouldn't have owned to begin with if not for their crimes.

So Blakey invented a whole new category of forfeiture: criminal forfeiture. Under Blakey's law, once prosecutors convicted a crime boss, they could take away his illegal profits. If those profits were invested in a legitimate business, the government could take that business away, too. In criminal forfeiture, losing the assets was part of the punishment. Here was a law with teeth.

To the civil libertarians who objected, Blakey had this response: unlike civil forfeiture, criminal forfeiture requires the government to prove beyond a reasonable doubt that the person losing the assets is guilty of a crime. In 1970, nobody envisioned what would happen if the clear line between the two types of forfeiture were to blur — if prosecutors started using the extended reach unique to criminal forfeiture with the lack of due process unique to civil forfeiture. It would take another decade and a half, and the declaration of a new kind of War on Drugs, for that to occur.

Central to Blakey's new forfeiture idea was a vastly broadened definition of what constituted "organized crime." It wasn't just whiskey and casinos; it also included brokerages and banks, anywhere the modern syndicates could extend their moneyed tentacles. Blakey wrote a list of acts that would constitute the elements of organized crime; if any two were committed, he told Congress, a criminal "conspiracy" would have taken place, a criminal "enterprise" formed, and the crime was considered "organized." As the bill wound its way around the Hill, the list of "criminal acts" grew and grew. By the time it reached President Nixon's desk, the definition of criminal "enterprise" was so broad it could consist of one person. To be guilty of "conspiracy," a person didn't need actually to commit a crime; merely knowing about it, or being an active participant in the organization that committed it, was enough.

As usually happens in the making of big law, Blakey's began piecemeal. He and his colleagues tinkered with the Corrupt Organizations Act, which covered criminal syndicates. They also made adjustments to the Infiltrated Businesses Act, which covered legitimate businesses penetrated by organized crime. But as the two bills moved through congressional committees, legislative alchemy blended them into one.

Meanwhile, the gangster image that most often came to Blakey's mind was that of Edward G. Robinson as the vicious gangster Rico Bandello in the 1930 movie *Little Caesar.* In that movie, Rico is killed by police, but his respectable patron, "Big Boy," is left untouched. Blakey wanted his law to get Big Boy, and when it came time to send his blended bills to the Senate floor he combined their names into Racketeering Influenced and Corrupt Organizations Act: RICO.

To this day, Blakey keeps a lifesize painting of Edward G. Robinson as Rico Bandello hanging above his desk.

John Mitchell's Justice Department was appalled by RICO, Santarelli in particular. The essence of good criminal law, to Santarelli, was its narrowness. RICO was sweeping and imprecise. It failed to spell out exactly what constituted a criminal enterprise, for example, leaving that decision up to every cop and lowly assistant U.S. attorney in the field. Its vague language regarding conspiracy and dirty money meant virtually any wealth even remotely connected to a crime could be subject to forfeiture.

The Justice Department, when asked by Congress, objected that RICO's breadth "would result in a large number of unintended applications."

~

Senator James Eastland, Democrat of Mississippi, figured he would put an end to all the shilly-shallying about marijuana. As chairman of the Subcommittee on Internal Security, he opened hearings with the grandiose title "The Marijuana-Hashish Epidemic and Its Impact on United States Security."

Keith Stroup was not invited to testify.

"We make no apology for the one-sided nature of the hearings," Eastland said as he opened them. "They were deliberately planned that way."

But Congress couldn't afford to dismiss marijuana easily, not when ten or twelve million Americans were smoking it. Not when a constitutional amendment was in the works lowering the voting age to eighteen. Not when marijuana smokers were organizing themselves into a political constituency under the NORML banner. There was a need at least to appear to take seriously the suggestion that the drug wasn't the gravest threat to the Republic since Quemoy and Matsu.

As Eastland was working his side of the street, a young rep from New York named Ed Koch rose to propose a formal commission to study the impact of marijuana on America's health, legal systems, and social fabric. "It is an outrage and a tragedy that young men and women should be imprisoned for the possession of marijuana," Koch said. "The appalling conditions and practices in many of our penal institutions can do infinitely more damage to a young person than his use of marijuana." Only a blue-ribbon panel with a chairman appointed by the president, Koch said, would have the authority to settle once and for all the complex legal, medical, and social questions raised by the newly popular drug.

Egil Krogh had no objection. Marijuana didn't interest him much; he saw his job as bringing down the crime rate, and unlike heroin, marijuana wasn't associated with crime. If a presidential commission could make the marijuana issue go away forever, that would be fine with him. Krogh ordered his staff to arrange a presidential commission on marijuana.

~

Among the items that reached the president's desk that summer was a Burns-Roper poll of a thousand college students. Conventional wisdom said "most" college students smoked pot, but this poll found only a quarter had tried marijuana, and only about half of those had smoked it more than once. Nixon, ever-conscious of the countercultural link between marijuana and antiwar activism, sent the poll back to Haldeman with a note penned in the margin: "They aren't as radical as most assume."

~

Just because drug panic was usually a ticket to ride didn't mean it was always a ticket to ride — as Congress learned when it tried to blame marijuana for the massacre at My Lai.

CBS aired a film clip of an American soldier in Vietnam smoking marijuana out of the barrel of his rifle, and Senator Thomas Dodd, Democrat of Connecticut and chairman of the Juvenile Delinquency Subcommittee, jumped right on it. He held a day of hearings about marijuana in Vietnam and made the mistake of including among his expert witnesses the GI who first reported My Lai to the army and Congress.

Ron Ridenhour, a helicopter door gunner in 1968, had flown over My Lai while Charlie Company was burying the bodies. He asked enough questions to figure out what had happened, but kept his mouth shut for a year, until he was out of the service. Perhaps Ridenhour was paranoid, but he believed it possible that a GI who reported such a thing would find himself assigned to a suicide mission.

Having survived Vietnam, Ridenhour filed a report, but by the spring of 1970 it looked to him as though only Lieutenant William Calley was going to take a fall. Ridenhour was convinced that guilt for the massacre went much higher. A senior at Claremont Men's College in California, Ridenhour could hardly concentrate on anything else. He was, as he liked to put it, "one seriously pissed off young man."

Then one day two members of Senator Dodd's staff showed up at Claremont and started asking questions. They kept asking about marijuana among the troops, and slowly it dawned on Ridenhour that they were cooking up a theory about My Lai, that the massacre was nothing more than a drug trip turned homicidal. Dodd's aides asked Ridenhour to fly to Washington to testify at the hearings about pot in the army.

"You assholes," Ridenhour told them. "We were *all* potheads." But he agreed to talk to Congress after getting an "absolute guarantee you won't ask me if I smoke marijuana." Ridenhour still believed he could help establish higher-up responsibility for the massacre.

But when Dodd got Ridenhour in front of the committee, he didn't ask a single question about My Lai. Witness after witness already had suggested a marijuana link to the massacre, and Ridenhour, the sole eyewitness to the scene at My Lai, was never given a chance to talk about it. He dutifully answered general questions about pot smoking in Vietnam — as many as 80 percent of the men in his own unit smoked it, he said, gritting his teeth. When Ridenhour burst out of the committee room moments later, reporters were waiting, cameras clicking and whirring.

"Dodd is stacking the evidence," Ridenhour told the cameras. Then he reminded everybody he'd been at My Lai. "Nobody mentioned drugs at My Lai after it happened," he said. "And they would have been looking for any excuse." Ridenhour finished with his opinion about the investigation of the slaughter: "Many, many Americans are looking for any reason other than a command decision."

A member of Dodd's staff pushed through the reporters, took Ridenhour's arm, and whispered that the senator wanted to see him.

"Take your fucking hands off me!" Ridenhour snapped. Click-click. Whirrrrrrr.

That same day, the Pentagon issued a statement saying that while drugs were "a serious problem in South Vietnam" there was "no evidence that any unit engaged at [My Lai] was under the influence of marijuana or other narcotics."

~

Nixon expected opposition from the Democratic-controlled Congress to his drug and organized-crime bills. "The administration's position in the crime field depends on our ability to shift blame for crime bill inaction to Congress," Egil Krogh's Domestic Council wrote in preparation for midterm elections.

To the surprise and delight of the Nixon staff, though, Congress passed everything the White House wanted, and a big part of it was a massive expansion of the Law Enforcement Assistance Administration. In a single jump the LEAA, whose two-year-old mandate was to beef up local cops, grew from a $75 million mouse to a half-billion-dollar-a-year lion. Suddenly, the federal government had an enormous presence in local police departments everywhere.

The thrust of that presence was in the kind of hardware citizens can see with their own eyes — new police cars, radios, riot training, and guns. Only tiny portions of the new federal funds went to corrections and the courts. The front of the criminal-justice pipeline was opened wide, the back end left largely untouched. Thus began a judicial bottleneck that would later choke the courts and the prisons.

~

After a year of clipping newspapers for Harry Dent, Gordon Brownell was ready for a new challenge. The most exciting Republican race at the moment was Ronald Reagan's reelection campaign in California. Brownell had met Reagan — in fact, had given him his first tour of the White House — and loved his brand of conservative politics. In May 1970, he left the White House to be Reagan's assistant campaign manager.

Brownell, who smoked a little pot in law school, had given it up while working at the White House. In California, though, most people of his age — of all political stripes — got high now and then. Brownell started toking up occasionally, too; it was no big deal. Then he met a young woman he liked a lot and they drove across the desert to spend a weekend at the Grand Canyon. While camped on the North Rim, Brownell and his sweetheart took a couple of hits of mescaline.

Brownell felt his mind leap out of his skull and hover over the Canyon. He felt the grim gray tones of his career washed away in joyous psychedelic hues. Why on earth, his spirit seemed to be asking him, are you working for a mean-spirited, war-mongering, prison-loving generation, an army of blue suits who would just as soon annihilate you and those you love? Within a month Brownell had quit the Reagan campaign, burned his suits, and gone to live in a shack overlooking the ocean at Mendocino. He was finished with the politics of death; all his efforts went into writing a "drug novel" that he called *Jessica's Story.*

~

Look at this, Jeff Donfeld said to his boss, Egil Krogh.

Rough crime figures were in for the District of Columbia. In the five months since Bob DuPont had begun treating addicts with methadone, the monthly number of street crimes was noticeably reduced. Krogh and Donfeld were amazed; they'd hoped for results, but this was awesomely quick.

Krogh and Donfeld started talking about doing nationally what DuPont was doing in D.C. — reducing crime by treating addicts instead of simply locking them up. Go look at the best drug-treatment clinics in the country, Krogh told his young assistant. See what works.

In 1970, there weren't many such clinics, and the one Donfeld liked best was the state of Illinois's, which used methadone in ministering to the state's 6,000 known addicts. The psychiatrist running the Illinois program was a short, wry, Jewish liberal Democrat named Jerome Jaffe.

After touring Jaffe's clinic, Donfeld asked him to assemble a team of experts outside government and prepare a report on what could be done about addiction in the United States if there was, say, $50 million to spend. Donfeld placed three conditions on Jaffe: the report could not exceed 100 pages, it had to be finished in six weeks, and if it leaked to the press it would be useless. This was, Jaffe thought, an extraordinary request. He didn't have a clue what the White House was up to.

Furthermore, it put him in a tough spot; Jaffe wasn't sure he could find any "experts" who would give the Nixon administration the time of day. The drug treatment field was dominated by liberal Democrats bound by a common loathing of Richard Nixon. Nobody in the field had forgotten that barely a year ago, Nixon had angered the health professions by giving the attorney general the power to schedule drugs.

Jaffe also thought Donfeld was leaning too hard on the drugs-and-crime link. In his own experience, heroin addicts made most of the money they needed for a fix by selling heroin to other addicts, not burglarizing homes or mugging people. Most of those who were crooks were crooks before they were addicts. Also, Jaffe had met productive working people who were heroin addicts — musicians, butchers, you name it. The assumption that drug addiction was responsible for rising crime made him uneasy.

But he understood that the drug-crime link was a political tool that wasn't going to be buried by sober talk about statistics. Besides, Jaffe reasoned, clearly some addicts do commit some crimes. The link wasn't entirely spurious, he told himself, just overstated.

And fifty million pre-inflation dollars was a lot of money.

So Jaffe began asking around, avoiding the doctors who were too rabidly anti-Nixon, and in a couple of weeks had an informal group put together that was beginning to jot down ideas.

What Jaffe didn't know was that Donfeld was simultaneously commissioning a second report from experts inside government. The rank-and-file staff at HEW, the National Institutes of Health, and the Food and Drug Administration were mostly civil-service holdovers from eight years of Democratic rule. They disliked the Nixon administration, and the feeling was mutual. Their recommendations were exactly what Donfeld expected; they came straight out of the "root causes" philosophy of Ramsey Clark and the Great Society. The gist of them was that heroin addiction is a symptom of society's failures — racism, alienation, and lack of opportunity. If government wanted seriously to address addiction, the "in-house" report said, it would pour money into housing, jobs, youth — the whole dreary laundry list of expensive liberal solutions that the Republican Party disdained. If the government insisted on Band-Aids in the meantime, the in-house crew said, psychiatry was useful for treating addicts, and civil commitment had its place. Therapeutic communities weren't so hot, they said, and the worst idea of all, they said, was methadone — a simplistic "magic bullet" that treated individual addicts as patients with no consideration of social context. The in-house team specifically recommended against a "massive methadone maintenance program": it simply wouldn't work.

Jaffe saw his marching orders differently from the government team. Donfeld had made it amply clear that the administration's antidrug priorities did not include providing "health care for the long-haired anti-establishment types who did not want to go to regular medical clinics." No, Donfeld said, the goal was simply to reduce crime by addicts. Willing to believe the worst about Nixon and his men, Jaffe assumed they wanted a recommendation of massive "civil commitment" of addicts, a solution Jaffe wanted no part of. Instead, he and his group focused on the estimated 30,000 addicts in the country who had applied for treatment but couldn't get it for lack of slots, and who were presumably tempted to mug old ladies for a fix. Yes, heroin addiction was a complex problem, Jaffe's report said, but methadone was the one type of therapy that demonstrably reduced crime by addicts. It should be made available to all who want it.

As Jaffe's group was coming to this conclusion, Donfeld hectored them with critical questions. Jaffe didn't know why. He didn't know his research was in competition with that of the government's own social scientists. He didn't know Donfeld was shuttling between the two groups. He didn't know Donfeld's criticism was intended to make the Jaffe report as strong as possible. Jaffe believed he was forcing treatment down the throat of a punishment-oriented administration. He didn't know his finished report was exactly what Donfeld and Krogh wanted.

Methadone had dual attractions for Donfeld and Krogh. It was an inexpensive way to reduce street crime by drug addicts, which was Krogh's primary concern. But Donfeld and Krogh were not political naifs; they knew, as the HEW bureaucrats did, that methadone was a way to discredit calls for massive social spending on the "root causes" of crime. A methadone program would define addiction as a disease suffered by individuals, not a social pathology. Furthermore, adoption of such a program would cut all those hostile social-service bureaucrats off at the knees. As an added bonus, methadone would put a humane face on Nixon's Drug War, deflecting criticism that his only answer to the drug problem was more law enforcement.

Jaffe didn't know all that. He got a nice note from Richard Nixon thanking him for his work, and that, he figured, was that.

~

December 16, 1970

To: Mr. Egil Krogh Jr., Deputy Assistant to the President for Domestic Affairs

From: John E. Ingersoll, Director, Bureau of Narcotics and Dangerous Drugs

This is in response to your memorandum of December 10, 1970 requesting a definition for "hard drugs" to show that much more than 15 percent of the seizures [in 1969] were of hard drugs.

So began a two-page memo on a sticky White House problem. Published reports showed many tons more of marijuana than heroin being seized by federal agents. Heroin, however, was the dragon the public wanted slain; the country wasn't yet convinced that marijuana — the "soft drug" — was worth fighting. Krogh knew public support for the War on Drugs depended on success on the heroin front and, as John Mitchell had ordered, on making the federal drug-fighting apparatus as visible and impressive as possible. He asked Ingersoll if there wasn't a way to jigger the figures.

The problem, Ingersoll replied in his memo, was that "comparing weights of drugs seized is like comparing apples and oranges." A few milligrams of heroin is plenty to get a mainlining addict high, Ingersoll explained, while a joint of marijuana passed around by a college kid could weigh a thousand times that much.

Rather than redefine the drugs, Ingersoll wrote, the government should report seizures some way other than by weight. "Alternatives," he wrote, "might be the illicit street value. . . . By using the illicit value concept, the hard drug figure would increase by at least a factor of 100 in relation to marihuana."

Street value varies widely depending on how heavily the drug is diluted. It likewise depends on how many middlemen's profits are factored in. So many variables can go into figuring street value that it is a meaninglessly protean yardstick. But born of a need to show triumph on the heroin front, street value became the yardstick by which progress in the War on Drugs would be measured. It is for the War on Drugs what the body count was for the Vietnam War; and it has been about as accurate a predictor of success.

~

The year ended on an odd note for the War on Drugs. Four days before Christmas, Egil Krogh's phone rang. It was Dwight Chapin, from Bob Haldeman's staff.

"The King is here," Chapin said.

"King who?" Krogh asked. "No kings on the president's schedule today."

"Not just any two-bit king," Chapin answered. "*The* King. Elvis. The King of Rock."

Elvis Presley had appeared that morning at the Northwest Gate of the White House and handed the guard a nearly illegible six-page letter on American Airlines stationery. He was an admirer of the president, Presley wrote, and he wanted to help spread Nixon's antidrug message. He was well positioned, too: "The drug culture, the hippie elements, the SDS, Black Panthers, etc. do *not* consider me as their enemy or as they call it The Establishment." To dispel any doubts as to his own loyalty, Presley added in bold underline, "*I call it America and I love it!*"

Then Presley made his pitch. "I can and will do more good if I were made a Federal Agent at Large. . . . All I need is the Federal credentials."

Presley was registered at a nearby hotel under the name Jon Burrows. "I will be here for as long as it takes to get the credentials of a Federal Agent," Presley wrote. "I have done an in-depth study of drug abuse and Communist brainwashing techniques and I am right in the middle of the whole thing where I can and will do the most good."

Though he didn't mention it in the note to Nixon, Presley was a collector of police badges. And he was a dopehound of legendary excess. But in the squareball Nixon White House, Presley found perhaps the only people in the United States who didn't know that.

Krogh certainly didn't. He took the letter at face value.

At 12:30, the King was relieved of his present for the chief executive — a nickel-plated .45 automatic, complete with ammunition — and ushered into the office of the president.

Nixon was dressed like Nixon: blue suit, white shirt, tie. Elvis was dressed like Elvis: black velvet jacket, chest hair, gold medallions, sunglasses, and a belt buckle big as a dinner plate. He pulled up a sleeve to exhibit cufflinks the size of hamsters. As Nixon bent close to examine them, Elvis launched into a tirade against the Beatles, whom he accused of being anti-American.

"You know," Nixon said, "those who use the drugs are the protesters. You know, the ones who get caught up in dissent and violence. They're the same group of young people."

"Mr. President," Elvis said, "I'm on your side. I want to be helpful. And I want to help get people to respect the flag because that's getting lost." Then Elvis got to the point. "Mr. President, can you get me a badge from the Narcotics Bureau?"

Krogh was afraid of this. He'd already called the number two man at BNDD, who earlier that day had thrown Elvis out. Elvis had gone there before stopping at the Northwest Gate and offered a $5,000 "donation" to BNDD in return for a badge.

Nixon, not knowing any of that, looked uncertainly at Krogh. "Bud, can we get him a badge?"

"If you want to give him a badge, I think we can get him one."

"I'd like to do that. See that he gets one."

Elvis then did something nobody had ever done in the Nixon Oval Office; he gathered the president up in his arms and gave him a big bear hug. The staff was stunned; the photographer didn't even get a picture. Nixon endured it stiffly, handed out presidential tie clasps, and dismissed the King with a hearty pat on the shoulder.

And so it came to pass that on the day Elvis Presley died of a drug overdose in 1977, he was a credentialed Special Assistant in the Bureau of Narcotics and Dangerous Drugs.

~

- Number of Americans who died in 1970 from legal and illegal drugs: 1,899.
- Number who died from the flu: 3,707.
- Number of prescriptions for psychoactive drugs written in 1970: 214 million.
- Amount spent by Americans on legal spirits, wine, and beer: $24 billion.
- Estimated size of the illegal drug market: $2 billion.

3

Pee House of the August Moon
1971

Uppers are no longer stylish. Methedrine is almost as rare, on the 1971 market, as pure acid or DMT. "Consciousness expansion" went out with LBJ. And it is worth noting, historically, that downers came in with Nixon.

— *Hunter Thompson,* Fear and Loathing in Las Vegas

IN MAY 1971, two congressmen stepped off a plane in D.C. bearing grim tidings. Robert Steele, Republican of Connecticut, and Morgan Murphy, Democrat of Illinois, had just come from visiting the troops in Vietnam, where, they reported, a horrifying number were addicted to heroin. As many as 15 percent — maybe 40,000 men — were hooked on smack. "The soldier going to South Vietnam today runs a far greater risk of becoming a heroin addict than a combat casualty," Steele told reporters.

"This is the kind of issue that can change the whole situation," intoned Republican senator Jacob Javits of New York, an opponent of the war. "The American people could get so fed up that the troops will all be out of there faster than McGovern, Hatfield or anybody else ever dreamed up, regardless of the consequences."

Bells went off in Egil Krogh's office. Here was a problem fairly humming with disaster. The country was wildly conflicted about the war already; if people thought they were sending their sons to defend Democracy, only to have them return as wretched junkies, Nixon's already frayed support for his handling of the war might snap. Left-wingers would use addiction as a metaphor for the whole mess; right-wingers would use it as a call to stop waffling and get serious about winning the war. The message Krogh got was: fix this one, and fast.

Krogh called the Pentagon and summoned the person in charge of military drug abuse. The man who came to see him was a white-haired admiral, in full uniform with ribbons. A former navy man himself, young Krogh was at first intimidated. But within a few minutes Krogh was angry.

"Excuse me?" he asked, leaning across his desk. "*How* many addicts does the Pentagon estimate are in the military?"

"One hundred," the admiral repeated. "Maybe two hundred."

"Admiral," said Jeff Donfeld, who was sitting in, "may I ask how you calculate that? Because Congressmen Steele and Murphy . . ."

"I know what they say," the admiral said. "But these are the data we have. This is the number of men we've arrested for using illegal drugs."

Donfeld and Krogh looked at each other. It was patently absurd. Even accounting for hyperbole on the part of the congressmen, the admiral's one or two hundred was a ridiculous number. Krogh looked back at the admiral. Either the Pentagon doesn't have the data, he thought, or it isn't going to give them to me. Either way, I'm on my own.

Now the press was on the story. "As common as chewing gum," *Time* said of drugs in Vietnam. The *New York Times* estimated that as many as a quarter of the privates fighting in Vietnam — some 60,000 men — were hooked on smack. ABC News aired a one-hour special, "Heroes and Heroin," that showed soldiers handing little packets to each other and then snorting up. Heroin made even the increasingly rapid withdrawal from Vietnam a problem. "The specter of weapons-trained, addicted combat veterans joining the deadly struggle for drugs [in the streets of America] is ominous," reported *Time*. The article went on to quote Iowa senator Harold Hughes: "Within a matter of months in our large cities, the Capone era of the '20s may look like a Sunday school picnic by comparison."

Krogh flew to Vietnam. He took no entourage, only a set of fatigues and a pass to travel wherever he wanted.

He flew all over the country, from the DMZ to the southern Delta, visiting twelve firebases. Krogh was thirty-one. By himself, in fatigues, and calling himself "a member of the White House staff," he looked like a harmless underling, not the man in charge of national drug policy. What amazed him was how candid the men were. Krogh would sit with them in their bunkers as they passed joints back and forth or cracked out vials of heroin, which they bragged was 90 percent pure and which they usually snorted, smoked in cigarettes, or mixed with alcohol and drank. Nobody was inhibited even when officers were around. There didn't even seem to be a "drug culture" among the troops he could delineate from the straight culture. Everybody smoked pot, and a lot of the men were using heroin.

The heroin problem Krogh was seeing was created largely by the Pentagon itself. The army had figured out in 1968 that a lot of its troops in Vietnam were smoking pot. The army then began an all-out campaign to cut off the supply — with pot-sniffing dogs, searches of men's billets, and mass arrests for possession. It also endeavored to reduce demand through a "reefer madness"–style propaganda campaign on Armed Forces Radio. Marijuana use declined, but when the Pentagon sent a researcher to study the campaign's effects two years later, he reported that the real results of the army's antimarijuana campaign were disastrous. "Human ingenuity being what it is — and the desire for an intoxicant in Vietnam being what it was — many soldiers simply switched" to heroin, which was odorless, far less bulky than pot, and in Vietnam, extremely inexpensive. Within two years field officers would miss the good old days when their troops merely smoked pot. One commanding officer told the Pentagon researcher, "If it would get them to give up the hard stuff, I would buy all the marijuana and hashish in the Delta as a present."

The worst drug in America — the most feared, the most taboo — has long been heroin. By clamping down hard on marijuana, the army not only created a big health problem in its ranks, it also pushed its soldiers across a line. If thousands of soldiers could casually accept heroin as "normal," what chance did the army have of controlling any kind of drug use?

~

Shaken by his trip, Krogh withdrew from his files the two reports on addiction treatment that Donfeld had commissioned. He looked at the lead name on the outsiders' report, the one that had recommended methadone rather than massive social spending. He buzzed his secretary and asked her to get Jerome Jaffe on the phone.

Krogh asked Jaffe to come up with a plan for dealing with heroin addiction in Vietnam. There's no time to set up a committee or anything, he told Jaffe, just give us your own ideas.

Jaffe sat at his kitchen table in Chicago and wrote a plan. Technology has just been improved, he said, to detect opiates in urine on a mass scale. (Marijuana wasn't yet detectable.) Only one such machine — a behemoth the size of an office desk — was actually in use. The army should order one and begin widespread testing, Jaffe wrote, first of troops on their way home, and eventually of all personnel. Anyone who tests positive should be kept in Vietnam for detox and held there long enough to be tested again, to discourage drug use and detect relapse. Soldiers are so eager to get out of Vietnam, Jaffe wrote, that the prospect of being held there longer will be a powerful motive to stop using drugs. Testing will also give a clearer view of the scope of the problem. As before, Jaffe had no idea how his recommendations would be received. Random drug testing had never been done. Jaffe assumed it would be ruled unconstitutional, but he sent his report to Krogh anyway.

The response was stunningly quick. Would Jaffe fly to Washington to brief the Pentagon on his recommendations?

Uh, sure, Jaffe said.

Met at the airport by a White House limo, he was whisked to Krogh's office in the executive mansion and then to the Pentagon, where he and Krogh were ushered into a room full of high-ranking generals and admirals. By this time, Jaffe felt he was truly through the looking glass. Yesterday he was a psychiatrist laboring in relative obscurity, today he was being introduced to the Pentagon's top brass as "consultant to the president." In training, appearance, and temperament, Jaffe couldn't have differed more from the square-jawed military men around him, who were eyeing him with obvious distaste. Vietnam is painful enough for the Pentagon, Jaffe thought. Now this.

Jaffe ran through his plan for the generals, all of whom had already received copies from Krogh. They were polite, but cool. They responded that the Defense Department itself was looking into the matter of addicted servicemen and in four or five months might be able to adopt a plan resembling Jaffe's.

"Gentlemen," Jaffe said, "I believe the White House wants something done about the problem a little sooner than that." Then he added, by way of being helpful, "I feel certain that I can find a few civilians who will be willing to aid me in getting this effort under way." Suddenly, the atmosphere in the room changed completely. The generals and admirals sat upright in their chairs, said they'd be back in a few minutes, and left the room.

When they returned ten minutes later, they said they would cooperate completely. If Jaffe could line up the testing machine and have it delivered to an airbase in California, the army would begin testing its soldiers in Vietnam on June 16, a little more than two weeks away.

Jaffe was thunderstruck at their turnaround. What he didn't know was that nobody tells two- and three-star generals what to do, except four-star generals and the president. Introduced as a "consultant" to the president, the generals assumed that when Jaffe spoke, it was Nixon talking. His comment about finding "a few civilians" to do the job hit the generals as a threat to take away their authority. When all this was finally explained to Jaffe afterward, he thanked heaven for his ignorance; had he known the way things worked, he would have been way more diffident and probably would have qualified everything: "Now this is only my opinion" and "While I don't speak for the president . . ."

There was another problem that Jaffe took up with Krogh. Random testing of everybody in Vietnam was going to place a lot of men in legal jeopardy. Addiction or even drug use is an infraction of military code and automatically results in a dishonorable discharge. Soon after the meeting at the Pentagon, Nixon sent a one-page memo to the secretary of defense that ordered that drug use no longer be considered a crime under the military code of justice. With that single memo, Nixon — acting as commander in chief — reversed decades of military policy and opened the door to the massive treatment of drug abuse.

He also introduced random urine testing for drugs as an instrument of public policy.

~

Keith Stroup was furious. The new Presidential Commission on Marijuana was shaping up to be a reefer-madness folly. Its chairman, handpicked by Nixon, was the retired Republican governor of Pennsylvania, Raymond Shafer, a known drug hawk. The commission was stacked with conservative doctors. Senator Harold Hughes of Iowa — who never tired of frightening Congress with drug horror stories — was one of four congressional members. Of the rest, only Jacob Javits could be said to be remotely reasonable, and even he was no legalizer. Worst of all, the commission's executive director — the man who decided whom to call for testimony — had been involved in some of the darkest recent episodes in drug policy. His name was Michael Sonnenreich.

Sonnenreich, a friend of John Dean, had started his career as a prosecutor and moved to the criminal division of the Justice Department under Ramsey Clark. Sonnenreich had been part of the legal team that engineered the consolidation of drug enforcement in the Justice Department. Although a Democrat, Sonnenreich had been asked to stay at Justice after the Republicans took over in 1969. He helped draft the drug-classification sections of Nixon's first big drug bill — the bill that gave the attorney general instead of the surgeon general the power to determine exactly how dangerous various drugs are.* As a reward, Sonnenreich was made deputy general counsel of BNDD — the drug police. A smart lawyer, Sonnenreich was also politically shrewd. In a long memo to Egil Krogh, he laid out BNDD's plan for a secret operation against the twenty biggest known heroin traffickers in the U.S. "This operation will remain underground," he wrote to Krogh. "If we succeed, the President can spring it on the public — if it fails, we can continue the rhetoric of routine law enforcement rationalizations." All in all, Michael Sonnenreich was the last person Stroup wanted managing the Presidential Commission on Marijuana.

When Stroup wrote to ask if he could address the commission, Sonnenreich said no. Stroup then called Ramsey Clark, now in retirement, and asked if he would address the commission on behalf of liberalized marijuana laws. Surely the commission would have to allow a former attorney general to speak. Clark agreed, but Sonnenreich again refused. "Clark can submit a written statement," he told Stroup.

Stroup called a friend, Brit Hume, who worked as a researcher for Jack Anderson's powerful "Washington Merry-Go-Round" column. Hume worked a mention into Anderson's column that the Marijuana Commission was refusing to hear from either NORML or the former attorney general. The same day the column ran, both Clark and Stroup received invitations from Michael Sonnenreich to testify.

A big peace demonstration was scheduled for May 3 in Washington, and these always put Nixon in a foul mood. He argued with his staff: Nixon wanted to tell the demonstrators, "The party's over, and it's time to draw the line," but everybody thought that was too harsh. Haldeman had to call John Mitchell and get him to talk Nixon out of it.

* While at Justice, Sonnenreich also was pressed into service as a temporary federal magistrate to help mass-arraign Norman Mailer and the hundreds of other protesters from the big antiwar demonstration at the Pentagon.

Mitchell and Haldeman offered Nixon something in return: they'd go hard on the demonstrators by sending narcotics agents to raid them early the day before the march. Using the "preventive detention" law Santarelli had written for D.C., they'd arrest and hold as many as possible on pot charges until after the demonstration was over. D.C. police ended up holding 8,000 people in Kennedy Stadium.

Immediately after the demonstration, a reporter asked Nixon what he thought of Keith Stroup's being invited to address the Marijuana Commission.

"I am against legalizing marijuana," Nixon said sternly. "Even if the commission does recommend that it be legalized, I will not follow that recommendation."

Two weeks later, the director of the National Institute of Mental Health, Bertram Brown, said in a speech he thought marijuana offenses should be treated "like a parking ticket." Nixon fired him. He ordered Haldeman to find a way to take all remaining responsibility for drugs away from HEW and give it to Justice, because at HEW "they're all on drugs anyway." Two days after firing Brown, Nixon exploded to Haldeman that he wanted "to put out a statement on marijuana that's really strong, one that really tears the ass out of them." Haldeman also recorded in his diary that Nixon wanted to know "why all the Jews seem to be the ones that are for liberalizing the regulations on marijuana."

~

Alert to what was coming, the army tried to get ahead of the White House and begin cracking down hard on heroin. Whole battalions of troops were diverted from combat against the NVA to try to catch suppliers, smash supply lines, seize sampans full of smack. The vials of heroin that Egil Krogh had seen in the bunkers went from $3 to $12 apiece, and their purity dropped. To the army, as to generations of policemen, this was a sign of success. But as health policy, it was a catastrophe. When Krogh saw men snorting, smoking, or drinking heroin with alcohol, he was seeing the luxurious effects of low prices and high purity. Nobody likes sticking a needle in his own arm (at least not at first); early heroin users find it far more pleasant to snort or smoke or drink, and those practices are far less likely to get them addicted. But all three ways require the user to consume a good deal of the powder, which is a luxury he cannot afford if the price quadruples and the purity drops. Then the user has to find a way to get more bang for his buck, and the most direct way to get heroin to the brain is to inject it directly into a vein, which is how addicts are made. By cracking down on marijuana, the army had pushed its troops into snorting heroin. By cracking down on snorting heroin, the army pushed its men into mainlining.

~

An opinion survey landed on Nixon's desk in May, showing that 23 percent of Americans now believed drugs were the country's number one problem, up from 3 percent in 1969. Drugs were now the number four domestic issue, under inflation, pollution, and unemployment. A few days later, at a press conference, Nixon was asked again about marijuana.

"I can see no social or moral justification whatever for legalizing marijuana," he said. "I think it would be exactly the wrong step. It would simply encourage more and more of our young people to start down that long, dismal road that leads to hard drugs and eventual self-destruction."

~

On June 14, *Time* delivered a one-two punch to the White House, opining that "the fallout from drug abuse in Vietnam could continue to focus attention on the American presence there and make the war an issue even after troop levels are down to 40,000 or 50,000." The article also noted "growing concern as drugs creep in to Nixon's natural middle-class constituency. Reston, Virginia, for example, the planned community once heralded as an American dream suburb, has a drug problem. Two weeks ago, a 14-year-old runaway from the community, Carolyn Ford, died from a heroin overdose."

Jaffe's phone came alive in Chicago. Egil Krogh calling, asking him to fly to Washington to brief the president and the cabinet personally on his recommendations to the Pentagon. Jaffe agreed, but he knew his department chair at the University of Illinois Medical School was starting to get a bit irate at all the gallivanting to Washington, especially for the dreaded Nixon.

Jaffe was thirty-seven. Much as he disliked Nixon and the war, he was thrilled and awed to enter the White House Cabinet Room to meet the president of the United States and his principal advisers. Marshaling his composure, Jaffe described the findings of his ad hoc team — that methadone, as part of a comprehensive treatment strategy, was a far better tactic than civil commitment. He described his conversation with the generals at the Pentagon. And another thing, Jaffe said: You need better coordination among your drug-abuse agencies.

"Well this is what we're going to do," Nixon told everybody in the room. He would announce immediately — tomorrow — the formation of a Special Action Office for Drug Abuse Prevention, or SAODAP. It would operate out of the Executive Office of the President with the highest authority in the land, enough authority to "knock heads" at FDA, BNDD, HEW, and every other agency with a piece of the drug-abuse budget.

That's not all, Nixon continued. He would tomorrow ask Congress to appropriate $371 million for SAODAP, so it can set up a comprehensive testing and treatment program for the soldiers in Vietnam — and also fund a vast network of state-run methadone maintenance clinics in the U.S. Let nobody tell another sentencing judge he committed a crime because he was addicted, Nixon said.

Jaffe was impressed. Nixon was following his group's recommendations to the letter. All this running back and forth to Washington would soon be over.

Finally, Nixon said, I want to introduce the new director of SAODAP, the man who will oversee our nation's antidrug effort. He extended his hand in Jaffe's direction. "Jerome Jaffe."

It took Jaffe a moment to realize what had just happened. Although the term hadn't yet entered the lexicon, Jerry Jaffe had just become the nation's first drug czar.

"You're going to do *what?*" Jaffe's wife asked when he called her that evening. "We're going to move *where?*"

"When the president of the United States asks you to do something, it's very hard to say no," Jaffe replied.

Which was nothing like the conversations Jaffe had with his department chair and the rest of his colleagues in the drug-abuse field. To them, and liberals like them both in and out of government, addiction and drug abuse were symptoms of a sick society, not sick individuals. The very act of creating a presidential office to deal solely with drug abuse was wrongheaded; it focused attention on the symptom, not the cause. Any hope that the perceived drug crisis might pry extra social-services spending out of the Nixon administration evaporated with the establishment of SAODAP and acceptance of methadone. Although most of Jaffe's colleagues acknowledged methadone *did* help addicts get off heroin and live a productive life, they felt its institutionalization as national policy, at a time of social-spending cuts, was a tightwad, conservative coup. The drug problem was now firmly written reports of the previous day's enemy attacks — in every corner of the country and all at once — were horrifying enough. Then the news film from Saigon started arriving on 707s via Guam and Hawaii. Over dinner, Americans watched jerky hand-held footage of their own embassy under attack, heard the shooting and the screams, witnessed helicopters crashing and men weeping, an illusion of quick victory blown to bits.

Within weeks of the Tet Offensive, the *Wall Street Journal* editorialized that "the whole Vietnam effort may be doomed," and Walter Cronkite broke with tradition to offer not news, but his opinion, to nine million viewers, that the United States was "mired in stalemate." Within a month, public opinion reversed from mostly supporting the war to mostly opposing it. Rather than face the country's wrath, Lyndon Johnson announced he wouldn't run again.

As he entered the primaries, Richard Nixon knew he wasn't going to be able to use Vietnam as a campaign issue; rather, he would need to avoid it. The country was riven straight down the middle on the war. Neither a strong stand for nor a strong stand against would carry him to the White House. So when it came to the most emotional and divisive issue of the day, Nixon said nothing, except to mumble enigmatically about a "secret plan" both to withdraw from the war and to win it. "Peace with honor," he called it.

Nixon knew his substitute campaign issue lay just outside the window, reeking of tear gas, burning tires, and marijuana smoke. Vietnam was a million miles away, but right here at home life was becoming unbearably chaotic for the middle-class white majority. Although Americans were turning against the war, most despised the movement trying to stop it. This didn't change even after Chicago police were televised savaging protesters at the Democratic Convention. Most Americans sided with the police. The protesters, they said, had asked for it. "My people," Nixon called that majority.

Nixon looked at "his people" and found them quaking with rage and fear: not at Vietnam, but at the lawless wreckers of their own quiet lives — an unholy amalgam of stoned hippies, braless women, homicidal Negroes, larcenous junkies, and treasonous priests. Nixon's genius was in hammering these images together into a rhetorical sword. People steal, burn, and use drugs not because of "root causes," he said, but because they are bad people. They should be punished, not coddled. Ramsey Clark had it exactly wrong, in Nixon's view: crime established as a problem of *individuals*. The solution would be to get those individuals to stop using drugs. "Root causes" was well and truly dead.

~

The press conference the next morning was torture for Jaffe. First of all, he looked terrible. When Nixon had dropped the bombshell on him, Jaffe hadn't been prepared to spend another night in Washington. He asked a White House flunky to go out and buy him a shirt, and the kid came back with one cut for a seventeen-inch neck. Jaffe appeared before the cameras looking like his head was poking out of a storm drain.

The questions turned, inevitably, to marijuana. Everybody agreed heroin was worrisome; marijuana was where there was still some political play. Egil Krogh gave the White House view: it is dangerous. "That is our position," he said, "and we continue to take it."

The cameras swiveled to Jaffe. As the new drug chief, did he agree?

Torture! Jaffe didn't give a hoot in hell about marijuana; his specialty was heroin. He didn't even like mixing up the two issues. To him, marijuana wasn't worth worrying about. It didn't seem to do anybody much harm, and he didn't buy the gateway drug line, either. Most junkies smoked cigarettes and drank alcohol. And ate fried food. You could as well say they were the gateway drugs. He looked into the lights, bent toward the nearest microphone, and said, "I think the president has made his position clear on that."

"What is your position?"

"Do you agree with the president?"

"What is your position?"

"Well, I have discussed this with the president," Jaffe said. Not true! he thought wildly. I'm already lying to the press! "I think that the issues are not always what the dangers are, but are the dangers such that we can safely legalize this substance at this time, and on this particular issue I have no disagreement with the president." Please God, he thought, grant that I made sense and that they'll drop it. But no! A reporter bored in and specifically asked him if he thought marijuana use led to harder drugs. Jaffe took a deep breath.

"It is a very, very complicated question," he said, stalling desperately. He paused, hoping that would do it. But the microphones were still pointed his way, so he babbled on. "I think that in one sense, and in a limited sense, you have to say that any time somebody steps over the bounds of using a drug which is not currently totally approved by society, he has broken a boundary, he has in fact put himself outside the conventional limits and to the extent that one begins to experiment beyond the conventional limits, one is more susceptible to experiment with other non-conventional and non-socially approved illegal substances. To that extent, I think one has to accept the idea that moving across the boundary does in fact increase the use of other drugs."

In other words, it isn't *marijuana* that leads to other drugs, it's the *laws against* marijuana, and the act of breaking them, that lead to other drugs. Luckily for Jaffe, the microphones swung away; none of the reporters caught his logic. By rambling dryly, and failing to deliver a snappy quote, he'd wriggled out of answering the question.

Welcome to Washington, Dr. Jaffe.

~

In his message to Congress that day asking for the authorization and money for his new drug agency, Nixon hammered at the theme of addiction causing crime. Egil Krogh and Jeff Donfeld had specifically tried to warn the White House away from hitting this too hard, writing in a Domestic Council decision paper that spring that "even if all drug abuse were eradicated, there might not be a dramatic drop in crime statistics on a national level, since much crime is not related to drug abuse."

Still, Nixon plowed ahead. Heroin addicts, he told Congress, steal over $2 billion worth of property a year to support their habits.

This was patent nonsense. In 1971, the total value of *all* property stolen in the U.S. — whether in burglaries, robberies, or thefts — was $1.3 billion. So Nixon was blaming a quarter of a million addicts for 153 percent of the property crime committed in the U.S. Nobody thought to question the figure. It was widely reported as holy writ.

~

Heavy-handed drug enforcement wasn't just making drug problems worse in Vietnam. It was doing so at home as well.

Until November 1970, the Detroit police had done little more than harass heroin dealers. They would identify a "shooting gallery" — an apartment where addicts bought dope and shot up — and then bang on the door without a warrant in the hopes of scaring the pusher into flushing the dope down the toilet or throwing it out the window. They would arrest a lot of people — more than 9,000 in 1970 — but only about a sixth of those would come to trial.

Then Detroit got itself a new police commissioner who switched tactics. Instead of just harassing dope dealers, Commissioner John Nichols set out to bust them solidly and send them to prison. He doubled the city's narcotics unit and ordered the narcs to gather the kind of evidence that would stand up in trial. The narcs began to raid the shooting galleries *with* warrants. The statistics were impressive. In seven months, Nichols closed 300 shooting galleries and arrested 1,600 people, almost all of whom went to trial.

But Nichols reaped the whirlwind. An all-out war broke out among heroin dealers desperate to hang onto their piece of the Detroit market. "So far this year," *Time* reported in June, "[the war] has claimed 40 lives, one every four days. The dead: penny-ante pushers and some major dealers grabbing for a larger piece of the action and killed by their peers." After years of drugs being thought of as a generator of property crime, the era of something new called "drug violence" was dawning.

~

John Ingersoll, chief of the federal Bureau of Narcotics and Dangerous Drugs, didn't want any part of what he saw in Detroit. Small-time pushers should be left to local police, he thought. Federal narcs should go after the big traffickers. That was the better use of scarce federal resources. And the government shouldn't be in the business of federalizing every crime.

But Ingersoll's BNDD had a public relations problem. To go after the big guys, it kept its operations secret until after a bust. It took months or years to work up a big drug investigation, and then what did you get? One press conference with powder on the table. All it took was a big football game that day and the news coverage was nil. Nobody ever got to see the federal government doing anything about the drug problem. Mitchell had specifically ordered BNDD to boost its public image. Nixon grumbled often about Ingersoll, said he was a do-nothing.

Nixon's kind of law enforcer was Myles Ambrose. At forty-four, Ambrose was the youngest commissioner of Customs in the nation's history. Gruff, handsome, bull-shouldered, and sporting a walrus mustache, he was a central-casting Irish cop, and his two-fisted style was welcome around the White House. It was his Customs Service that in 1969 bludgeoned the Mexicans into compliance with Operation Intercept.

Ambrose and Ingersoll fought constantly over how drug enforcement should be done and who should do it. Customs and BNDD each claimed authority, for example, to investigate drug traffickers overseas. So hostile were the two agencies that they hid evidence from each other, kidnapped each other's witnesses, and in one memorable case got into a gunfight with each other. It was a never-ending nightmare.

Ambrose knew how to undercut Ingersoll, and he outlined his plan in a memo to his boss.

Federal narcotics agents should get into street-level enforcement, Ambrose wrote in his memo to the undersecretary of the treasury, and here's why: Addiction spreads at the street level. An addict turns on a nonaddict and then you have a new addict. The government needs to step in and break that chain.

You don't catch the big guys without first catching the little guys and making them talk, Ambrose argued. For example, the case against Vito Genovese, the Mafia "boss of all bosses" who was recently sent to prison, started with an eighth-ounce heroin purchase in 1955 by an undercover cop.

Narcotics is the one area of law enforcement where the biggest corruption problems occur, Ambrose continued. There's big money in the narcotics business, the chance of undercover cops getting cozy with pushers is high. The best way to prevent that is to have various law enforcement agencies work together, to keep an eye on each other. If the feds work alongside the NYPD, each will keep the other honest.

Ambrose wanted a new agency using federal, state, and local narcs to work low-level arrests. And the public should know that the feds are everywhere, working every level of the drug trade, from the lowliest street pusher up to the international smuggler.

Not only would every drug pusher know the feds were everywhere, so would a law-abiding electorate expecting law and order from its government. Ambrose didn't mention in his memo the political value of street-level federal enforcement. He didn't have to.

~

Over the objections of the State Department, Nixon embarked on a plan to put diplomatic pressure on the countries that grow opium and either produce or transship heroin. He asked Congress to change the law to allow American drug officials to talk with countries on the "no contact" list, such as Cuba. He recognized that American-made amphetamines and barbiturates were finding their way into foreign countries and asked Congress to do something about it. He pledged more money to the United Nations' antidrug effort. He recalled the American ambassadors to Turkey, Mexico, France, Luxembourg, Thailand, and South Vietnam for consultations on how to reduce drug trafficking to the U.S., but really to put those countries on notice that he was going to make them share the blame for American addiction. "We want good relations with [these] countries," Nixon had said to Congress on June 17, "but we cannot buy good relations at the expense of temporizing on this problem."

For a brief period, Nixon and his advisers considered simply buying up the world's illicit opium crop. One afternoon, Pat Moynihan, Henry Kissinger, John Mitchell, and Myles Ambrose were knocking around the idea and Moynihan was arguing in favor. What would it cost? Fifty million dollars a year? A hundred? Would that do it? The idea had a certain free-market appeal. Then Mitchell turned to Ambrose and asked him what he thought.

"Mr. Mitchell," Ambrose said, "I feel like Alice in Wonderland at the tea party. If you put this policy into effect I'd consider going into the opium business *myself*." That ended the discussion.

In his boldest move, Nixon ordered Krogh quietly to arrange $35 million in "aid" to the government of Turkey to wipe out all but a tiny portion of its opium crop. A press conference was arranged for June 30 with Nixon and the Turkish ambassador to the United States; a young speechwriter named David Gergen prepared remarks for Nixon that called heroin "the number one public enemy in the United States" and hailed the Turkish government's "decision" to end all further opium production. No public mention was made of the $35 million.*

The public-relations value of the Turkey deal was lost, however. That same day, the Supreme Court upheld the right of the *New York Times* to publish the Pentagon Papers. Nixon became obsessed with finding out who leaked them and with plugging other leaks from the White House. Egil Krogh was called into Ehrlichman's office and given the job. He commandeered a room in the White House basement and recruited as his chief operative the man who had been in on the planning of Operation Intercept and who was now a member of the White House staff: G. Gordon Liddy. Since they worked in the

* Ultimately, the payment to Turkey worked so well that within a year there wasn't enough opium around to produce legitimate supplies of morphine and codeine, and the U.S. had to quietly ask Turkey to resume growing a little more. By then, though, Turkey wanted another payment, other opium-producing countries were talking about payments to them as well, and it quickly became apparent that the U.S. was sliding into a position of being expensively blackmailed. It quit paying countries not to grow opium and fell back on enforcement and crop eradication as its principal ways of getting farmers in developing countries to stop growing their most lucrative crop.

basement and were supposed to plug leaks, Liddy and his crew gave themselves a cute nickname: the White House Plumbers.

Krogh's attention was thus diverted from drug policy, never fully to return.

~

But he flew to Vietnam one more time. The army now had two testing machines, one at Long Binh and the other at Cam Ranh Bay, testing the urine of men scheduled to rotate out. As Jaffe predicted, the number of men testing positive was dropping rapidly as word got out that everybody had to pass through the "Pee House of the August Moon" and that a positive test would keep you in Vietnam for an extra week of detox. Congress had authorized only a single week of detox and three weeks of stateside follow-up, a ridiculously short period of treatment to get an addict off heroin. Moreover, the army wasn't using methadone, but only counseling. So even more surprising than the rapid drop in positive urine tests was the success the army was having in keeping its men off heroin. Most of those who had been addicts in Vietnam simply stopped using when they got home. The nightmare vision of swarms of killer Nam-vet dope fiends never materialized. Take a man out of a pestilential jungle where people he can't see are trying to kill him for reasons he doesn't understand, and — surprise! — his need to shoot smack goes away. If there was a lesson there about environmental factors contributing to drug abuse, it went unlearned.

~

Drugs hit number one on the hit parade of national problems in July. Haldeman put the latest Roper poll on Nixon's desk: drugs, Vietnam, racial tensions, lack of respect for the Golden Rule, and lack of strong leadership, in that order. Only after all that came the economy. The way Nixon read it, people are as discouraged about their kids as they are about the war, and it's all because naysayers are saying "everything is going to hell." What's needed, he said, was an "administration offensive on what's right with America." Noted Haldeman in his diary that night: "Maybe we have to demagogue it."

~

Meanwhile, back at the Marijuana Commission, the winds were starting to shift.

Keith Stroup of NORML and Ramsey Clark gave the kind of testimony Michael Sonnenreich had expected. What neither Sonnenreich nor the commission members expected was the testimony they got from such "straight" witnesses as Governor Richard Ogilvie of Illinois, the Drug Abuse section of the American Bar Association, and the San Francisco Committee on Crime, which was established with LEAA money. "In the past we have been guilty of a kind of overkill in the way we punished and criminalized some marijuana users," Governor Ogilvie said. "It would seem that sometimes the punishment meted out was more damaging to individuals and to the whole of society than was the use of the drug itself." The ABA passed a resolution calling for the elimination of all marijuana-possession penalties. And the San Francisco group flatly concluded that "criminalization has failed; we suggest that society now try non-criminalization."

Even more surprising to Sonnenreich was a comparison of state marijuana penalties. Depending on where you were caught with a joint for the first time, you could be sentenced either to no time in jail and a $250 fine, as in Arkansas, or, just across the state line in Texas, to life in prison. This wasn't just theoretical, either. State-level marijuana arrests had risen 1,000 percent since 1965; hundreds of thousands of people were in prison on marijuana charges at enormous expense to taxpayers. Clearly, too, marijuana laws were being used politically, to lock up the kind of people local police wanted locked up; Black Panther Otis Lee Johnson had recently been given a thirty-year sentence in Texas for passing a joint to an undercover cop at a party.

Sonnenreich was no ideologue. He'd been assigned to gather the facts about marijuana use, and these were the facts he was finding. He also hadn't yet heard any medical evidence convincing him the stuff was as dangerous as the "reefer-madness crowd" liked to say it was. The gateway theory, he thought, was "crap." One afternoon, while poring over some medical research in his office, Sonnenreich suddenly looked up at his assistant and said, "There's nothing the matter with this drug."

Having come to that conclusion, and appalled by the waste of court time, corrections money, and young lives on the altar of marijuana prohibition, Sonnenreich and his staff set out to move the president's commissioners in the direction of legalization. It wasn't that he thought marijuana was "good"; he still believed smoking it was foolish. But it was clear to his lawyer's eye that criminalizing it was cheapening the criminal justice system and overwhelming the prisons. He held well-publicized hearings that were carefully designed to appear "balanced." But there was no open-meeting law in 1971, so Sonnenreich and his staff could easily weight the bulk of the testimony in favor of lenience. In secret sessions, he brought in psychiatrists and pharmacologists to talk about medical effects, criminologists and corrections officials to talk about the cost of prosecuting marijuana offenses, and sociologists to talk about the social problems arising from waging war on the country's young people.

Knowing where he was taking the commission, Sonnenreich thought it only fair to warn his friend at the White House, John Dean.

"What?" Dean asked. "The commission is going to say *what?*"

~

Nixon's first two choices for seats on the Supreme Court, Clement Haynesworth and Harold Carswell, were rejected by the Senate; Nixon's consolation prizes were Warren Burger and Harry Blackmun. Then, in the fall of 1971, Justices Hugo Black, appointed by FDR, and John Harlan, a Truman pick, announced their intentions to retire. Nixon, who considered the term "loyal opposition" an oxymoron, went into the double nomination process with a good deal of bitterness. He decided to find a "real right-winger," Haldeman noted in his diary, and "stick it to the left."

But one after another, potential nominees were ruled out. Nixon briefly considered Senator Howard Baker of Tennessee and Mildred Lilley, a California Supreme Court justice who would have been the first woman on the Court.* But Egil Krogh, on whose shoulders the job of investigating potential nominees fell, didn't think either candidate was satisfactory. He called a meeting in his office with Mitchell, Ehrlichman, John Dean, and, representing the Justice Department's office of legal counsel, William Rehnquist.

Krogh gave Mitchell the bad news: they were back to square one. Mitchell was furious and flew into one of his ten-minute tirades. As he ranted on, Krogh's eyes wandered around the room until they rested on William Rehnquist. Hmmm, Krogh thought. Smart, conservative, an ally of the president; Nixon was sure to remember that Rehnquist had declared the invasion of Cambodia legal. What was it Mitchell once said of Rehnquist? "The only lawyer I know who would willingly

* Nixon probably came to regret he didn't put Baker on the Court. It was Baker who, as a member of the Senate Watergate Committee, coined the devastating line "What did the president know and when did he know it?"

defend the Sheriff of Nottingham." Krogh wrote a note on his yellow pad and handed it to Ehrlichman: "How about Rehnquist?"

Ehrlichman's eyebrow went up; he folded the note and put it in his pocket.

~

Don Santarelli by now was administrator of the LEAA: thirty-two years old, with a billion-dollar budget, accountable to nobody. Absurd requests were pouring in from police chiefs: Frank Rizzo of Philadelphia wanted a whole new fleet of police cars, and, being a prominent Democrat loudly supporting Richard Nixon, he got them. Several police chiefs wanted tanks, and Ed Davis of Los Angeles wanted a submarine. Santarelli put his foot down there. Many tiny police departments wanted "tac squads" to deal with potential riots. Too often for Santarelli's taste they got them. Santarelli had envisioned LEAA as a way to spread new ideas and professionalism to police departments everywhere, but it was turning into merely a kind of giant quartermaster for the nation's cops.

Watching the full flowering of the law-and-order presidency and Congress's embrace of RICO, Santarelli was starting to have second thoughts about the laws he had written. No longer did he believe in restricting defendants' rights the way no-knock and preventive detention had. His new goal was to inject the principles of the marketplace into the criminal justice system, to increase the body of *victim's* rights and let them clash in what he called a "healthy" way with defendants' rights. The administration around him was too single-mindedly conservative, though, and his own agency too big to control. He had a rule — no grants to prosecutors without matching grants to public defenders — but the money still seemed to flow almost entirely to prosecutors. It drove him crazy.

The big change that started Santarelli thinking differently, though, was the Supreme Court. Trading Earl Warren for Warren Burger was exactly the kind of thing Santarelli hadn't been able to envision. And now, of all people, William Rehnquist. A conservative Court!

Still, the job had its pleasures. Now that he was so important in Washington, he had been elected to the board of visitors of his beloved University of Virginia Law School. On one of his trips there, he met a young law professor who Santarelli thought was simply terrific — brilliant, erudite, conservative in the liberal tradition Santarelli revered. Santarelli wanted to bring him to Washington, get him connected, set him on the road to bigger things. Swinging his clout, Santarelli pried him away from UVA and wangled him the job of general counsel to the White House office of telecommunications.

His name was Antonin Scalia.

- Number of Americans who died in 1971 from all legal and illegal drugs: 2,313.
- Number who died in gun accidents: 2,360.
- Number who died choking on food: 2,227.
- Number who committed suicide: 24,097.

4

To the Streets
1972

> Narcotics suppression is a very sexy political issue. It usually has high media visibility. Parents who are voters are worried about narcotics. They listen to a politician when he talks about drug suppression just as they seem to tune him out when he makes speeches about the energy problem. Therefore, the White House often wants to be involved in narcotics problems even when it doesn't need to be. . . . For example, the Feds went into street enforcement partly in response to the obvious political mileage to be gained.
>
> —*former White House domestic policy adviser John Ehrlichman, in testimony to the Senate Subcommittee on Investigations, July 28, 1976*

A FEW DAYS BEFORE CHRISTMAS, 1971, John Ingersoll, director of the Bureau of Narcotics and Dangerous Drugs, tuned his television to a John Chancellor special called "A Day in the Life of the President." It was innocuous enough; Nixon talked with Canadian prime minister Pierre Trudeau and debriefed Treasury Secretary John Connally about his recent trip to Rome. But then Ingersoll's mouth dropped open: there on the screen, Richard Nixon was introducing Chancellor to his new "Special Consultant to the President for Drug Abuse Law Enforcement." It was a position Ingersoll, the nation's top drug enforcer, had never heard of. And standing next to Nixon was Myles Ambrose.

As Nixon stood there chatting with his hand on Ambrose's shoulder, Ingersoll realized the direction of federal drug enforcement was about to change. That gangbuster Ambrose wanted federal agents making street-level drug arrests: penny-ante buy-busts, shooting-gallery raids, you name it. Ingersoll braced for a directive that his agency alter its mission.

Instead, Nixon created an *additional* federal drug agency to operate alongside Ingersoll's BNDD. It was just what Ambrose had asked for in his memo. The new drug-fighting agency would be run directly from the White House, though technically Ambrose was to become a special assistant attorney general. When Ingersoll called John Mitchell the morning after the John Chancellor special, the attorney general didn't even know about it.

Although Ambrose said the new agency's purpose was "to stop the proliferating addict population," its puny size made it clear the real purpose was showbiz. No new money was appropriated. Ambrose detailed BNDD and Customs agents to his new agency, while BNDD and Customs continued to pay their salaries. Likewise he took prosecutors from Justice and detectives from state and local agencies. At its zenith, the Office of Drug Abuse Law Enforcement, or ODALE, fielded about 300 agents, just enough to give the feds a telegenic presence on the street. As one White House deputy put it, the feds need to bust street dealers for the same reason Mafia dons occasionally knock off a rival in public — just to show we can do it. ODALE was designed to showcase all the new tools provided by the big drug and crime bills of the past few years: RICO, no-knock, preventive detention, and "special investigative grand juries" with the power to question witnesses and suspects under oath and jail them indefinitely if they resisted. Moreover, it wasn't permanent; it had a sunset provision of eighteen months — long enough to take Nixon through the coming election.

~

A fearsome apparition rolled onto the War on Drugs battlefield in early 1972: the newborn addict.

"The symptoms are unmistakable," reported the *New York Times Magazine* in the first article of its kind. "The baby is racked by a peculiar coarse tremor. Its arms twitch. Its knees jerk convulsively toward its chest. Sometimes its tiny hands claw at its face and arms until they are raw. All the while the baby cries out with a tense, high-pitched shriek."

The *Times* reported an estimated 550 addicted babies born in New York the previous year out of a total of 117,000. Although about 11,000 babies were born underweight in New York that year — two and a half kilos or less — and 1,600 died from various causes in their first

28 days, the *Times* chose to focus on newborn heroin addicts as "an epidemic."

And the villain in this melodrama was clear. "Almost always the mothers are from the black, Puerto Rican and slum areas of town," the *Times* reported. "They have no joy of motherhood. They do not know who the father is, or how to care for themselves during pregnancy. . . . Suspicious, impatient, secretive, they are quickly turned off by either a cold or an overly sympathetic attitude."

~

Heroin addicts constituted about one-quarter of one percent of the population in 1972, yet they loomed large and terrifying in the public mind.

The conservative Hudson Institute estimated that New York City's 250,000 heroin addicts were responsible for a whopping $1.7 billion in crime, which was well more than the total amount of crime in the *nation*. "Narcotics addiction and crime are inseparable companions," said presidential candidate George McGovern in a speech on the Senate floor. "In 98 percent of the cases [the junkie] steals to pay the pusher . . . that translates into about $4.4 billion in crime." Senator Charles Percy of Illinois saw McGovern's bid and raised him. "The total cost of drug-related crime in the United States today is around $10 billion to $15 billion," he said.

In fact only $1.28 billion worth of property was stolen in the United States in 1972 (the figure actually had fallen slightly from the previous year). That includes everything except cars, which junkies don't usually steal because they can't easily fence them, and embezzlement, which also isn't a junkie crime. The combined value of everything swiped in burglaries, robberies, and muggings, everything shoplifted, filched off the back of a truck, or boosted from a warehouse was $1.28 billion. Yet during the heroin panic of Nixon's War on Drugs, junkies would be blamed for stealing as much as fifteen times the value of *everything* stolen in the United States.

"Addicts spend an estimated $17 million daily on heroin, a total of $6 billion a year," Myles Ambrose said in a speech in Los Angeles. "Most of that money is obtained through crime."

"The total costs [of drug abuse] attributable to property loss are estimated at $6.3 billion," said Dr. Robert DuPont, who by this time had moved from the D.C. methadone clinics to become Jerry Jaffe's number two man at SAODAP, the White House drug-treatment agency. DuPont later described to Congress a dizzying formula he used to arrive at that amount: take the number of addicts, figure in the proportion of their habit supported by income-producing crime, the days per year they're using drugs, the average cost of their habit every day, and the percentage of value stolen they receive in cash and — presto! — you come up with $6.3 billion. Not a single legislator noticed that DuPont's number was five times the value of *all* property crime.

Such inflated assertions weren't just for public consumption; Nixon's drug warriors spoke this way to each other. "If we assume that 60 percent of the estimated 560,000 heroin addicts steal property to support their habit, more than $18 billion worth of property is stolen each year to pay for heroin addiction," wrote Richard Harkness, an NBC reporter hired by the White House to manage public relations for the Drug War, in a confidential memo in May to drug officials throughout government.

Surely somebody could have glanced at the government's own crime figures and noticed that Harkness was off by a factor of 15.

~

Assuming addicts aren't stealing the equivalent of the NASA budget every year, how *do* they make their money?

The most authoritative study of junkie economics was published in 1985, a tome called *Taking Care of Business*. Seven researchers from a handful of colleges, along with a corps of graduate students, examined the junkie population in New York for eight years and found some surprises.

Almost all addicts commit *some* crime to get by. Most of that crime, though, is selling heroin to other addicts. Innocent citizens are not, by and large, hit over the head by heroin addicts. In fact, if drugs were legal, most addicts would be leading largely law-abiding lives. Many hold jobs, or do legitimate spot work, to earn most of their money. Moreover, most who steal were thieves *before* becoming addicted, so the theory that addiction leads to crime is dubious.

Egil Krogh would testify to Congress in 1976 — when he was no longer making drug policy — that he and his staff used to discuss whether drug enforcement was making the problem worse, whether it would "lead to a shortage, increase the price, and thus compel addicts to commit more crime to feed their habits." Krogh's Vietnam experience told him enforcement could worsen the health consequences of drug abuse. And doctors at the Centers for Disease Control were discovering that, contrary to expectations, demand for treatment increases during times of abundant heroin. But given the political momentum for drug enforcement, Krogh chose to believe the opposite.

~

The inevitable finally happened: the National Commission on Marihuana and Drug Abuse delivered its report to the White House. Michael Sonnenreich gave the document a name he felt captured the essence of the pot issue: *Marihuana, A Signal of Misunderstanding*. The conclusion: marijuana should be legalized.

Health effects are minimal. The "gateway drug" theory has no basis. If anything, smoking marijuana *inhibits* criminal behavior. "Since the beginning of our official life," the report read, "we have grappled with the threshold question: why has the use of marihuana reached problem status in the public mind?" The answer, it said, lies not in its pharmacological properties. "Many see the drug as fostering a counterculture which conflicts with basic moral precepts as well as with the operating functions of our society." Idleness, hedonism, and sexual promiscuity are cultural factors linked with the drug, the report explained, and " 'dropping out' or rejection of the established value system is viewed with alarm. Marihuana becomes more than a drug; it becomes a symbol of the rejection of cherished values."

This was President Nixon's own commission and, from the White House point of view, the report went downhill from there, audaciously siding with the "counterculture."

> Our youth cannot understand why society chooses to criminalize a behavior with so little visible ill effect or adverse social impact. . . . These young people have jumped the fence and found no cliff. And the disrespect for the possession laws fosters a disrespect for law and the system in general. . . . On top of this is the distinct impression among the youth that some police may use the marihuana laws to arrest people they don't like for other reasons, whether it be their politics, their hair style or their ethnic background.

The commission was telling Nixon, in effect, that the real marijuana problem wasn't the drug, but the war on the drug. The war was alienating young people, turning "straight" society against the counterculture, and leading police to use pot laws as political weapons. Marijuana prohibition, the commission concluded, is not in the national interest.

"I read it and reading it did not change my mind," Nixon told reporters during an impromptu Oval Office press conference a couple of days after its release. He offered no reason for his decision. None of the big newsweeklies reported on the commission's findings. After years of emotional back and forth about the medical, legal, and social implications of the boom in marijuana use, a commission of Nixon's own choosing recommended legalization, and the press let Nixon bury the story.

~

A reporter asked the new White House drug enforcer, Myles Ambrose, about a survey that had just been published: "I wondered if you are pleased with the trend among youth, particularly college kids, away from marijuana and back to booze?"

Ambrose chuckled paternally and said, "It recalls a happier day in which those of us who had the good fortune of going to college indulged in booze on more than one occasion, as I recall. It was beer. Let's say beer mostly. Yes I am very much pleased in that respect."

That same year, 55,000 Americans died in highway accidents, most of them believed to be alcohol-related. Another 33,000 died from alcohol poisoning or cirrhosis of the liver.

No death from marijuana has ever been recorded.

~

In September 1972, the State Department called home staff from fifty-four embassies abroad to hear President Nixon announce a stunning new policy. In keeping with his "total war" on "the slave traders of our time," Nixon was ordering the Central Intelligence Agency to join the drug fight. Traffickers, the president said, "must be left no base in any nation for their operation. . . . They must be hunted to the end of the earth."

It would be hard to imagine a better deal for a CIA bent on fighting wars Congress wouldn't finance: authority to operate wherever it liked, and a perfect cover for insinuating itself into a business saturated with loose cash. Throughout his tenure at the White House, Egil Krogh heard reports that even as he tried to keep Southeast Asian heroin out of the United States, the CIA's Air America was helping fund the secret war in Laos by flying the dopelords' smack. (Krogh never got to the bottom of it before having to resign in the Watergate fiasco.) A decade later the CIA would get caught doing the same thing, this time subverting Congress's specific prohibition against funding the Nicaraguan Contras by making unholy and lucrative deals with cocaine dealers. Nixon already had built a big federal drug-abuse bureaucracy whose institutional life depended on a "drug crisis." Now he added the CIA to the list of those with a powerful interest in keeping the War on Drugs alive.

~

After his mescaline conversion at the Grand Canyon and stint as a novelist in Mendocino, Gordon Brownell hung out in the Haight, doing his best to join the counterculture of San Francisco and northern California. It wasn't easy, because every now and then someone would ask what he'd been doing lately and he couldn't bring himself to answer, "Working in the Nixon White House, and then trying to get Ronald Reagan elected governor." By 1972, though, he was ready to come clean and put the political skills he'd acquired to work for a new cause. NORML needed a West Coast organizer, and Brownell got the job. The big issue was Proposition 19, the California Marijuana Initiative, to make California the first state to decriminalize possession.

Brownell shaved his beard, cut his hair short, bought a Brooks Brothers suit, and roamed the halls of the state house in Sacramento. He signed up as supporters of Prop 19 such assemblymen as Willie Brown, who would later become the Speaker of the Assembly and the second most powerful person in California; Henry Waxman of Los Angeles, who would soon be on his way to Washington as a U.S. congressman; and future San Francisco mayor George Moscone. The California Bar Association joined too, as did two different police associations. "If marijuana were decriminalized, [people] could grow it in their own healthy environment," said the president of the San Francisco Deputy Sheriffs' Coalition. "So it is reasonable to state that crime in general could drop."

More people ended up voting on Prop 19 — both for and against — than on any other proposition on the ballot. Statewide, the California Marijuana Initiative garnered only a third of the votes. It passed in only one county, San Francisco. But read another way, the first major city in the United States had voted to decriminalize. When NORML activists analyzed the returns, they discovered to their astonishment that several precincts that had gone for Richard Nixon also had voted to decriminalize marijuana.

This didn't particularly surprise Gordon Brownell. He himself had been the kind of conservative who believed in minimal meddling with individual freedoms. He'd gotten his political start in the 1964 Goldwater campaign and knew the country was full of the kind of conservatives who didn't want to spend taxpayer money intruding on citizens' privacy. In an interview with the *Los Angeles Free Press,* Brownell said his break with Nixon was only partly a matter of his mescaline epiphany; it was also that he felt betrayed. "I took a lot of these people at their word that when push came to shove, they'd favor the individual over big government," he said. "That hasn't been the case." Lyn Nofziger, Governor Reagan's political adviser, tore out the page and scrawled a note to Brownell across it: "Gordon, if this kind of drivel comes from smoking Pot it's the best reason I have yet to see for not using it. Lyn."

Nixon wanted his War on Drugs to hammer the political left, but 1972 saw the opening salvos of conservative opposition to the War on Drugs. In time, both economist Milton Friedman and Secretary of State George Schultz came to advocate legalizing drugs. Criticism from the right is a continuing problem for drug warriors; when people like Friedman or Schultz speak out for decriminalization, it's hard to dismiss them as radicals or drug users. Long before either of them joined the resistance, however, the Second Front of the Drug War was opened by one of the organizers of the right-wing student group Young Americans for Freedom: a Texan named Richard Cowan.

Cowan, then fresh out of college, wrote an article titled "American Conservatives Should Revise Their Position on Marijuana" and sent it to the most powerful publication of the American right: William F. Buckley's *National Review*. Buckley not only printed it; he put it on the cover, under the headline "The Time Has Come; Abolish the Pot Laws." Cowan laid out the arguments in conservative language: harsh laws engender disrespect for the laws, foster bureaucratic incompetence, and inspire fiscal waste. Marijuana has "tribal value" to the counterculture, he argued. "Any attempt at interference with so fundamental a part of the new social life is doomed to failure in a free society."

To the amazement of the conservative establishment, Buckley tacked on an editorial saying he agreed. On this big, emotional issue, the most eloquent voice of conservative America was more closely allied with Haight Ashbury and the left than with Richard Nixon.

As was Buckley's wont, he also printed a dissenting column. Jeffrey Hart, one of Buckley's stridently conservative writers, reversed Cowan's "tribal" argument. Yes, marijuana laws attack young people at their tribal core, he wrote, and that's good. "[Marijuana laws] aim to lean on, to penalize the counterculture," he wrote. "They reflect the opinion, surely a majority one, that the counterculture, and its manners and morals, and all its works are *bad*. Marijuana became an *issue* during the 1960s with the rise of the counterculture. It will cease to be one about six months from now with the death of the counterculture" (emphasis in the original).

In laying out the pages Buckley put his own editorial after the other two, but the last word, historically, would be Hart's.

- Federal drug-enforcement budget in 1969: $65 million.
- Federal drug-enforcement budget in 1974: $719 million.

5

Truce
1973–1976

The right to be let alone — the most comprehensive of rights and the right most valued by civilized men.

— *Justice Louis Brandeis*

DESPITE Buckley's silver-tongued urbanity, mainstream American conservatives were moving in the opposite direction, with the issues of drugs and crime leading the charge. Rather than taking a Libertarian turn toward small government and minimal interference with the individual, conservative thinkers were pushing the country toward accepting — and even demanding — an ever-larger government role in policing individual conduct.

What became William Bennett's best-selling "values" topic of 1993 was a muted dialogue among conservative academics in 1973. Cornell professor Walter Berns was arguing that "the purpose of law is and must be to promote virtue." A Yale law professor wrote in 1971 that there is no such thing as a "victimless" crime in a moral society. "No activity that society thinks immoral is victimless," he wrote. "Knowledge that an activity is taking place is a harm to those who find it profoundly immoral." That professor's name was Robert Bork. Four years after the "southern strategy" won Richard Nixon the White House, conservative academics were building an intellectual framework around it.

So strong was the new moral voice of conservatism that the *New York Times Magazine* ran a long article analyzing it in the winter of 1973. Queens College professor Andrew Hacker argued that conservatives have come to believe people are essentially *bad*. They will take drugs, commit crimes, and loaf on welfare if given the chance, and the duty of government is to correct such reprehensible behavior. Conservatives have been pushed to this belief, Hacker argued, as a reaction against the Great Society thinking of the 1960s. They are convinced that "to assume that we know enough to diagnose causes (derelict housing, bad schools, unemployment) or to bring about cures (jobs, slum clearance, better education) is a monumental delusion."

In the new conservative world view, Hacker wrote, personal depravity *is* the root cause of crime. Social pressures — racism, poverty, lack of jobs, bad education — are essentially immaterial, and as "proof" conservatives could point to the majority of poor blacks who didn't commit crime or use drugs. The corollary of such a view, of course, is that the relatively wealthy white mainstream is not responsible for ameliorating the conditions liberals insist cause crime. It was around this time that Governor Ronald Reagan of California first invoked the so-called welfare queen, with a "tax-free income of over $150,000," to argue for lower taxes and reduced social spending. Rather than attack "root causes," Hacker wrote, "the conservative prescription [for crime] is to bring criminality under control. Force has been a corollary of conservative thought: how else do you deal with perversity?"

As if to prove Hacker's point, the *New York Times Magazine* that same winter ran a second article in which another academic, conservative Harvard political scientist James Q. Wilson, summarized his forthcoming treatise on the value of proper punishment, *Thinking About Crime*. Wilson predicted much of the War on Drugs for the next two decades, arguing Americans have been getting unsatisfactory results from their criminal justice resources because they have unreasonable expectations. Prisons can't rehabilitate people who are essentially bad, and the good people will eventually go straight without special rehabilitative efforts. "Suppose we abandon entirely the rehabilitation theory of sentencing and corrections," Wilson wrote. "Instead we would view the correctional system as having a very different function — namely, to isolate and to punish." John Ehrlichman cut out the article and sent it to the president's desk with a memo urging him to read it.

Wilson argued for short, standardized prison sentences. Judges are reluctant to impose long terms, he reasoned, and confronted with long mandatory sentences, they will simply encourage plea bargains, defeating the attempt to deliver severe punishment.

As it turned out, Wilson never quite got his way. Instead of choosing between short, certain sentences and long, uncertain ones, Congress ultimately would combine the worst of both, opting for *long, mandatory* sentences, such as ten years without parole for a first-offense cocaine-dealing charge.

This would be a continuing pattern in the War on Drugs — the fusion of two unrelated or contradictory schemes into explosive policy. The reach of RICO's criminal forfeiture would combine with the low burden of proof in civil forfeiture to let police legally confiscate the homes and bank accounts of innocent people. Don Santarelli's no-knock and preventive detention laws would mix with an "unthinkably" conservative Supreme Court to create a decade-long assault on the Fourth, Fifth, and Eighth Amendments. And the parallel notions of long sentences and certain sentences would join to become a prison-filling monster so harsh and expensive that William Rehnquist would eventually come to denounce it.

Wilson called his proposal for a stern and standardized system of punishment "hopelessly utopian."

"It will be opposed by judges unwilling to surrender their authority to do as they please. It will be opposed by legislators [desiring] massive sentences that are rarely imposed. It will be opposed by taxpayers' groups that do not wish to foot the bill for . . . new correctional facilities. . . ." Wilson was, respectively, right, partly right, and flat wrong. Judges certainly opposed mandatory and guideline-driven sentencing. Legislators passed laws for massively long prison sentences *and* saw to it they were frequently imposed. And the one function of government that taxpayers consistently have supported is the building of more prisons.

~

Bob Randall was depressed. At twenty-five, he was going blind from glaucoma, a disease that elevates pressure inside the eyeball. A year earlier, he'd been forced to give up driving a cab. Now, teaching speech at Prince Georges College outside Washington, D.C., he'd be almost completely blind by evening. His intraocular pressure would rise steadily as the day progressed, and as he walked home every evening the world would be nothing but colored halos surrounding cars' headlights. None of the standard drugs seemed to be helping.

One night he smoked a couple of joints with some friends. A little while later, he looked out the window at the street lamp on the corner and realized suddenly there was no halo around it. He could see clearly for the first time in months. Excited, he tried smoking pot the next night when the halos started closing in. The same thing happened; his vision cleared. Marijuana seemed to be doing what the doctors' expensive drugs could not.

~

He'd never wanted the job to begin with, but Jerry Jaffe could look back on the previous two years as drug czar with a good deal of pride.

While the government never reached the point of providing help to every addict who wanted it, treatment had come a long way; 400 federally funded treatment centers were operating around the country, with a capacity of about 100,000 addicts. More important, Jaffe had managed to set up a sensible reporting system whereby cities could estimate the number of treatment "slots" needed and government could allocate funds accordingly. Heroin deaths were dropping. Addiction research had been vastly expanded. Lloyd Johnston at the University of Michigan — who had canvassed the high school class of 1969 on their drug use — had been signed up to do an annual nationwide survey of high school seniors that would become one of the most important measures of illegal drug use in the country. Methadone had become legitimate. The federal drug budget was ten times bigger than when Nixon came to power, and until the current budget cycle, treatment had gotten more money than law enforcement. Jaffe had to hand it to Nixon: he'd quietly done a lot of good.

But verbally he'd done a lot of damage. All of Nixon's harsh rhetoric about marijuana — combined with a good deal of ignorant media coverage — was starting to make the public think all drugs were equally dangerous. Nixon's vitriol further increased the chance that the public would turn against helping addicts recover. And the president was clouding an important public health issue with political and cultural hostility that, from Jaffe's point of view, couldn't do the nation any good. Jaffe once expressed misgivings to Nixon about all the "war" rhetoric surrounding White House drug policy, and Nixon had quoted Corinthians back to him: "If the trumpet give an uncertain sound, who shall prepare himself to the battle?" That was the problem, Jaffe thought, thinking of the effort to reduce drug abuse as a "battle."

What's more, Jaffe thought, the administration's split personality on drugs — destructive rhetoric alongside sensible policies — was starting to unify itself the wrong way. The big treatment budgets Jaffe had enjoyed in 1972 and 1973 were to be reduced in 1974 as part of Nixon's overall austerity program. The White House was going to maintain the illusion of "doing something" about drugs by sending ODALE's police teams into the field. Egil Krogh was up to his neck in the Plumbers, and more and more, the enforcers were taking over drug policy. Jaffe adopted a philosophy he'd heard from a friend on Wall Street: "Don't fight the tape." Enforcement was the new zeitgeist and Jaffe wasn't going to buck it. Soon after Nixon's second inauguration in January 1973, Jaffe resigned his position at the White House drug-treatment agency and returned to Chicago.

~

Armed with the Marijuana Commission's recommendation to legalize, Keith Stroup and NORML hit the road. Stroup arranged hearings before state legislatures throughout the country to discuss abolishing or at least reforming marijuana laws. He brought along a powerful ally: the retired number two man at BNDD, a white-haired, steely-eyed narcotics enforcer of the old school who believed marijuana wasn't worth the time of agents who had a heroin war to fight.

NORML enjoyed some early success. By the fall of 1973, Georgia had reduced first-offense possession of marijuana to a misdemeanor. Texas had gone from having 800 marijuana possessors in prison (serving an average of nine years each) to ruling possession of two ounces or less a misdemeanor with a five-month maximum sentence. Oregon had become the first state to decriminalize possession completely. And the American Bar Association — not usually associated with radical causes — voted that year to support a federal bill decriminalizing pot. "With the ABA behind decriminalization of pot," *Time* asked, "can the rest of the nation be far behind?"

Well, yes. The California legislature voted to reduce pot possession to a misdemeanor, only to have the bill vetoed by Governor Ronald Reagan. Half of all drug arrests in Massachusetts were still for pot. And New York pushed the panic button. Calling for "brutal honesty" regarding narcotics addiction in New York, Governor Nelson Rockefeller told his state legislature that New York's addicts steal $6.5 billion worth of goods and money a year — five times that year's total for the nation. But Rockefeller insisted that "addicts are robbing, mugging and murdering day in and day out for the money to fix their habit" and asked the legislature to pass the toughest drug laws in the nation, including mandatory life in prison for heroin pushers and addicts who commit violence while high. "Had it come to that?" *Newsweek* asked rhetorically. "In truth, Rockefeller's hard line seemed designed more as an opening gambit than a serious bill."

But Albany went for it big time, imposing up to fifteen years for an ounce of marijuana and life in prison for possessing less than an ounce of "a substance containing heroin." This was the most severe marijuana law yet, but the language on "substance" in the heroin section was the real bombshell: nine-tenths of an ounce of milk sugar mixed with a tenth of an ounce of heroin counted in the law as an ounce of heroin. The law also forbade plea bargaining in cases of serious drug crimes. To help handle an expected crush of cases, the law created thirty-one new courts.

Still, within a year and a half, the backlog of drug cases in New York's courts had reached 2,600, and the time required to dispose of a drug case had almost doubled, not only because of the plea-bargaining restriction but because with the stakes so high, more than twice as many defendants were demanding jury trials. The law's effect on addiction was nil, according to a study by the New York City Bar Association: heroin use was as widespread in 1976 as it was before the 1973 law. Likewise, during the next two years, the increase in New York's crime rate was identical to that in nearby states.

"Crime does not go down when you take addicts off the streets," argued one New York City Police captain. "In fact, there is some evidence that [crime] increases, that the preoccupation with addicts lets more serious criminals to act more freely."

Regardless, two-thirds of Americans polled at the time thought the Rockefeller drug laws were "a good idea."

Nixon scowled at the speech and slashed it with his pen. This was to be his big speech on crime and drugs, and young David Gergen on the speechwriting staff hadn't made it nearly tough enough. "Namby-pamby," Nixon called it in a memo to John Ehrlichman. He wanted "stark, tough language" filled with "controversial, hard-line proposals." Mandatory sentences for heroin dealers. A federal death penalty. No marijuana legalization. And damn the legalities. "I know most of the legal eagles in the Justice Department as well as on the White House staff will disagree on what would appear to be rather sound legal grounds with my decisions on all three of these items," Nixon wrote. "This happens to be one of those cases, however, where I have convictions that run contrary to those of many of my staff and despite their opposition I intend to go forward full bore."

Next morning, Ehrlichman sent the speech back to the president filled with references to Americans' right to "freedom from the fear of crime." The Ehrlichman version derided "permissive judges [who] are more considerate of the pusher than they are of his victims." But the speech dealt first with marijuana. "The line against the use of dangerous drugs is now drawn on this side of marijuana," Ehrlichman wrote. "If we move the line to the other side and accept the use of this drug, how can we draw the line against other illegal drugs?" Now the marijuana argument was openly a matter of cultural politics, not health. It wasn't damage to the smoker that required the continued ban, but the potential perils that legalizing the drug posed to the overall Drug War effort.

The other important shift in the speech was Nixon's demand that Congress pass a five-year minimum sentence for anyone convicted of selling heroin: ten years to life "for major traffickers" and "life *without parole* for a second offense" (emphasis in the original).

The severity of the punishments was the least of it. By making a loud public demand that Congress pass tough federal sentences for "everyone convicted of selling heroin," Nixon was inviting all drug cases into federal court. At the time, almost all narcotics offenses were investigated by local police and handled in state courts. The Nixon speech had immediate appeal for local cops, who measure their success by how many years in prison the suspects they catch are given. If a two-bit heroin dealer will get only probation or a year in prison in state court but a mandatory five-year sentence in federal court, the incentive is strong to ask the feds to take over the case. Especially when the federal government is fielding a whole new agency — Myles Ambrose's ODALE — to sweep up street dealers.

Along with the muscular rewritten speech, Ehrlichman gave Nixon a memo guessing what the headlines would be the day after the State of the Union address: "President to seek mandatory jail for pushers," "Nixon for life in jail for drug sellers," "President: 'Strike harder against drug pushers,' " and " 'Law and order' not code for racism or bigotry, says Nixon."

~

Herbert Giglotto, a twenty-nine-year-old boilermaker, and his wife, Evelyn, were asleep in their Collinsville, Illinois, home when their front door exploded from its hinges. The Giglottos watched in terror, clutching each other, as five longhaired men with guns rushed down the hall toward their bedroom. "My God, we're dead," Giglotto moaned. "The hippies have come to kill us."

The men grabbed Giglotto, threw him to the floor, and pressed a gun to his head, while one of them screamed, "Where's it at? Where's it at?" Another held a shotgun on Evelyn and yelled, "Who's this whore in the bed?" When Giglotto tried to answer, the one holding the pistol on him growled, "You son of a bitch, you move and you're dead."

Then the men started smashing furniture, pulling pictures off the wall, dumping drawers. "Where's it at?" they yelled. "Where's it at?" Slowly it dawned on Giglotto that the hippies were some kind of police. He couldn't imagine what they were looking for. After an hour of fruitless searching, their ardor seemed to dissipate, and they collected themselves to leave.

"That's it?" Giglotto asked them. "You just kicked in my door, threatened my life, called my wife a whore and a bitch. Can you explain to me why you did this?"

The leader spun on his heel and knocked Giglotto to the floor. "Shut your mouth, boy," he said, and they disappeared into the night.

The men were agents of ODALE. From the Giglottos' house, they drove across town and kicked in the door of Donald Askew, a forty-year-old gas station operator, whom they proceeded to terrorize, along with his wife, Virginia, and their sixteen-year-old son, Michael. They ransacked the house for an hour and left as suddenly as they did from the Giglottos'. Virginia Askew, who had a history of psychological problems, was so shaken by the raid that she spent weeks thereafter in the psychiatric unit of a local hospital.

The White House finally got some drug-enforcement publicity, though not the kind it wanted. When reporters started asking questions, they learned this had happened before, though never twice in one town on the same night. The ODALE practice of gathering cops from disparate jurisdictions, pinning a federal badge on them, filling their ears with complicated new laws, and then turning them loose was turning into a recipe for massive violations of civil rights. ODALE director Myles Ambrose suspended the officers involved in the Collinsville raids, but he was hardly apologetic: "Drug people are the very vermin of humanity," he said. "Occasionally we must adopt their dress and tactics."

Later in 1973, Congress voted on Nixon's plan to combine ODALE, BNDD, and the drug-fighting functions of Customs into a single agency: the Drug Enforcement Administration. Like BNDD, the DEA would be a division of the Justice Department, putting more police muscle into the same agency that fields prosecutors. Wary of giving so much power to a Justice Department besmirched by Watergate — especially in an enforcement field stained by Collinsville — Congress placed tough restrictions on the DEA. "The use of DEA agents to supervise ODALE-type operations against street-level pushers should be avoided. . . . The primary mission of DEA should be to interdict the highest levels of the illicit drug traffic." It might have been a fine goal if drug enforcement weren't — in John Ehrlichman's words — such a "sexy political issue."

Time magazine wrote:

> The dinner party on Manhattan's fashionable East Side included all the chic refreshments. It began with perfectly mixed martinis, followed by a fine vintage French wine with the main course. With dessert, guests puffed the finest marijuana. Then, after coffee and cognac, the young hostess presented the evening's *pièce de résistance,* a glass jar filled with white powder. "Would anybody like a hit of coke?" she inquired casually, as if offering another drink. Indeed they would.
>
> "It's the height of fashion," says a well-heeled snow freak, "because it shows success."

It drove Michael Sonnenreich crazy. During hearings for the Marijuana Commission, he had looked at other drugs as well. One study in particular stuck in Sonnenreich's mind: When researchers offered various drugs to monkeys, the beasts wouldn't touch LSD after the first time, and would soon tire of marijuana and the opiates. For cocaine, however, the monkeys had an insatiable appetite, and if given the choice between cocaine and food, they would literally starve themselves to death ingesting cocaine. Of all the drugs Sonnenreich had looked at, cocaine was the one that seemed the most likely to do real harm. All that kept him from truly panicking was cocaine's high price; it was out of reach to anybody but the jet-setters portrayed in the *Time* article.

By the summer of 1973, drug abuse was low on the list of concerns at the Nixon White House. The Watergate hearings were daily television fare, and each broadcast seemed to bring closer the end of Nixon's presidency. Egil Krogh, who had incubated the first national drug-treatment program, was on his way to federal prison for ordering Liddy's "Plumbers" to burgle the office of the psychiatrist of Pentagon Papers leaker Daniel Ellsberg. Krogh's drug-policy staff was reduced and scattered; nobody had replaced him as manager of law enforcement issues for the White House. ODALE had been wrapped into the DEA, so the White House had no direct enforcement role. Congress, emboldened by the scent of Nixon's blood, picked apart any White House request for money. It was hard to believe that only a year earlier a confident Nixon had told Congress the country was "turning the corner" on heroin abuse. Treatment funding was cut, and addiction and crime rates started back up. Bob DuPont, who had stepped into Jerry Jaffe's old position as head of the federal treatment program, could barely keep it from disintegrating entirely. Just before SAODAP was dragged down by a sinking Nixon, DuPont himself bailed out, to a civil service position in research at the National Institute on Drug Abuse (NIDA). There, he couldn't be fired when the administration changed. And if he couldn't dictate national drug policy, he could at least influence it.

By the time Nixon resigned a year later, the country was so consumed with Watergate that the "drug epidemic" — luridly vivid just two years earlier — had dropped off the national radar. A glance through the *Reader's Guide to Periodical Literature* shows heroin got only five mentions in all of 1974, as opposed to two years earlier when it was worth several stories a week. The problem of addiction hadn't gone away, but with so much else to think about the country didn't need a War on Drugs.

~

By 1975, Bob Randall was smoking an ounce of marijuana a week to keep his glaucoma under control. Being stoned didn't seem to interfere with his work as a college professor, but it did keep his vision from deteriorating. Rather than assume the expense and risk of buying so much pot on the street, Randall grew his own — four weak plants in the bathroom of his D.C. apartment.

Upon returning from a short vacation that August, he found his apartment ransacked, the plants gone, and lying on the kitchen counter both a D.C. police search warrant and a letter inviting him to turn himself in. He did so, and in preparing for his trial did what most people did in those days when in trouble for marijuana. He called NORML.

NORML referred him to scientists at NIDA, the DEA, and the FDA, all of whom told him that yes, research has demonstrated that marijuana can help control glaucoma. Other drugs work too, they said, but not for everybody. A Howard University researcher added that glaucoma strikes blacks at eight times the rate it strikes whites.

Randall was furious. The government *knew* marijuana was useful in treating a disease that was otherwise hard to treat, and yet it both kept that information secret and the drug itself banned. Randall decided to fight his case on the grounds of medical necessity, an argument he learned had been tried only about a dozen times in the United States, never successfully.

~

The treatment network Krogh and Jaffe launched survived the transition to the Gerald Ford administration. Although Ford never established an equivalent to SAODAP, treatment had acquired a life of its own and the funding continued, albeit at lower levels. Years later, Jaffe would say that his greatest achievement was institutionalizing drug treatment. Its funding could be diminished, but never scrapped entirely.

In September 1975, a little more than a year after Ford climbed atop a wobbly executive branch, a skeleton drug-policy staff at the White House, along with DuPont at NIDA, produced a thin "white paper" on the state of drug abuse in the U.S. It was a gloomy and pessimistic report, befitting an administration that was unelected, understaffed, and tainted by Ford's pardon of Richard Nixon. "We must be realistic about what can be achieved and what the appropriate Federal role is in the war against drugs," it said. "We should stop raising expectations of total elimination of drug abuse from our society."

Federal drug enforcement should be directed only at the highest levels of trafficking organizations, the report said. All other efforts should be directed not at "wiping out drug abuse," but at "minimiz-[ing] the adverse social costs of drug abuse." Heroin was still the most fearsome drug, it said, and the federal Bureau of Prisons should drop its resistance to methadone and start using it. Outpatient methadone clinics, with treatment "slots" costing a clearly defined $1,700 apiece, are the most cost-effective way to reduce the harm of drug abuse, the report said.

As for cocaine, the data in the report showed that "as currently used, [it] usually does not result in serious social consequences such as crime, hospital emergency room admissions, or death."

A year later, the Ford administration would retreat even further from the Drug War. Its 1976 *Federal Drug Strategy*, published the same month Jimmy Carter won the White House, returned to "root causes," mentioning heroin addicts' "poverty, unemployment, alienation, or lack of opportunity." It engaged in lengthy hand-wringing over the distinction between a *real* drug problem and a *perceived* drug problem, arguing that an individual's drug abuse isn't always a problem if it doesn't affect the wider society. It directed attention for the first time to alcohol, "the most widely used drug in the United States today," stating that "its abuse is related to more deaths and injuries than any other drug." Finally, President Ford's *Federal Drug Strategy* suggested "seriously studying" the decriminalization of marijuana.

~

The War on Drugs had drifted into a wavering truce. Its general had been toppled, and new crises had captured the public imagination. In the lull, the armies of legalization continued marching; ten more states in addition to Oregon voted either to remove penalties for marijuana possession or reduce them to the equivalent of a parking ticket. A group of senators led by Indiana's Birch Bayh held a day of hearings to give voice to Keith Stroup and a long list of legalization advocates and then introduced a bill to decriminalize marijuana possession. The DEA's own chief counsel opined that the U.S. could legalize marijuana possession without violating any international narcotics treaties. Running for president, Jimmy Carter said he thought jailing pot smokers was counterproductive.

The *Washington Post* editorialized in favor of decriminalization. Rockefeller's successor in New York, Governor Hugh Carey, toyed publicly with scrapping the state's draconian drug laws in favor of civil fines for pot possession. The Michigan Court of Appeals voided a key drug-enforcement tool by ruling unconstitutional the practice of charging people with "intent to sell" simply because they possess a certain quantity of drugs.

The drug culture now had its own magazine, *High Times*, which started in 1974 with a pot dealer's $10,000 investment and two years later was a $5 million giant whose editors partied publicly with the likes of Jack Nicholson. A multimillion-dollar industry had grown up around drug paraphernalia; bongs and roach clips were a big and legitimate part of the annual Boutique and Gift shows in New York. "I'm like a bottle maker during Prohibition," a millionaire rolling-paper tycoon told the *New York Times*. "When [marijuana] is legalized, I'll make even more money than I do now."

The legalizers, flush with a feeling of imminent victory, graciously welcomed defectors from across the lines. When NORML held its annual conference in 1974, NIDA director Bob DuPont — formerly Richard Nixon's drug czar — was the keynote speaker and added his voice to those calling for an end to the jailing of marijuana users. "Criminal penalties have clearly failed to prevent widespread use of marijuana," he said. "Law and health are two entirely separate issues."

~

Congress even took on the DEA in 1975 and 1976, something it would not find the courage to do in subsequent years. Senator Henry "Scoop" Jackson's Permanent Subcommittee on Investigations loosed an investigator named Philip Manuel, who returned with a report accusing the DEA of being entirely off its congressional leash: ignoring its mandate, inflating its statistics with small-quantity busts, falsifying records, and failing to police itself against corruption.

John Ehrlichman, under whose aegis the modern War on Drugs was launched, sat down before the committee and said the effort he'd once championed was a sham. "I think there is a genuine hypocrisy in all of this," he said. "The people in the federal government [are] just kidding themselves and kidding the people when they say we have mounted a massive war on narcotics when they know darned well that the massive war they have mounted on narcotics is only going to be effective at the margins. If they don't know it, they ought to know it. Maybe we can use the money some other way."

~

A woman in suburban Atlanta threw a birthday party for her thirteen-year-old daughter during the summer of the Bicentennial. This birthday party, which started calmly enough, with the children dancing to records in the sticky heat, would be remembered as the moment when a new front opened in the War on Drugs. After Ashley Schuchard's birthday party, the heavy artillery of the Drug War began wheeling around from the heroin target to marijuana, a substance no drug czar yet had taken seriously. The woman who started the process was Ashley's mother, a spare, intense, self-described liberal-Democrat professor named Marsha.

Known all her life by her middle name, Keith, Schuchard grew up in Texas and taught English at Emory University along with her husband, Ron, who taught poetry and literature. They lived with their children in a spacious old house near the campus.

During Ashley's birthday party, Schuchard was amazed to see twelve- and thirteen-year-olds stumbling around red-eyed, giggling, and obviously stoned. She saw the flicker of matches in dark corners of the backyard. She could smell burning reefer. Schuchard knew what she was seeing; everybody got high during grad school at the University of Texas, and she herself had enjoyed more than one panful of pot brownies. Schuchard didn't think of herself as a prude, but seventh-graders smoking marijuana seemed beyond the pale. These were children! No sooner had the balloons and crepe paper come down than she and her husband crawled around the backyard, confirming what they'd suspected. Roaches lay everywhere, along with papers, clips, and plastic bags containing crumbs of pot leaf. Schuchard decided to call the parents of the kids who'd been at the party, to tell them what she'd found. The reactions surprised her.

Some parents didn't care; "it's only pot," they'd say. Others were furious that Schuchard was "snooping" on their children and accused Schuchard of being a hypocrite: "Don't you drink? What's the difference?" Many simply denied any such thing had taken place or that their children were involved.

Being an activist by nature, Schuchard invited all the pot-smoking kids' parents for an informal meeting to share information and talk about what might be done. At least thirty showed up, but not all were friendly. Many parents couldn't believe their kids were involved, and when presented with evidence to the contrary, argued that marijuana was no big deal anyway. Some walked out, calling Schuchard a hypocrite and a prude. But as the evening wore on, several confessed that their children seemed to be going downhill, acting even more withdrawn and furtive than they expected of an adolescent. They began blaming each other, accusing each other's kids of being ringleaders and pushers. But by evening's end, the parents had agreed to meet again in three days.

What they found in those three days appalled Schuchard. The police knew about teenage pot smoking, but didn't think it worth their time. "Pot is like the air, it's everywhere," one police official said. The school guidance counselor told them not to worry. "Marijuana isn't addictive," he said, "and all kids experiment a little." They asked the school principal, who simply denied the school had a drug problem. They asked a therapist, who said at least their son wasn't drinking or doing hard drugs. Local merchants knew kids were smoking pot in their parking lots, but considered it only a loitering problem. Even school drug-abuse books dismissed marijuana as less harmful than tobacco or alcohol; one advised kids to use a water pipe to cool the smoke and to avoid burning holes in their clothing. The experts were telling the parents not to worry, but the parents felt they could see with their own eyes that this drug was harming their children.

Sensitized, the parents also started noticing how pervasive drug culture was. Posters in their kids' bedrooms, magazines lying around, rock-and-roll lyrics, album covers, and even TV shows all seemed to reinforce a message that getting high was cool. Schuchard went to see the Cheech and Chong movies the kids liked so much and couldn't believe her eyes. People debilitating themselves was supposed to be funny! The parents also started putting two and two together, realizing that those odd, foul-smelling pieces of colorful bent plastic they'd seen around the house were pipes for smoking pot.

By the time the Atlanta parents reconvened, they were in a drug-fighting mood. They drew up a list of rules that all would agree to enforce. Kids would be grounded for the next two weeks, during which they would also be forbidden to use the phone. After that, all outings would be planned and chaperoned. All phone callers would have to identify themselves, and no calls could be made or taken after 9:00 at night. A common curfew — 6:00 on school nights, 9:00 on weekends — was agreed upon. The parents assured each other it was okay to search their kids' rooms, read their diaries, listen in on their phone calls. Some opted out, feeling these measures were too severe. Others drifted away, thinking the effort was hopeless anyway.

Predictably, the kids were stunned and furious. But Schuchard's group, which started calling itself the Nosy Parents Association, was suddenly everywhere, lurking in the corners of school dances, cruising parking lots, showing up at parties. To most kids and many parents of the neighborhood, Schuchard and her Nosy Parents were a damned nuisance.

At the same time he was building his medical-necessity defense for his trial, Bob Randall filed a petition with the Department of Health, Education and Welfare to receive marijuana directly from the federal government's experimental pot farm at the University of Mississippi. After a one-day bench trial, the judge delayed delivering a verdict. HEW, worried that Randall would be acquitted on medical-necessity grounds without having a policy in place to deal with cases like his, told him that he could get government pot if he met certain conditions.

First, HEW said, he would have to be hospitalized constantly and receive the marijuana only in the hospital. Barring that, he would have to drive to the hospital to smoke it. When Randall suggested that would mean driving home stoned, HEW countered that he could keep the pot at his house provided he stored it in either a 750-pound safe or a 250-pound safe embedded in concrete and bolted to the floor.

Meanwhile, the judge sat on his verdict, and HEW got more and more nervous. Okay, HEW said, we'll give you the pot, but you can't tell anybody about it. Furious, Randall called CBS News and the *Los Angeles Times,* both of which reported on his case.

HEW relented on November 12, 1976. Randall was handed a square tin containing three hundred long, straight-walled U.S. government–issue marijuana cigarettes, along with a promise that he could get more when they ran out. Twelve days later, the judge acquitted him of growing marijuana, on the grounds of medical necessity. It was the first time in U.S. history that anyone had beaten a drug charge on those grounds. Bob Randall was now the only legal marijuana smoker in the United States.

- Number of DEA agents in Chicago in 1975: 111.
- Number of cases they worked that year: 138.
- Number that involved less than a pound of drugs: 119.
- Amount the DEA paid to buy evidence and pay snitches in 1969: $750,000.
- In 1976: $10 million.

6

Civil Punishment
1977

Congress should definitely consider decriminalizing possession of marijuana. . . . We should concentrate on prosecuting the rapists and burglars who are a menace to society.

— *U.S. Representative Dan Quayle, March 1977*

AS JIMMY CARTER walked up Pennsylvania Avenue on the cold, sunny day of his inauguration, one thing he didn't have to carry was Nixon's antidrug baggage. Vietnam was over. His constituency didn't demand a war on the "counterculture." Addicts were being cared for. Crime was off page one. No particular advantage was to be gained by making an issue of drug abuse. And Carter had a trusted friend in charge of drug policy: thirty-eight-year-old Peter Bourne.

Like the previous two drug czars — Jerry Jaffe and Bob DuPont — Bourne was a psychiatrist. British born and raised, Bourne had emigrated to Atlanta at seventeen to attend Emory University and then Emory Medical School. After a stint in the army — studying combat stress in Vietnam — he simultaneously completed a psychiatry residency and a master's degree in anthropology at Stanford University. Then he stayed in the Bay Area to help open the Haight Ashbury Free Clinic. By the time he returned to Atlanta in 1969, his experience among the Haight's hippies made him the closest thing Atlanta had to a drug expert. So when Jimmy Carter was elected governor in 1970, he hired Bourne to manage the state's drug-abuse program and the two men became close friends. Bourne made good use of the methadone program Jaffe was setting up, and by 1972 he had just about all of Georgia's 6,000 addicts in treatment. Though a lifelong Democrat, Bourne had to admit Nixon had done right by legitimizing methadone and funding nationwide treatment.

In one of their first sessions together after the inauguration, Bourne and Carter talked about Birch Bayh's marijuana-decriminalization bill making its way through Congress. Would Carter support it or not? Although candidate Carter had come out in favor of the eleven states' decriminalizing pot possession, President Carter said he didn't want to support the bill. Why do it? he wanted to know. What's to be gained? Bourne followed their conversation with a memo, telling Carter that in light of what he'd said during the campaign, his new position was "almost impossible to justify." He asked Carter for five more minutes to discuss it.

Still resisting, Carter argued that removing federal penalties for marijuana possession would send the wrong signal. Even NORML doesn't say marijuana is completely harmless, he said; everybody agrees it's worthwhile to discourage people from smoking. Bourne concurred, but stressed that prison was more harmful than pot, so if the goal really was to protect people's health, the prison terms for possession had to be abolished. Also, decriminalization made good fiscal sense; the National Governors Conference had just published a study of the states that decriminalized, and found "substantial" savings of tax dollars with no increase in marijuana use. Even Bob DuPont, the Nixon holdover running the National Institute on Drug Abuse, favors decriminalization, Bourne said; DuPont had just spoken publicly in favor of legalizing home cultivation. That way, DuPont argued, pot smokers "would no longer be in contact with dealers who may offer other illicit items for sale."

The compromise Bourne got Carter to buy was an intricate and subtle one more typical of an anthropologist/psychiatrist and a Baptist deacon than of two people savvy in the ways of image politics. The president would advocate replacing the *criminal* penalties for pot possession with a *civil* fine. That way, they thought, the government would be registering its disapproval of marijuana smoking while not ruining the lives of harmless potheads. Bourne also reasoned that because some judges are reluctant to send pot smokers to prison, the civil penalty would be more widely imposed and therefore satisfy the James Q. Wilson standard requiring certainty of punishment.

Fine, Carter said, sharing Bourne's trust that the public would be able to tell the difference between criminal and civil punishment. Carter's domestic policy adviser, Stu Eizenstat, advised against making an issue of drugs so early in the presidency. But Carter stuck by his young friend Bourne and overruled Eizenstat. Neither Carter nor Bourne understood marijuana's emotional importance as a cultural symbol; to them, it was merely a mildly dangerous substance whose use was worth discouraging. Just as the next Democrat to win the White House would choose gays in the military as his first big issue, Jimmy Carter selected marijuana — a topic equally resistant to reasoned debate — as the topic for an early presidential stand.

The speechwriter assigned to draft Carter's drug message, Griffin Smith Jr., felt he needed a quick education in marijuana's legal status nationwide, and the most knowledgeable person in Washington on that subject was Keith Stroup at NORML. At the time, no stigma attached to NORML; it was simply a player in the drug debate. Bourne himself spoke to Stroup frequently and had hosted him at the White House mess. Smith called Stroup and asked him to come to his apartment in the Watergate that evening, to talk over some matters of law for a presidential statement. Over a beer, the two wrote the marijuana section of Carter's message to Congress on drug abuse.

Smith ended up delivering a draft so radical that Eizenstat felt moved to intervene. "I am very concerned about the marijuana section of this message," he memoed Carter. "This will certainly be the headline story." While Smith mentioned removing criminal penalties, the proposed civil penalties were left out. "In general, I believe the section on marijuana is written in an almost laudatory tone," Eizenstat wrote. "Sentences such as 'marijuana has become an established fact throughout our society and the sky has not fallen,' 'research studies indicate it may have beneficial uses in the treatment of certain types of illness,' and a suggestion that the states should repeal their criminal prohibitions, 'thus bringing to a close an unhappy and misguided chapter in our history,' almost seem to be a positive recommendation of the drug." Every one of those phrases was written by Keith Stroup. Two decades later the NORML founder still chuckles and shakes his head to think how close a president came to pronouncing them.

Even toning down the message to Congress, Jimmy Carter became the first American president to advocate decriminalizing marijuana possession. Carter's drug statement, delivered to Congress barely six months after he assumed the presidency, nodded briefly in the direction of tougher enforcement — directing the Justice Department to "study the need for" stiffer trafficking penalties. But Eizenstat was right; the new president's position on pot was the news:

> Penalties against possession of a drug should not be more damaging to an individual than the use of the drug itself; and where they are,

> they should be changed. Nowhere is this more clear than in the laws against possession of marihuana in private for personal use. . . . Therefore, I support legislation amending Federal law to eliminate all Federal criminal penalties for the possession of up to one ounce of marihuana.

He went on to advocate civil fines for pot smokers, to assure Congress he still wanted drug *dealers* prosecuted, and to allow states "to adopt whatever laws they wish concerning the marihuana smoker." The press was kind; conservative *Time* magazine, for example, gave the new president credit for being more sensible than the public on this one and recognized what Carter missed, that marijuana has power beyond its pharmacological properties. Carter's idea was likely to go nowhere, *Time* said, only because "polls still show that most Americans still believe that pot is addictive, harms users physically and usually leads them to hard drugs. None of this has been proved in more than ten years of scientific studies."

~

The principle guiding Peter Bourne's drug policy was a long-established doctrine, developed in the Netherlands, called "harm reduction." Eliminating all drug use is impossible, goes the reasoning; the proper role of government is to reduce the harm that drugs do individuals and society. For addicts, addiction isn't the problem; only the *harm* the addiction causes is to be addressed. Therefore, perpetual addiction to methadone is appropriate.

In the harm-reduction context, "harm" is defined broadly, considering also the harm done by ham-fisted efforts to reduce drug abuse. If stiff pot-possession penalties do more harm than the drug itself, reduce them. If heavy street enforcement makes dealers more violent and more inclined to adulterate their drugs with poison, back off. Harm reduction is the kind of policy one might expect from a drug czar like Peter Bourne, who also is a physician, who has taken a Hippocratic oath that begins: "Do no harm."

If avoiding harm is paramount, other priorities must be abandoned. A harm-reduction drug policy cannot, for example, also make a punitive moral statement about drug abuse, because doing so might cause harm. It can't necessarily work as a political cudgel against the young, the poor, and the black, because some aspects of reducing harm — such as refusing to imprison teenagers for pot smoking — run contrary to such a political goal.

One of the principal American gurus of harm reduction was a

Harvard Medical School psychiatrist named Andrew Weil, a flamboyant writer and speaker whose foot-long hair cascaded from a shiny bald pate. Harvard Med School, of course, is notorious for producing counterculture drug advocates: Timothy Leary taught there, as did Richard Alpert (later known as Ram Dass). Weil had been a college roommate of Carter's favorite speechwriter, Rick Hertzberg, so the White House was in easy contact with him. In his book *From Chocolate to Morphine,* Weil made the revolutionary argument that "any drug can be used successfully, no matter how bad its reputation, and any drug can be abused, no matter how accepted it is. There are no good or bad drugs; there are only good and bad relationships with drugs."

Here was the antithesis of the demonization of drugs that Richard Nixon had started with his harsh anti-marijuana rhetoric. No drug is evil unto itself; the harm it does the individual and society depends entirely on the relationship the individual and society make with it — on its social context. Government doesn't need to act as some kind of knuckle-rapping schoolmaster went the harm-reduction argument; leave people alone and most of them will use drugs in a way that harms nobody. The few that fall off the cliff into addiction can be gently nursed back to health.

Gerald Ford's drug strategy, prepared by Bob DuPont, had hinted in the harm-reduction direction. But Peter Bourne accepted it, and Weil's logic, with a whole heart. Carter's midterm drug strategy read:

> Drugs cannot be forced out of existence; they will be with us for as long as people find in them the relief or satisfaction they desire. But the harm caused by drug abuse can be reduced. We cannot talk in absolutes — that drug abuse will cease, that no more illegal drugs will cross our borders — because if we are honest with ourselves we know that is beyond our power. But we can bring together the resources of the Federal Government intelligently to protect our society and those who suffer.

That was the last White House drug strategy to use such terms. It was the last to make delineations between hard and soft drugs and between types of penalties (criminal or civil). It even tried to draw a hairbreadth distinction between drug *abuse* — "non-therapeutic use of any psychoactive, including alcohol, in such a manner as to adversely affect some aspect of the user's life" — and drug *misuse* — "inappropriate use of drugs intended for therapeutic purposes."

Bourne was intensely proud of elevating drug policy to a high intellectual plane of fine distinctions and measured rhetoric after what he viewed as the relative barbarity of Nixon. "I am not sure that we will end up making the right decisions," he wrote to Andrew Weil in 1977, "but I do feel that unlike previous administrations we will have made the very best effort to get the most knowledgeable input before arriving at any conclusions."

By the end of Carter's presidency, though, such a cool, haughty attitude toward an issue as emotional as drug abuse would number among the nails in Carter's political coffin. And then President Ronald Reagan would use them to deepen Carter's political grave. "We cannot talk in absolutes," the Bourne-Carter strategy said, but talking in absolutes about drugs was the American way before Jimmy Carter and it has been that way ever since. The short reign of Peter Bourne as drug czar stands as the high-water mark of technocratic, scientific, unemotional drug policy. It also stands as the high-water mark of drug-policy naïveté.

~

Something else happened in the strategy that the public never knew: all references to tobacco were removed. A draft of the strategy filed in Carter's presidential papers includes such references as "excessive use of . . . tobacco," "an estimated 55 million Americans smoke cigarettes daily," and an assertion that while illegal drug abuse costs the country $10 billion a year, cigarette smoking costs the country $25 billion. But all were crossed out by an unknown hand, and tobacco disappeared from White House drug strategies for the next seventeen years.

~

Cocaine got a mention in Bourne's drug strategy — placed as a priority just below barbiturates and just above marijuana.

Bourne thought little about cocaine. Harm reduction was the order of the day, and though Bourne knew cocaine use was rising, few people appeared to be harmed by it. Those with the most to worry about, he wrote in late 1977, were the Latin American countries whose economies were being undermined by the big cartels. He asked Andrew Weil to think about ways to get Andean cocaine farmers to switch crops, and Weil rather typically suggested instead "expanding legitimate uses of the leaf, such as research and medicinal ones, which might decrease diversion to the illegal traffic." Bourne fairly gushed in response. "It is extraordinarily helpful to have somebody such as you available to us as a resource," he wrote back. "We greatly appreciate your help and will try to make decisions that will make you proud of us."

In a 1977 article practically selling cocaine as "de rigueur among hostesses in the smart set of Los Angeles and New York" — like "Dom Perignon and beluga caviar" — *Newsweek* quoted Bourne saying "there's not a great deal of evidence of major health consequences from the use of cocaine." By year's end cocaine wasn't even on the list of eleven items Bourne wanted discussed at an upcoming staff meeting. Heroin was still the big bad drug, and aside from some disturbing recent deaths of methadone patients, the heroin problem appeared to be under control. The country was rapidly approaching the goal Richard Nixon had established: to provide treatment for every heroin addict that wanted it.

The bottom line on cocaine, Bourne told *Newsweek,* was that only the very rich can afford to snort cocaine, and they don't do it enough to do themselves any harm. But, the article ended, "Bourne . . . believes that if cocaine were less expensive and more easily obtained, users would indulge more heavily, perhaps creating greater health problems."

~

Bourne was walking into a trap and taking Jimmy Carter with him. Several things were happening that Bourne either could not or would not recognize.

High school kids were smoking more and more marijuana; what Keith Schuchard's Nosy Parents Association was seeing in Atlanta was evidence of a demonstrable national trend. Lloyd Johnston's first high school survey, in 1975, showed 6 percent of seniors were toking up every day. By 1977 it was over 9 percent. Although Bourne noticed the trend, it was fourth on his written list of concerns at the end of that year, right after heroin-addiction in Europe. Moreover, Johnston was asking kids about their *attitudes* about marijuana; fewer and fewer each year believed it harmful or disapproved of its use. If Bourne was reading the survey, it was not dawning on him that Carter's push to decriminalize — and the administration's studied nonhysterics about drugs — would someday catch the blame for young people's easing attitude toward marijuana.

Similarly, Bourne was unaware of what was really happening to all those swanky cocaine snorters. Cocaine doesn't drag the chronic user down suddenly; the desire for more creeps up slowly. Many of the beautiful people tooting nose candy in 1977 were going to find themselves strung out and desperate by about 1982. Bourne would have had to have been a psychic to know this, though. Hardly any researchers were doing serious work on cocaine in those days. Focused on heroin and lacking data on the obscure amusement known as cocaine, Bourne didn't know a monster was growing right under his nose. Come the crisis, all of his blithe comments about "the lack of major health consequences from the use of cocaine" were going to come screaming back at him in a vituperative snarl.

And then there was something starting to occur in South America that even the most visionary weren't fully comprehending in 1977. That summer, Nick Kozel was on the streets as a drug-abuse researcher for HEW. Nine years had passed since the D.C. jail study that had touched off Nixon's War on Drugs and started Kozel's career in drug-abuse research. Despite his misgivings about that study's linking of addiction and crime, Kozel had to admit the addiction-treatment effort that the study helped spawn was impressive.

Kozel worried about cocaine breaking out of the smart set and thought HEW should try to stay ahead of the curve. He convinced his boss to send him to a conference in La Paz, Bolivia, on the production, refining, and use of coca.

The conference was hosted by a Bolivian psychiatrist named Niels Naya, who ran a ward for addicts in La Paz's central hospital. Naya invited Kozel to visit the ward to look at some cases of severe cocaine poisoning. Among Naya's most worrisome patients, he told the young American researcher, were about twenty men who had scrambled their brains smoking coca paste, a chemical precursor to cocaine the locals call "basuco." It's becoming quite a fashion, Naya told Kozel, and it has me scared. Smoking cocaine drives the drug into the brain much faster than snorting it. It really makes people crazy for more, he said. They can't get enough.

~

The resistance Keith Schuchard was getting from the parents in her area made her furious. All these righteous old hippies who wouldn't let their kids touch white sugar or a hot dog were allowing — practically encouraging — them to smoke pot.

There had to be a way, she thought, to sever marijuana from the liberal, counterculture values these parents espoused. Pot was all wrapped up with the old opposition to the war, with the civil rights movement, with all of the good, healthy rebellion of the sixties in which Schuchard herself believed. It wasn't enough just to get the conservatives on her side; the liberals' kids smoked as much pot, if not more.

In the meantime, she started paying attention to the rhetoric out of Washington. Jimmy Carter — her old governor, the man she worked so hard to elect — was advocating decriminalization! His drug czar was on record saying not only was marijuana relatively harmless, cocaine was too. The director of NIDA, Bob DuPont, wanted not only possession but home cultivation of marijuana legalized. Didn't they know, Schuchard wondered, that children were smoking pot? Apparently they did but didn't care; Carter's Cabinet Committee on Drug Abuse had concluded that drug experimentation by young people "is not particularly distressing." Didn't Bourne and DuPont see a difference between children and adults? Didn't they understand that by downplaying the dangers of marijuana they were encouraging kids to smoke it?

Schuchard wrote Carter a letter — "as a Carter supporter and loyal Democrat" — warning him that he not only was inadvertently doing kids harm, he also was setting himself up for a heap of political trouble. It was a four-page, single-spaced letter, followed by three pages of footnotes. She got a form letter in return. Peter Bourne wouldn't return her phone calls.

But she also fired off a long letter to Bob DuPont at NIDA, and there she struck pay dirt.

DuPont read the letter, and something in it rang a bell. First of all, like Bourne, he had attended Emory Med School and could picture Schuchard's neighborhood exactly. The image of drugged kids in that leafy, idyllic setting was alarming. It was true, he thought; he hadn't thought much about the implications for children when he'd called for decriminalization. Maybe the "soft" talk from Washington did have something to do with the rising use of pot by kids.

DuPont also instantly understood what Carter and Bourne missed: parents were the future of drug policy. They were the only ones with a real stake in it. All the doctors and experts and commissions in the world could drone on about marijuana's relative harmlessness, but parents lived with the real-world consequences every day. No force in nature is stronger than a mother's anger, DuPont believed, and if parents were organizing around marijuana, they were going to have far more energy for the fight than all the graybeards in Washington, D.C. Also, DuPont knew, the image of tearful, angry mothers was going to blow the "experts" right off the evening news.

Maybe this is how it should be, he thought. Maybe we experts really have let the country down. He picked up the phone and dialed

Schuchard himself. My father lives in Atlanta, he told her, and the next time I'm down I'd like to pay you a visit.

~

Peter Bourne testified often to Congress on the administration's efforts against drug abuse, and every time he did the subject of marijuana decriminalization came up. What a bore! Bourne thought. Marijuana is an issue of no consequence. But in his mellow and refined English diction, he would again walk the solons through the administration's desire for civil penalties for possession, to replace the criminal penalties now in effect. But let's talk about the real drug problem, he'd say. Let me tell you about our efforts against heroin addiction. . . .

And every time, he'd open the paper next morning and find it written that "Peter Bourne advocates legalizing marijuana." Couldn't these people tell the bloody difference? he'd fume. Couldn't they keep their minds on what's important?

~

Living across the street from Keith Schuchard was a young mother named Susan Rusche, wife of an Emory professor and, like Schuchard, a self-described liberal Democrat. Rusche was friends with many of the parents both allied with Schuchard and opposed to her, and she had tried to act as a go-between. She felt herself removed from the fray, because her own sons were only seven and eight, far too young to be affected.

One afternoon in 1977 she took the boys to the local record store to buy the new *Star Wars* soundtrack album. She found the record, but when she looked up, her sons were at the far end of the store, fascinated by something else. It turned out to be what looked like a Star Wars ray gun. When Rusche looked closer she saw it had a mouthpiece and a little bowl with a screen in it. A marijuana pipe, the clerk told her.

Rusche looked at the other items in the case. A kind of Frisbee with a dope pipe built into it. Beautifully colored water pipes and stash boxes. A "practice rolling kit" complete with a little bag of shredded alfalfa. A board game called Dealer McDope. A magazine was lying on the counter: *High Times*. After thumbing through it for a few minutes, Rusche grabbed her sons' hands and stormed out of the store.

Like Schuchard, Rusche had tried marijuana when she was younger and hadn't given it too much thought since then. Until

Schuchard began her antipot crusade, she hadn't been aware teenagers were smoking. And until she went into the record store, she hadn't known the "commercialized drug culture" — as she came to call it — was so blatantly targeting children her own kids' age. She found fifteen stores selling paraphernalia in the county, six of them in the university district within walking distance of her home. She asked the owner of one why he sold such things, and he told her it was all that got the Emory students into his store. So Rusche bought a bagful of the stuff and brought it to the next PTA meeting. Look at this, she said.

Paraphernalia was a godsend for Keith Schuchard. As soon as the bongs and roach clips spilled across the table at PTA, it seemed, the denial she'd been facing melted away. Here was a concept all those old hippie parents could grasp. It isn't just drug dealers that want your kids toking up, Schuchard said, it's big capitalist paraphernalia corporations, too. Suddenly, her phone rang constantly.

Bob DuPont's visit had been so exciting — the gangly NIDA director could barely contain his enthusiasm for the Nosy Parents Association — that Schuchard and Rusche were emboldened to keep after Peter Bourne. Finally, he agreed to drop in the next time he was in Atlanta.

They prepared for the drug czar's visit by assembling a big collection of magazines, record albums, posters, and paraphernalia. They laid it out on a big table, along with heaps of drug-abuse literature downplaying the dangers of marijuana and mountains of scientific studies showing the drug harmed everything in the body from the lungs and the immune system to the cerebellum and the gonads. Bourne arrived, ever charming and polite, and looked over the things on the table. Fascinating, he said.

You're missing something important by focusing only on heroin addicts, they told him.

Hmm, he said.

Look at the information that even the federal government is putting out, telling people how to use drugs responsibly instead of not to use them at all.

Yes yes, he said. I can see that's confusing.

Schuchard and Rusche explained their activism, how they were trying to take control of their kids and keep them away from drugs.

Marvelous, he said, glancing at his watch. Do keep me informed. And he breezed out, never to be heard from by the Nosy Parents again. Marijuana wasn't a problem worthy of his time, he figured. Besides, he thought he knew all about people like Schuchard and Rusche.

He lumped them in with the Georgia right-wingers always looking to oppose anything Jimmy Carter did.

The White House correspondence section told Bourne that a torrent of angry mail was arriving daily from parents in Atlanta. Bourne told Carter about it, and the president's response was "don't answer them." That was fine with Bourne. Bourne was a doctor after all, a psychiatrist, an architect of White House policy. If anybody was going to change his mind about marijuana, it certainly wasn't going to be a group of untrained, hysterical southern parents. Drug policy simply wasn't made that way.

By turning his back on the nascent parents' movement, Bourne made himself a very large enemy at precisely the moment he was going to need all the friends he could get.

7

You Didn't Get This from Me

1978

> Between 1977 and 1992 a conservative cultural revolution occurred in America. It was called the drug war.
>
> *— John Walters, deputy drug czar from 1989 to 1993*

IT WAS THE PARTY OF THE YEAR. The elegant mansion off Washington's DuPont Circle throbbed with music and glittered with the beautiful and the famous. Journalists, congressional aides, White House staff members, activists, and even straitlaced scientists from NIDA pressed against each other, sipping wine, swapping gossip at the tops of their lungs, gobbling up the caviar that circulated on silver trays.

This being NORML's annual Christmas party, fat joints of sinsemilla circulated as well; the air was thick with reefer smoke and alive with the harsh snarl of cocaine disappearing up fashionable noses. Dramatically gutted by its architect-owner, the house afforded a view from basement to top floor, giving everyone a view of everyone else. The only privacy was in a bedroom on the top floor, its door guarded by a former Secret Service agent, where Keith Stroup hobnobbed with Christie Hefner, Hunter Thompson, and other luminaries.

A ripple went through the crowd. Walking through the front door, shaking hands this way and that, was Peter Bourne. The drug czar at a NORML party! Truly the kingdom of heaven was at hand if the president's principal drug-policy adviser would appear openly at a pot-smoking party of legalizers. Stroup immediately swooped down on Bourne, fending off the proffered joints, and led him upstairs to the bedroom. "Good evening, everybody," Bourne said, as he shook hands all around. After a few pleasantries, somebody produced a bullet-shaped vial of cocaine and frosted his nose. He handed it off — sniff — it was handed off again — sniff — and then, making its way around the circle, the vial of cocaine was offered to Peter Bourne.

~

Enraged by her visit to the record store, Susan Rusche went after drug paraphernalia with the zeal of a grizzly sow protecting her cubs. She pressured the PTA into writing the fifteen head shops in the county, asking that the drug-oriented products be withdrawn. When the head shops refused, Rusche convinced the county commission to revoke their business licenses on the grounds they posed "a hazard to the health, welfare, or safety" of the county. (The businesses successfully sued, but in the meantime twelve of them closed or got rid of the paraphernalia.) She formed an organization, Families in Action, that convinced the owners of a new Oz Records chain store to drop their usual line of paraphernalia. Families in Action put leaflets in every mailbox in the county, asking for support. And then Rusche stumbled on a tactic that brought her and the suburban Atlanta parents movement into the limelight of the national press. She convinced her state legislator to introduce a bill banning paraphernalia outright.

Indiana had tried such a law but it had been overturned by a federal judge. Georgia went ahead, though, and passed not one but three bills; one banned selling any device "primarily intended for use in injecting, inhaling, or smoking" any illegal drug; another banned selling paraphernalia to minors; and the third made it illegal to sell or display printed materials that advocate the use of illegal drugs. As soon as Governor Busbee signed them, lawsuits were filed in federal court in Atlanta challenging their constitutionality. Rusche drove down to the courthouse to pick up copies. They'd been filed, she read, by the Georgia Paraphernalia Association, the owners of the affected head shops, and an organization Rusche had never heard of: the National Organization for the Reform of Marijuana Laws, a.k.a. NORML.

~

For NORML, the paraphernalia laws seemed an opportunity, not a problem. How could a piece of plastic bent a certain way be ruled illegal? How could the law distinguish between a tobacco pipe and a marijuana pipe? Ludicrous! Defeating such laws would only bring glory to the legalization cause. For star power, William Kunstler was recruited to lead the legal fight.

Paraphernalia seemed such an easy issue to win that NORML largely ignored it. Likewise, Stroup and his lieutenants paid no more attention to what was happening in Atlanta than Peter Bourne had. For every study the prohibitionists produced showing marijuana's harmful effects, NORML could produce an equally prestigious one debunking it. After all, Richard Nixon's own presidential commission had ruled marijuana relatively safe. The medical question was settled, Stroup thought. If anything, he and the legalizers thought it to their advantage to have the prohibitionists arguing on the basis of health effects. The forty million Americans who'd tried pot and come away unscathed would certainly recognize all the shrieking about immune-system damage and testosterone levels as nothing but another wave of "reefer madness."

What neither Stroup nor NORML understood until too late, though, was that the harmlessness argument was impossible for the legalizers to win. The reverse was true, too; for every study NORML could produce showing marijuana's safety, the prohibitionists could produce one showing its harms. And like Bourne, NORML and Stroup weren't paying attention to the declining age of marijuana smokers. It didn't occur to them that people could simultaneously believe marijuana relatively benign for adults and dangerous for children. NORML was so fixated on proving marijuana harmless that it didn't feel the ground shifting under its feet.

At just this moment, as a whole new front was opening in the marijuana wars, NORML attacked in an entirely different — and suicidal — direction. Rather than articulating a clear policy against marijuana smoking by children and publicly urging head shops to stop marketing to minors — thereby co-opting the distinction between children and adults in favor of the legalization cause — NORML ignored parents and kids altogether. Instead, NORML threw itself into stopping what it thought was the most serious threat to marijuana smokers: the spraying of Mexican marijuana with the herbicide paraquat. In choosing this fight, NORML was selecting as its enemy the presidential administration that had done the most to advance NORML's cause. Of all of NORML's many blunders over the years, this would be its biggest. By the time the paraquat issue burned itself out, NORML would have all but destroyed the legalization cause with its own friendly fire.

G. Gordon Liddy had first suggested defoliating marijuana fields in his infamous 1969 memo on Operation Intercept. By 1978, the DEA was directly assisting the Mexican government with spraying opium crops with 2-4-D, a dioxin-based defoliant similar to Agent Orange. (There being no addict lobby comparable to the pot smokers' lobby, nobody in the U.S. made a fuss about that.) But Mexico also was buying paraquat from England and spraying marijuana crops from the same U.S.-supplied helicopters they were using in the opium spraying. NIDA rushed out a report estimating that as much as a fifth of the marijuana imported from Mexico — some 500 tons — was contaminated and that some samples were tested at 44,000 times the maximum safe level. HEW Secretary Joseph Califano warned that "if an individual smokes three to five heavily contaminated marijuana cigarettes each day for several months, irreversible lung damage will result." Senator Charles Percy of Illinois, a sponsor of the decriminalization bill and an enemy of federal drug enforcement ever since ODALE's Collinsville raids, called for an investigation.

Bourne sent a delegation to Mexico to talk about ways to ameliorate any possible harm to American pot smokers. Among the group was the man who would come to personify the national obsession with stamping out marijuana. Thirty-seven-year-old Carlton Turner, a former disk jockey, was assistant director of the University of Mississippi's five-acre "pot farm." The Old Miss marijuana project was the only legal source of research marijuana in the country, and Turner, a cheerful, easygoing Alabaman with degrees in pharmacology and organic chemistry, was considered one of the world's top experts on the drug.

For a long time, Turner was a scientific noncombatant whose allegiance seemed up for grabs; in the early seventies, when most research was showing the drug to be fairly harmless, Keith Stroup thought he might enlist Turner as a full-blown ally. Turner himself had harbored plans of becoming a defense attorney for drug dealers and had even been stoned once, when he accidentally inhaled a headful of smoke during a lab experiment.

In 1971, though, the federal drug agent in charge of Mississippi press-ganged Turner into setting up a marijuana-education program for police. "Either you help me educate cops about drugs and I'll ensure your system runs smoothly," the agent had told Turner, "or don't and I'll put you out of business." By 1978, Turner was convinced marijuana was the deadly drug police liked to say it was and was eager to throw his scientific credentials behind saying so. More cancer in a joint than in a Camel, he liked to say. He wasn't a very public figure, though, and his views weren't well known. When Bourne sent him to Mexico City, he thought he was sending an impartial scientist.

In a meeting at the U.S. Embassy in Mexico City, the group

considered asking the Mexicans to mix into the paraquat a bright yellow dye to warn smokers their pot had been sprayed, but that was no good; it would only make the pot look like high-quality "Acapulco Gold." Then they hit on the idea of mixing in a powerful odorant as a warning, but the question was raised: if a pothead smokes it, and the odorant permeates his carpet and drapes, would the U.S. government be liable?

"You've got to be kidding," said Turner. "If that happens, you arrest the son of a bitch and throw him in jail for being a criminal."

The U.S. never did get a chemical warning mixed in with the paraquat, and among people interested in the pot debate — like the parents in Atlanta — word began spreading that Carlton Turner, "the country's foremost authority on marijuana," was firmly in the prohibitionist camp.

Bourne testified to Congress that while the U.S. was involved in the opium spraying, the marijuana spraying was Mexican policy, not American. Bourne traveled to Mexico personally to admonish the Mexican attorney general to use the helicopters for their intended purpose only. Still, NORML filed suit against the U.S. government to stop the spraying and launched a loud, angry campaign against Bourne and Carter. Bourne explained to Stroup personally — several times — that he should be blaming the Mexicans instead, but Stroup seemed to Bourne beyond argument. All of the old congeniality between the two men was gone; Stroup appeared to be personally furious at Bourne over the paraquat spraying — furious to the point of irrationality. They'd run into each other, and Stroup would pointedly snub him. Bourne would open the newspaper or turn on the television and find Stroup denouncing him again and again.

Gradually, it began to dawn on Bourne that he had, in a way, created this problem for himself. The Carter administration had been so friendly with the reform movement that the sense of crisis NORML needed to sustain itself had passed. Pot smokers didn't feel the need to rally 'round NORML — and send it their money — with Jimmy Carter and Peter Bourne in the White House.

Had they been speaking at the time, Stroup would have agreed. NORML's membership was dropping, and paraquat was a sufficiently alarming issue to keep pot smokers active. But only because the threat was, in Stroup's eyes, real. Stroup felt genuinely betrayed by the spraying. When he confronted Bourne about the danger of inhaling pot smoke laced with paraquat, Bourne had said, "But Keith, it's illegal."

"Does that mean it's right to sentence pot smokers to lung damage and maybe death?" Stroup shouted back.

The U.S. could stop the spraying, Stroup believed, and it was unconscionable not to. The two men hadn't spoken since.

It also bears saying that like a lot of young, hip Washingtonians in those days, Stroup was developing a personal, apolitical taste for cocaine, and that, he would recall, "leaves you ragged on the edges, and made us more belligerent than we should have been."

After one particularly acrimonious exchange of letters between Stroup and the White House, Stroup hinted to Bourne that he knew a lot about the after-hours marijuana smoking of several young members of the White House staff, and it was common knowledge in Stroup's circles that the president's son Chip liked to toke up. Bourne worried about this; he knew several members of Chip's Secret Service detail had asked for reassignment because they didn't like being compromised by Chip's pot smoking. In February 1978 — well into their feud — Bourne tried to make peace with Stroup, writing to him, "I want you to know of the very high personal regard in which I hold you and the remarkable leadership that you have provided to NORML under conditions that I know have not always been easy. I will look forward to continuing to work closely with you in the future."

~

The various agencies involved in giving Bob Randall his legal marijuana had never been happy about it, and in January 1978 he was notified by HEW that he no longer would get any. Immediately, Randall filed suit.

A month later, New Mexico became the first state to pass a resolution recognizing the medical value of marijuana. But since the federal government controlled all legal supplies of the drug — at Carlton Turner's marijuana farm — any New Mexico patient that wanted it would have to apply to the same bureaucracies that now were fighting Randall over his.

Having been shown smoking legal marijuana on television, Randall was becoming famous among those who also felt they could benefit from medical marijuana. Oncologists called to tell him how useful pot was in fighting the nausea caused by chemotherapy; many said they secretly recommended that their patients try it when all conventional drugs failed. Legislative aides from New York to California were calling to ask his advice about writing state laws similar to New Mexico's.

In May, Randall was invited to observe a meeting at the National Cancer Institute on the medical benefits of marijuana and its main psychoactive ingredient, delta-9 tetrahydrocannabinol, or THC.

In addition to the NCI researchers, present were representatives from NIDA, the FDA, and the DEA.

One problem with THC, the FDA official said, is that it's a natural substance, so it can't be patented, and if it can't be patented, no pharmaceutical company will make it. Eli Lilly has asked us to approve a synthetic THC they've made called Nabalone, the FDA contingent said. We'd really like to get this on the market to stop people asking for legal marijuana, so we're going to allow "double tracking" — human research concurrent with animal research. It's unusual, but the pressure's on.

Randall, sitting silently against the back wall, was amazed. Marijuana contains more than 400 distinct chemicals, of which THC is only one. THC is the drug that gets people stoned, but in 1978 there wasn't any research that showed it was the drug that reduced pressure inside the eyeball or fought nausea. Since THC was the pot chemical about which there was the most research, that was the one the FDA wanted synthesized for medical use. It was crazy.

A pill presented other problems as well, Randall thought. Once swallowed, it delivers its whole dose at once. One of the nice things about marijuana, in Randall's view, was that the patient can smoke a little, see how it's working, and if necessary smoke a little more. Also, if the issue is nausea, expecting a chemotherapy patient to hold down a swallowed pill was ludicrous.

Randall knew, though, that asking the medical/pharmaceutical community to accept marijuana was going to be a tough fight. No therapeutic drugs in Western medicine are smoked; pill or injection are the ways this society takes its medicine. The medical community also is oriented toward single-drug therapies narrowly targeted at specific conditions, whereas marijuana is a complex miasma of chemicals whose total effects may never be fully understood. The DEA was still in charge of scheduling, or categorizing, drugs by their dangerousness, and it was committed to keeping marijuana in Schedule One, meaning highly dangerous, having a high potential for abuse, and having no medical value. Cocaine, occasionally used as a topical anesthetic, was a Schedule Two drug, but marijuana was classified as being as deadly and useless as heroin. Finally, as one FDA official put it, marijuana will never be a legal drug because "there's no profit incentive to develop marijuana"; anybody can grow it.

So the NCI meeting broke up with the federal government determined to develop synthetic THC to offer to those requesting marijuana.

By the end of 1978, Illinois, Florida, and Louisiana had followed

New Mexico's lead and passed laws recognizing marijuana's therapeutic value. HEW also had settled Randall's suit by creating a program called Compassionate Investigative New Drug, or IND, which considered marijuana a drug under study and allowed for the grievously ill to receive it on an experimental basis. Randall started getting his pot again. IND, though, required the patient to file reams of forms. Patients also needed the sponsorship of a physician willing not only to process the forms but also to suffer unscheduled spot checks by armed DEA agents flashing badges in their waiting rooms in the middle of the workday. As a result, only a handful of cancer patients were receiving legal pot by the end of that year, and Randall, recognizing that the medical-marijuana campaign was going to be a long one, began preparing the lawsuits to challenge IND.

That November, Eli Lilly reported to the FDA problems with its synthetic THC, Nabalone. Dogs given the drug would be fine for fifty-three days, and on the fifty-fourth would go into seizures and die. Luckily, no humans had been harmed in studies, and the drug was quickly withdrawn from testing. The government was back where it started, lacking a manufactured synthetic substitute for medical marijuana.

Peter Bourne was not completely lacking a will for drug enforcement. In his view, though, the best way to cripple the big trafficking rings was — as Deep Throat once told Bob Woodward — to follow the money.

It was during Bourne's tenure that the two halves of forfeiture law were sewn together to create the great forfeiture monster that stalked the eighties and nineties. Traditionally, narcotics agents seized only civilly — that is, without first convicting somebody — either the dope itself or equipment directly and obviously related to the trade, like guns, cars, and boats. If narcotics agents wanted to confiscate drug money or legitimate assets bought with drug profits, they had to first convict the owner under RICO or the other 1970 organized-crime laws.

An incident in early 1978 impressed Bourne with the need to change the law. A suitcase was abandoned at Miami International Airport. After watching it spin around on the baggage carousel for a few hours, police opened it and found $3 million in cash. Bourne was stunned. If the drug cartels could afford to abandon $3 million, they must have been positively awash in cash. DEA administrator Peter

Bensinger brought the suitcase to a Senate hearing and opened it on the witness table.

The law Congress passed in 1978 let the DEA seize money and "derivative proceeds" without even charging — let alone convicting — the owner; the low burden of proof required under civil forfeiture now was combined with the extended reach of criminal forfeiture. Now drug agents could, on suspicion alone, confiscate not only cars and boats but also bank accounts, stock portfolios, anything they suspected of being bought with drug money.

But Congress drew the line at real estate; that would come later. Also, passing a law and enforcing it are two different things. Congress cocked the gun and placed it in the Justice Department's hands, but Justice, under Attorney General Griffin Bell, didn't pull the trigger. It had no political, ideological, or institutional need to devote itself to impoverishing drug suspects, so it simply didn't do it. Bourne would discover, as many have before and since, that lawmakers aren't the only ones who decide who does and doesn't get arrested. Police and prosecutors have enormous powers of discretion and exercise them daily. From the attorney general down to the cop on the beat, law enforcement is constantly deciding where to put its time and resources, understanding full well it can't enforce *every* law *every* minute of the day. In 1978, confiscating every drug-tainted dollar in America was not a Justice Department priority.

~

Late one torpid afternoon that summer, a member of Bourne's staff, twenty-six-year-old Ellen Metsky, asked if she could have a private word with Bourne. She was in the midst of breaking up with her boyfriend, she said, and hadn't slept in days. She was afraid it was going to start affecting her work. As a doctor, she asked, would you write me a prescription for something to help me sleep?

Bourne reached for his prescription pad. Oh, by the way, she added, I'd hate for it to get back to anyone in the White House that I'm taking sleeping pills. Could you make it out to another name? Certainly, Bourne said. Having taken a strong stand against the overprescription of barbiturates, Bourne didn't think he could very well dispense one. Instead, he wrote the scrip for fifteen tablets of methaqualone, a nonbarbiturate sedative marketed under the trademark Quaalude. He also made up an alias for Metsky: Sarah Brown.

Metsky asked a friend named Toby Long to fill the prescription for her. By chance, a state pharmacy inspector was in the Woodbridge,

Virginia, pharmacy when Long asked for the Quaaludes, and her ears pricked up. Quaalude was fashionable then as a sex-enhancer and was widely abused. Knowing this, the inspector asked to see the prescription. When Long couldn't identify herself as "Sarah Brown" and there was none in the phone book, the inspector called the police, who arrested Long. Then police turned their attention to the doctor who'd written the phony scrip.

Jimmy Carter was on his first state visit through Europe when the Bourne story hit the papers. Bourne did his best to control the damage. I am a physician, he said, and Quaalude is a legal drug. The false name was a minor infraction on the rules, not a criminal offense. But a decriminalizer drug czar writing queer prescriptions for aphrodisiacs for his young female assistant was too good a story. Bourne appeared on *The Dick Cavett Show,* which was uneventful until Rona Barrett's Hollywood gossip show reported incorrectly that, on *Cavett,* Bourne had "advocated the use of cocaine." Bourne personally called Barrett, who wouldn't come to the phone; a staff member said no, Miss Barrett didn't *personally* hear Bourne say that, but a "member of her staff" did. Then the *New York Post* ran a story about a big drug arrest in New York that involved a man who happened to have been treated in Bourne's addiction clinics in Georgia years earlier. The *Post* played up the "connection" to Bourne, adding that "questions remain about Bourne's other connections to the ring." John Chancellor delivered an editorial on the NBC evening news and said, "Bourne has long advocated the legalization of marijuana." Bourne felt like he was in the middle of a grass fire on an summer day; he'd stamp on a blaze here and two more would flare up there.

~

Keith Stroup's phone rang. Gary Cohn, another of Stroup's friends on columnist Jack Anderson's staff, wanted to see him right away. Meet me at the office, Stroup said.

We've got to talk about last Christmas, Cohn said.

What? asked Stroup.

For eight months, Cohn continued, I've sat on the story about Bourne using coke at the Christmas party. But now with this prescription mess we have to go with it. If I don't break it, someone else will.

Cohn hadn't been in the room when the cocaine was offered to Bourne, and Stroup knew it. Cohn wanted Stroup to confirm the rumor that Bourne had snorted. I can't do that, Stroup said.

You were all doing blow in there, weren't you? Cohn asked. Did Bourne? Did Bourne snort any? He did, didn't he?

Stroup still wouldn't discuss it. Look, Cohn said, we're going with the story. I just want to know if we're way off base, if we're going to get sued for saying he was doing coke at the party.

It was early in the day for Stroup. He was tired, and maybe a little jangled from all the cocaine he was enjoying in those days. And the mention of Bourne piqued his anger over paraquat. Off the record, Cohn kept saying. I didn't get it from you. I just want to know if I'm going to lose my job if we go with this story. Come on, Keith, off the record. Yes or no. Are we going to be completely wrong if we run this story? Are we?

No, Stroup muttered, but you can't use me as a source.

I don't need you as a source, Cohn said, scrambling for the door.

Just after 7:00 the next morning, Jack Anderson announced on *Good Morning America* that drug czar Peter Bourne — currently under investigation for procuring 'ludes for his comely young assistant — had sniffed cocaine at NORML's Christmas party last year. By nightfall it was the top story everywhere. Bourne denied it, said he'd been *in the room* when the coke was snorted but hadn't had any himself. It was hopeless. Republican senator Orrin Hatch of Utah offered the airwaves the measured assessment that Peter Bourne "has done more harm than any public official in the history of the government."

Jimmy Carter, due to arrive from his European trip next day, already had one staff disaster to untangle: UN Ambassador Andrew Young said in a speech that week that the U.S. held "hundreds" of political prisoners who were in prison "much more because they are poor than because they are bad." Public opinion was running 100 percent in favor of Young's being fired. Bourne knew that if he continued fighting the charges against himself in the press he, and not Carter's accomplishments abroad, would hog the spotlight. On July 20, Bourne wrote his old friend Jimmy Carter a rambling, disjointed letter of resignation. In it, he acknowledged how alienated he was from the law enforcement community, and how police, whose lore held that Bourne wanted to "legalize drugs," now were exacting their revenge. "In the last 18 hours," he wrote, "I have seen law enforcement officers release to the world the name of my patient, other articles containing the grossest innuendo and obviously emanating from law enforcement sources, a prosecuting attorney discuss my case on national television. . . ."

With the end of Peter Bourne's tenure as drug czar, so ended the era in which national policy toward psychoactive drugs would be managed by a psychiatrist. Thereafter, drug policy would be steered by a social worker, a general, a chemist, a pediatrician, a prosecutor, a philosophy professor, a politician, and a policeman. Each would bring his own particular style and priorities to the job. None, though, would consider drugs primarily a matter of public health.

Bourne knew his blunder fumbled forever the reins of science-based, health-oriented drug policy, and he ended his resignation letter on a particularly gloomy note. "I fear for the future of the nation far more than I do for the future of your friend, Peter G. Bourne."

8

PRIDE Before the Fall
1979–1980

There was, of course, no admission that any change had taken place. Merely it became known, with extreme suddenness and everywhere at once, that Eastasia and not Eurasia was the enemy.

— *George Orwell*, 1984

FOUR DAYS AFTER BOURNE'S RESIGNATION, Jimmy Carter sent the following memo to his senior staff:

I am deeply concerned over recent reports that some members of the White House Staff are using illegal drugs.

I expect every member of the White House staff to obey the law. Whether you agree with the law or whether or not others obey the law is totally irrelevant. You will obey it, or you will seek employment elsewhere.

I expect that you will convey my feelings directly and in no uncertain terms to every member of your staff.

(signed) Jimmy Carter

~

When Peter Bourne resigned, his deputy, Lee Dogoloff, took over. Dogoloff, thirty-nine, was a social worker by training — the first White House drug czar who wasn't a psychiatrist. Dogoloff's experience in drug policy began in 1969 as Bob DuPont's deputy at the D.C. treatment agency; then he worked under Jerry Jaffe at SAODAP, and during the Ford administration he moved to the Office of Management and Budget to coordinate drug treatment funding. When Carter was elected, he became Peter Bourne's deputy and labored quietly until Bourne self-destructed. Short, pudgy, and bespectacled, with a reedy voice and Baltimore accent, Dogoloff cut a contrast with the debonair, British Peter Bourne.

Dogoloff considered himself a "right-wing Democrat." He had opposed the Vietnam War, but hadn't made a spectacle of himself doing so. He'd married and started a family young, and had spent his twenties and thirties working hard. He wasn't drawn to the flashy Washington crowd, didn't aspire to hobnob with the glittery and famous, and had thought all along that Bourne was making a fool of himself cozying up to Keith Stroup and NORML. Lee Dogoloff would never have gotten himself compromised at a legalizers' ball.

As he took over Bourne's job, Dogoloff took stock. The country wasn't taking drugs as seriously as it once had, he thought. Every day on his way to lunch Dogoloff had to skirt a sidewalk vendor of dope pipes and bongs, not two blocks from the White House. And the new Cheech and Chong comedy, *Up in Smoke,* was said to be the most profitable movie ever made (in part because it cost so little to make). "Don't come straight to this movie," the posters urged. Dogoloff was stunned at such open advocacy of drug abuse.

Maybe the Vietnam War had something to do with it, Dogoloff thought. Kids had said the war was bad and drugs were good, and when it turned out the war *was* bad, a lot of people seem to have accepted at the same time that drugs were good. The sixties had turned everything upside down. Parents now were using their teenagers as role models — growing their hair long, smoking pot, listening to rock and roll — instead of the other way around. Dogoloff found that disgusting.

When he thought about it, another reason the country wasn't concentrating on drugs was that its worst problem — heroin — was being managed pretty well. The treatment "slots" system was working; state agencies established how many treatment slots they needed, and applied for federal aid at $1,700 a pop. Any time Dogoloff's old friends at OMB wanted to cut treatment funding, Dogoloff could say, "Okay, which slots do you want to cut? In which cities? Which addicts should we say we're no longer going to treat?" The "slots" system let Dogoloff speak in such human-specific terms; OMB had no stomach for choosing which addicts to cut adrift, so they left his treatment budget alone.

With the heroin problem under control, Dogoloff looked around for something else to do. Talk of "prevention" was floating around, and Dogoloff didn't really know what that meant. He called in a group of fifteen "prevention experts" to brief him for two days on how people could be taught to stay away from drugs. By the end of the day, it still didn't make sense.

"Prevention is something you all talk about because it makes you feel good," he said, dismissing the group. "But none of you have told me how it works, or whether it works."

It was frustrating.

~

Buddy Gleaton had been teaching drug-prevention courses for eight years, and though he didn't know Lee Dogoloff, he shared the new drug czar's frustration.

Gleaton had escaped a childhood of poverty in rural Alabama through a scholarship to the state's university, where he majored in physical education. He went on to a doctorate in education and, in 1970, a job at Georgia State. As it happened, he was hired right around the time one of the Georgia regents was wrestling with a child's drug problem and prevailing on the state's public-education officials to "do something." The order came down: Georgia's teachers colleges would make sure every primary and secondary school teacher attended a drug-education course. As the new guy on staff in physical education at Georgia State, Gleaton was saddled with the job.

He knew nothing about drugs, so he gathered information from wherever he could. There were mishaps. He once asked a local pharmacist to address a class, which was fine until the man concluded, "Nobody ever gets off drugs except through Jesus Christ," and wouldn't you know it? One of the students was a Jew.

Gradually, Gleaton came to believe that information available on drugs didn't take the substances seriously enough. A government-made drug-education film, *Brian at 17*, implied that the teenage protagonist drank and smoked pot because his mother was divorced and neglectful. The drugs, in other words, weren't the source of his problems, just a symptom. Gleaton kept hearing of kids strung out on drugs and sent to psychologists, only to learn their real problem was "mama spanked me" or "my parents are divorced."

Everybody wanted to look for excuses for drug abuse, Gleaton thought. Nobody seemed to believe that the drugs themselves were harmful. Even the government wasn't helpful; Gleaton once called the National Institute on Drug Abuse to get information on marijuana, and they referred him to NORML.

By 1978, Gleaton had organized three regional conferences on drug education. Teachers came from all over the Southeast, but Gleaton couldn't help feeling something wasn't quite clicking. The whole field of drug-abuse prevention needed a shake-up. Then Keith Schuchard walked through his door.

Schuchard was talking a mile a minute about her Nosy Parents Association and her research into marijuana. Did you know, she said, that THC is fat soluble and stays in the body for *weeks*? What about the studies showing reduced testosterone levels? Have you heard about amotivational syndrome? And I haven't even *started* telling you about immune-system damage!

Whoa, whoa, okay, Gleaton said. I'm with you.

Gleaton and Schuchard decided to hold a workshop for parents and see if they could generate interest in a town as small as Dublin, Georgia, where Gleaton's in-laws lived. The response was overwhelming. Teenagers in Dublin apparently were every bit as sullen, secretive, and amotivational as their Atlanta counterparts; the Dublin parents flocked to the workshop and hungrily snapped up the information Schuchard and Gleaton brought. Driving back to Atlanta, Schuchard told Gleaton she wanted to start a national organization to educate and empower parents to reassert proper parental control. The name had come to her in a dream, she said — PRIDE: Parents Research Institute for Drug Education.

Gleaton said they should change "Research" to "Resource" to "make it a little more friendly."

~

Lee Dogoloff was sitting in his office in the Old Executive Office Building one afternoon not long after becoming drug czar when an aide dropped the new edition of Lloyd Johnston's high school survey on his desk. Dogoloff leaned back in his chair, put his feet on his desk, and looked at the percentages of students who admitted using various drugs in the past thirty days. Interesting: cigarette smoking was down a bit. Alcohol was up less than a percentage point. Pills were down. Cocaine was up, but still insignificant. Heroin remained pretty much nonexistent. The LSD craze seemed well and truly over.

He turned to the percentages of students using drugs daily and found more good news: *both* alcohol and tobacco were down. Pills, too. Cocaine was flat. And nobody was using heroin or LSD every day, thank goodness. Then Dogoloff planted his finger next to the percentage of seniors smoking pot every day.

He rocked forward and banged his feet onto the floor. He made sure he was looking at the right number. "Holy shit," he whispered. Almost 11 percent of high school seniors — one in nine — was getting stoned *every day*. The percentage had doubled in three years. This wasn't occasional use or "experimentation"; this was *daily* pot smoking. He buzzed his staff. Come in here, he said. You've got to see this. Finally, Dogoloff called Lloyd Johnston at the University of Michigan, to be sure it wasn't a misprint.

No, Johnston said. No misprint. You know I'm not much of an alarmist, but that seemed troublesome to me, too.

Dogoloff retrieved a letter from his files, a recent one that had caught his eye, signed by somebody named Schuchard in Atlanta. We're doing interesting things down here involving marijuana and high school kids, the letter said. I'd like to come tell you about it.

Dogoloff asked his secretary to set it up.

~

Keith Schuchard and Buddy Gleaton arrived in Dogoloff's office carrying a bulky duffel bag. Schuchard leapt into her high-speed lecture on marijuana. Have you heard of gynomastitis — breast enlargement — in teenage boys? Do you understand the drug's effect on the pleasure receptors in the brain? Dogoloff's eyes started to glaze over. As Schuchard sped through the current research on fatty-tissue retention of delta-9 THC, Gleaton walked around Dogoloff's office, looking at the pictures on the walls. He stopped in front of a framed photograph of Dogoloff's children, the oldest of whom was thirteen, and the family's border terrier. "These your kids?" Gleaton asked, in his soft Alabama drawl. "This your dog?"

We want to talk to you not as drug czar, Gleaton said, but as a parent. He tapped a finger on the photo. We want you to think about your daughter here. You may tell her it's wrong to smoke marijuana, but look at all the influences telling her to go right ahead. He dumped the duffel bag onto Dogoloff's desk: bongs and pipes and copies of *High Times* tumbled out. This is a billion-dollar industry, Gleaton said. Have you seen those Cheech and Chong movies? Have you noticed the way illegal drug use is glorified on TV and in rock and roll? Look at that new movie, *9 to 5*: there's Jane Fonda and Dolly Parton sitting around getting stoned like it's the most natural thing in the world. And surely you've noticed the *Seventeen* magazine ads for "Opium" perfume, or for eye drops that will "get the red out." That's the red that marijuana puts there.

Gleaton rested his knuckles on Dogoloff's desk and leaned across it. The *commercialized drug culture* wants to take your little girl away from you, he said. It isn't only drug dealers who are getting rich when your baby gets stoned. It's big business, too. In this country we can't ban those magazines and movies and music, but we can mobilize against them.

That's exactly what we're doing down in Atlanta, Schuchard said. We tell our kids no, you can't smoke pot. You can't go to places where people do. We listen to our kids' music, we read their magazines, and if we find drug messages, we take them away. As long as our kids are living in our house we see nothing wrong with searching their rooms, going through their drawers, whatever it takes to keep them away from dope.

Part of the problem, she continued, is that we're making this crazy distinction between hard and soft drugs. There's no such thing as a soft drug when you're talking about thirteen- or fourteen-year-olds, she said. Drugs are drugs. We're trying to get schools down in Georgia to develop strict codes of conduct. Any drug use — doesn't matter hard or soft — and that's it, you're out of school.

Then Gleaton leveled a long hard look at Dogoloff and delivered the line that clinched it. We're not afraid of our kids, Mr. Dogoloff. We love them too much.

Dogoloff leapt to his feet. "That's it!" he cried. "*That's drug prevention!*"

~

HEW Secretary Joseph Califano cleaned house in the summer of 1978, and among those to go was the director of the National Institute on Drug Abuse, Bob DuPont. DuPont's last public pronouncements on marijuana — when Peter Bourne was still drug czar — had been in favor of legalizing possession and home cultivation. But as he left NIDA for private practice in August 1978, DuPont gave an interview to *U.S. News & World Report* in which he climbed aboard the anti-marijuana bandwagon.

DuPont still thought civil fines were more effective at discouraging pot smoking than jail time, but after years of soft-pedaling marijuana's health effects and even speaking at a NORML conference, he now told the magazine that "no issue was more frustrating to me in five years as director of NIDA" than "the difficulty of communicating the risks of marijuana use." He predicted the marijuana culture would have harsh consequences for "health, social activities, family living, and work performance" and warned: "Those people going around today emphasizing the benignness of marijuana are going to have a tough time with their consciences."

The last thing DuPont did before leaving NIDA was hand Keith Schuchard a contract to write a NIDA handbook on the parents' movement and the medical dangers of marijuana. That Schuchard had no scientific qualifications to write a government drug-abuse booklet was, to DuPont, refreshing. The "experts" had let the country down, he thought, and it was time to put power in the hands of those with a real stake in the future of drug policy.

Parents, Peers & Pot is an eighty-page tirade against rock and roll, the "commercialized drug culture," and working parents who let their children come home to empty homes. It devotes twenty-three pages to studies on marijuana's health risks without once mentioning either Nixon's Marijuana Commission or any of the other voluminous research demonstrating marijuana's relative innocuousness to adult occasional smokers when compared to alcohol, tobacco, or other psychoactive drugs. Schuchard blames marijuana for causing heart disease, sterility, cancer, and other maladies, but doesn't explain why, if so many kids were toking up, no epidemics of these diseases had emerged. Beautifully written and terrifying to read, *Parents, Peers & Pot* is larded with stories of strung-out, surly, combative, furtive, anti-authoritarian teenagers whose only "problem" is marijuana. They drop out of sports, use foul language, and let their grades go to hell. "There is no such thing as recreational use," Schuchard writes.

Though leaning heavily on Johnston's 1978 high school survey, Schuchard's book fails to mention that almost half of all students had *never* smoked pot and two-thirds didn't use it even monthly. At the same time, 30 percent were smoking cigarettes every day and 40 percent were getting drunk about every two weeks.

Although she was by now well known among the parent advocates as Keith Schuchard, she wrote the book under a pen name combining her little-used first name and her maiden name: Marsha Mannatt. She said her daughter Ashley was taking too much grief from her peers for being related to the supreme Nosy Parent. Schuchard wanted to spare her any more.

DuPont's successor at NIDA, William Pollin, was equally unconcerned about Schuchard's credentials as a drug-abuse expert, and he wrote the booklet's introduction. Since its publication, *Parents, Peers & Pot* and its sequel have become the federal government's official word on the subject of marijuana and teenagers. Still in print, the booklet is the most-requested publication in the agency's history.

~

In the nine years since convincing Congress to pass his anti–organized crime brainchild — RICO — law professor Bob Blakey had been traveling the country trying to get prosecutors to use it. He had little luck. The law was too complicated and too unusual to be quickly grasped by overworked prosecutors. In one meeting with the U.S. attorney's office in New York, a prosecutor listened for fifteen minutes before storming out. "You don't know what you're talking about," he said. "You're wasting my time." Federal prosecution of criminal organizations had gone nowhere since 1970 despite the powerful law on the books.

In the summer of 1979 Blakey convinced Cornell University in Ithaca, New York, to let him hold seminars on campus for detectives, FBI agents, and prosecutors. If he could get them away from their desks and their phones for a week, he thought, he might be able to make them understand the power of RICO.

Use the tools Congress gave you, Blakey exhorted. Wiretaps! Forfeiture! Conspiracy! You no longer need to catch the crook with the gun smoking in his hand. Follow the money, and when you trace it back to a crime, take it away. Blakey's students learned well. In the years following, several went on to nail mobsters John Gotti and "Matty the Horse" Ianniello on RICO charges.

And while they were at it, they spread the gospel of wiretap, forfeiture, and conspiracy to those working on small-time drug cases as well. Though passed in 1970, RICO wasn't launched as a Drug War weapon until the summer of 1979.

That same summer, a young United States senator, angling for a senior position on the powerful Judiciary Committee, noticed that RICO and the other laws enabling police to confiscate drug-tainted assets had hardly been used. Invoking his privilege as a member of Congress, he asked the General Accounting Office to study the laws' potential and their use in the field. It seemed a good law-and-order issue to stiffen the liberal image of Senator Joe Biden, Democrat of Delaware.

~

Dogoloff took to the road preaching the new gospel of parent power. He stayed two days in Naples, Florida — going in August so nobody could accuse him of boondoggling — and heard from parents who had set up a phone tree to keep an eye on each other's kids. When a parent recognized in another's child the red eyes of a doper, it was the duty of that parent to alert the other. Dogoloff flew next to Thousand Oaks, California, and was amazed to find parents there doing the same thing, completely ignorant of the effort in Naples.

Dogoloff spoke at the PRIDE conference in Atlanta that fall, rewriting his speech at the last minute to make it "tougher." By now, Dogoloff saw his mission as drug czar not only to stamp out drug use but to reverse the erosion of parental authority in general — to save the American family. He conducted public meetings on "The Teenage Drug Problem," telling parents they could "regain appropriate control of their children through the drug issue." Often somebody would stand up and ask, "How do you respond to my kid who says, 'You drink alcohol, why shouldn't I smoke pot?' " Dogoloff was dismayed: the question indicated to him how fearful of its teenage children the country had become. "There are all kinds of things I do that my twelve-year-old doesn't do," Dogoloff would fire back, drawing himself up at the podium and glowering like a Pentecostal preacher. Dogoloff was so excited by the potential power of the parents' movement that he tried to get Carter to welcome a PRIDE delegation to the Rose Garden. Carter declined.

~

Also present at PRIDE's Atlanta conference was a sad-eyed, soft-spoken pediatrician from Clearwater, Florida, named Donald Ian Macdonald. Forty-nine years old, Macdonald had spent years caring for sullen, lazy adolescents without ever thinking they might be suffering from anything other than adolescence. Then his own teenage son, Andy, collapsed during a binge of alcohol and marijuana and had to be hospitalized. Grief-stricken, Macdonald started attending parents' meetings in his hometown. Instantly, he was mobbed. A doctor! There's a doctor here! A doctor who understands how bad marijuana is! Will you sit on a panel? Will you sign a letter to the editor? Write a book, doctor, write a book. He did: *Drugs, Drinking & Adolescence*. Suddenly, Macdonald was in demand everywhere, appearing on panels with Carlton Turner and Bob DuPont to lend medical weight to the anti-marijuana cause. Reading the civil rights movement of the fifties and sixties as one of rights granted rather than justice restored, Macdonald liked to blame drug abuse on the civil rights movement's legacy. The problem, he liked to say, is the movement evolved into a right-to-smoke-pot movement. The civil rights and Woodstock eras brought a revolution against authority in general, he'd say, and drugs were the symbol of that revolution. We shouldn't have to prove marijuana is harmful, he'd say to wild applause. The burden of proof should be on *them* to prove it isn't! Now it was clear to Macdonald that all those unpleasant adolescents he'd been treating were drug abusers; he had simply been too blind to notice! When a urine test was announced that was "95 percent effective" at detecting marijuana, Macdonald, now president of the Florida Pediatric Society, became one of the first to advocate random urine testing for all children in the sixth grade or older. "It can save time and money needlessly spent on batteries of tests when, in fact, pot proves to be the sole cause of the problem," Macdonald said. Along with the Nosy Parents, Macdonald was doing on the family level what Nixon started on the national level: shifting responsibility for problems out of context — in this case, off parents' shoulders — and onto the substances and the individuals who use them.

~

Like Lee Dogoloff, Keith Stroup of NORML also was criss-crossing the country. He was trying to get more states to join the first eleven and decriminalize marijuana possession. But everything was getting harder.

Legislatures were less willing to hold hearings, and when they did, the testimony was heavily stacked with prohibitionists. The central issue — marijuana's relative harmlessness and the injustice of jailing users — was getting lost, Stroup thought. Prohibitionists would wave around little mirrors they'd bought in head shops and yell about cocaine. We're not *talking* about cocaine, Stroup would insist, eager for the hearing to end so he could have a toot himself. Damn those head shop owners, he'd think. Those mirrors and razor blades and cocaine grinders they'd started selling recently were confusing everything. Stroup would meet paraphernalia moguls at cocktail parties and tell them, you're going to kill us all by selling cocaine toys. Stick to marijuana. But they didn't listen. And Stroup was finding himself attacked about cocaine paraphernalia, which was crazy. It had nothing to do with NORML. There was no constituency for cocaine like there was for pot.

Wherever Stroup went those days, pickets were waiting for him. This too was new; the groups looked organized. And they all seemed to have the word "parents" in their names. But whenever he left Washington, he'd pass the inevitable group of Lyndon LaRouche crazies in National Airport shouting about the marijuana cabal led by Henry Kissinger, the Queen of England, and Keith Stroup; and when he got off the plane at his destination he would be met by the hollering parents' groups. Stroup figured they were all the same thing — the lunatic fringe, easily ignored.

NORML never convinced another state to decriminalize.

~

Among those threatened by the post-Nixon slide toward easier marijuana laws was the Drug Enforcement Administration. Were marijuana legal, the country's problem with illegal drugs would shrink to the tiny number of heroin and cocaine users, obviating a federal drug-enforcement budget the size of the DEA's. So now that Peter Bourne was gone, the DEA began pushing for a harder line on marijuana.

As soon as Bourne resigned, DEA administrator Peter Bensinger told reporters he wanted to see the federal penalties for marijuana increased, not eliminated. He also said any notion that marijuana is a valuable therapeutic drug — for reducing nausea in chemotherapy patients, for example — is hogwash. "The American Cancer Society," he said, "confirms that marijuana represents a more serious cancer threat than cigarettes."

Which took the Cancer Society by surprise; it had said no such thing and in fact believed just the opposite. "We have no national policy on marijuana and cancer," a spokeswoman said in response to Bensinger. "We're interested in it, though, for treatment of pain for cancer victims."

Still, Bensinger pressed on. Speaking at the annual convention of the International Association of Chiefs of Police, Bensinger contradicted federal policy and declared marijuana a dangerous drug warranting heavier penalties and tougher enforcement. He ordered new operations against marijuana traffickers and invited the press in to photograph the seizures. The DEA cooperated with *Time* on a cover story in January 1979: "The Colombian Connection — How a Billion Dollar Network Smuggles Pot and Coke into the US." The story, which ran six pages, showcased the planes and boats and supersleuths of the DEA in their never-ending battle against the armies of darkness. And then *Time* — which barely a year before had dismissed marijuana as benign — tacked on a twelve-inch sidebar quoting the most extreme studies on marijuana's harmfulness. The tide was turning.

In April, the issue holding together NORML's constituency evaporated when the Centers for Disease Control squelched the paraquat scare. A yearlong study, it said, indicated that all the initial reports of contaminated pot were based on bad data. Less than one percent of the marijuana confiscated in the past year showed traces of paraquat. Not a single verifiable case of paraquat poisoning had ever been recorded.

Three weeks later, Jimmy Carter's White House announced a new "war on marijuana." More effort would go toward busting dealers, stopping smugglers, and confiscating assets. Street enforcement would be beefed up. And there would be open support for spraying in Mexico, Colombia, and the United States. All White House mention of decriminalization was dropped. Finally, Carter's White House was hip to marijuana's emotional power.

That same month, Keith Stroup resigned from NORML, hinting darkly in an interview that, given what he knew about drug use among White House staff, Peter Bensinger of the DEA must be "blackmailing" Carter and the White House. His insinuation that White House staff were indulging in illegal drugs was dismissed as the disgruntled mutterings of a bitter cokehead loser . . . until August rolled around.

~

A new Drug War combatant stepped onto the field of battle in the summer of 1979. Peggy Mann, a writer of children's books, devoted herself to unearthing all marijuana research that showed the drug was harmful. She was tired of fancy Harvard psychiatrists telling Congress about "casual" and "recreational" drug use, implying that marijuana was harmless and that it was possible to use drugs responsibly. Drug use was wrong, she felt. It was bad for kids and bad for adults.

Mann began turning out pieces for the *Reader's Digest, Saturday Evening Post,* and *Ladies' Home Journal,* magazines that reach millions of housewives while being all but invisible inside the Beltway. In two years, Mann published half a dozen articles on the danger pot smokers pose on the highway, parents who give two-year-olds marijuana to smoke, and the "proven" links between marijuana and heart attack, cancer, infertility, sterility, impotence, loose sex, and big breasts on teenage boys. They weren't necessarily new findings. Studies demonstrating the dangers of marijuana had been around as long as the studies demonstrating the drug's relative harmlessness. What was changing was the side of the debate to which the press was giving credence.

The overall problem, Mann wrote, is teenage culture. "A recent survey in Atlanta, Georgia, showed that while one third of non-drug-using kids listen to rock music on the radio three hours or more a day," she wrote, "virtually all drug-using youngsters listen to three or more hours a day . . . to such lyrics as Eric Clapton singing, 'Cocaine, cocaine, it's all right, it's all right.' " In one year, the *Reader's Digest* sold three million reprints of Mann's first article.

∾

Andy Kowl frowned as he hung up the phone. That was the third call from a panicked head-shop owner in a week; something was up.

Kowl, a tall twenty-eight-year-old New Yorker with fashionably long hair, elegant clothes, and a neatly trimmed beard, was the nexus of the paraphernalia industry. He had been the organizational and editorial genius behind *High Times* magazine and had piloted it from an underground quarterly to a $5-million-a-year monthly in just five years. Paraphernalia made up the bulk of *High Times*'s advertising, so Kowl knew everybody in the business. After he had a falling-out with the magazine's publisher in 1978, he started his own newsletter, *Paraphernalia Digest,* to serve what was by then — depending on how you computed it — a billion-dollar industry. It was great fun; the industry was full of characters like Burt Rubin, who noticed one day that most potheads stuck two cigarette papers together before rolling a joint. Rubin manufactured one twice as wide, gave it the pun name "E. Z. Wider," and ultimately sold the business for $6.2 million.

But suddenly a chill was in the air. Kowl was getting calls from all over the country about legislatures debating laws to ban paraphernalia. Indiana had passed one, but it got beat in the courts. Now Georgia had one, and surely NORML would beat that one, too. Still, the sheer number of new laws being talked about was worrisome.

∾

Having reduced its penalties for marijuana possession earlier in the decade, Texas by 1979 was building up a powerful urge to get tough on drugs again. Sensing this, Governor William Clements decided to launch a "Texans' War on Drugs" and needed somebody bold and flamboyant to lead it. The first person he thought of was the state's richest and best-known businessman, H. Ross Perot.

When Clements called Perot he learned he was in Turkey, assembling a team to free a group of his employees captured in the Iranian revolution. Perfect, Clements thought. Not only will the derring-do enhance Perot's reputation, he isn't here to object to my appointing him. Clements announced the Texans' War on Drugs, with H. Ross Perot as its leader, while Perot was in Turkey. When Perot got back and learned about it, he was furious. But he was more angry when the *Dallas Morning News* editorialized that Perot's was a stupid appointment because Perot didn't know anything about drugs.

I'll show them, Perot told his staff.

~

For Jimmy Carter's White House, a new hard line on marijuana was politically delicate; it could anger and alienate the country's 40 million pot smokers. On the other hand, the 1980 election was looming, and Carter needed to protect his right flank. In a nation rapidly becoming so conservative it would ultimately elect Ronald Reagan, advocating marijuana decriminalization no longer looked like such a good idea.

The challenge for Eizenstat and Dogoloff was backing away from decriminalization without making an issue of doing so. Dogoloff achieved this merely by pretending no such policy ever existed. When a Treasury Department official publicly opined that the DEA's shift toward pot enforcement "does not adequately or directly address the changing social attitudes regarding marihuana use" and suggested "we explore a full range of options," Dogoloff responded equally publicly that so doing "would, in itself, be a major change in Federal policy because we have made it clear that we will not consider legalization."

This reversal of Jimmy Carter's marijuana policy may have escaped the notice of the chief executive himself. Fifty-four American hostages were rotting in Teheran, and every night Walter Cronkite was closing his evening broadcast with the running count of the days they'd been held. Inflation was well into the double digits, gasoline was over a dollar a gallon, unemployment was high, and the Republicans were getting ready to send Ronald Reagan into battle against him. Drug abuse was likely the farthest thing from the president's mind.

~

That summer, the Internal Revenue Service closed in on one of the era's defining characters: Steve Rubell, owner of the famous Studio 54 disco in New York. Studio 54 was at its zenith of hip and nightly hosted the rich, the famous, the beautiful, and the decadent. IRS agents had been building a tax-evasion case against Rubell for months, and when they sprung the trap and arrested him in August he offered a deal: White House chief of staff Hamilton Jordan, he said, had snorted cocaine right here in the disco. If I testify against him will you go easy on me?

It took nine months, 65 witnesses, and 100 interviews, and cost the taxpayers $121,000, but Hamilton Jordan ultimately was cleared of any wrongdoing. In the meantime, though, the media had lots of fun with the story. After the Bourne disaster, the Carter White House was so closely identified with drugs that coke snorting by its chief of staff was too juicy a story not to wring for all it was worth. *Time*, for example, ran a story about "the scandal" in all four of its issues the month the story broke (and then one four-inch item, buried deep, when Jordan was cleared). One reporter got a real scoop: Peter Bourne — Dr. Quaalude himself — had prescribed an "obesity drug" for Jordan two years earlier, and the White House reporters jumped all over press secretary Jody Powell to unearth what kind of obesity drug it was. "Obviously," Powell said, utterly deadpan, "one that didn't work."

It probably didn't help that the "Ham and Coke" story broke the same week Carter was attacked by a rabid bunny rabbit while fishing.

With all the attention on the hostages, the economy, Ham Jordan, and the upcoming presidential race, nobody paid much attention to a dry article published that December in the journal *Science*. A University of California psychiatrist wrote that snorting cocaine is self-limiting, because as a vasoconstrictor — or vein-tightening agent — cocaine slows absorption to the brain even while it's being snorted. When cocaine is smoked, though, it hits the brain almost instantly, creating a "rush" that starts to dissipate in about ten or fifteen minutes. Then, continued the article, the smoker "may begin to become depressed and require another 'hit' to maintain an equilibrium."

Widespread in South America, the smoking of cocaine "could become a serious problem in the United States as well," the article concluded.

Carlton Turner's secretary at the Old Miss marijuana farm told him one afternoon that a Mr. Parrot had called from Dallas while he was out to lunch. The name meant nothing to Turner, and he forgot all about it. The next morning his phone rang before his secretary was in, so Turner picked it up himself. "This is H. Ross Perot," a high, twangy voice said. "I hear you know something about marijuana."

"Little bit," Turner twanged back, "but nobody knows more."

They talked for forty-five minutes. Texas is woefully lax on drug pushers, Perot said, and we have to turn around public opinion. Perot wanted Turner to come help him, he said, because marijuana was the drug to concentrate on; too few people have any experience with the others. Turner called Keith Schuchard, and, sharing what Turner called "common views about what America ought to be," they together created a "road show" of hearings and town meetings on the dangers of marijuana and paraphernalia, the importance of parent power, and the need to make marijuana penalties tougher, not lighter. They spent months traveling through Texas on Perot's money, speaking at PTA meetings, Lions Club luncheons, ladies auxiliary teas, anywhere they could gather a forum of concerned parents. Usually Perot would lead off with his folksy ramblings, then Turner would chime in with the horrors of marijuana, and then Schuchard would wrap up with a seminar on how to organize parents against the commercialized teenage drug culture.

Perot had his corporate lawyer write legislation, too: mandatory life without parole for selling pot to a minor, complicated reporting requirements for pharmacists, expanded wiretap and search authority for police, and more. The legislature wouldn't bite, so Perot, Turner, and Schuchard organized a drug-education seminar for the male legislators' wives the day before the legislature opened in 1980. They really raised the roof and simultaneously organized busloads of parents to arrive from all over Texas the day the session opened. "You're either for us or against us," Perot told the legislators through a press conference that morning. His legislation passed.

One night soon after the legislative victory, Turner and Perot were sitting in their hotel suite in Abilene talking about the upcoming presidential election. Ronald Reagan is going to run Jimmy Carter straight out of Washington, Perot told Turner. And you, my friend, are going to the White House. We're going to put the pressure on, you'll see. Be ready.

~

By the fall of 1980, Andy Kowl felt like he was trying to keep the *Titanic* afloat. State after state was passing paraphernalia laws, gradually banning his entire industry. Some of the laws were stupid, Kowl thought; others were downright crazy. In several states, the way police could determine the legal status of a pack of cigarette papers was to see whether the store also sold *High Times*. If so, the papers were "drug paraphernalia"; if not, they were legal. The laws were fightable, but Kowl's industry group spent a million dollars on lawyers in a single year and still there was no way to keep up. William Kunstler would sally forth to fight one court case, and six more laws would get passed. Often, the industry would win in court, only to have the legislature rewrite the law and start enforcing it, driving NORML and the industry back into court.

Then police began their own campaign against paraphernalia, whether there was a law on the books or not. Again and again Kowl heard about police arresting convenience-store clerks because the store sold both *High Times* and cigarette papers. Kowl would call the store owners and plead — we'll send you lawyers, we'll pay the bills. But given the choice between taking on the communities in which they did business or simply dropping *High Times* and the papers, the owners invariably did the latter. The big Drug Fair chain took rolling papers off its shelves and made a big public to-do over it. Kowl changed the name of his newsletter from *Paraphernalia Digest: Newsmagazine of the Industry* to *Accessories Digest: The Magazine of Lifestyle Marketing*, but to no avail. The DEA, with Susan Rusche's help, drafted a model drug-paraphernalia law containing a fifty-five-word definition of "paraphernalia" and banning not only the manufacture and sale of the stuff, but the advertising of it as well. Dogoloff used White House funds to circulate the model law to every state legislature. Congress held hearings on paraphernalia with an eye toward passing federal laws banning it.

On the *Today Show*, Kowl invented a myth to show how silly it was to try to identify this or that piece of plastic as paraphernalia. "The little stirrers you get at McDonald's are the most popular cocaine spoon in the country," he joked, waving one. Within days, McDonald's announced with great fanfare it was recalling all its coffee stirrers and replacing them with a new design. Kowl could see what was coming. Late in 1980 he abandoned his paraphernalia newsletter and went back to editing *High Times*. Right around then, the DEA began investigating his advertisers, contending that running an ad in *High Times* meant the papers or pipes you were selling constituted drug paraphernalia.

"This is wonderful," Kowl said sarcastically to his staff. "Advertise in *High Times!* Buy an ad, get a subpoena!"

∾

On September 28, 1980, the *Washington Post* ran on page one a story depicting the life of "Jimmy," a black eight-year-old who had been a heroin addict since the age of five. Splendidly written by staff reporter Janet Cooke, "Jimmy's World" described the needle sliding into "the baby smooth skin of his thin brown arms . . . like a straw into a freshly baked cake," Jimmy's mother watching her "live-in lover" "plunging a needle into [Jimmy's] bony arm, sending the fourth grader into a hypnotic nod," the violence and rapes of the neighborhood, and the DEA's confirmation of "Golden Crescent heroin" flooding the city.

So disturbing was the piece that Mayor Marion Barry launched a citywide search for the boy, ordering police and teachers to inspect the arms of every child in the District of Columbia. A $10,000 reward was offered for Jimmy's whereabouts. The *Post* assigned six reporters to find another "Jimmy," on the theory that if there is one, there must be others. After days of searching, neither Jimmy nor any other child addict was found.

When Cooke said she "couldn't find" again the house she had described so vividly, her editor, Milton Coleman, suspected the story was a fake and shared his suspicions with the other *Post* editors. They decided to do nothing, however. Six months later, the Pulitzer Prize committee asked for nominations and put the *Post* editors in a bind; if they didn't nominate Cooke's story, it would look like they didn't believe it. "In for a dime, in for a dollar," said assistant managing editor Bob Woodward. So the piece was sent up to Columbia University in New York, where the Pulitzer committee was meeting.

Among the judges was Roger Wilkins, who had won a Pulitzer of his own writing editorials for the *Washington Post* and who had written the *New York Times*'s urban-affairs column for five years. When someone suggested that the story might be a fake, Wilkins stood up and angrily reminded the judges that on any day of the week at the corner of Frederick Douglass Boulevard and 116th Street — just a few blocks from where they were sitting — you could find little children heavily involved in the drug trade. Nobody chose to argue with one of the nation's most distinguished black journalists about it, and "Jimmy's World" got the Pulitzer. Right after that, the *Post* got Cooke to confess to making it all up, and returned the prize.

How could such a thing happen to one of the most respected newspapers in the country, to a street-savvy mayor, and then to the judges of the nation's top journalism prize? From Milton Coleman to Marion Barry to the Pulitzer judges, everybody was willing to believe that the same addicts who need to "rob, steal, and kill" to support their habits would give away precious heroin to a five-year-old. Knowing how most children feel about vaccinations, they were willing to accept that "Jimmy" allowed himself to be injected daily. Despite their sophistication, they bought the notion that junkie mothers are so monstrous they would sit by and watch their "live-in lovers" pump their babies full of dope.

Most amazing of all, everybody was willing to believe all this even after a citywide search for "Jimmy" not only failed to find him, but failed to find any other child addicts. Newspapers had been making "trends" out of isolated tragedies for years. Now one of the country's top papers had created one out of whole cloth and won the Pulitzer Prize for it. "Frankly," Wilkins summed up, "in those days I could have believed in an eight-year-old junkie quicker than I could believe the existence of a black woman at the *Post* with fake credentials and who's a liar who puts lies in the newspaper. This was, after all, the *Washington Post*."

~

Laboring in the background of drug policymaking for the past seventeen years was a retired army officer named Richard L. Williams. Stocky and businesslike, Dick Williams had fought as a paratrooper in Vietnam but his real specialty was management; he'd attended the Industrial College of the Armed Forces and had served as an army comptroller. Nixon hired him in 1973 to manage the creation of the DEA. After the resignation, he stayed on to man Gerald Ford's thin drug-policy staff. He left the White House briefly to work on Capitol Hill, and then, being a proven manager, was hired by Jimmy Carter to see to it Peter Bourne's staff ran smoothly. He was an organization man, "focused on the trees and not the forest." But with the ascension of Lee Dogoloff, Williams stepped from the shadows.

His mission, as he saw it: "to close the debate."

Williams had learned in the paratroops that clear objectives boldly stated were the way to motivate people. All that "harm reduction" business during the Ford and Peter Bourne days was nonsense, he thought. It was stupid for the White House to say eliminating all drug use was impossible. Even if that's true, he'd argue, you don't tell a platoon to come as close as they can to wiping out an enemy position, you order them to wipe it out. Let's start talking about making America "drug free."

Also, he argued to a very receptive Dogoloff, all those fine distinctions Peter Bourne loved so much are doing us more harm than good. Let's stop talking about drug use, drug abuse, and drug misuse. Fact is, there's no way to make distinctions like that unless you want to write a four-paragraph disclaimer every time you want to use such a term. Same thing with saying "casual" or "recreational" use. They make it sound like fun. Let's end the use of those terms forever.

Another distinction to get rid of is the one we make between "hard" drugs and "soft" drugs, Williams argued. It's all bad news, from smoking a little pot to mainlining heroin, and if we're trying to discourage that behavior, let's call all of it drug abuse and be done with it.

Finally, Williams convinced Dogoloff to all but forget about heroin addicts and instead play to the strengths of the moment: the parents' movement and the public's newfound alarm about marijuana. Forty million pot smokers versus half a million heroin addicts: we reach more people taking a firm stand on marijuana.

While he was at it, Williams decreed that marijuana would henceforth be spelled with a "j" instead of an "h" in all government documents. "People are making fun of us because we don't even know how to spell it," he told the Justice Department, which objected to the change. "I say it's 'j,' so it's 'j.' "

By the middle of 1980, heroin was all but gone from Dogoloff's agenda. The way he now saw it, there was no point talking about heroin to a group of parents in Kansas City when the drug problem they faced was marijuana in the schoolyard. In a long memo on the state of his drug policy to Carter political adviser Gerald Rafshoon that July, Dogoloff didn't even mention heroin. Instead, he trumpeted his "major adolescent drug campaign" involving a wide array of what he called "grass roots community groups" that had no particular expertise in drug abuse: the PTA, the Boy Scouts, and the National Football League. Dogoloff likewise took Williams's advice on eliminating talk of hard and soft drugs. "On several recent occasions," he wrote, "I have said that when it comes to adolescent drug use, we have neither the luxury of time nor the opportunity for esoteric debate over the effects of a particular drug. We must move forward now with a sense of purpose to turn the tide of youthful drug abuse."

Lee Dogoloff and Dick Williams together effected the biggest change in drug policy since Nixon launched the Drug War. They took the leadership away from doctors and scientists and handed it to untrained, emotionally motivated parents. They then directed federal policy not at the most dangerous drugs, but at the one parents worried about as much for reasons of family politics and culture as health.

With Dick Williams whispering in his ear, Lee Dogoloff also permanently rewrote the function of the War on Drugs. No longer was it an exercise merely in reducing drug abuse and stopping the drug traffic. Beginning with Dogoloff, the Drug War also was seen as a way to change the way Americans think. "We always talked about the three-legged problem: supply, demand, and international," Dogoloff said. "The part that was missing was social attitudes, the permissive social attitudes toward drug abuse." The harm the chemicals actually do was no longer the issue; the permissive social attitudes they accompany were every bit as harmful to society's overall health. "We have passed from a time when the nonmedical use of any drug was considered the first step toward certain drug addiction to the present situation where, unfortunately, drug abuse is looked upon by some with benign tolerance," wrote Dogoloff in Jimmy Carter's last *Annual Report on the Federal Drug Program.* "A permissive societal attitude has posed particular difficulties for law enforcement officials and teachers in the performance of their duties, as well as for parents who are striving to impart the values and attitudes of responsible citizenship to their children."

The time had come to end all the "esoteric debate." As Dick Williams succinctly put it, "Let's declare drug abuse wrong and get on with it."

9

Hour of the Hard Chargers

1981

I was hired by the President of the United States to clean up America.

— *Carlton Turner*

BY A TEN-TO-ONE MARGIN in electoral votes, Ronald Reagan flushed Jimmy Carter out of the White House and launched the most radical reorganization of government since FDR. Government, the new president was fond of saying, is not the solution. It's the problem.

Within two months of taking office, Reagan signed the biggest package of tax and budget cuts ever. To free American business, he lifted regulations on pollution, workplace safety, consumer protection, discrimination, and the savings-and-loan industry. The best candidates for such positions as director of the Environmental Protection Agency or energy secretary, in Reagan's view, were those committed to abolishing their own agencies. Reagan's Washington noisily endeavored to put itself out of business, to withdraw from the lives of its citizens.

During one of his first cabinet meetings, Reagan's boyish budget director, David Stockman, discussed his plans to reduce or eliminate various federal agencies. He was going along fine until he mentioned his intention to trim the Justice Department's 54,000-strong workforce by 2,000. Attorney General William French Smith smacked his palm on the gleaming oak cabinet table.

"The Justice Department is not a domestic agency," Smith snapped. "It is the internal arm of the national defense."

This was a new one to Stockman. As diplomatically as he could, Stockman argued there wasn't much the Justice Department could do to preserve American security. He pointed out that under the Constitution, state and local police handle almost all crime. "They always have," Stockman said, "and I hope they always will."

Smith disagreed. "Restoring a strong federal law enforcement capacity is going to be highly popular with the American people," he said.

"Bill is right," Reagan intoned from the head of the table. "Law enforcement is something we have always believed was a legitimate function of government."

⁓

"Law enforcement," however, is a broad term. Civil rights law, labor law, and environmental law all require enforcement. Securities fraud, embezzlement, and other white-collar crime have at times been targeted for vigorous federal enforcement.

But that wasn't what Ronald Reagan and William French Smith had in mind. They wanted to fight *crime* crime, the kind citizens lock their doors against — violent, personal, telegenic crime. Eight years had passed since Andrew Hacker described the emergent conservative impulse to substitute heavy policing for social spending. Now, the first conservative government elected since then was making that impulse a centerpiece of its small-government domestic policy.

Beefing up federal law enforcement wasn't so much an exception to Reagan's small-government revolution as it was a facilitator of it. To the extent criminals could be portrayed as a distinct population of inherently bad individuals, the easier it would be to justify cutting the social programs Reagan wanted eliminated or diminished. The criminal, Attorney General Smith told the National Press Club that first year, "has gained the upper hand over society itself. Too frequently, Congressional failure to act has invited the courts to fashion makeshift approaches that favor the accused over the accuser."

Never mind RICO, John Mitchell's drug laws, the widening of forfeiture authority, or Nixon's conservative additions to the Supreme Court. America is *still* soft on crime, Smith said, and the new administration aims to "restore the proper balance between the powers of law and the rights of the lawless." Reagan's chief adviser, the former prosecutor Ed Meese, articulated the administration's immediate goal this way: "We must," he said, "increase the power of the prosecutor."

⁓

As English composition, the Fourth Amendment is a clunky thing, a classic run-on sentence, oddly punctuated and archaically capitalized. It reads:

> The right of the people to be secure in their persons, houses, papers and effects, against unreasonable searches and seizures, shall not be violated, and no Warrants shall issue, but upon probable cause, supported by Oath or affirmation, and particularly describing the place to be searched, and the persons or things to be seized.

No prizewinner as English, it worked well for almost 200 years, requiring police to convince an impartial judge they had good reason to search a citizen's property. It was a radical document when ratified in 1791 and remains unique on the planet in the standards it sets for police.

For most of this century, the Fourth Amendment was routinely upheld and even strengthened. In 1966, the U.S. Supreme Court made mandatory in all states its strongest Fourth Amendment requirement, which came to be known as the "exclusionary rule": any evidence obtained illegally by the police must be excluded from court. The rule had not been seriously questioned since. Even John Mitchell — who once boasted his administration would "take the country so far right you won't recognize it" — hadn't tried to challenge it.

Ed Meese and William French Smith, though, placed repeal of the exclusionary rule at the top of their legislative agenda. "Perhaps the interest of justice would be best served by the complete abolition of the exclusionary rule," Smith told the National Press Club, "so that reasonable, good-faith action by law enforcement does not result in release of the lawbreaker." Police might kick in the wrong door, search a place not listed in their warrant, or even have no warrant at all; Meese and Smith still wanted the evidence to be admissible so that "thousands" of lawbreakers wouldn't be released each year "on a technicality." Smith bolstered his argument with a study by his own Justice Department finding the rule had a "major impact," weakening prosecutions in California.*

To further strengthen the prosecutor's hand, Smith and Meese wanted police released completely from the *Miranda* burden of reading suspects their rights. They wanted more authority to hold defendants without bail. They wanted tax law and the Freedom of Information Act rewritten to make it easier for police to gain access to Social Security

* The study later was shown to have used tiny samples, ignored data, and generally overestimated the rule's impact by a factor of between five and fifteen. Prosecutors at the time of the study were rejecting fewer than 1 percent of felony cases because of illegal searches.

and other files federal agencies keep on citizens. In a highly unusual move, Chief Justice Warren Burger publicly signaled his receptivity to Reagan's tough new agenda by complaining in print about plea bargaining: "Should we be surprised," he asked *U.S. News & World Report*, "if word gets around . . . that you can commit two or three crimes for the price of only one?"

Though Smith himself was not a prosecutor by training, he assembled around him a team of self-described "hard chargers." Among them was the tall and cool Lowell Jensen, who as a young assistant DA in Oakland had helped Ed Meese prosecute Mario Savio and 772 other activists of the Berkeley Free Speech Movement. Smith's number three was the dark and intense Rudolph Giuliani, the former chief of the federal drug-prosecution office in New York who came into office publicly decrying "one procedure after another that glorifies the rights of the accused above everyone else's."

Through Giuliani, Smith ordered his ninety-four U.S. attorneys around the country to confer with local police and prosecutors and answer the same question Richard Nixon's Justice Department had wrestled with: how can the federal government claim a greater role in fighting street crime?

The answer that came back was much the same as in 1969: one type of crime crosses state lines, fields organizations too big for local police to handle, and is associated with plenty of violence and theft. If the government wanted to deploy a "strong federal law enforcement capacity" in a "highly popular" manner, in William French Smith's words, the way to do it was with a federal War on Drugs.

∾

Ann Wrobleski needed an issue for her client.

Her client was Nancy Reagan. Wrobleski, a poised, graceful blonde of twenty-seven, was the First Lady's new projects director, and these early months in the White House had been difficult. The media were making a big deal out of Mrs. Reagan buying china and other baubles for the White House. Was that so terrible? Wrobleski wanted to know. Jackie Kennedy had done the same thing, and the public had loved her for it. But there was no talking sense to reporters. The sooner the First Lady had a new image, the better.

When Wrobleski had interviewed for the job, Mrs. Reagan talked about wanting to "do something" about drug abuse. She didn't want to chair a presidential commission, the way Rosalynn Carter had for mental health. She didn't want a policy job. And no, she didn't want a budgetary role. Ronnie was elected to run the country, she said, not I. I just want to be "helpful." And I'd like it to be related to drug abuse. And kids.

At the time, Wrobleski didn't give it much thought. Drug abuse? Yuck. She had in mind something "nice," like historic preservation or foster grandparenting. Communications director Michael Deaver wouldn't hear of drug abuse, either.

Drug abuse is a downer, Mrs. Reagan, he told her. Can't you talk about something fun? Volunteerism or something?

No, Mrs. Reagan said. When Ronnie and I were in the picture business we knew a lot of people whose kids got into trouble with drugs. I'd like to do something about drug abuse.

Mrs. Reagan gave Wrobleski marching orders: Our friend Ross Perot is speaking next week at some kind of parents' drug-abuse convention in Atlanta. You go down there and tell me what you find.

∾

Pat Burch, wife of Republican Party chair Dean Burch, swept into the annual PRIDE conference in Atlanta and just about took the place over. What a *wonderful* thing, she said. Why, if *parents* take up the fight against drug abuse, the federal government can get out of it altogether! It's another government function we can scratch off the list!

Burch was potentially a terrific ally for Buddy Gleaton — energetic, committed, and connected. But Gleaton didn't want his parents' movement to become a mere tool of the Republicans' New Federalism. Keeping Burch from taking over would be tricky. So Gleaton created another parents' organization to operate alongside PRIDE and put Burch on its board. Her National Federation of Parents for Drug Free Youth proved to be a mixed blessing. When wealthy friends of the Reagans wanted to write checks to stop drugs, who got the money — a group of nobodies from Georgia, or the wife of the chairman of the Republican National Committee?

∾

Requested by Joe Biden during the Carter administration, the General Accounting Office's report on drug enforcement and forfeiture was delivered to Congress at precisely the moment the Reagan administration was girding the loins of its "strong federal law enforcement capacity." Running seventy-five pages, the report was a call to battle. While RICO and Peter Bourne's 1978 forfeiture law have given police extraordinary power to confiscate the assets of drug dealers, the GAO said, police hadn't made use of them. "The government has simply not exercised the kind of leadership and management necessary to make asset forfeiture a widely used law enforcement technique," the GAO wrote. Bob Blakey couldn't have said it better himself.

Upon returning to work after surviving John Hinkley's pistol shot, Reagan announced that he had done what no other president had been able to do: he'd enlisted the FBI in the War on Drugs. Now that J. Edgar Hoover had been dead a good eight years, the premier federal law enforcement agency was finally going to become active in drug investigations. FBI director William Webster made his agency's mission clear: agents would look for ways to use RICO to round up trafficking rings and take away their assets.

The new Congress, seeded with Reagan-coattails freshmen and led in the Senate by Republicans, was in a perfect mood to receive the GAO report recommending tougher use of forfeiture. The biggest impediment to fighting the War on Drugs, one Florida Democrat said, was the laws of the United States. "In the war on narcotics, we have met the enemy, and he is the U.S. Code," Congressman Earl Hutto said. "I have never seen such a maze of laws and hangups."

~

What drug problem, exactly, was the Reagan administration and Congress gearing up to fight?

Heroin was a nonissue; nobody talked about it officially or in the press. Although the number of addicts hadn't shrunk since Nixon's day, it hadn't grown, either. The problem was stationary, and therefore invisible.

About cocaine the country had not yet made up its mind, and its ambivalence was typified by *Time*'s cover story that summer displaying a martini glass full of white powder under the legend "High on Cocaine: A Drug with Status — and Menace." In small and occasional doses, *Time* said, cocaine "is no more harmful than equally moderate doses of alcohol and marijuana, and infinitely less so than heroin." An Illinois appeals court had just ruled there was "no causal connection between the ingestion of cocaine and criminal behavior." It was still the drug of the "smart set"; all the cokeheads in the story were people otherwise enviable for their wealth and fame — Richard Pryor, Keith Richards, and a long string of well-heeled yups.

But the drug was starting to show its dark side. "After one hit of cocaine I feel like a new man," said one young executive. "The only problem is, the first thing the new man wants is another hit." *New York* magazine ran a long feature around the same time about a thirty-one-year-old financier, "worth at least $10 million," strung out on cocaine and trying to kick the habit. Amid loving descriptions of lavish apartments, panoramic offices, and racy cars, both pieces described the consequences of cocaine as the evaporation of disposable income and a stint in a cushy treatment program. Neither even suggested cocaine users might end up in prison. A Chicago cop quoted in *Time* explained why: "These people," he said, "are not the dregs of society."

~

Heroin was invisible, and cocaine wasn't yet a demon. That left marijuana.

The crisis — youthful pot smoking — was already abating on its own. Lloyd Johnston's high school survey in 1981 showed the first decline in teenage marijuana use in six years. Likewise, teenage *disapproval* of marijuana was rising, which confirmed that the decline was real. Drug use historically rises and falls in cycles; people try a drug, like it, get bored with it, and then a new generation discovers it; this may have been a "boredom" stage. The parents' movement can probably take some credit, as can the overall conservative swing that put Ronald Reagan in the White House. "There is less adolescent rebellion now," Lloyd Johnston told reporters upon releasing the figures, "so youth is more apt to listen to the cautions of their elders and less apt to use drugs as a form of social protest." Tobacco use also was in decline; kids may have overall been turning off the idea of drawing hot smoke into the lungs. For whatever reason, youthful marijuana use was diminishing. At that particular moment, with adolescent pot use dropping, cocaine a problem only for the very rich, and heroin off the national radar, there was as little need for a War on Drugs as at any time since Richard Nixon declared his in 1969.

~

Dick Williams didn't believe in statistics. By the time somebody shows up in statistics, he'd say, they're already a disaster for themselves, their families, their school, and society as a whole.

Reagan hadn't yet chosen a drug czar, and Williams — the manager behind the throne for the three prior administrations' drug offices — was helping the new administration assemble its policy. Treating addicts was a waste of money, he thought. The government can spend its whole budget and not help more than a fraction of them. As for methadone, well, swapping one addiction for another isn't something the government should pay for. The people the government should concentrate on, he said, are those who are just starting to try drugs. They're the only ones we have a prayer of affecting. So there's no point making a big federal deal out of heroin or cocaine; beginners aren't tempted by those. The drug we need to focus on is marijuana.

~

Such thinking dovetailed nicely with the project under way in another corner of the Old Executive Office Building. There, David Stockman was dismantling as much of the civilian federal government as he could. When he came to drug abuse, Stockman found myriad agencies squirreled away in many departments, in aggregate funding the "slots" system that sent federal money where the need was greatest. But that kind of direct federal funding was exactly the kind of budget item Stockman was looking to cut. In the Reagan philosophy, direct spending not only was expensive, it undermined state and local authority because federal dollars came with federal regulations. It also bears pointing out that drug-treatment dollars under the "slots" system were flowing to the places where the junkies were — New York, Detroit, and other cities that traditionally were Democratic strongholds — whereas it had been suburbs and rural areas that had elected the new president.

By redefining the national drug problem from heroin to marijuana, Dick Williams opened up some enticing possibilities for Stockman. Drug treatment — methadone especially — suddenly was no longer a priority. Those most visibly susceptible to marijuana — the middle-class white kids spotlighted by the parents' movement — had comfortable support systems to fall back on. The federal government was hardly needed there at all. So when it came to the "soft" side of drug policy — treatment and prevention — there really wasn't much of a role for the federal government if the primary drug of concern was marijuana.

To cut the budget and return "proper authority" to state and local governments (and, incidentally, cease favoring urban over rural districts), Stockman proposed the government cease direct federal funding for the methadone "slots" and phase out its own treatment programs. Instead, it should hand out big block grants to the states to spend as they wished. With the 1982 budget came the beginning of the end of the federally funded drug treatment network that four drug czars had worked a decade to build.

Just about the only federal programs that fared worse than the "soft" side of drug abuse in the 1982 budget were child nutrition (down 34 percent), urban development action grants (down 35 percent), education block grants (down 38 percent), school milk programs (down 78 percent), and energy conservation (down 83 percent). In keeping with Williams's desire to "close the debate," drug-abuse research suffered a 15 percent cut.

On the other hand, the "hard" side of drug-abuse policy, drug enforcement, enjoyed increases as big as 44 percent (the Coast Guard), with the FBI's drug budget swelling by more than half, the prison system's by almost a third, and the DEA's by a sixth.

And for all the talk of empowering the states, total federal aid to state governments actually dropped in Reagan's first budget for the first time in thirty years.

~

William Von Raab, a spare, taut attorney of thirty-nine from one of New York's oldest families, was working in his New York law office when his secretary buzzed to say that Richard MacNamar was on the phone.

Von Raab had worked with MacNamar back in 1972 in Richard Nixon's Federal Energy Commission. MacNamar said he'd just been named deputy treasury secretary and was recruiting a commissioner of Customs. Would Von Raab like the job?

It sounded like fun and Von Raab took it, finding that a lot of people who'd been his low-level colleagues in the Nixon administration were filling middle- and high-level slots in the Reagan administration. In their first meeting, the gruff ex-marine treasury secretary, Don Regan, gave Von Raab a short list of directives: Don't let anybody at Customs earn more than me (some low-level inspectors at the time were collecting massive overtime checks); find a private plane for me, since the attorney general has one and I don't; and don't take any mediocre political appointments from the White House.

And one more thing, Regan said; increase your drug seizures.

This, Von Raab learned, would be delicate. Under the 1973 agreement that created the Drug Enforcement Administration, Customs gave up its drug-fighting charter. It now had only 600 investigators, none of whom was trained or experienced in drug enforcement.

But Von Raab liked the idea. Deeply conservative, with the tight-lipped intensity of a folded switchblade, he began firing off memos to his inspectors and investigators: I want more emphasis on imported narcotics and less on pursuing every undeclared gift. Democrats look for socks, he was fond of saying, Republicans look for drugs.

Soon after, Customs in New York stumbled upon a big shipment of heroin and scheduled a press conference. Von Raab flew up, positioned himself in front of the cameras at the DEA's New York office, and called the bust "the most important since the French Connection" of 1973. DEA was livid, but Von Raab couldn't have cared less. As he saw it, he was on a mission.

~

"I'm not the guy for the job," Carlton Turner said into the phone, drumming his fingers on his desk at his marijuana farm at the University of Mississippi. On the other end of the line was Ron Frankum, deputy director of Reagan's domestic policy office. "Not that I don't support y'all," Turner said. "I do. But you want someone with more prestige."

Ross Perot's magic must have worked, Turner thought. And that pretty young thing from Nancy Reagan's office he introduced me to at the PRIDE conference in Atlanta must have put a word in the ear of the First Lady. Frankum was recruiting a drug czar.

Turner let himself be persuaded to fly to Washington and talk with Dick Williams. Then he was invited back a second time. The third time back, Michael Deaver spent thirty seconds with him in a hallway, but Ed Meese invited Turner to sit down and say what he'd do as drug czar.

"Strong law enforcement" was the first thing the chemist said. "You've got to do interdiction, crop eradication, and have a good international program on something besides heroin." Meese nodded. In addition to Ross Perot's endorsement, he had in his desk a sheaf of letters from parent activists all over the country recommending Turner for the job. "It is hoped by legions of hopefuls," urged one such letter, from the author of the prohibitionist manifesto *Bitter Grass: The Cruel Truth About Marijuana*, "that the government in Washington will come forward with a new approach to the whole drug problem in America, which will mean turning the nation away from the wretched Drug Culture that is rotting it at the core."

Turner went on. "Most of all," he told Meese, "you've got to clean up society. You have to create a climate in which society will take a stand. Get people involved who have a vested interest — parents, insurance companies, the medical community. Stop talking about whether marijuana's good or bad for you; I'm here to tell you it's bad. The scientists will tell they can't say for sure because as soon as they do they get no more research money."

Meese stood and shook his hand warmly. There was some awkwardness when the White House learned Turner was a member of the Democratic Party. He explained, though, that nobody survives at the University of Mississippi as a member of Abraham Lincoln's party, and his Democratic membership was a front. In truth, he'd been a Republican supporter for years and had the canceled contribution checks to prove it.

Meese called a few days after their meeting to say things "looked good."

~

The philosophical change at the Justice Department began filtering immediately to the army of federal prosecutors around the country.

Sid Lezak had been U.S. attorney in Portland, Oregon, since John Kennedy's day. He'd seen administrations come and go, the executive branch handed back and forth from party to party. A self-described "Adlai Stevenson Democrat," he'd weathered the sea change from Ramsey Clark to John Mitchell and survived the turmoil surrounding the Saturday Night Massacre. His office had grown steadily from seven to twenty prosecutors, and he had acquired a reputation within the department as excellent on civil rights, securities, and antitrust cases. Being about as far from Washington as any U.S. attorney, he long felt largely unaffected by the shifting of political winds there. He'd always set his own agenda.

Until now. The memos emanating from Justice all seemed to talk about nothing but drugs. Not only was this emphasis new, so was the department's attempt to set priorities for the U.S. attorneys in the field. Lezak had never experienced a Justice Department like it and was especially surprised given this administration's anti-Washington rhetoric. He called one of his new superiors to talk about it and was told outright: beef up your effort on drugs, forfeit assets, adopt big drug cases from the locals, start bringing dealers into federal court. If you have to take prosecutors away from other work, do so.

But I have some excellent white-collar and civil rights cases in the works right now, Lezak responded. My prosecutors are maxxed out.

You'll have to pull them off, came the response. This administration is committed to the War on Drugs.

Lezak, however, was not. Big drug cases were appropriate fare for a U.S. attorney, he thought, but the little ones they were urging him to adopt from state court were silly. Building up drug-prosecution statistics was not why he joined the Justice Department.

Lezak was one of the grand old men of Justice and had recently attended a U.S. attorneys' dinner in his honor. He'd hoped to serve until he was sixty-five but couldn't stomach being recruited into so patently a political crusade.

At fifty-seven, after more than two decades' service under six administrations, Sid Lezak resigned.

~

Joseph Russoniello, however, the newly appointed U.S. attorney for San Francisco, was in prosecutor heaven. *This* was an administration with fire!

Russoniello, a handsome, sturdy man of thirty-nine with a fine head of thick dark hair, was a former FBI agent. As assistant district attorney in San Francisco, he had run for his boss's job when DA Joseph Freitas let Dan White walk away from killing Mayor George Moscone and Supervisor Harvey Milk by using the infamous "Twinkie defense." Although Russoniello lost that election and moved to a private firm, he became visible to the state party machine because charismatic law-and-order Republicans were scarce in San Francisco.

In his interview with Rudolph Giuliani, Russoniello knew at once that working for the Reagan Justice Department would be worth the $50,000 salary cut. At the time, U.S. attorneys were held in low esteem; it was the local DAs, prosecuting sexy violent crime, that the public heard about, never U.S. attorneys. But Giuliani was determined to change that. We're going to become much more involved in the kinds of cases DAs handle, he told Russoniello. The DAs we spoke to say state laws are inadequate for the kind of crime fighting they want to do. We have wiretap authority; they don't. We have secret grand juries — with no transcripts published — which lets us use grand juries as an investigative tool; they don't. Forfeiture is stronger on the federal side, Giuliani said.

We are after nothing less than the enhancement of the prosecutor's role in this society, Giuliani said. What we want are hard-charging prosecutors, men who understand that a weakening of the prosecutor's role has taken place and are determined to reverse that. We're taking criticism because most of those we're hiring are white men, but screw it, that's who the hard-chargers are.

It was clear to Russoniello that to a certain extent the new Justice Department was using the drug problem as an excuse for increasing the power of the prosecutor; all of its new initiatives had to do with drug enforcement. Russoniello had no problem with that. A lot of violent crime was connected with the drug trade. Also, Russoniello was educated in Catholic schools and a Jesuit college and simply believed using drugs was wrong. He was glad the new Justice Department was going to get tough on users as well as dealers; users were the real problem. It wasn't enough, he thought, to offer treatment. Anybody could quit using drugs if he wanted to; treatment is just a government-sponsored crutch. Methadone, Russoniello believed, only prolongs addicts' dependence. What drug users need, Russoniello and Giuliani agreed, is the *stick* to make them go through with getting clean.

~

The Democrats in Congress wanted the president to have a Senate-approved drug czar, not only to give senators a chance to grandstand on this deliciously volatile topic during the confirmation hearings, but also to give Congress the authority to yank the drug czar up to the Hill to testify whenever it saw fit. (Presidential appointees who aren't approved by Congress must be formally subpoenaed.) Ed Meese and Ronald Reagan, though, didn't want any part of that. Congress was working on an omnibus crime bill containing the creation of a Senate-confirmed drug czar's position, and Reagan threatened to veto the whole thing if he had to, just to avoid having a congressionally approved drug czar. Until then, he quietly hired Carlton Turner to serve as his acting drug-policy adviser. Right after the Fourth of July, 1981, Nancy Reagan invited him to visit.

"Carlton," she said. "We've been in the White House six months already. When are we going to *do* something?"

~

The man could barely finish two sentences back to back without waves of applause cutting him off. Ronald Reagan was in New Orleans during the first September of his presidency, speaking to a conference of police chiefs.

His War on Drugs, "one of the single most important steps that can lead to a significant reduction in crime," would include the following: an end to the exclusionary rule (applause), injecting the military into the drug fight (applause), bail and parole "reform" (read "abolition"), enlisting the FBI into the War on Drugs, and "the responsible use of herbicides" (applause). Sitting among the policemen was Carlton Turner, Reagan's unannounced drug czar, nodding approvingly and noting with excitement the enthusiasm with which Reagan's agenda was being received.

The most important part of the speech, though, didn't concern specific legislation at all. In a few paragraphs, Ronald Reagan simultaneously changed the rules of engagement in the War on Drugs and redefined the country's essential drug-and-crime problem. "Controlling crime in American society is not simply a question of more money, more police, more courts, more prosecutors," he said. "It's ultimately a *moral* dilemma, one that calls for" — another surge of applause — "one that calls for a moral or if you will, a spiritual solution."

Close the debate!

> More law and order rhetoric may be justified. The studies and surveys may still be needed. The blue ribbon panels may keep investigating. But in the end, the war on crime will only be won when an attitude of mind and a change of heart takes place in America, when certain truths take hold again and plant roots deep in our national consciousness, truths like: right and wrong matters; individuals are responsible for their actions; retribution should be swift and sure for those who prey on the innocent. (applause)

Reagan was redeploying the tactic Richard Nixon used to batter "root causes" in 1968: shift the blame for social problems away from inequality, racism, injustice, and the like and place it on the immoral acts of bad individuals. That way, government has no greater role than to mete out "swift and sure" retribution.

"[Crime is] a problem of the human heart and it's there we must look for the answer," he said. "Men are basically good but prone to evil, and society has a right to be protected from them." (applause)

~

- Percentage of men imprisoned in 1981 who held jobs before prison: 50.
- Percentage of the same group who held jobs after prison: 19.

10

Rotten Behavior

1981–1982

What we do to our children they will do to society.

— *Pliny the Elder*

CARLTON TURNER WAS RIGHT. He *was* arguably the country's premier expert on the botany and pharmacology of marijuana. He knew the Latin names for every part of the plant, could reel off marijuana's 420 distinct chemicals and 61 cannabinoids, had studied the effects of herbicides on pot plants, had experimented growing plants under different kinds of artificial light and at different levels of moisture, had purified THC any number of ways. There wasn't much Carlton Turner didn't know about *cannabis sativa*.

The medical, social, and policy experience he brought to the drug czar's job, however, was nonexistent. Lee Dogoloff had taken drug policy away from psychiatrists. Turner, a chemist, explicitly rejected a government role in handling drug abuse as a disease. "Our philosophy," he explained to his new staff, "is 'get rid of the psychiatrists.' They're trained to treat, and treatment isn't what we do." Unlike Jaffe, DuPont, or Bourne, Turner had never run a drug-treatment clinic, worked with addicts, or wangled support from a legislature. Moreover, he was as inexperienced in the ways of Washington politics as the most derided Carter crony. And he had only a layman's understanding of heroin and cocaine; his experience was limited to one drug: marijuana, a drug that had never caused a documented death and about which the medical community was far from consensus.

"I'll hear any man's point of view," Turner was fond of saying, "but

I'll never see it so clearly that I forget my own." In fact, Turner actively limited dissenting views. Former NIDA director Bob DuPont, now an oft-quoted independent authority on drug abuse, privately questioned Turner's appointment. Turner heard about it and, in keeping with Dick Williams's desire to "close the debate," barred DuPont from the White House. When he heard that DuPont was scheduled to appear with Nancy Reagan at a drug-prevention event in Florida, he called the organizers to say "if Bob DuPont is there the First Lady won't be."

Researchers at NIDA were as appalled as DuPont at Turner's appointment; one wrote to tell Turner that when he left the White House he'd never get another contract from NIDA. Turner wrote back to say "when I leave the White House, you won't *be* at NIDA," and Turner made good on his word.

Turner embraced Dick Williams's idea of making marijuana the designated bad guy. No point in talking all the time about heroin, he'd say; hardly anybody uses it. If you make a big deal about heroin, someone can always come back and say, well, marijuana isn't as bad. The thing to do, he told his small staff, is to draw the line at the drug considered the *least* harmful. Then nobody will argue with you about heroin or cocaine. When somebody suggested Nancy Reagan make a photo-op visit to a methadone clinic, Turner vetoed it.

"With methadone you're saying 'when people get bad enough and progress to heroin, we'll use methadone,' " he said. "But we can't afford that luxury. We have to create a generation of drug-free Americans to purge society."

When Turner quoted marijuana studies on fat solubility, sperm counts, and immune-system damage, he was selective. He never cited Nixon's marijuana commission, which found the drug relatively benign for adults and recommended decriminalization. Nor did he acknowledge researchers at Harvard Medical School and elsewhere who were reporting similar conclusions with remarkable consistency. While nobody was saying that drawing hot, psychoactive smoke into the lungs was good for one's health (except perhaps in prescribed medical circumstances), many researchers were saying that a society that tolerates alcohol, tobacco, and bacon-double-cheeseburgers cannot on medical grounds justify jailing people for smoking marijuana.

Simultaneous with Turner's appointment as Reagan's behind-the-scenes drug adviser, the press suddenly dropped cocaine like a hot rock. As though a switch had been thrown, all drug coverage turned to marijuana.

It started in *Science News,* which reported a University of Kentucky study "proving" marijuana "is a cause of heroin use." Like other "gateway drug" theorists, the researchers looked in only one direction, asking heroin and cocaine users if they first used marijuana and predictably finding that a great many had. They didn't ask, though, whether the addicts had first used alcohol, tobacco, or caffeine — any of which might also be described, under the study's methodology, as the "gateway." More important, the researchers failed to track marijuana smokers on how many graduate to harder drugs. Whenever the question is asked that way, the percentage is in the single digits.

The "gateway drug" theory — that marijuana leads to harder drugs — had been a staple of the antidrug movement since pot first hit the big time in the late 1960s. Under Carlton Turner, though, it became holy writ. As an anti-marijuana tool in an age when millions of Americans have smoked pot without feeling themselves harmed, the gateway theory is perfect. Sure, you're okay now, but what about tomorrow? Susan Rusche, the anti-paraphernalia activist, had a word for recreational pot smokers: "pre-addicted." Bob DuPont told *Education Digest* he considered "marijuana use to be the single most serious new threat to our nation's health" and was about to publish a book about it: *Getting Tough on Gateway Drugs.*

The gateway theory is lunatic. The number of Americans who have smoked pot has skyrocketed in the past thirty years — to as many as 70 million — while the number of heroin addicts is about the same in the mid-1990s as it was in 1970: about half a million. Still, the gateway theory endures by holding each of us *equal* in our power (or lack thereof) to resist drug abuse, no matter our social history or milieu. Rich kid, poor kid, secure or alienated, cherished or abused, mentally healthy or deeply depressed, optimistic about his future or sensibly pessimistic — it doesn't matter. Take any kid and add pot, goes the theory, and an addict results.

Even the Kentucky researcher quoted in *Science News* conceded it is the act of criminalizing pot smokers, rather than the pharmacological properties of the drug itself, that is the real gateway to harder drugs. "By throwing subjects into a subculture that elicits heroin use," he said, "even moderate marijuana use can weld the first link of a causal chain leading to heroin."

The most consistent and passionate media attacks on marijuana, though, appeared in the conservative mass-market press, with Peggy Mann single-handedly striking blow after blow against the evil weed. In the *Saturday Evening Post, Family Circle,* and *Reader's Digest,* Mann seesawed between well-researched warnings against driving stoned and such histrionics as calling marijuana "a slow erosion of life" and "the devastation of personality." Dr. Harold Voth of the Meninger

Foundation's School of Psychiatry identified marijuana-induced "Organic Brain Syndrome" whose symptoms included "diminished will power" and "hostility toward authority." Voth and Mann tidily concluded that failure to believe them constituted proof that they were right. "Another pernicious symptom," Mann quoted Voth as saying, "is the element of denial — refusal to believe the hard medical evidence that marijuana is physically and psychologically harmful."

For Carlton Turner as for Richard Nixon, launching a war on marijuana was as much about culture as health, and he made no secret of it. In an article titled "White House Stop-Drug-Use Program — Why the Emphasis Is on Marijuana," the magazine *Government Executive* profiled Turner and summarized his views this way: Marijuana, like "hard-rock music, torn jeans and sexual promiscuity," was a pillar of "the counter culture."

> Point is, illegal, i.e. non-prescription, use of drugs . . . is not only a perverse, pervasive plague of itself, though it is that. But drug use also is a behavioral pattern that has sort of tagged along during the present young-adult generation's involvement in anti-military, anti–nuclear power, anti–big business, anti-authority demonstrations; of people from a myriad of different racial, religious or otherwise persuasions demanding "rights" or "entitlements" politically while refusing to accept corollary civic responsibility.

It would be hard to think of an era in which the "counterculture" was more thoroughly dead than during the early 1980s. Old hippies were throwing off their anti-military, anti–nuclear power, anti–big business attitudes and showing up in MBA programs like sinners pouring out of the hills to be baptized. "Yuppies" entered the lexicon, picking up where "the me generation" left off. John Sayles made his low-budget movie *Return of the Secaucus Seven* about a bunch of former activists wondering where their politics went, and then Lawrence Kasdan made his big-budget *The Big Chill* on the same theme. In 1982, even the poets laureate of the Woodstock era, Crosby, Stills and Nash, repudiated their hippie days, reuniting to sing regretfully, in "Wasted on the Way," about the time squandered getting high instead of rich. The song was a hit.

Yet Turner ordered an updated version of Keith Schuchard's *Parents, Peers & Pot* that identified the early 1980s as "an age of permissiveness" in which "there has been a growing tendency among parents, particularly those with a college background, to try to blend their roles as parents with adjunct roles as 'pals' to their children." The appropriate relationship between parents and teenagers, the booklet advised, is full-scale combat. "The number ONE and number TWO rules for today's parents should be 'Don't be afraid to be a strong parent; Don't be afraid of your children.' "

~

Parents and teenagers always fight; the conflict between them is one of the great power struggles in American life. Acting combative, secretive, and thoroughly unpleasant is how teenagers carve out their new proto-adult identities. Suddenly, their childhood friends are dorks, time spent with the family is a sentence, and their music is deliberately awful. Chuck Berry once said rock and roll has to have three elements: it has to be danceable, the lyrics have to speak to the concerns of young people, and parents have to hate it. "If any one of those is missing," he said, "then it isn't rock and roll."

To the parents' movement and its new ally in the West Wing of the White House, though, symptoms of teenagehood equaled symptoms of drug use. "Is your child keeping late hours?" asked *Parents, Peers & Pot: An Update*. "Has his schoolwork suddenly gone bad? Has he lost weight? Has her appearance changed and does she look sloppy or dirty? Is she often vague and withdrawn? Is he furtive about phone calls?" The book sensibly suggests parents spend more time with their kids and ask them frankly about their drinking or drug use. But "if he denies use, intensify your investigation of your child's friends, activities and environment." "Is the child not doing chores, late coming home, tardy at school, forgetful of family occasions (birthdays, etc.), not cutting grass, allowing room to be untidy?" asked Buddy Gleaton in a pamphlet for the Georgia War on Drugs. "Has the child a new group of friends; the language of new friends, hairstyles of new friends; switched clothes styles . . . become very interested in rock music and concerts . . . ?" If so, no manner of excess — searching the kid's room, banning certain friends, even calling the police — was inappropriate.

With America's Number One Problem Drug identified as the one teenagers are most likely to use, and every sneer, slammed door, and blast of Joan Jett pegged as evidence of a "drug problem," the War on Drugs became a powerful weapon for parents to use in their struggle with their teenagers. Blaming drugs for kids' troubles also worked within the family just as demonizing individuals' drug use worked in wider society: it obviated concern for "root causes" and let parents take their own behavior off the hook. If drugs were, as the Florida pediatrician Ian Macdonald liked to assert, a problem teenager's "only" problem, then parents needn't examine their own role in their children's troubles — divorce, career obsession, neglect — or for that matter falling wages, the need for both parents to work long hours, and slashed funding for education and after-school programs. While some nasty kids *did* have drug problems that required intervention, the parents of *all* nasty kids were urged — in magazine articles, PTA handouts, TV spots, and exhortations from the White House — to band together and "fight back." And in 1982, the most bellicose pro-parent, anti-child manifesto of them all rocketed up the best-seller list: *Toughlove*.

Its authors, forty-five-year-old Phyllis York and her fifty-three-year-old husband, David, were counselors by profession. But their own children — whom they describe as "rotten" — taught them that psychological counseling "only prolonged the problems by looking for the causes in the family's behavior." A child's rotten behavior was exclusively the child's fault, they wrote, and the most appropriate response was banishment. The Yorks' crowning achievement of "tough love," as they tell it, was refusing to post bail for their teenage daughter when she was arrested for drug possession just before Christmas. When their other daughter "threatened" to post the bond, Phyllis screamed at her, "I'll kill you! You will not make her bail!" And when an intern at the rehab center came to ask them to visit their troubled daughter, Phyllis slammed the door in her face.

Some children, the Yorks explained, are simply too horrible to continue nurturing. Among the two pages of banishable offenses the Yorks list are "living in filthy bedroom and saying that it is their room and they can do what they want, leaving dirty dishes around and claiming that they did not do it, fighting with their siblings and saying that their brothers and sisters started it, fighting with their parents and saying that Mom or Dad was nagging them . . ." as well as wrecking the family car, shoplifting, and getting stoned.

"The common denominator is rotten behavior," the Yorks wrote. "Despite a wide range of geographical, social, and economic backgrounds, our young people today behave with stereotypical predictability. Like clones stamped out in some satanic laboratory, they share an underlying selfishness and similar ways of demonstrating it."

The trick is to band together with other parents — "your support people" — who are doing the same thing to their bad children. And most of all, stay away from doctors and therapists. "We do not support the use of counselors who 'psychologize' the problem," the Yorks wrote, "but we encourage the patronage of counselors who will cooperate with our TOUGHLOVE strategies."

Even children whose parents didn't subscribe to Toughlove

felt — quite literally — the hot breath of the older generation's wrath. Trained dogs were employed in many schools to search students for drugs. "A dog has an emotional impact on kids," ex-FBI-agent-turned-dog-trainer Daniel Brainard told *Nation's Business* magazine in an article about the burgeoning industry. "A dog has credibility."

~

The Drug War on America's teenagers was not only rhetorical, it also was violent.

Seventeen-year-old Karen Norton of Jacksonville, Florida, was forcibly imprisoned for eighteen months in a facility where she was denied food, denied sleep, refused permission to use the toilet alone, led everywhere by a belt loop, and thrown against walls. No court sent Karen to this prison. It was entirely a private decision by her parents, who paid thousands of dollars. The reason for Karen's imprisonment: her "drug problem."

Karen was what the Yorks might have called a "rotten" teenager. She had friends her parents didn't like. She found school boring and got mediocre grades. She considered her father a hypocrite for sneaking beers even while attending AA meetings. She smoked the odd cigarette. She came home drunk from a party one night. Once, in eleventh grade, she skipped school and went to the beach. Karen had dropped acid twice, ate mushrooms once, and took speed a couple of times. She also smoked pot when it was around, but never with enough regularity that she'd buy any herself.

Her parents didn't trust her, and the feeling was mutual. When she was raped by a stranger at thirteen, and then by a friend's older brother at fifteen, Karen didn't tell them.

The cult-like prison in which Karen spent a year and a half was operated by a private company called Straight Inc. At its zenith, Straight operated seven "drug treatment centers" and twelve "family service centers" in fourteen states, "treating" more than 5,000 children ages twelve to eighteen, and sometimes young adults as well. By all accounts, Karen's experience was fairly typical. Court papers and complaints to state health agencies document dozens of similar cases of food and sleep deprivation, beatings, forced confessions, and complete isolation from family and friends. Under a different trademark, Straight's owners had earlier run an identical drug-treatment program that Florida health officials compared to the techniques used on prisoners of war by North Korea.

Straight was successfully sued more than a dozen times before being forced to shut its last facility in 1993. A jury ultimately awarded Karen Norton $721,000 in damages.

Her ordeal began one weekend in March 1982, soon after her seventeenth birthday. After a wild night of partying, Karen slept at her cousin's house. Next morning, her father arrived with the police.

According to her court deposition, he wrapped a belt around her arms so she couldn't escape and dragged her to the police car, which drove her home. At five o'clock the next morning, her father woke her up and told her to get dressed. No breakfast, no shower; with her father holding one arm and her uncle the other, Karen was led to the car for a four-hour drive to St. Petersburg. "We're going to get you help" was all her father would say. They drove to an unmarked warehouse in an industrial part of town. Karen had no idea where she was.

"You are in a Straight, Incorporated, drug rehab," said one of four girls who joined her in a windowless room. Karen was amazed. Although she occasionally used drugs, she didn't believe she had anything like "a drug problem." She politely told the girls she wasn't going to stay and tried the door. It was locked. The girls then called in the staff psychiatrist, Dr. Virgil Miller Newton.

"You are a little bitch, aren't you?" Dr. Newton said. "I don't know who you think you are." When Karen tried to brush past him, he threw her against the wall. Karen "had no right to try to leave," Dr. Newton said.

Then he tried another tack. If she signed, he said, she could try the program for fourteen days and then leave if she wanted to. "Your parents don't want you," Dr. Newton said. "Nobody wants you, you're scum and not worth anything anywhere and you're lucky we'll even take you in."

By this time Karen was thoroughly frightened and figured it would be easiest to endure the fourteen days and then split. When her parents came in to say good-bye her mother said, "We'll see you in fourteen days."

Karen was strip-searched and then led by the belt loop into a big windowless room in which a large group of teenagers was sitting on hard chairs. "Group, listen up," the girl holding her said. "This is Karen Norton, age seventeen, and she has done these drugs." The girl listed some Karen had tried and others that she hadn't. In unison, everybody shouted back, "Hey, Karen, we love you!"

Karen thought she was going crazy.

That first night, Karen was kept awake with no dinner until 3 A.M. writing a "moral inventory" of her transgressions. Then she was whisked in a car to a locked bedroom in her "foster home," the home of two "oldcomers."

Karen's daily routine at Straight went like this:

Beginning at six o'clock in the morning, Karen and the others spent twelve to eighteen hours sitting erect on the hard chairs in the windowless warehouse. Children who used the back of a chair for support would be "restrained" — others would grab them and hold them against the floor. Children were forbidden to speak to each other or even to make eye contact. They wrote countless "moral inventories" and then stood in turn to denounce themselves and each other for drug abuse and whatever other depravities they could conjure up.

Karen wasn't allowed to go anywhere, even to the bathroom, without "oldcomers" holding on to her belt loop. For three months, Karen told the court, she was unable to move her bowels because she was never left alone.

For lunch, the children were given "choker sandwiches," thick smears of peanut butter on stale bread, and they usually ate the same thing at night, with a cup of water or Kool-Aid. No hot meals. But it didn't much matter to Karen because, being unable to move her bowels in others' presence, she had all but stopped eating.

On day fourteen Karen told the staff she wanted to leave. They tore her initial agreement into shreds and told her she "wasn't going anywhere." Then, for speaking up, she got "confronted."

To be "confronted" in Straight meant undergoing "spit therapy," in which an "oldcomer" screamed insults and obscenities into her face, spitting, for what seemed like hours. Anyone who resisted would be jumped by the group and sat upon until he or she stopped struggling.

Karen wasn't allowed to call her parents or talk with them privately when they visited. Instead, all parents came into the big windowless room to hear the denunciations and self-denunciations. She heard the staff tell her parents she was such a bad "druggie" that if she left the program she'd be dead in six months. Other Straight alumni say their parents were told the same thing in precisely those words. At the time, parents were relieved of $6,000 up front and thereafter paid $900 to $1,600 a week to keep their children in Straight.

Eventually, Karen was allowed to attend the nearby high school, but was always in the company of an "oldcomer," even in the bathroom, an arrangement the high school accommodated. After school, she was taken straight back to the warehouse for more indoctrination, and then "home" late at night to a "choker" or bowl of cold cereal and a locked bedroom door. Most nights, Karen got only a few hours' sleep.

Karen thought a lot about escaping. She'd heard of one boy

who'd jumped straight through the glass of his foster home's window and made a run for it. But he was caught. Another girl escaped into a neighbor's house and managed to dial her brother's number, but Straight "oldcomers" barged in and before the horrified eyes of the neighbors pried the phone from her hand and dragged her back. She'd also seen escapees dragged back to Straight by their own parents.

Finally, six months after her eighteenth birthday, Karen slipped out of school and made it to a pay phone. She called the Florida Department of Health and Rehabilitative Services (HRS) and was connected with someone who believed her. An HRS official picked Karen up at school, drove her to Straight, and witnessed her sign herself out.

Eighteen months after being imprisoned for a drug problem she didn't agree she had, Karen Norton was free.

Straight's "Written Plan for Professional Services" didn't mention "spit therapy," sleep deprivation, choker sandwiches, or denial of bathroom privacy. Instead, it described its "peer counseling . . . which has its origins in the Twelve Steps of Alcoholics Anonymous" and an "Intensive Therapeutic Process." Instead of noting hours of insults from "oldcomers" and being thrown against the wall by Dr. Newton, the pamphlet promised "a formal evaluation (by the therapeutic staff) of the prospective client." It also stated that the "client must have a diagnosis of chemical dependency or abuse." It didn't mention that the diagnosis can come from resentful parents or untrained "oldcomers" inflicting on others what was done to them.

The average stay was twenty months long, and among the four goals for the corporation written in the literature was "To Admit Fourteen Clients Per Month." Most paid an average of $14,000 for the treatment.

Straight was founded in 1976 by two wealthy real estate developers in St. Petersburg: Mel Sembler and Joseph Zappala. Each would later become newsworthy for contributing more than $100,000 to George Bush's 1988 presidential campaign and being rewarded with ambassadorships (Sembler to Australia and Zappala to Spain, even though he spoke no Spanish). As early as 1979, allegations of abuse — beatings, food deprivation, forced detention, and the like — began appearing in the *St. Petersburg Times*, along with assurances that Florida health officials were investigating. In 1983, the year Karen Norton was released, an escapee from the same St. Petersburg facility won a $220,000 judgment against Straight for precisely the kind of abuse Karen Norton experienced. According to an internal report by a Florida inspector, threatening phone calls from high officials repeatedly kept Florida from revoking Straight's license.

All the while Straight was brutalizing what it called "druggies," the company enjoyed the praise of the White House. Nancy Reagan visited Straight facilities twice, once with Princess Diana along to see "the miracle of recovery." Bob DuPont, the founding director of NIDA, called Straight "the best program of its kind in the country."

11

The Battle Flag
1982–1983

The mood toward drugs is changing in this country and the momentum is with us. We're making no excuses for drugs — hard, soft, or otherwise. Drugs are bad and we're going after them.

— *President Ronald Reagan, in a Radio Address to the Nation, October 2, 1982*

THE NATIONAL ACADEMY OF SCIENCES had commissioned a study of marijuana's health effects in the middle of Jimmy Carter's presidency and in 1982 was ready to release the results. Acknowledging that it had come up with "politically inconvenient scientific knowledge," NAS found "no convincing evidence" that pot permanently damages the brain or nervous system, or decreases fertility.

As for the legal question, small-quantity possession should not be a crime, the report said. "Alienation from the rule of law in democratic society may be the most serious cost of the current marijuana laws."

Heresy! The new president of the NAS, Frank Press, hotly disavowed his own agency's report. The committee that prepared it had "insufficient data," he said, and had rendered a "judgment so value laden that it should have been left to the political process."

"The report," mused *Time*, "may have ignored the temper of the times."

~

Dick Williams had been around the block with sloganeering; during the Nixon days the line had been "Stop Drugs at the Source," and all that did was raise the expectation that the government actually would stop drugs at the source. Williams spent what seemed like half the Nixon presidency explaining to small-town mayors and police chiefs that the federal government was doing all it could. So when the Ad Council — the advertising industry's public service arm — offered its services to Carlton Turner's office, Williams — now Carlton Turner's deputy — was cautious. If there was going to be a new slogan, Williams said, it had to be something that didn't even imply the federal government was responsible for solving the drug problem.

After much back and forth, the Ad Council produced two campaigns — one for parents, one for kids. The theme of the parents' campaign was "Get Involved." For the kids, the theme was "Say No to Drugs." The spots ran, but nobody paid them much attention.

Something, Turner thought, is missing.

~

"Which drugs," *U.S. News* asked Nancy Reagan in an interview, "do you see as the greatest threat to young people today?"

"All drugs are bad," she responded. "Too many kids have the idea that there are hard drugs and soft drugs, dangerous drugs and safe drugs. There is no such thing as a safe drug. . . . The report years ago that said marijuana was harmless did more harm than anything else."

"What are the signs of drug abuse that parents should be watching for?"

"Children get very laid back and cool," the First Lady said. "They undergo a personality change, become combative, secretive, unable to get along with the family . . . they become messy about the way they dress."

"How strict should parents be with a child who has a drug problem?"

"It is lovely to say 'yes' but sometimes you've got to say 'no.' The Toughlove technique is the kind of strict discipline parents can use."

Then the interviewer dared a tough question. "Federal drug treatment programs have been cut about 30 percent under the Reagan administration," he said, referring to the precipitous drop in methadone treatment slots. "Do you have any evidence to show that private groups are in fact taking up the slack, as you have urged them to do?"

"Yes. The number of antidrug parents' groups has grown from about 1,000 to over 3,000 in the last year and a half."

It was apples and oranges. Methadone programs for stabilizing heroin addicts were giving way to suburban parents' support groups for surveilling surly teenagers.

~

Dependent as it was on presenting marijuana as Public Drug Enemy Number One, Reagan's War on Drugs couldn't withstand scientific debate. Placed against heroin — or for that matter alcohol, tobacco, poor prenatal care, workplace accidents, and myriad other public health problems — marijuana pales by comparison. So rather than invite opponents onto the playing field of science and data, Turner and his colleagues attempted to ban the game altogether.

Over at the National Institute on Drug Abuse, director William Pollin ordered his staff to read the drug-abuse publications his agency had published and remove any containing the word "social."

Pollin then sent a list of suspect documents to every librarian in the country along with a letter explaining: "These publications reflect preliminary marijuana and cocaine research findings that often found equivocal results. I strongly suggest that you purge your collection of these old materials."

The list included sixty-four NIDA booklets, papers, and monographs dating from 1972. Among the newly condemned were "Drug Abuse Prevention Films: Multicultural Film Catalog" (1979), "Can Drug Abuse Be Prevented in the Black Community?" (1977), "Multicultural Perspectives in Drug Abuse: An Annotated Guide to the Literature" (1977), "The Rap Kit: Resources for Alternative Pursuits" (1975), and "A Woman's Choice: Deciding About Drugs" (1979).

~

Bill Hughes hated "crime bills."

Not that he was soft on crime: Hughes, a Democratic representative from southern New Jersey, was a former prosecutor and favored such law-and-order measures as confiscating convicted drug dealers' assets.

But as chair of the House Subcommittee on Crime, Hughes disliked omnibus bills that wrapped lots of new criminal justice laws together into one package. The process allowed too much eleventh-hour mischief. Bad laws were passed with the good ones in unholy deals. Amendments were tacked on in the heat of a floor debate. Important provisions were hidden in mountains of dry language where potential opponents might miss them. Hughes preferred passing small, separate bills so Congress could focus on the merits of each.

Hughes understood, though, that crime bills are a narcotic on Capitol Hill. Crime is the one area of public life in which everybody considers himself an expert. Voting for a "tough" crime bill sells at home, which is why such bills always appear in the summer of even-numbered years, just in time for election day. Hughes also knew his Republican colleagues were fond of omnibus bills, because if they didn't pass, the blame fell on the Democratic majority.

From 1980 to 1982, Hughes's subcommittee reported half a dozen crime-related bills on such specifics as penalties for bribing jurors, tampering with consumer products (this was right after the Tylenol poisoning case), and asset forfeiture in drug cases. Along the way, Congressman John LeBoutillier, Republican of New York, tried to include the Arctic Penitentiary Act, which proposed shipping criminals to a rocky island in the Gulf of Alaska. That one withered in committee. On the whole, Hughes was pleased with the pieces of crime legislation he sent, separately, to the Senate for consideration.

But there, Hughes's six bills were tossed into a hopper with other crime-related bills to become the Omnibus Crime Bill of 1982. Among the many provisions that made it into the big bill was one that required the president to nominate a drug czar who would have to be confirmed by the Senate.

Reagan made good on his threat to resist having a Senate-confirmed drug czar and vetoed it. Wanting to torpedo the drug czar provision, Reagan was obliged to sink the whole bill, and two years of Bill Hughes's work on juries, asset forfeiture, and Tylenol went down with it.

∾

On June 24, 1982, Ronald Reagan stood in the White House Rose Garden and declared his War on Drugs.

"I was not present at the Battle of Verdun in World War I," he said. "But from that battle I learned of that horrendous time of an old French soldier who said something we could all heed. He said, 'There are no impossible situations. There are only people who think they're impossible.' "

With a finely aimed chop at Jimmy Carter, Reagan added, "I want to get away from the fatalistic attitude of the late seventies and assert a positive approach." His federal government would abdicate all responsibility save the rough stuff. "We can put drug abuse on the run through stronger law enforcement, through cooperation with other nations to stop the trafficking, and by calling on the tremendous volunteer resources of parents, teachers, civic and religious leaders, and State and local officials."

Only one drug earned specific mention. The country must "mobilize," Reagan said, "to let kids know the truth, to erase the false glamour that surrounds drugs, and to brand drugs such as marijuana exactly for what they are — dangerous, and particularly to school-age youth."

He then signed an executive order bringing Carlton Turner out of the shadows of his undefined "adviser" role and naming him director of a new Drug Abuse Policy Office, whose authority derived entirely from the Oval Office.

"We're taking down the surrender flag that has flown over so many drug efforts," Reagan said to applause. "We're running up a battle flag."

The reference to Verdun was odd: the battle is famous for killing half a million men on each side while resolving exactly nothing.

≈

Turner swaggered his new presidential authority over to the Office of Management and Budget and directed it to require every federal agency to submit a "drug budget" when requesting money. Dick Williams followed up by calling the OMB liaisons at every department and asking how much they were spending on the fight against drug abuse. Usually the answer was "What?"

The White House, Williams would growl, would like to know how much your department is spending on the national crusade against drug abuse.

Oh. Uh, let me get back to you.

Little by little, figures began trickling in. Williams had on his desk one of the first personal computers at the White House and was happy to have numbers to crunch. But he also knew merely asking for the numbers was half the battle. Every agency now had to think about the War on Drugs.

With Nancy Reagan's help, Turner convinced the president to let him sit in on cabinet meetings and impose an overarching drug agenda on the cabinet. "Let's go around the table," Reagan would say, pointing to Defense Secretary Caspar Weinberger. "Cap? What are you doing for the War on Drugs? And Malcolm?" — Labor Secretary Malcolm Baldridge — "what about you?" Soon every cabinet secretary — John

Block at Agriculture, Andrew Lewis at Transportation, even the star-crossed James Watt at Interior — knew he had to have an answer ready when the president of the United States asked about his and his wife's national crusade against drugs. Carlton Turner was thrilled. No other single issue swings such authority over every function of government, he liked to gloat. I'm manipulating the damn world.

~

It was time to put the war into the War on Drugs.

One of Reagan's first legislative victories was the revision of a 103-year-old law that kept the military out of civilian affairs. The 1878 law was written as an offering to the southern states after the Civil War; Congress banned military participation in domestic law enforcement. The Posse Comitatus Act, as it was called, made it illegal for the military to act as police on U.S. territory or waters.

Since 1971, though, the military had been providing sporadic Drug War assistance to law enforcement personnel. The law allowed "passive" or "indirect" assistance, vague terms occasionally interpreted to let the navy, for example, pass along word to the Coast Guard that a suspicious-looking ship was entering U.S. waters. No formal mechanism for such cooperation existed, however, and it didn't happen often.

Ed Meese and William French Smith wanted a clearly defined and active role for the military in the War on Drugs. As they put it, imported drugs were a threat to the security of the United States. Drugs from abroad maimed and killed Americans as surely as any other foreign enemy. The navy and air force were constantly training in the Gulf of Mexico and southern Atlantic; why shouldn't they keep their eyes open and radar tuned for smuggling? Not only would the drug fight be enhanced, the smugglers also would provide live, unpredictable "targets" for training.

The Pentagon brass was divided. Some officers believed the Drug War would dilute the military's traditional mission. Also, there was no way to declare victory in the War on Drugs, and the last thing the Pentagon needed was another unwinnable war. "All they want the military for is to serve once again as a whipping boy when their posturing and bluffs fall through," said one colonel. Others welcomed the fight. "The Latin American drug war is the only war we've got," said General Maxwell Thurman of the Southern Command, who would later lead the attack on Manuel Noriega. "If there are resources tied to it, why, you'll see the services compete for those, and probably vigorously," said Joint

Chiefs of Staff chairman Admiral William Crowe. "We take pride in being accomplished bureaucrats as well as military men. And I think it's legitimate for military men to try to perpetuate their institution."

One officer pleased with the rising tide of drug warfare was Admiral Paul Yost, chief of staff of the U.S. Coast Guard. Yost, who had commanded coastal patrols in Vietnam, was unhappy with the direction the Coast Guard had taken since World War II. Having performed as an effective fighting force in that war, the Coast Guard had degenerated into a bureaucratic agency responsible for hull and boat-license inspections, the lighthouse service, and boating safety. In a cold-war environment in which the danger of sabotage and infiltration was high, Yost believed, the Coast Guard should look and act like a branch of the armed forces. Now came a mission — drug interdiction — that fit those capabilities exactly. The navy, oriented toward fighting big battles in the open ocean, was neither trained, equipped, nor oriented for the seaborne drug war, Yost believed. The War on Drugs would nudge his Coast Guard in exactly the direction he wanted it to go.

Defense Secretary Caspar Weinberger didn't want any part of it. "Reliance on military forces to accomplish civilian tasks is detrimental to both military readiness and democratic process," he wrote. Past experience did not bode well, either. In a yearlong experiment in 1978 and 1979, Customs agents participated in 97 flights of AWACS radar jets. Although 268 potential "targets" were identified, communication between agencies was so poor that Customs planes were able to intercept only 31 of them. And not one turned out to be a smuggler.

But Caspar Weinberger didn't have Ed Meese's clout with Ronald Reagan. The White House pushed for a relaxation of Posse Comitatus, and Congress approved it with hardly a murmur. Military units now were directed to spot, track, and follow suspected smugglers. They couldn't arrest them, but were ordered to report them to civilian law enforcement, including the Coast Guard, a unit of the Department of Transportation.

With the ascension of Carlton Turner to drug-policy director, escalation of the military Drug War was rapid. In five years Pentagon funding for it went from $1 million to $196 million. Air force AWACS — huge four-engined jets with powerful radar domes mounted on their backs — and navy Hawkeyes — scaled-down AWACS built on twin-engine turboprops — were lofted on antismuggling missions. "Aerostats" — stationary blimps carrying radar — were hoisted over Key West and along the Tex-Mex border.

Liaison among agencies was spotty, however. The navy and Coast Guard traditionally loathe each other. Military men and policemen live in different worlds. And from the time of Myles Ambrose, Customs and the DEA have thirsted for each other's blood, jurisdiction, and funding.

~

As far as Reagan's people were concerned, Richard Nixon's disastrous attempt to deploy federal agents against street drug dealers — the violent and repressive ODALE — might never have happened. Barely a decade later, Reagan's White House announced it was establishing a South Florida Drug Task Force with Vice President George Bush at the helm.

The cocaine trade was so big in Miami that it was shockingly visible to the law-abiding community. A quarter of the city's murders were being committed with machine guns, and plenty of bystanders were hit along the way. Existing law enforcement wasn't up to the job, the White House said. The FBI and DEA pulled agents out of other posts and sent them to Miami. The Justice Department likewise sent prosecutors. Coordination was the key; navy intelligence with the Coast Guard, the Coast Guard with the DEA, and everybody with the media. The task force produced a string of big drug seizures, a bevy of impressive prosecutions, and plenty of photo opportunities for a shirtsleeved George Bush astride bales of confiscated marijuana.

"There is significant evidence the crackdown is working," *Newsweek* crowed. The evidence, though, was bizarre. Police usually claim credit for an increase in drugs' street value on the theory they're making drugs scarce and too pricey for marginal users. But the price of cocaine was continuing to fall in South Florida, so Bush's chief of staff bragged to *Newsweek* that the task force's success was ruining the market for drugs and thereby driving *down* the price of cocaine.

However they wanted to spin price fluctuations, it was clear the level of smuggling into the United States wasn't dropping, only the level of smuggling into South Florida. Nearby states began seeing big increases in drug smuggling. "I'm afraid they're going to close the front door and leave the back door open," complained one Tennessee DA. "We're the back door."

~

Three weeks before the 1982 midterm elections, Reagan launched the biggest offensive ever in the War on Drugs. "In recent years," Rudolph Giuliani told Congress, "this nation has been plagued by an outbreak of crime unparalleled in our history and unequaled in any other free society."

Not true. The rate of violent crime — the number of crimes per 1,000 people — was *lower* in 1982 than in the previous year and was less than one percentage point higher than in the dark, "permissive" days of Jimmy Carter. The rates of rape, assault, theft, burglary, and car theft all were lower in 1982 than in 1977. Robbery, though up slightly from 1977, was down from the previous year. The number of people reporting personal experience with either burglary or robbery was unchanged or slightly lower than in the mid-seventies. And the murder rate had been falling steadily since 1979. There was no new "plague" of crime, despite what Giuliani — the number three official of the agency tallying crime statistics — was willing to tell Congress.

Still, Congress allocated $125 million to hire more than a thousand new FBI agents, DEA agents, and federal prosecutors to man twelve new regional drug task forces modeled on that of South Florida. Altogether, the corps of federal drug fighters increased by about a quarter, and existing personnel also were taken off other duties to work on the drug task forces. With all the Justice Department's other pressing duties — discrimination, immigration, commerce, banking, and the environment, to say nothing of forty-two categories of federal crime — drugs and organized crime were to be the sole purview of this massive new effort.

Reagan also announced plans for a presidential commission of "experts" to study organized crime and drug trafficking. Chairing the commission was Judge Irving Kaufman, remembered for censoring Lenny Bruce and sentencing the Rosenbergs to death. Among the other "experts" was the editor of the *Reader's Digest*.

In announcing the new initiative on October 14, 1982, Reagan stood in the Great Hall of the Justice Department before the friendliest of audiences and heaped more soil upon the grave of "root causes." The "rise in crime," he said, is the result of "a misguided social philosophy."

> At the root of this philosophy lies utopian presumptions about human nature that see man as primarily a creature of his material environment. By changing this environment through expensive social programs, this philosophy holds that government can permanently change man and usher in an era of prosperity and virtue. In much the same way, individual wrongdoing is seen as the result of poor socioeconomic conditions or an underprivileged background. This philosophy suggests in short that there is crime or wrongdoing, and that society, not the individual, is to blame.

The American people, he said, "utterly reject this point of view" and "are reasserting certain enduring truths — the belief that right and wrong do matter, that individuals are responsible for their actions, that evil is frequently a conscious choice, and that retribution must be swift and sure."

In case anybody missed his point, "fact sheets" were distributed that declared "official inaction has been a major part of the problem. When the Reagan Administration took office, it discovered that during the prior Administration the government had lost more than 1,000 FBI and DEA agents. . . . Through the inaction of public officials who should have known better, going back many years, the Nation had lost a whole generation to drugs." And in case *that* wasn't plain enough, a Q & A sheet about the new program asked outright:

"Q: Is the Carter Administration really to blame for a lot of the current narcotics problem?

"A: Certainly drug enforcement and law enforcement did not receive the emphasis they needed during the Carter years."

~

The new racheting up of the Drug War wasn't just a matter of more agents and prosecutors. Reagan wanted radical changes in the law, too. The new corps of "hard-charging" U.S. attorneys submitted their wish lists to the Justice Department, which in turn drafted Reagan's legislative agenda.

First on the list was the conservatives' nemesis, the exclusionary rule. Reagan demanded its repeal "so that evidence is not thrown out and defendants freed on minor technicalities in an otherwise solid case." Reagan wanted the Posse Comitatus Act further relaxed to let soldiers and sailors make arrests. He wanted new wiretap authority. He wanted to expand preventive detention. He wanted to let police officers serve on secret grand juries.

Reagan's Justice Department also demanded broad new powers to confiscate citizens' property upon *suspicion* — not proof — of drug trafficking. Neither the 1970 RICO laws nor the 1978 forfeiture laws went far enough for Ed Meese and William French Smith. They didn't let the government take real estate, for example. Stash pads, marijuana farms — and, for that matter, people's homes — were therefore immune. The current laws also prevented the government from seizing assets until after an indictment was returned, on the theory that at least the minimal evidence needed to indict a person should be required before their property was confiscated. Reagan's Justice Department wanted all that reversed, along with the law requiring police to give people notice that their property was about to be seized. Better to grab the assets first, went the thinking, and then file the notice or present the evidence to a grand jury for indictment.

Finally, the Justice Department wanted a new authority — never hinted at in previous law — to seize "substitute" assets, assets that are completely legitimate but equal in value to the allegedly tainted goods.

Overall, the Reagan Justice Department wanted further to blur the line between the low standard of proof inherent in civil forfeiture with the long reach of criminal forfeiture. Justice wanted a "new criminal forfeiture statute" that would let prosecutors seize anything believed — not proven — to be either drug related, bought with drug proceeds, or equal to the value of drug proceeds. The desired law, which would apply only in drug cases, would create what Justice called "a permissive presumption, or more correctly, an inference" that anything bought "within a reasonable time" after a drug deal was bought with drug money and therefore seizable. Such a seizure could take place upon a showing only of "probable cause," the same low standard required for mere search warrants. No proof would be required. The person would not have to be charged — let alone convicted — of a crime.

A suggestion by Congressman Bill Hughes that innocent people whose property was wrongly confiscated should be allowed to sue for its return was rejected by Justice. Better for them to petition the attorney general and seek "administrative relief" than to bring "further litigation in our already overburdened courts," a Justice official explained to Congress.

The final item on the Justice Department's wish list was a bounty-hunter provision. A quarter of any assets taken — up to $50,000 — should be set aside to pay the snitch who got the case going.

Deputy Associate Attorney General Jeffrey Harris was assigned to appear before Congress to present a formal request for these laws. But it turned out the Reagan administration didn't need to lead Congress on this one. It didn't even need to rely on the Senate Republican majority. Harris's testimony was delayed five weeks, during which everything the Reagan administration wanted was included in a new bill designated S.2320. The new bill was introduced not by Jesse Helms, Strom Thurmond, or any other stalwart of the Republican Right, but by Democrats Joe Biden and Hubert Humphrey. All Harris had to do when he finally gave his prepared statement was cross out references to Justice's "proposal" and pen in "S.2320." Though originally conceived as a Republican strategy, the Drug War now was fully bipartisan. Democrats and Republicans were marching in lockstep to its martial beat.

~

By geography and cultural design, Humboldt County is a world unto itself. Tucked into the far northwestern corner of California, the county is a warren of steep canyons and dense forests of redwood, fir, and pine. Logging once employed the few people who lived there, but by the 1970s the last of the profitable trees were gone and the timber jobs with them. The canyons of Humboldt County, accessible only by a maze of tangled dirt roads, became a refuge for the kind of people who wanted nothing more than to be left alone. Back-to-the-land hippies, broody Vietnam vets, artists, and other assorted hermits were attracted by the mild weather and cheap land. People arrived, threw up a tarpaper shack or parked a microbus, planted a garden and a little pot. They lived without benefit of phones, electricity, or a daily newspaper. It was, for a certain type of person, the perfect place to sit out the Nixon and Ford years. They didn't bother the conservative establishment of such nearby towns as Eureka, and the distanced respect was mutual.

In 1972, Andrew and Susan Camarda bought forty remote acres in Humboldt County at $235 an acre to start a horse-boarding ranch and riding school. Four years later, their peaceful idyll had vanished. Perhaps because of federal efforts to intercept imported marijuana, American-grown pot was becoming a lucrative business, with prices shooting from about $150 a pound to as much as $1,000. Humboldt County — remote, inaccessible, well-watered, and sunny — suddenly started looking good to a different type of person.

Armed bikers roared through the canyons to and from big pot plantations. Trucks full of men with guns patrolled the roads. Guard towers with searchlights started appearing. A woman the Camardas knew was murdered when pot-farm hands broke into her house to burgle it. Another longtime Humboldt resident blundered into a boobytrap and was blown up. Several locals were shot at for venturing too close to pot fields. The owner of the huge spread next to the Camardas had dozens of acres planted in marijuana and liked to practice at night with his .30 caliber machine gun, lighting up the sky with tracer bullets. Camarda asked the sheriff why he didn't stop it, and the sheriff replied he didn't have the resources to field more than eight pot-farm raids a year. He frankly told Camarda he didn't have the man- or firepower to storm the bigger, better-armed plantations.

By the early 1980s another big change was apparent in Humboldt County. It wasn't only well-armed gangsters new to the area who were growing pot. A fair portion of the county's back-to-the-land counterculture was getting rich off the marijuana boom too, and starting to swing real clout in the community. Suddenly, there was a well-funded "Environmental Protection Information Center" in Eureka and an alternative radio station. The "hippies" of the county opened their own community credit union and financed a new medical center. The transformation of the county's economy from timber to marijuana was shifting the power in the area from the old-line establishment to the longhaired newcomers of the early seventies. The government doesn't care if we're machine-gunned to death up here, Camarda said to his wife one afternoon in 1983, but now that the hippies are taking over I'll bet we see some action.

~

For northern California's U.S. attorney, Joseph Russoniello, and California's new attorney general, John Van de Kamp, the "emerald triangle" of Humboldt County was, as the Jesuit-trained Russoniello liked to say, "an open wound on our prayer hand." The remote county was starting to show up regularly in homicide reports. TV and the papers showed vast acres of Humboldt reefer swaying in the breeze. By 1983 the area had come to the attention of Carlton Turner, who constantly pressed Russoniello and Van de Kamp to do something about it. You're undermining our entire foreign policy, Turner told them. We can't pressure other countries to stop growing marijuana if we're allowing it in our own backyard.

One afternoon in the summer of 1983, the Camardas were eating lunch and listening to local talk radio when callers began phoning the station to ask what was going on. There are helicopters all over the place, the callers said. Is there a forest fire? An escaped convict? A lost plane? In the distance, the Camardas could hear the roar of helicopters. It sounded like a small war, and so it was. CAMP — the Campaign Against Marijuana Production — had begun.

Russoniello and Van de Kamp marshaled the DEA, state and local police, an amalgam of four-wheel-drive enthusiasts' clubs, and the California National Guard into a single, high-profile, effort to wipe out Humboldt County's new cash crop. The Camardas and their friends at first were delighted. The air force was flying U-2 missions over the county to spot the big pot fields; then helicopters would descend, disgorging battalions of armed and fatigue-clad troops to scythe down the reefer and burn it. Few arrests were made that summer, but vast swatches of marijuana were put to the torch. Those hardest hit were those with the biggest pot fields, the people the Camardas wanted to see driven off anyway. By the end of the summer, Humboldt County felt like a quieter and safer place.

But the helicopters of CAMP returned the following year, and this time there weren't any big commercial pot farms to hit. Now the helicopters were searching for smaller pot fields, like the ones the Camardas' friends planted for their own use. To find them, the choppers had to zoom in low, so low they'd break windows and spook horses and kick up dust clouds so thick that cars would be driven off the road. For a solid month, the clatter of helicopters was never absent from Humboldt County. CAMP roadblocks started hauling whole families out of cars and holding them at gunpoint while searching the vehicles without warrants. CAMP troops — some of them National Guard, some troopers of the California Highway Patrol, and others untrained and quickly deputized amateurs — went house to house kicking in doors and ransacking homes, again without warrants. Van de Kamp bolstered the raiding squads with borrowed LA policemen who, Van de Kamp knew, looked on two weeks of raiding hippie shacks in Humboldt as "summer camp." Many were Vietnam veterans, and watching them, Camarda thought they looked on Humboldt's teepees and homebuilt cottages as the hooches of the Mekong Delta. They'd kick them apart, wave guns at the terrified owners, and storm off in a cloud of dust and helicopter exhaust.

A local attorney — who'd retired to Humboldt from San Francisco to "relax" — began gathering complaints. A CAMP team rousted a family from their home at gunpoint and shot their dog. A CAMP helicopter chased a nine-year-old girl down a dirt road and pointed guns at her. Another hovered so low over a woman taking an outdoor shower that she could see the pilot laughing. CAMP troops were searching without warrants not only the homes of suspected pot growers but also all the neighbors' homes as well, ostensibly to "protect themselves." Once inside, the troops would empty the refrigerator, pilfer what they wanted, and leave empty beer cans on sofas and counters. No home or vehicle in Humboldt County was immune from a helicopter assault and a warrantless search. The citizens of the county, who had first welcomed CAMP as a way to get rid of dangerous lawbreakers, now viewed the operation as an occupying army.

California wasn't the only place this was happening. CAMP was the biggest of the state/federal marijuana eradication projects, but similar assaults were under way in Missouri, Florida, Maine, and elsewhere. The War on Drugs had become a real war.

The last time the government had launched an attack specifically on marijuana was in Vietnam. As Egil Krogh learned to his dismay, cracking down on pot in Vietnam made heroin cheaper and easier to find, and then cracking down on heroin led soldiers to mainline instead of snorting it. But to Carlton Turner's drug warriors, the age of Egil Krogh was no more relevant than the Peloponnesian Wars. Their latest war on marijuana would bring results; pot would become harder to find. And there would be cocaine, waiting.

12

The Least Dangerous Branch
1983

> It is a fair summary of history to say that the safeguards of liberty have frequently been forged in controversies involving not very nice people.
>
> —*Justice Felix Frankfurter*

THE RISING TIDAL WAVE of antidrug orthodoxy failed to break against that final bulwark against temporal excess, the United States Supreme Court.

Alexander Hamilton called the judiciary "the least dangerous branch of government." Appointed for life, federal judges are presumed immune from the political passions that seize elected politicians. But even Supreme Court justices are only people, appointed for their politics by politicians seeking political gain. By the early 1980s, the Court had swung decidedly and reliably to the right. Earl Warren had been replaced by Warren Burger; William O. Douglas, Hugo Black, John Harlan, and Potter Stewart had given way to John Paul Stevens, Lewis Powell, William Rehnquist, and Sandra Day O'Connor. The last time a Democratic president had named a Supreme Court justice was when LBJ nominated Thurgood Marshall in 1967. The "permanently liberal" judiciary that Don Santarelli had counted on to counterbalance his harsh criminal laws was but a memory.

In response to the activist Court of Earl Warren, conservatives adopted a rallying cry that judges "shouldn't legislate from the bench." But in decision after decision throughout the 1980s, the Supreme Court assembled by Nixon, Ford, and Reagan rewrote the Fourth

Amendment's protections against police excess as actively as any Congress. The Court let police stop cars at roadblocks and search them without a warrant. It let police crack open a traveler's suitcase or a piece of private mail on the say-so of a barking dog. It permitted the use of "courier profiles" — lists of such characteristics as "black with Jamaican accent" that constitute sufficient grounds to search a person in an airport without a warrant. It let police spy through windows from low-flying helicopters and *then* get a warrant on the basis of what they see. It permitted compulsory urine testing for federal employees. It essentially revoked the Fourth Amendment rights of schoolchildren by allowing warrantless searches of their lockers and pockets. And it ruled that even if fenced and posted "No Trespassing," the fields, barns, and outbuildings surrounding a home are not protected by an "expectation of privacy" and may be searched without a warrant.

Every one of the 1980s cases that weakened the Fourth Amendment had one thing in common: they all involved drugs. The Court shared both the national distaste for illegal drugs and the conservative desire to use that distaste to empower the prosecution. Drug trafficking, the Court ruled at one point, "is as serious and violent as the crime of felony murder." The Court followed the Drug War agenda of Reagan's White House so closely that conservative Justice John Paul Stevens lamented in writing that the Supreme Court had become little more than "a loyal foot soldier" in the War on Drugs.

Perhaps no case of the era so clearly demonstrated the Supreme Court's political intent as *Illinois v. Gates,* decided in 1983. The principle established in *Gates* was precedent-shattering: that it is legal for police to obtain search warrants on the basis of anonymous tips. But in his eagerness to be an ally of Ed Meese against the exclusionary rule, Warren Burger ordered the case argued so oddly that William Rehnquist, writing for the majority, ultimately was compelled to apologize in his decision. The story of this case — typical in some ways and extraordinary in others — begins five years before the decision, on the morning of May 3, 1978.

~

Bloomingdale, Illinois, is one of the older, leafier suburbs of Chicago. Nestled in the hardwoods between the Glendale Country Club and the Mallard Lake Forest Preserve, a comfortable hour's drive from the Loop, Bloomingdale prided itself on being a world away from big-city crime. Detective Charles Mader of the Bloomingdale police was going through his mail one balmy spring morning and came across an envelope postmarked the day before. Inside he found the following note, handwritten and all spellings *sic:*

> This letter is to inform you that you have a couple in your town who strictly make their living on selling drugs. They are Sue & Lance Gates, they live on Greenway, off Bloomingdale Rd in the Condominiums. Most of their buys are done in Florida. Sue his wife drives their car to Florida, where she leaves it to be loaded up with drugs, than Lance flys down and drives it back. Sue flys back after she drops the car off in Florida. May 3 she is driving down there again and Lance will be flying down in a few days to drive it back. At the time Lance drives the car back he has the trunk loaded with over $100,000.00 in drugs. Presently they have over $100,000.00 worth of drugs in their basement.
>
> They brag about the fact they never have to work, and make their entire living on pushers.
>
> I guarntee if you watch them carefully you will make a big catch. They are ~~wit~~ friends with some big drug dealers, who visit their house ~~freek~~ often.
>
> Lance & Sue Gates
> Greenway in Condominiums

Mader, a squat, burly man with dark curly hair, weighed the note in his hand. No signature, he noticed, and no return address. That was a problem. Long-standing case law laid down a "two-prong" requirement for tipsters if their information was to be used to get a search warrant. First there must be sufficient basis of fact in the tip, and second the informant must have a demonstrable knowledge of those facts. This note was exceptionally specific. But because the tipster was unknown, there was no way to determine whether he knew what he was talking about. There was no second prong.

Mader decided to do some preliminary checking. Sure enough, there was a Lance Gates at the Greenway address in the phone book. He checked to see if either Lance or Susan had a criminal record; neither did. Then Mader called the airlines, and bingo, an L. Gates was reserved on a flight to West Palm Beach on Friday. This was Wednesday, May 3, the day Susan Gates was said to be heading to Florida in her car. Now Mader was excited.

He asked a Chicago DEA agent to watch the plane and confirm that Lance boarded. On Saturday morning, the agent got Mader out of bed to say the DEA had followed Gates from the West Palm airport to a motel, where a woman answering Susan Gates's description let him into a motel room. The Gateses' gray Mercury, he said, was parked in front. Next morning, the agent called again to say Lance and Susan had climbed into their car and swung onto the freeway, heading north. Everything was happening exactly as the note had predicted.

Mader drove to the home of Ken North, a blond, beefy, and jovial local prosecutor who had been a policeman years before. Mader laid out the details. It's a tough one, North said. The courts don't like anonymous tips because they worry about police making them up, or people with a grudge using the police for revenge. In cases like this, courts tend to insist on the two prongs — fact and the informant's reliability — like salt and pepper. We have here a hundred pounds of salt, but not even a pinch of pepper. It would be interesting to see if that's good enough.

North's wife cooked the men a pot of spaghetti, and then, being a legal secretary, typed up the warrant affidavit while they ate. At ten o'clock that night, Mader and North brought the affidavit to the home of a local judge, who signed it on his kitchen table.

It was a quiet, civilized bust. Just before dawn, the Gateses' gray Mercury rounded the corner and stopped in the driveway of their house. Mader walked up, showed his badge, and said he had a warrant to search the trunk. Gates didn't run, didn't pull a gun; he just handed Mader the keys and asked, "May I call my lawyer?" When Mader popped the trunk, the smell told him he'd scored big; the pungent aroma of fresh marijuana almost knocked him over. There were seven burlap bags full of the stuff, about 350 pounds by later count, more drugs than Mader had ever seen in one place. North, parked nearby, ran up to take a look.

A few minutes later a Bloomingdale police cruiser appeared in the dawn's early gloom. There's been a noise complaint, the officer said. A couple of guys have been yelling and whooping and giving each other loud high-fives.

~

James Reilley of nearby Des Plaines was home reading the Sunday papers and chain-smoking Newports when Lance Gates called. You're a defense attorney, right? Gates asked. Right, Reilley said. I got your name from a friend, Gates said. My wife and I are in trouble.

After bailing out the Gateses and looking over Mader's paperwork, two things were clear to Reilley. First, Lance and Susan Gates were professional drug dealers. But more important, the search that led to their arrest was illegal. The tip that inspired the search warrant didn't meet the two-prong test.

Reilley, a flamboyant dresser with a white pompadour and bristle mustache that gave him a Caesar Romero look, had been a narcotics prosecutor before becoming a defense lawyer. He knew search and seizure law well. This case was hardly worth worrying about. He filed a motion to suppress the search warrant with trial judge William Hopf, who discussed the case with an appellate judge he knew. The man laughed. "If you allow anonymous letters, I know four cops who will take pen in hand right now," he said. Hopf agreed. Invoking the exclusionary rule, he decided the search was illegal and the marijuana therefore inadmissible as evidence.

~

Ken North filed an appeal and the appellate court sided with Hopf and Reilley. But North didn't want to let it go, so he appealed the case to the Illinois Supreme Court.

This guy, Reilley thought when he got the notice, is a glutton for punishment.

Illinois's highest court agreed with Reilley and Hopf, too. Even if ten pounds of salt could equal a pinch of pepper — and it doesn't — all of the actions the letter said Lance and Susan Gates would take were legal ones. Booking a flight, staying in a motel, and driving home are all innocent, the Illinois Supreme Court ruled, and "the corroboration of innocent activity is insufficient to support a finding of probable cause. . . . Judgment affirmed."

~

By now it was 1981. Ronald Reagan had been inaugurated, shot, and catapulted to new heights of popularity. William French Smith's "hard-charging" U.S. attorneys were lobbying to garner more power for the prosecution. Ed Meese and Ronald Reagan were openly calling for repeal of *Miranda* warnings and the exclusionary rule. State and local prosecutors were asking the Justice Department for a new federal War on Drugs.

Reilley opened his mail one morning and found notice of a petition to have the Gates case heard by the U.S. Supreme Court. His first reaction was to laugh out loud. Never happen, he thought. But the Court agreed to hear the case the following year. Reilley was surprised, but not worried. Nothing in the case so far indicated any willingness anywhere to reverse the long-standing two-prong test.

On October 13, 1982, the day before Ronald Reagan's big Drug

War speech to the Justice Department, Reilley arrived at the Supreme Court for oral arguments. Despite a cold rain, a big crowd of people was waiting outside for seats. Among them were Lance and Susan Gates, along with their parents. Reilley nodded to Paul Biebel of the Illinois attorney general's office, who was arguing the other side. On Reilley's table, by tradition, was the white quill feather given to all who argue before the country's highest court. Reilley put it in his briefcase.

What impressed Reilley most this day was how unprepared the justices seemed. Questions from the judges included: "Where does all this 'prong' lingo come from?"* One justice was ready to criminalize overnight trips to Florida, asking, "Can you seriously maintain that this was consistent only with innocence, when you have the quick flight to South Florida and the non-stop trip back?" Another asked whether judges *ever* deny search warrants to police. Still another didn't seem to know that reliability of a tipster was required by law. "If this isn't probable cause, I don't know what is. . . . No one in their right mind would conclude that this was not a reasonable action on the part of the police."

"My answer to that, Your Honor, is specifically this," Reilley said. "This Court said that hearsay cannot be the basis for a search warrant."

~

Reilley walked out of the court feeling good. Nothing Biebel said refuted his argument that the law forbids police from getting a search warrant on the strength of hearsay. Reilley expected a decision in about six months.

Six weeks later, though, he received a registered letter from the U.S. Supreme Court ordering him back to D.C. on March 1, 1983, to reargue *Illinois v. Gates*. In the meantime, the Court was making an extraordinary request.

It ordered both sides to brief it on the following issue: should the exclusionary rule be "modified" to allow illegally seized evidence to be used in court, provided the police had a "reasonable belief" the search was legal?

Reilley was stunned. The Supreme Court was suggesting the exclusionary rule be made a sometimes thing; if the police illegally obtained a warrant, anything they found would be admissible provided

* Supreme Court transcripts don't specify the justice asking a question. Questions from the bench are indicated only as "question."

they said they thought the warrant was legal. Such an exception would effectively make the Fourth Amendment optional. Police could be as repressive as they liked, provided they said they had a "reasonable belief" they were acting legally.

But that the Supreme Court was trying to work this into *Illinois v. Gates* was more mind-boggling. The Court's own rules forbid any new point of law to be introduced at the Supreme Court level. If the issue hasn't been raised in a lower court, it cannot be raised at the Supreme Court. A "good faith exception" to the exclusionary rule had been discussed in lower-court cases around the country, but never in *Illinois v. Gates.*

Weird, Reilley thought, brushing cigarette ash from his vest and frowning at the letter. It seems they can't wait for the issue to reach them; they're jumping the gun to dismember the exclusionary rule.

Reilley explained in his brief that the Supreme Court legally had no jurisdiction over the good-faith-exception question. He further pointed out that Illinois was one of a handful of states that had the exclusionary rule on its books *before* the Supreme Court extended it to all states in 1961. So even if the Court did create a good-faith exception to the exclusionary rule, it wouldn't apply in the case of Lance and Susan Gates. He also attached thirty-eight supporting briefs from parties as diverse as the ACLU and an Ohio policeman's association. The exclusionary rule rarely causes good cases to be lost, the policemen wrote, but it does keep cops honest.

Paul Biebel wasn't happy about this turn of events, either. He thought his original case had merit; that anonymous tips as good as the one in this case demonstrate the informant knows what he's talking about and satisfy the second prong requirement. Biebel wanted to redefine the standards for probable cause so citizens could give meaningful assistance to police; he didn't want to argue about the exclusionary rule. He said as much on the day of the reargument: "We think the Court ought to clearly establish the role of probable cause in search warrants."

A justice asked: "You're not contending, in other words, that the good faith of the police officer is enough?"

"I don't think the subjective police officer's good faith is enough," Biebel said. "That's correct."

Biebel's argument shifted as the justices' determination became apparent. Provided the police don't show malice, he said, the exclusionary rule should not apply. "The imposition of the exclusionary rule in this case for purely technical reasons would deter police officers, it seems to us, from doing their job."

Reilley argued that the Court didn't have jurisdiction to introduce the exclusionary rule in this particular case. He then summarized the supporting brief of an Iowa prosecutor who cited 6,487 cases, of which only 13 were dismissed because of the exclusionary rule. "That's two out of a thousand that were dismissed because of the exclusionary rule," Reilley said. "I think that is probably the most meaningful statistic I've ever seen."

If the Court creates a good-faith exception to the exclusionary rule, Reilley said, "the police will really be telling the Court what the Fourth Amendment means."

~

Reilley walked out convinced he'd won. He figured the decision would come down in another six months. But in half that time, he got a call from a local reporter in Des Plaines. How did he feel about the decision handed down that day in *Illinois v. Gates?*

A decision already? Reilley asked, reaching for another Newport.

Yeah, the reporter said. You lost.

In a speech later that year, William Rehnquist summed up his opinion this way: "It was a classical case of one side having the facts, and the other side having the law. . . . A majority of us felt that the facts simply reeked of probable cause." The law, in other words, was of less consequence to the Supreme Court than the facts of an overnight trip to Florida and 350 pounds of marijuana.

In overturning the "two-prong test" and allowing police to obtain search warrants on the strength of anonymous tips, the Court removed the last obstacle to police writing such tips themselves or reporting to a judge that "somebody" called with a tip. Similarly, nothing now prevents people from inflicting a legal police search on their unwitting enemies simply by calling in a phony tip to the authorities.

But *Illinois v. Gates* did more than that. It broadcast the Court's political intentions. In writing the 6-3 opinion, Rehnquist acknowledged that the Court had blundered in raising the exclusionary rule. "We decide today, with apologies to all, that the issue we framed for the parties was not presented to the Illinois courts and, accordingly, do not address it." He then went on to invite others to bring such a case to the Court. "We reserve *for another day* the question of whether the exclusionary rule should be modified" (emphasis added). Byron White went further in his concurring opinion, stating, "I continue to believe that the exclusionary rule is an inappropriate remedy where law enforcement officials act in the reasonable belief that a search was consistent with the Fourth Amendment."*

"They put a big neon sign on the roof of the Supreme Court," Reilley said afterward. " 'Bring us a reason to dismantle the exclusionary rule!' "

Nineteen days later, somebody did.

* Justice White also cited the same California study of the exclusionary rule that William French Smith had quoted in his first attack on the rule, and misrepresented it exactly the same way. Prosecutors, White wrote, "rejected approximately 30 percent of all felony drug arrests because of search and seizure problems," an exaggeration by a factor of fourteen.

13

Nineteen Eighty-Four
1984

To understand the nature of the present war — for in spite of the regrouping which occurs every few years, it is always the same war — one must realize in the first place that it is impossible for it to be decisive.

— *Emmanuel Goldstein*

AS 1982 GAVE WAY to 1983, it became known, with extreme suddenness and everywhere at once, that cocaine and not marijuana was the enemy.

Cocaine was still a Caucasian thing. Throughout 1983 and 1984, almost all the users portrayed in *Time* and *Newsweek* and on the evening news were white and middle-class. *U.S. News* ran a cover story — "How Drugs Sap the Nation's Strength" — picturing an elegant white woman snorting coke. Two University of Michigan researchers tallied the race of cocaine users portrayed on television news, and from 1981 through 1985 whites constituted nearly 80 percent. The face of cocaine looked like flamboyant car tycoon John DeLorean, busted for trying to smuggle cocaine (and who ultimately proved entrapment); comedian John Belushi, who died of a cocaine-and-heroin shot; Yankees pitcher Steve Howe and actor Stacy Keach, both arrested for possession.

Now there was real money to be made on the legal side of the cocaine wave. Treatment was becoming a major industry, with ads for fancy cocaine clinics displayed in *Variety, Hollywood Reporter,* and *Billboard* beside ads for *Terms of Endearment, The Killing Fields,* and *Ghostbusters.* From 1978 to 1984 the number of for-profit psychiatric hospitals quadrupled, with the number doubling again in the next seven years. The 1-800-COCAINE hotline opened in 1983, revealing "a deep sickness in our society," as Dan Rather reported. Turned out, the "service" was sponsored by National Medical Enterprises Inc., a health-care giant seeking to identify insured potential customers for high-priced drug treatment. When the hotline referred people to doctors for treatment, they usually were NME doctors. NME's own annual report praised the hotline, which was receiving 2,200 calls a day by 1987, for being an "innovative outreach program" that helped boost the occupancy rates at NME's fifty psychiatric facilities. As reported by *Advertising Age* magazine, the hotline "became a model for direct-response healthcare marketers of how to use the phone to mix public service with revenue generation."

Except for sensational cases like DeLorean's, cocaine wasn't usually discussed in the media as a crime problem. "Police and prosecutors know that they have no great public mandate to wage a war on cocaine," *Time* said in April 1983, "a war they admit, realistically, they could not win." Cocaine's glitter status was in its waning days, though. "If cocaine trickles down far enough," *Newsweek* portended, "at least the snob appeal may be gone from its glamour." A psychologist quoted on CBS News used the same Reaganomics metaphor: "It's trickling down. . . . It's not uncommon to have the average blue-collar worker in a factory using cocaine on a regular basis."

~

With those words began a curious new phase of the War on Drugs. Throughout 1983 and 1984, the Reagan administration and the press churned out a steady stream of warnings that America's "competitiveness" was being compromised by an "epidemic" of drug use in the workplace. "The scourge of drugs," *U.S. News* rumbled, "is now so widespread among adults that it threatens to sap the nation's strength at a critical juncture in its history. . . . No one has measured how all this pill popping, injecting, and inhaling has affected the national output. Yet the growth of US productivity has been lagging behind that of other major industrial nations, none of which has a drug problem as serious."

"Joint by joint, line by line, pill by pill," *Newsweek* reported, "the use of illegal drugs on the job has become a crisis for American business. . . . Some experts even suggest that one reason the United States is losing its industrial leadership to Japan is that America's work force is so stoned." Peggy Mann chimed in as well with a characteristic piece in the *Reader's Digest* on "The Hidden Scourge of Drugs in the Workplace." And the magazine *Government Executive* put a particularly political spin on it:

> While OSHA [Occupational Health and Safety Administration] was created (in itself, a result, in part, of political pressure in Washington by anti–Big Business activists) and gushing regulations having to do with workplace machines and procedures, corporations themselves began attacking a major part of the problem where it really was — in alcohol and drug use by employees.

True enough, American industry was in trouble. Manufacturing jobs began disappearing in the 1980s for the first time since the Great Depression. In every decade since World War II, at least a million and a half new factory jobs had been created; in the eighties, 300,000 were lost.

But dope-smoking workers were not the problem.

Industrial America was collapsing because companies were putting their money not into developing products and building factories to make them, but rather into buying and selling each other. (Oilmen had a cheerful term for it: "drilling for oil on Wall Street.") Worse, companies were borrowing money to buy and sell each other, running up a corporate-debt total for the 1980s of more than a trillion dollars. American corporations paid more in interest during the eighties than double their interest payments during the previous forty years combined — enough money to create seven million $25,000-a-year jobs had they chosen to do so. For the first time in history, companies were spending more on interest payments than on new plants and equipment.

Reagan repeatedly fought Congress's attempt to do the one thing that might have slowed the disastrous rate of corporate borrowing: repeal the tax deductibility of corporate interest payments. Additionally, the Reagan administration actively encouraged businesses to move factories and jobs to Mexico, further weakening the country's industrial base. The "crisis" of workplace drug abuse was a convenient diversion. Much better to focus instead on pernicious individual workers.

The complicated economics of the country's industrial decline was a difficult story for the media as well, being hard to wedge into ten column inches or a thirty-second news segment and offering little in the way of visuals. Workplace drug abuse, on the other hand, was easy to explain and exciting to film, and it put the story — as journalists like to say — down where the goats can get it.

Somehow, despite all the "pill popping, injecting, and inhaling," corporate profits hit record highs in August 1983, the same month *Newsweek* called drugs "a crisis for American business."

~

The National Endowment for the Humanities is not a big government agency. In 1980 it distributed about $130 million for research, exhibits, films, and television programs to promote national familiarity with history, philosophy, and literature. A gentle, diminutive agency, it rarely attracts attention. In all likelihood, most people couldn't name a past chair of the NEH. Until, that is, Ronald Reagan nominated a broad-shouldered, blunt-spoken thirty-seven-year-old philosophy professor who ultimately would escalate the War on Drugs to its furthest extreme. His name was William J. Bennett.

By Bennett's own account, he got the NEH job because he was one of precious few academics in the country who had supported Reagan's campaign. Well-read and exquisitely articulate, Bennett was artful at making such sly references as those to his admiration for "the public Martin Luther King," inoculating himself against a racism charge while subliminally suggesting J. Edgar Hoover's unproven allegations of King's sexual misconduct. When Reagan found him, Bennett was director of a conservative think tank in North Carolina. He easily won confirmation from the Republican-led Senate.

To an administration determined to close debate, Bennett was a godsend — an anti-intellectual intellectual. Though both a Ph.D. in philosophy and a Harvard-educated lawyer, Bennett liked to rail against "elites" and "intellectuals"; scholars and scientists, in Bennett's view, were not to be trusted. Anybody quoting "facts" or a "study" was suspect. Scholars, Bennett wrote, "have hitched their intellect to the service of ideology."

But at NEH, Bennett himself wielded a profoundly ideological sword. By 1983, he'd cut funding to projects focused on women by more than a third. He'd cut grants to labor unions from six to zero. He'd approved a $30,000 "emergency grant" to the right-wing Accuracy in Media to produce a conservative response to a PBS series on the Vietnam War. He'd turned down a host of projects focused on peace, multiculturalism, and other matters of what he called "cultural relativism." In his first month on the job, Bennett set the tone of his tenure by publicly vilifying an NEH-funded documentary about Nicaragua. "Unabashed Socialist-realist propaganda," Bennett huffed. "A hymn to the Sandinistas."

But more important than the politics of the moment, in Bennett's view, was "an ongoing and intensifying cultural war" between "the most important beliefs of most Americans and the beliefs of a liberal elite" dominating the media and education. "The American people's sense of things" — which he defined variously as "family, community, freedom and self-restraint" or "conventional morality, patriotism, Ronald Reagan . . . 'Rocky,' light beer, cookouts [and] Disneyworld" — is "in most instances right," Bennett declared. The "liberal elite's" sense of things is "in most instances wrong." Questioning, debate, delineation between science and hysteria — these constituted "the politics of radical nihilism" and were deserving of scorn. For Bennett, things were that simple, and the NEH was his first national platform from which to say so.

~

Stephen Jacobs was an idea man. He'd managed public relations for Jimmy Carter's Energy Department and had come up with the idea of a comic book, financed entirely by the Campbell Soup company, featuring the villainous superhero Energy Waster. Before that, Jacobs was public relations director for New York University, where he worked alongside William Von Raab. Now commissioner of Customs, Von Raab called Jacobs at his private consulting firm and suggested he pay a visit to the White House Drug Abuse Policy Office.

There Jacobs found one courtly southern gentleman, one plain-spoken ex-army colonel with his own computer right there on his desk, and two secretaries operating out of a tiny warren in the Old Executive Office Building. We have no budget, Carlton Turner told Jacobs, and no statutory power. But I sit in on cabinet meetings and we swing a lot of clout. The First Lady is making drug abuse her issue. This administration is going to be as tough on drugs as on the Soviet Union. Now what do you have in mind?

Well, Jacobs said, what I do best is comic books.

Perfect, Dick Williams said. Comic book people understand what we're trying to do here. They do it every day: black and white, good and evil. A drug-free society is our goal. Go for it, Williams told him. As long as it doesn't take any federal money, go for it.

At the time, a DC Comics series called "The New Teen Titans" was the biggest seller among the fourth-, fifth-, and sixth-graders Jacobs wanted to reach. Jacobs blocked out an antidrug story line for DC and as sponsor lined up the Keebler cookie company. The deal was that no ads could appear in the comics, but the trademark Keebler "elf" could pop up in the margins to pose such challenges as "At this point in her life, DRUGS were more important to Anna than anything else. Have you ever thought about what things are most important to YOU?"

The first comic — titled "Plague!" — appeared in 1983, and as Dick Williams directed, the drug dealers were portrayed as leather-jacketed, sunglasses-wearing creeps who lurked around schoolyards or as highly organized businessmen who laughed over the deaths of their pubescent customers and escaped in fleets of helicopters. The kids in the comic, though studiously multiracial, all came from intact middle-class suburban families. Nobody in the comics had any reason to do drugs other than peer pressure, weak character, or the predatory tactics of drug dealers. When the Teen Titans found the pushers, the violence was extreme — FOOM! SKREE-BLAMM! And though the Titans never kill — because, says the masked Protector, "then we're as bad as they are" — the half-man half-robot Cyborg throws his enemies through walls because "nothin' says I can't *enjoy* beatin' their heads in." SPA-BOOOOOM! "Plague!" ends with a small blond girl admitting she's "taken pot, hash, uppers, downers, cocaine and PCP. I'm a DRUGGIE, and yes, I'm gonna STOP!"

To lend weight to the series, Jacobs emblazoned across the cover, "In Cooperation with the President's Drug Awareness Campaign." There was no such campaign; Jacobs made it up. But nobody at the White House minded him taking the liberty. Nancy Reagan was so pleased with the effort she wrote a letter for the inside front cover urging kids to join the "battle" against drug abuse and reminding them that "the President feels as strongly as I do about winning this battle. His Drug Awareness Campaign put this material together and generous corporations paid for it."

It took Jacobs a while to realize why Carlton Turner and Nancy Reagan liked the comic books so much. It wasn't just that he did it without federal funds. Unlike movie stars or sports heroes, cartoon characters couldn't endorse the First Lady's cause one day and get picked up for buying cocaine the next.

~

Susan Rusche, the parents' advocate who started the movement against drug paraphernalia, threw an empty Cheez-Its box into the wastebasket beside her desk and reached for a fresh package. Cradling the phone between ear and shoulder, Rusche cracked the box open and helped herself to a handful. I'll hold, she said into the receiver.

After the legislative and legal battles to ban bongs, Rusche's little DeKalb (County) Families in Action had swelled into National Families in Action, with member parents' groups all over the country. She published pamphlets on setting up parents' antidrug groups, monitored hearings and legislation related to marijuana and paraphernalia, distributed copies of Peggy Mann articles, circulated research papers demonstrating the dangers of marijuana, and wrote her weekly syndicated column, "Striking Back," for parents. As she flew around the country lecturing parents on the dangers of drugs, she realized the cigarette balanced in the corner of her mouth was a hypocrisy and replaced her three-pack-a-day habit with heavy doses of little square cheese crackers. A box was always nearby.

Rusche hadn't voted for Ronald Reagan, but she had to admit the country had come a long way under his leadership. Carlton Turner was an open ally of the parents' movement, singing its praises in speeches and cabinet meetings, bringing Nancy Reagan to a PRIDE conference, and organizing a meeting of First Ladies from around the world to talk about the role of the family in fighting the commercialized drug culture. It was a far cry from the days of Peter Bourne, whom Rusche thought had written off the parents' movement as a bunch of right-wing flakes.

But now Rusche was starting to think that the Reagan White House saw the parents' movement as little more than a vehicle for Reagan's federalist revolution. Kind words from the White House were nice, but Rusche thought it was time for some — ahem — financial support. Volunteerism isn't free, she liked to say. People may give their time without expecting pay, but there was rent to pay, and electricity bills, phone bills, office machines, staples, postage . . . the list of expenses for her volunteer organization was long and growing. She received private donations, but the big money went elsewhere. When Nancy Reagan convinced the Sultan of Brunei to donate $500,000 to the parents' movement, the check was made out not to Rusche's group but to the National Federation of Parents for Drug-Free Youth, run by the wife of the Republican National Committee chairman, which seemed to spend all its time using the drug issue to unseat Democrats. When the Reagans' wealthy supporters lined up to donate to the First Lady's cause, the money was directed to the Nancy Reagan Drug Abuse Fund. One such donation occurred while the Reagan administration was considering a Saudi request for AWACS planes; King Fahd gave the Nancy Reagan Drug Abuse Fund $1 million. By the end of the Reagan presidency, the fund held almost $5 million. (According to Nancy Reagan biographer Kitty Kelley, only about 10 percent of that was distributed to drug-abuse causes; the rest was transferred to the Nancy Reagan Foundation in Los Angeles, where it remains.)

It galled Rusche that the parents' movement got no real support from Washington. Even Jimmy Carter's administration — blithe about drug abuse though it was — came up with a little dough; ACTION, the parent agency to the Peace Corps and Vista, gave National Families in Action $50,000. Turner and Reagan hadn't yet offered a dime. Now Rusche was calling Turner himself to ask him directly: will this administration fund parents' organizations like National Families in Action or won't it? Rusche put another Cheez-It in her mouth and told the secretary again that yes, she would hold for Dr. Turner. Rusche, she said. R-U-S-C-H-E. He knows me.

When Turner came to the phone and heard Rusche's request, he was tempted to slam the phone down. How *dare* you come to us for money, he yelled. Don't you understand the politics of this administration? The only way I could sell the president on supporting the parents' movement was to say it wouldn't cost anything. A big reason this administration *likes* the drug issue is that so much of it can be handled by volunteer groups. You're white middle-class folks, Turner fumed. You're the last people that need government handouts.

And then, with a few pleasantries and words of encouragement, Turner excused himself to a cabinet meeting and hung up.

~

The high school principal in Lewisville, Texas, (pop. 24,000) began offering a $100 reward to any student who would turn in another for drugs. To finance the plan, he asked local businesses for contributions, and so much money poured in that he asked them to hold up after just a few days.

"You'd be astonished how well the students are cooperating," the school's assistant principal told the *Dallas Morning News*. "Some have even turned in their best friends."

~

Bob Randall, the country's only legal pot smoker, was by now working full-time on improving legal access to medical marijuana. His Alliance for Cannabis Therapeutics, which the Playboy Foundation helped launch with a $5,000 grant in 1981, got dozens of calls every week from people suffering from cancer, glaucoma, multiple sclerosis, and many forms of paralysis. Paraplegics, Randall learned, are prone to spastic seizures that can be dangerous when patients are, for example, lowering themselves into a bathtub. Marijuana appeared to control paraplegics' spasticity. In March 1983, a young quadriplegic in New Jersey, Michael Tate, had been hauled off to jail for possessing marijuana he said he used to control seizures. His case was pending.

It was hard for Randall to understand how the government could believe a quadriplegic smoking pot in his own home was doing anybody any harm. Still, the number of people legally receiving marijuana under the Compassionate IND program could be counted on one hand; Reagan's Department of Health and Human Services was even more hostile to the idea than Jimmy Carter's.

But now there was added urgency to Randall's work. A strange virus was gnawing its way into the homosexual community. One of its worst symptoms was a complete loss of appetite; patients wasted away quickly simply because they couldn't bring themselves to eat. Suddenly, Randall's phone was ringing constantly. People afflicted with the disease were telling him pot was the only drug that kept nausea down and their appetites up. For people stricken with the newly christened Acquired Immune Deficiency Syndrome, marijuana munchies were serious business.

⁓

In July 1983, state troopers cruising the Florida Turnpike pulled over and arrested sixty-four people on drug-trafficking charges, four times as many as the month before. The reason: the Florida State Police had started using "drug courier profiles" that included such characteristics as "scrupulous obedience to traffic laws," "wearing lots of gold," and "doesn't fit vehicle" — characteristics that could apply to many of Miami's octogenarians. Another characteristic, though, was "ethnic groups associated with the drug trade," and most of those arrested were black. Troopers also stopped at roadblocks nearly 1,500 cars that month for "safety inspections"; while one officer examined the registration, another circled the car with a drug-sniffing dog. If the dog barked, the U.S. Supreme Court had just ruled, that's sufficient probable cause to ransack the car. Only one arrest came from the 1,500 stops, but Florida officials declared themselves pleased. "We want to send the message that we will be aggressive in the War on Drugs and will use every available tool," a Florida drug agent told reporters.

⁓

Every Fourth of July since 1970, the Yippies and the Citizens Against Marijuana Laws had held a marijuana "smoke-in" in Lafayette Park, across Pennsylvania Avenue from the White House. By 1983, though, the parents' movement — some 4,000 organizations strong — was in a position to provide opposition. A D.C. parents' group reserved the park a year in advance for a Family Celebration. The Grassland Singers and Jimmy Arnold's bluegrass band entertained the prohibitionist crowd. But the dopers went ahead with their march anyway, sitting down in the middle of Pennsylvania Avenue and blocking traffic. A long time had passed since 1970; the dopers were outmanned and outsung. SMOKE-IN SMOKED OUT BY THE JULY 4TH FAMILY DAY CELEBRATION, the *Washington Post* reported.

~

Keith Schuchard — a.k.a. Marsha Mannat — had launched the parents' movement and authored *Parents, Peers & Pot* and now was back on the road. Under the aegis of PRIDE, she began traveling the country to speak to junior high school classes.

One of the biggest dangers of marijuana, she was convinced, was in reducing testosterone in teenage boys just as they should be developing adult male characteristics. The evidence was everywhere. Healthy men have big shoulders, well-muscled chests, and rounded buttocks. But she'd look at men on itinerant construction crews, with their ropy arms and flat buttocks, and think: pot smokers. Figures a pot smoker would end up working construction.

Here was a message she knew would resonate with teenage boys eager to become big, attractive men. When she visited classrooms she'd pick out the scrawniest boy in the class, the one with the long hair and the sallow complexion and the Grateful Dead stickers on his notebook. She'd make him stand and take his shirt off in front of the others.

See what pot smoking can do to you? she'd say.

The kids would get very quiet.

~

The pressure was on. Eric Sterling could feel it.

Sterling was one of the faceless foot soldiers of Congress, a staff member of a House subcommittee. The halls of Congress teem with such people — young, pale, caffeinated, and staggering under armloads of files. Catch one in a hallway and she'll give you a breathless ninety-second analysis of why — depending on her boss — the ad valorem tax on sugar products needs repeal or aid to Estonia should be tied to Moscow's willingness to devalue the ruble. Senators and reps rely on their staff members to digest the data and come up with voting recommendations. In many cases, the staff underling virtually *is* the member of Congress when it comes to his or her particular area of expertise. That's the only way members can take positions on diverse and complicated subjects and still have time to campaign, schmooze, and appear on *Nightline*.

Sterling was thirty-four years old in early 1984 and was a relative old-timer on the Hill with five years' experience on various crime-related subcommittees. A former public defender with swept-back brown hair, wire-rimmed glasses, and an intense, unblinking stare, he now worked for the Crime Subcommittee of Congressman Bill Hughes, Democrat of New Jersey. Sterling had helped write Hughes's 1982 crime legislation that fell victim to Reagan's veto on the drug-czar issue.

Sterling had never before felt such a panic in the House to pass new drug laws. The Republican-led Senate had just passed Reagan's new crime bill that, cobbled together out of recommendations from Rudolph Giuliani's "hard-charging" prosecutors, broke new ground in boosting the power of the prosecution. The bill contained the sweeping police authority to confiscate property without trial. It established a "presumption" that drug defendants aren't entitled to bail. It ordered the formation of a National Drug Enforcement Policy Board, with the attorney general as chairman, to coordinate the domestic and international War on Drugs. It limited the use of the insanity defense, a shoo-in now that John Hinckley had been acquitted by reason of insanity of shooting President Reagan.

The biggest changes, though, were in sentencing. Federal judges had long retained absolute discretion in sentencing, and both liberals and conservatives thought that a problem. In one study, fifty federal judges were given identical files from real cases and asked to indicate the sentences they would impose. Sentences for a bank robbery ranged from five to eighteen years, for an extortion case from three to twenty years. Parole boards added another layer of discretion and disparity. Conservatives could point to dangerous criminals going free early. Liberals could convincingly show that poor blacks got stiffer sentences and less parole than wealthier white convicts.

So the Senate bill created a sentencing commission to write guidelines for judges. The commission was to come up with a complicated formula taking into account the seriousness of the crime, mitigating or aggravating factors, the defendant's record, and the degree to which the defendant accepted responsibility for the crime. A range of sentences then was to be offered, from which the judges weren't permitted to deviate without a written explanation. At the same time, Congress abolished federal parole, so under the new guidelines the sentence given would be the sentence served. The Senate passed the bill 91 to 1.

Now the ball was in the court of the Democrat-led House of Representatives, which shared Congressman Hughes's loathing of omnibus crime bills. Reagan held a press conference to say his crime bill was "long overdue" and that House Democrats should "stop dragging their feet," a theme House Republicans hammered repeatedly whenever a reporter's microphone was directed their way. Now the House Democrats found themselves in the treasonous position of *not* joining the president's War on Drugs. Sterling got the message: find ways to make us Democrats look tough on drugs and crime without having to pass this odious Republican crime bill.

It happened that around this time a couple of lobbyists from the National Association of Retail Druggists appeared in Sterling's cramped office. Pill freaks had knocked over several drugstores in recent years, and the druggists wanted a federal law against robbing a pharmacy. The powerful Republican congressman Henry Hyde of Illinois had tried to get such a bill into the 1982 law, but Hughes had blocked it. The whole idea was ridiculous, Hughes argued. Robbery is a local crime, and every state already has sufficient penalties.

Now, though, Hughes saw it differently. Sure there's no need for a law, he told Sterling. But what the hell difference does it make if we give them one? We can look tough and become heroes to the pharmacists. What's more, we make Hyde look good and build a nice relationship with a senior Republican when we need it. Go ahead and hold some hearings, Hughes told Sterling. Find a way to make it happen without completely dismantling the principles of federalism.

Sterling scheduled a hearing and alerted his contacts in the press. He began drafting the law, building into it the kind of language found in other federal criminal law: thresholds for value stolen, interstate aspects, significant bodily injury, use of a firearm. It took weeks. Hughes's crime subcommittee received it, debated it, and passed it along to the Judiciary Committee, which did likewise. Then the full House voted on it and sent it to the Senate. Four months after Sterling started the process, the Senate made it a federal crime to rob a pharmacy. "All this," Sterling said when it was over, "for a bill that everybody but the pharmacists in Nebraska knows is bullshit." The Justice Department took the bill lightly, forbidding its prosecutors to pursue any pharmacy-robbery cases without approval from Washington — further reducing the chances the law would ever be invoked.

≈

Mark Webb said thank you, good work, and hung up the phone. As U.S. attorney for the Western District of Arkansas, the responsibility for making the next phone call was his. He didn't relish it, but he wanted to do it before the press got wind of what had just happened in the grand jury room in Little Rock. He lifted the receiver and dialed the governor's mansion.

In a way, Roger Clinton was lucky. Indicted in 1984 on federal charges of selling cocaine and conspiracy, he was ultimately sentenced to two years in prison. He served sixteen months. His big brother, Bill, asked about drug policy in a televised presidential debate eight years later, referred to Roger's case. "I don't think my brother would be alive today if it wasn't for the criminal justice system," Bill Clinton said. "I think the justice system saved his life."

Had Roger's case come just three years later, his mandatory sentence would have been ten years without parole. No one will ever know if that would have changed Bill Clinton's answer.

≈

When the director of the U.S. Alcohol, Drug Abuse, and Mental Health Administration (ADAMHA) resigned, parent activists from around the country called Carlton Turner and recommended Dr. Ian Macdonald, the Florida pediatrician who had become such an effective speaker against marijuana. The man has been working his tail off for us, the activists told Turner, traveling to PTAs and parents' groups everywhere to lecture on the dangers of pot. He also believes in strict discipline: he put his son, Andy, in a Straight Inc. rehab center for ten months.

The director of ADAMHA is a crucial position. While the DEA implements the enforcement side of federal drug policy, ADAMHA sees to the "soft" side — treatment and education. Macdonald had no drug-treatment training or experience, and for that reason the secretary of health and human services, Margaret Heckler, objected to hiring him. But Turner knew and liked Macdonald from his days stumping for the parents' movement. As a pharmacologist suddenly elevated to national drug-policy director, Turner wasn't bothered by Macdonald's lack of treatment or policy experience. What was important was that Macdonald *believed*.

Macdonald shared Turner's and Williams's hostility to current drug-abuse research. He believed that the scientific community — NIDA, ADAMHA, and the other alphabet-soup agencies dealing with drug abuse — should serve their masters rather than pursue "their own tired agendas." Their research, Macdonald believed, should promote the ideas of the people who paid them: the administration in power.

Macdonald further shared Turner's view that adolescent drug use was a cultural problem as much as a health problem. The Woodstock era had condoned a tendency in young people to reject authority, a malignant legacy that lingered fifteen years later. An entire generation of children seemed to believe that whatever their parents told them was wrong, that they could make up their own minds about what was safe and acceptable. The outcome was such disasters as his own son, Andy, bingeing on alcohol and marijuana at fourteen.

Turner liked Macdonald's thinking. Besides, Macdonald had solid Republican credentials and Turner knew he would be appealing to Reagan's highly partisan White House.

So when Margaret Heckler objected to Macdonald's appointment, Turner went straight to Nancy Reagan for support. Then, when Heckler's chief of staff appeared in Turner's office to oppose Macdonald, Turner put his feet on his desk and said, "You tell Madam Secretary I don't work for her. I work for the president of the United States."

Just as the untrained Keith Schuchard was assigned to write the government's official word on adolescent pot smoking, Macdonald was elevated from pediatrician to manager of federal drug treatment and prevention. National drug policy slipped another notch further from the grasp of those with experience and training.

~

On July 4, 1984, Nancy Reagan visited Longfellow Elementary School in Oakland, California, where a class of fourth-graders had been assembled to visit with the First Lady about the nation's drug problem. Surrounded by reporters and cameras, and backed up by U.S. Attorney Joseph Russoniello, the First Lady sat with a semicircle of children and talked about the dangers to children of drinking alcohol and taking drugs. A fourth-grader asked Mrs. Reagan what he should do if his friends press him to smoke pot. Mrs. Reagan then spoke the magic words, adding the "something" Carlton Turner thought was missing from the Ad Council's "Say No to Drugs" campaign.

"Just say no," she said.

The cameras whirred, and the clip topped the evening news. The Reagans' critics had a ball, deriding them for substituting simplistic moralizing for a drug policy.

Mrs. Reagan's stated intention was to give kids the confidence to resist peer pressure, to supply a positive non-drug-using identity to which kids could gravitate. At best, it was naive. At a Just Say No rally some months later, she led the kids in yelling "no!" and concluded, "That's wonderful. That will keep drugs away."

But for the majority of kids who weren't using drugs, Just Say No may have been a reassuring message that there is a non-drug-using culture alongside the glamorously publicized drug culture. And it may even have emboldened some kids to say no. There is safety in numbers; Just Say No clubs began sprouting, and on Just Say No Day in 1985, rallies were held nationwide — 2,000 kids in D.C., 600 in Albuquerque, 500 in Los Angeles, 1,000 in Oakland.

Just Say No wasn't the worst part of the Reagan Drug War. It didn't put anybody in prison or diminish anybody's civil liberties. It didn't deploy armies of drug agents with inflated powers to wiretap and surveil. It didn't weaken the Fourth Amendment. It didn't ratchet up violence in the inner cities by fielding "sweeps" that disrupted volatile drug turfs and touched off gunfights. It didn't lead county officials to spend more on criminal justice than on education. It didn't dismantle a federally funded treatment system that took ten years to build. And it didn't jail people without trial, confiscate their property without due process, or deny them public housing, student loans, or federal benefits.

But Just Say No did something insidious. It finished Dick Williams's job of closing the debate. In fact, it reduced the debate to a single word. Don't talk about why people use drugs, the slogan said. Don't ask why Halcion and malt liquor are legal drugs while marijuana and cocaine are not. Don't talk about the difference between drug use and drug abuse. Don't talk about the tendency of prohibition to promote violence and the use of stronger and more dangerous drugs. Don't talk about the lives, taxpayer dollars, and civil liberties sacrificed for the Drug War. Don't talk about the culture and race wars waged under the Drug War battle flag. Don't talk about the medical potential of illegal drugs. Don't talk at all. Just say no.

The country's ability to discuss the problems of drug abuse and debate solutions had been withering for years under Williams's efforts to close the debate and the White House's hiring and promotion of untrained zealots openly hostile to science, data, and "intellectuals." Just Say No, ostensibly aimed at children, finished the debate off. What replaced it was an unquestionable antidrug orthodoxy that skewed the work of every government agency, elevated drug users to national enemies, and limited even the language permissible in drug discussions. From Reagan through Clinton, the merest suggestion that the country pursue any path but total prohibition has been tantamount to forbidden speech.

As Congress was building its big drug and crime bill that summer, Eric Sterling suggested to his boss, Congressman Bill Hughes, that he consider legally separating marijuana from more dangerous drugs. Nobody has ever died from smoking pot, Sterling argued, but cocaine and heroin are genuinely dangerous. He made the old argument: we're damaging the criminal justice system, respect for the law, and the public's health by falsely considering marijuana equal to the others.

You're one of the most respected anticrime members of Congress, Sterling pressed. You could do it.

"Look Eric," Hughes finally growled, "there are only two ways I could be defeated. One, I'm accused of stealing. Two, I talk about decriminalizing marijuana. Okay?"

Truth was, Eric Sterling was a believer in ending drug prohibition. It was a failure and a waste, he thought, and spawned unspeakably un-American laws and police conduct. He thought often about how drugs could be decriminalized — controlled through civil fines and other regulations. At times he found himself thinking that marijuana at least should be flat-out legalized — set entirely outside the law.

Working for Congressman Hughes meant walking a tightrope. Sterling was careful never to let his own beliefs betray Hughes's agenda. In fact, when the DEA sent over a bill to increase its authority to classify drugs, Sterling found it vague and rewrote it to the point where the DEA preferred his version to its own.

Sterling's legalizer friends would ask him how he could work for the Crime Subcommittee. How do you sleep at night, they'd ask him, knowing you write laws to put your friends in prison? Isn't it better, Sterling would reply, to have somebody like me in there, to be sure things don't get too crazy? If I lie awake at night, it's because I worry about being fired for being insufficiently hard-ass.

When reporters called Sterling to talk about the pharmacy-robbery bill, he tried to put their questions into a broader context. This is why we need to talk about legalizing drugs, he'd say. But this is off the record, he insisted. He made a sign reading OFF THE RECORD and taped it to his telephone to remind him to say it each time. No reporter ever betrayed him.

Whenever a new freshman class of representatives came to Congress, Sterling tried to identify those who might be reasonable. Larry Smith of Florida had been a defense attorney and a friend of the ACLU, so Sterling went to see him in his new office. Sterling delivered his standard legalization rap. Smith listened without saying much. A few days later, though, Smith gave a speech on the House floor saying "the most dangerous people in America are those who believe in legalizing drugs." Sterling was in the House Chamber at the time, and Smith glared right at him.

"Traitors," Smith fumed. "They're traitors."

~

Senator Strom Thurmond of South Carolina, chairman of the Judiciary Committee, tossed into the pending big crime bill a proposal to do what the Supreme Court had tried to do in *Illinois v. Gates:* create a "good-faith exception" to the exclusionary rule. Thurmond wanted to create a presumption in the law that policemen act in good faith. This would allow evidence seized under flawed search warrants to be used in federal court.

His bill passed the Senate three-to-one.

And then the House Democrats, who were determined to kill it, were rendered irrelevant by the Supreme Court. The day after Nancy Reagan's "Just Say No" comment in Oakland, the Supreme Court — assembled largely by conservative presidents who professed irritation with justices "legislating from the bench" — created its own good-faith exception to the exclusionary rule.

The Court took the case within days of broadcasting its eagerness to weaken the rule. The justices decided *Illinois v. Gates* on June 8, 1983; less than three weeks later, on June 27, they agreed to hear the case of Alberto Leon, busted in Burbank for selling Quaaludes. The search warrant that led to his arrest was ruled illegal by three lower courts. But after hearing arguments in January 1984, the Court overturned them, using language nearly identical to that in Strom Thurmond's bill. Evidence seized under tainted warrants is admissible provided the police met a subjective standard of "good faith," the Court ruled in *United States v. Leon.* Nothing now prevented police from lying on their warrant requests and claiming in court an honest mistake. Writing for the majority, Justice Byron White justified this extraordinary transfer of power by a cost-benefit analysis: the rule had no deterrent effect on police misbehavior, he decided, and "cannot pay its way."

Dissenting, John Paul Stevens vented that the Court was converting "the Bill of Rights into an unenforced honor code that police may follow at their discretion." William Brennan went further. "The Court's victory over the Fourth Amendment," he wrote, "is complete."

~

Republican congressman Dan Lungren of California came up with a parliamentary trick to force passage of the big new crime bill. On September 25 he made a motion to attach a brand-new House bill, identical to the Senate bill, to a "must pass" appropriations bill and send it to the full House for a vote. If the House delayed or failed to pass it, federal funding would freeze and the entire government would shut down. The House had spent months tinkering with the Senate bill, rewriting portions and adding new sections, but that work was out the window. What faced House Democrats now was a straight up-or-down vote on what was essentially the Senate bill they'd received in February. It was a 419-page bill, and under House rules only five minutes of debate was permitted.

"The American people have shown in the latest poll that this is the number one issue for them!" Lungren exhorted his colleagues. "Do not worry about next week! Do not worry about last week!" Faced with the choice of giving in or leaving the government with no money to run on, the House voted yay.

By the time the horse trading was over on October 11, the Omnibus Crime Bill of 1984 gave huge new powers to prosecutors. It substantially boosted maximum prison terms for drug crimes. It replaced parole with "supervised release," which let judges add a period of parole-like restrictions and supervision onto the end of a completed sentence. It let prosecutors appeal sentences — a right previously reserved for the defense. It stipulated that anybody charged with a drug crime that might result in a ten-year sentence is presumed dangerous and can be held without bail. It axed a long-standing program that expunged the records of first-time drug offenders between eighteen and twenty-six who'd served their time.

Prosecutors now could confiscate, with no more "proof" than was required for a search warrant, cash, cars, boats, homes, bank accounts, stock portfolios — anything *believed* to have been purchased with drug money or equal in value to the money *believed* earned from drug sales. No charge, indictment, trial, or conviction was necessary, and the burden of proof was placed on the person whose assets were seized. Drug offenses were the target; accused murderers, kidnappers, or rapists were in no danger of losing their assets without trial.

A "noncontroversial" provision was jammed into the bill in the final go-round: to restore a sense of "poetic justice," the new law allowed seized assets to be shared among the law enforcement agencies involved in the case. A fund would be created from seized assets, the law decreed, and beginning in 1986 state and local police could apply for a spoonful. By 1991, the fund would contain $1.6 billion, of which state and local police would enjoy more than $265 million.

This fund would soon further swell the federal court caseload with penny-ante drug cases. Many states had laws requiring seized assets to revert to the state treasury rather than to the police who seized them. But federal law supersedes state law. At a time of budget cuts and a nationwide property tax revolution that starved the budgets of local law enforcement, the "sharing" provisions of the new forfeiture law gave local police a powerful incentive to take their drug cases federal. Worse, it inspired police to make cases solely to bolster their own agencies' coffers. The age of free-market criminal justice was dawning.

Finally, the big new law gave prosecutors the power to wreck the relationship between a drug defendant and his attorney. The way the new forfeiture laws were written, the government could confiscate, before proving any wrongdoing, the money a drug defendant might use to hire a lawyer. The new law let prosecutors — in drug cases only — strip those presumed innocent of the funds needed to argue their innocence. Accused murderers or big-time embezzlers could hire any lawyer they could afford, but under the new law drug defendants would be forced to rely on overworked, underfunded public defenders.

"Under the Constitution, defendants are entitled to legal advice," a federal prosecutor wrote, "not to high-priced advice." To enforce the new law, defense lawyers could be subpoenaed to tell how much they received as retainer and how they were paid. Defense lawyers, in other words, would now be pressed into service as witnesses for the prosecution.

Reagan signed the Omnibus Crime Bill of 1984 the day after the Senate cleared it.

- Number of wiretap requests submitted to federal judges by the Justice Department in 1983: 648.
- Percentage change from 1982: +60.
- Percentage approved: 100.

14

No Such Thing
1985

Perhaps the most powerful influence of news, talk, and writing about problems is the immunity from notice and criticism they grant to damaging conditions that are not on the list.

— *Murray Edelman*

WHEN IT COMES TO DRUGS, the High Court decided early in 1985, schoolchildren have no Fourth Amendment rights. A fourteen-year-old Piscataway, New Jersey, girl had been caught smoking cigarettes and was taken to the office of assistant vice principal Theodore Choplick. Without asking the girl's permission, Choplick searched her purse, found some marijuana, and turned her over to the police. She was convicted of delinquency in Juvenile Court. The New Jersey Supreme Court invoked the exclusionary rule and called the marijuana evidence illegal: Choplick didn't have probable cause to suspect the girl of a drug crime and shouldn't have searched her purse.

The U.S. Supreme Court found, though, that citizens don't merit equal protection under the law until they graduate from high school. "In any realistic sense," wrote Justice Lewis Powell, "students within the school environment have a lesser expectation of privacy than members of the population generally." The New Jersey Supreme Court decision was overturned, the girl's conviction was upheld, and schoolchildren everywhere were written out of the Fourth Amendment. School officials could now frisk students, turn out their pockets, cut locks off their lockers, invade their privacy at will without obtaining a search warrant, and call the police with their findings. "The schoolroom is the first opportunity most citizens have to experience the power of government," Justices John Paul Stevens and Thurgood Marshall wrote in their dissent. "The Court's decision today is a curious moral for the Nation's youth."

~

The pursuit of drug users in the workplace was beginning to create a new industry with a powerful stake in keeping the Drug War alive. Urine testing was in 1985 a $100 million business. One small urine lab, founded in 1983, posted a 450 percent increase in profits between 1984 and 1985. In 1984, a fifth of the Fortune 500 corporations had some kind of urine-testing program. A year later, a quarter had such a program, and two years later it would be more than half. Carlton Turner said he expected that "every major corporation in the US within the next three to five years will have a preemployment screening," and the *Wall Street Journal* predicted that urine testing would be a $250 million industry by the end of the decade. (Actually, it turned out to be $300 million.) "The Gold Rush of the Eighties," as Abbie Hoffman called it, was on.

The National Institute on Drug Abuse kept alive the fear of drugs in the workplace with such warnings as one in *Business Week* of "an epidemic of [workplace] cocaine casualties every day." But at the same time, NIDA and the federal Centers for Disease Control were publishing in the *Journal of the American Medical Association* results of a nine-year study of urine-test reliability that found such testing terrifyingly flawed. CDC sent spiked and clean urine samples to thirteen labs and was generous in its ratings, deeming "satisfactory" any lab that tested samples correctly 80 percent of the time. (Given the corporate climate, with companies like Federal Express firing employees on the basis of a single positive drug test, the CDC was therefore willing to sacrifice the careers of twenty innocent workers out of every hundred.) Many labs in the survey didn't pass even the easy standards: false positives ran as high as 66 percent at some labs and false negatives as high as 100 percent. A Northwestern University study found a national false-positive average of 25 percent, and a UCLA study found that of 161 prescription and over-the-counter medications, 65 produced false-positives in illegal-drug urine tests. Clerical errors, sloppy lab work, and the limitations of the testing machines themselves all were blamed for the appalling results. At a conference of forensic scientists in Cincinnati, the chief toxicologist for North Carolina's medical examiner asked, "Is there anybody in the audience who would submit urine for cannaboid testing if his career, reputation, freedom, or livelihood depended on it?"

Not a single hand was raised.

~

DEA agent Enrique Camarena left the U.S. Embassy in Mexico City to meet his wife for lunch one afternoon in February 1985 and disappeared. Two weeks later, his body, and that of a DEA pilot, were found wrapped in plastic near a remote northern Mexico farm. The Mexican government was slow to start an investigation, and U.S. officials publicly accused the Mexican narcotics squad of corruption. Then an audiocassette surfaced of Camarena screaming in agony as he was tortured to death, and every DEA agent in the United States and abroad either heard it or was told of it in vivid detail. In the insular, suspicious, and violent culture of the DEA, no other event plays as crucial a role as the death of "Kiki" Camarena. More than a decade later, brows still lower and teeth still gnash at its mention — even among agents who weren't with the DEA at the time. Camarena's death deepened agents' belief that they were alone in the battle against drug dealers, that DEA agents can't trust even brother police agencies, that the War on Drugs is a fight to the death in which the mildest criticism is treason.

Around the same time, another gruesome audiotape was having the opposite effect. Baltimore narcotics detective Marcellus Ward had been wearing a wire during a routine drug buy from a street dealer. But something went wrong; the dealer pulled a pistol and shot Ward twice, killing him instantly. All of it was picked up by Ward's hidden tape recorder.

The chief state prosecutor in Baltimore was a young black attorney who knew Ward personally. Preparing for the trial of the killer, he listened again and again to the tape, until he started wondering: what exactly did Marty Ward die for? To bust some two-bit pusher who was replaced on the street within an hour? The state's attorney's office was processing hundreds of drug cases a month. For all that time, energy, and expense, none of it seemed to be denting the public's appetite for illegal drugs. Now Marty, a fine family man, had been sacrificed. The young prosecutor pressed the play button, listened to the horrible tape again, and shuddered. I wonder if there isn't some other way to cope with drugs, Kurt Schmoke thought, besides prohibition.

~

Cocaine was no longer merely a "high-class high" like "Dom Perignon and beluga caviar." Now, blared *Newsweek*'s cover on February 25, 1985, it was "Cocaine: The Evil Empire." After five pages of high-speed chases, shoot-out drug busts, massive seizures, and other examples of "the DEA fighting back with courage and energy," *Newsweek* wrapped up with a hint of the coming new front in the Drug War. "If we tried to target users, we'd be treading water — there are so many users, we'd accomplish nothing," commander John Ryle of the Chicago Police Department's narcotics section told the magazine. But, *Newsweek* said, "some experts believe that the only way to win the cocaine battle is to put pressure on the purchasers."

One such expert was the new attorney general of the United States, Edwin Meese III. The main thrust of the Reagan Drug War up until now had been the military/DEA/Customs effort to stop drugs coming into the country, and task forces deployed to break up high-level trafficking rings within the United States. In one sense, those two efforts had met with great success — huge drug seizures in terms of tonnage and value, and many, many arrests. On the other hand, interdiction was missing so much that the price of cocaine was falling through the floor, to under $100 a gram. Moreover, directed as it was against offshore targets and high-level crooks, federal law enforcement was becoming invisible again to the average citizen.

So it was time to try something "new." "We need to put pressure on the drug user," Meese told his National Drug Enforcement Policy Board, which included not only Carlton Turner, CIA director William Casey, national security adviser Robert McFarlane, and DEA chief Jack Lawn, but also Reagan and the full cabinet — including the new education secretary, William Bennett. "There are still millions of pot smokers in this country who are unaware of the health hazards posed by marijuana and oblivious to the legal sanctions. Many users don't seem to realize they are breaking the law. . . . If we are to eliminate the drug market, we need to go after users as well as dealers," Meese declared.

It might have been 1972 again, in the cabinet office of Richard Nixon, when ODALE was launched to "bring sanctions against the user" and put a federal antidrug presence in front of the TV cameras.

Meese laid out who he believed the users were. "The young people who got hooked on drugs in the 1960s and '70s took their habits with them as they grew older," he told the president and cabinet. "It is therefore no surprise to find that marijuana and cocaine are favorite 'recreational' drugs among the so-called 'young, upwardly mobile professionals.' . . . We can — and we must — discourage drug use among the successful and affluent."

Marijuana, of course, doesn't "hook" people. And Meese didn't explain why, if drug use is so debilitating, it goes along with being "successful and affluent."

Meese then turned the floor over to the new ADAMHA director, the Florida pediatrician Ian Macdonald, who took one of the legalizers' main arguments — that alcohol and tobacco kill far more people than illegal drugs — and turned it around to serve the Drug War. "Alcohol and tobacco are used by much larger populations than the illicit drugs and are related to fully 25 percent of deaths in this country each year," he told the cabinet, whizzing through a stack of charts. If legalized, Macdonald said, cocaine would be used by as many people as cigarettes. "Thus, in a sense, 90 percent of our cocaine problem is being handled by our current supply reduction efforts. . . . Conclusion: . . . supply reduction works."

Ironically, at that very moment the opposite conclusion was dawning on Lloyd Johnston, author of the widely respected Annual High School Survey. In his office at the University of Michigan, Johnston looked at three charts of his own. The first plotted marijuana use, which had peaked in 1979 and was falling steadily. The second plotted the percentage of kids who thought marijuana was harmful. Not surprisingly, it was a mirror image of the first, bottoming out in 1979 and then climbing at the same pitch as the first chart's line was falling. When Johnston superimposed them on each other, they formed an X. Attitudes were hardening against pot, and kids were smoking less.

Running along on top of the X was the line plotting the percentage of kids who said marijuana was easy to get — the availability line. It was dead flat from 1975 to 1985 at about 85 percent. Something was inspiring kids to smoke less pot, but availability wasn't a factor. Efforts to reduce supply — interdiction and law enforcement — apparently weren't affecting either pot's availability or use. As the parents' movement had suggested, attitude was everything.

Johnston, who gave more than a hundred media interviews a year, wrote up his findings and sent them to the "My Turn" guest column in *Newsweek*. Our attempt to close down the supply of drugs is an abject failure, he wrote, but we're having considerable success teaching kids not to use drugs. He figured *Newsweek* would snap it up; the magazine quoted him often and referred constantly to his survey, and here he was saying something newsworthy with the figures to back it up. But the magazine didn't even reply to his letter, and when Johnston finally got the "My Turn" editor on the phone he was told, "Oh, we've done something like this." Turned out, the "something" was a piece by a private drug-treatment executive, calling for an escalation in the military-and-police War on Drugs.

Such a war was under way in California's Humboldt County, where the helicopters descended for a month every August.

When it started, CAMP had plenty of twenty-acre marijuana fields to uproot. After those were gone, the agents went after the ten-acre plots. Then five, then two, then one, and now it was pushing the noses of its helicopters against people's windows to find single plants growing in window boxes. But the people of Humboldt, in conjunction with NORML, had filed a lawsuit, and on April 12, 1985, federal judge Robert Aguilar issued a strong injunction against the operation: for the next five years, he wrote, helicopters had to remain outside a 500-foot "bubble" around houses, vehicles, and people; CAMP troopers were forbidden to enter private property other than remote fields without a warrant; personnel had to be specifically briefed on their powers and duties before operations.

It was as strong a restraint on Drug War operations as any judge had ever written.

CAMP ignored it. The Vietnam-style raids continued as before.

AIDS, glaucoma, and paralysis patients, counseled by Bob Randall, continued filing special requests to the Food and Drug Administration to receive legal marijuana. The FDA continued to deny or delay them so long the patients either gave up or died. After the 1978 dead-dog disaster with Eli Lilly's synthetic THC, Nabalone, the FDA was desperate to have a legal substitute to offer. Eli Lilly wouldn't try again, so the FDA went to a small pharmaceutical company in Buffalo Grove, Illinois, called Unimed Inc. and asked it to develop a synthetic THC pill. Unimed had no prescription pharmaceuticals on the market, only two over-the-counter oral-hygiene potions. NIDA had spent tens of millions of dollars during the past decade studying the chemistry of marijuana, and that tax-funded research was made available to Unimed and to Unimed only.

In time, Unimed came up with dronabinol, a synthetic THC, which it brand-named Marinol. On May 31, 1985, the FDA approved Marinol for use by cancer patients. While all other drugs are scheduled by the DEA under their chemical names, Marinol became the first scheduled under its brand name. Thus was Unimed granted both a government monopoly to develop a drug using government research and the privilege of having its product's trademark enshrined in law. Sick people who called the FDA for a special dispensation to smoke marijuana were offered Marinol instead.

Demonizing marijuana as "immoral," the federal government now was pushing the "pot pill" — a powerful dose of the chemical in marijuana that gets people stoned. Unlike smoked marijuana, whose effects build slowly, Marinol delivers its whole dose as soon as its capsule dissolves; a half hour after being swallowed, the drug comes on like a kick in the head. There was still no conclusive evidence, though, that of marijuana's 420 distinct compounds it's the one that gets people stoned that relieves nausea. Like most drugs, Marinol worked for some cancer patients but not for others. Unlike other drugs, though, Marinol had no legal alternatives. What's more, the FDA approved Marinol only for cancer patients. For AIDS, glaucoma, and paralysis patients wanting marijuana's relief, the government offered nothing.

~

"I Want a New Drug," sang Huey Lewis and the News, and in 1985 the country got not one, but two. In the first instance, a handful of psychiatrists around the country reported phenomenal success with MDMA, a little white capsule that dramatically reduced inhibitions and made it possible for people to confront personal issues they previously could not. "Like a year of therapy in two hours," one patient said. Another said the drug let her confront memories of a rape she'd suffered, which in turn helped her end periods of depression and panic. "Not only did MDMA enable me to recover my sanity," she told *Newsweek*, "it enabled me to recover my soul." MDMA, the magazine said, "is not a hallucinogen, and it doesn't interfere with thinking. It is not a 'party drug' or one to help you through your 47th rerun of 'Casablanca.' " Being new and unscheduled, there was no law against it.

Unfortunately for its adherents, MDMA had an attention-grabbing street name: Ecstasy. It also wasn't the protected offspring of a publicly traded pharmaceuticals corporation but had been created by independent chemists. Within six weeks of hitting the mainstream press, MDMA was banned by DEA chief Jack Lawn under sweeping emergency powers granted him under the 1984 drug law. "All of the evidence DEA has received shows that MDMA abuse has become a nationwide problem and that it poses a serious health threat," Lawn said, offering no such evidence. By placing MDMA in Schedule I — along with heroin and marijuana — Lawn made it illegal for scientists even to experiment with it. Any potential MDMA may have had as a psychotherapeutic drug was sacrificed to the growing antidrug orthodoxy.

~

The second drug to appear that year had more staying power.

Nick Kozel was gazing out his office window at the spring blossoms when his telephone rang. Sixteen years had passed since Kozel had helped Bob DuPont conduct the much-misrepresented D.C. jail study, and now he was a researcher at the National Institute on Drug Abuse with a reputation for being good on the streets. On the line was NIDA director Bill Pollin, asking if Kozel would come see him for a minute.

Pollin had had an intriguing call from a colleague in Los Angeles. It seemed that a smokable form of cocaine was showing up around the country under the street name "basuco." So far it had appeared in New York, Phoenix, and Miami, Pollin told Kozel. The *Los Angeles Times* had run a piece about something that sounded similar, called "rock." I'd like you to do some checking around.

It sounded to Kozel like the coca paste he'd seen in the La Paz hospital eight years earlier, but he couldn't be sure. "Freebase," a smokable form of cocaine that was lovingly — and dangerously — manufactured by using highly flammable ether, had been around for years, and had become famous when comedian Richard Pryor immolated himself making it in 1980. Its use had tapered off, though. And nobody had ever called it "basuco" or "rock." Kozel told Pollin he'd look around.

He flew first to Miami but came up empty-handed. Then he hopped a flight to New York and on the way into Manhattan from La Guardia Airport stopped to see a friend who was working as a counselor at the Queens Youth Treatment Program. Yeah, the friend said, I've heard of basuco. A few of the people I've been seeing lately are smoking it. They have lots of names for it; some call it basuco, but others call it "bazooka" and some call it "chicle." Up in the South Bronx, he said, they call it "crack."

The next day, Kozel dropped in on another friend, Paul Goldstein, one of the authors of the landmark study of addict economics, *Taking Care of Business.* Goldstein was a longtime expert in the street culture of drug abuse and was well connected in the addict community. Kozel asked Goldstein to set him up with some streetwise junkies. They met the following day at Goldstein's office — five heroin addicts, Goldstein, and Kozel. Sure they'd heard of coca paste, the junkies said, but it wasn't very popular. Several attempts to distribute it had fallen flat. Kozel ran the street names past them, to see if they knew any more. When he came to "crack" the addicts laughed. You're mixing things up, they told him. Basuco isn't crack. Basuco is paste. Crack is little rocks of cocaine, and that stuff is everywhere. You smoke it like freebase, they told Kozel, but it's cooked with water and baking soda instead of ether, so it's much easier and cheaper to make.

What's new about it, the addicts said, is how cheap it is and how you can buy it in tiny single-hit doses. Kozel looked at the *Los Angeles Times* clip and asked, like $25 a hit? Nah, the junkies told him. Half that, maybe less. Really, really cheap. They call it crack here, but in LA they call it "rock" and in Miami, "growl."

Kozel wrote it all down, and on the plane back to D.C. he frowned into his notebook. The drug abuse research community hadn't worried too much about cocaine because they thought its high price would keep a lid on it. Kozel himself had always considered cocaine more of a "Hollywood production" than a threat to public health. But once dealers were marketing it at a few dollars a hit, anybody would be able to afford it.

Particularly scary that it was appearing only in places like the South Bronx, Kozel thought. At that moment, Reagan was readying another $20 billion cut in urban funding, bringing to 80 percent the total decline so far under his administration. This kind of policy toward the urban poor, Kozel thought, plus a new cheap form of cocaine, might soon spell disaster in the ghetto.

~

Ed Meese began drawing clear battle lines in the War on Drugs; either you're with us or against us, he felt; there was no room for fence-sitters. "I would like to suggest that there are no neutrals," Meese told a conference of professional neutrals — newspaper editors — in March 1985. "The message must get through and that's where you and I can work together." Meese exhorted the editors "to press hard on this story and connect the occasional cocaine user . . . with the governments that support this trade." Spencer Claw, editor of the *Columbia Journalism Review,* was offended. "That's exactly the role allotted to the press in socialist countries," he told Meese, "to educate people and persuade them about the truth as the government sees it."

Meese even wanted defense attorneys enlisted in the War on Drugs. Meese told a lawyers' conference in May that "there are no bystanders, not even the lawyers." Constitutional freedoms, the attorney general declared, should not be used as a "screen" to protect defendants who engage in "the evils of drugs."

Even as he spoke, the Justice Department was beginning to exercise its new powers to subpoena defense attorneys and force them to inform on their own drug clients. It also was stripping drug defendants of the money they might use to hire a lawyer.

"Governmental investigations of lawyers — including use of such tactics as informants, wiretaps, subpoenas, and office searches — have risen so dramatically in the last four years that they are almost common," the *National Law Journal* reported. The attorney who successfully proved entrapment in John DeLorean's cocaine case noted, "There's rampant paranoia among the criminal defense lawyers, and it's there with good purpose."

~

On suspicion alone, the Supreme Court ruled that summer, an international traveler into the United States may be strip-searched and then held incommunicado until he or she defecates into a wastebasket. Customs agents in Los Angeles had done that to Rosa Elvira Montoya de Hernandez, a Colombian citizen arriving from Colombia, because they suspected — rightly — that she was carrying cocaine-filled balloons in her digestive tract. After almost twenty-four hours locked in a room with only a hard chair to sit on, and denied permission to call an attorney, Ms. Montoya de Hernandez was taken in handcuffs to a hospital and put through a forcible rectal exam that revealed a cocaine-filled balloon. Over the course of the next four days, she excreted eighty-eight more such balloons under observation, and was charged with smuggling drugs. A federal appeals panel had overturned her subsequent conviction, questioning the "humanity" of such a procedure. A study at the time revealed that for every woman apprehended this way, five innocent women were put through the degrading experience.

Justice William Rehnquist reversed the lower court on July 1,

1985, saying the freedom to control one's own bodily functions is a justifiable sacrifice to "the veritable national crisis in law enforcement caused by smuggling of illegal narcotics." To strengthen his point, he listed some of the freedoms he had likewise helped diminish: "first class mail may be opened without a warrant on less than probable cause. . . . Automotive travelers may be stopped . . . near the border without individualized suspicion even if the stop is based largely on ethnicity . . . and boats on inland waters with ready access to the sea may be hailed and boarded with no suspicion whatever."

For Justice William Brennan, who had the year before declared the Court's victory over the Fourth Amendment "complete," the ruling was a disgrace. In a bitter dissent, Brennan compared the Customs agents to kidnappers. Furthermore, Brennan wrote, "Neither the law of the land nor the law of nature supports the notion that petty government officials can require people to excrete on command."

~

Gail Fischer called the police on July 26. Look at me, she said through swollen lips, as she opened the door to her mother's apartment and let the Chicago Police patrolmen inside. My boyfriend beat me up this morning and I want him arrested. His name is Edward Rodriguez and he's asleep in our apartment right now, she said. I'll take you to him.

Fischer led the police to Rodriguez's apartment, reached in her pocket for a key, and opened the door. Inside, the police found not only Rodriguez, but also enough cocaine to bust him for possession with intent to deliver. Rodriguez asked to call a lawyer.

As James Reilley listened to Rodriguez's jailhouse account of the bust, his eyes fell on the white quill feather he'd received from the Supreme Court when he'd unsuccessfully argued *Illinois v. Gates*. This case, obviously, was no *Gates*. Gail Fischer and her children had moved out of the apartment several weeks earlier and she shouldn't have had a key. Clearly she had no authority to let the police into Rodriguez's apartment, and since they didn't have a search warrant, the search was illegal. Anything they found was therefore inadmissible. The courts had long been clear that citizens must *themselves* permit warrantless searches of their own property.

This one looked easy. Sit tight, Reilley told Rodriguez as he sucked on a Newport. Then he got to work.

As expected, Reilley was able to convince Chicago circuit court judge James Schreier to exclude the cocaine as evidence. Rodriguez walked, and Reilley moved on to other cases. For a while.

~

This was the fifth phone call Claire Coles had gotten from a reporter in a week. Something was up.

Coles, a solidly built, no-nonsense woman of forty-three, had been studying babies at Emory University Medical School in Atlanta for five years. A Ph.D. in psychology, her specialty was infants damaged in the womb by their mothers' drinking. Fetal Alcohol Syndrome had been identified a dozen years earlier as causing permanent mental retardation and distortion of the facial features, but the attention (and funding) it received was minimal. When interviewing mothers and pregnant women about their drinking, Coles and her colleagues likewise asked about cigarettes — known to produce low-birthweight babies — and marijuana, which also caused low birthweight. Although they excluded heroin users from their study because so much research into its neonatal effects had already been done, Coles saw plenty of babies born addicted. She rarely received a reporter's phone call.

Now suddenly, in September 1985, every news organization in Atlanta wanted to talk about the effect of cocaine on newborns. It seemed odd. Few women Coles interviewed used the stuff. She knew, though, that the *New England Journal of Medicine* had just published a short article by Dr. Ira Chasnoff and others reporting that in twenty-three women under study cocaine appeared associated with miscarriage and "depression of interactive behavior" in their newborns. She'd read the article and found it interesting, but the sampling was tiny and a great many factors hadn't been controlled for.

What Coles didn't know was that on September 11, the CBS Evening News picked up the story. Reporter Susan Spencer filmed the baby of a cocaine user shaking with "withdrawal" and warned, "The message is clear. If you are pregnant and using cocaine, stop."

In the next few weeks, Coles hosted a stream of TV crews and reporters to answer questions about something they called "cocaine babies." Clearly cocaine isn't good for babies, Coles would say, but the ones exposed to it that I see usually are born to mothers with many other risk factors: poor prenatal care, poor nutrition, drinking, cigarette and pot smoking, and violence. How can anybody look at these babies and identify cocaine as the whole problem?

Upon rereading Chasnoff's study, Coles realized that all the women in his study drank alcohol, smoked pot and cigarettes, and had agreed to be in the study in return for substance-abuse treatment. Also, Chasnoff hadn't controlled for prematurity and, without considering the other risk factors, seemed to imply prematurity was an effect of cocaine. But Chasnoff himself warned against making too much of the study; it was small and imperfect, he wrote. It merely suggested further study.

Coles started paying attention to the TV reports on "cocaine babies" and was infuriated. Chasnoff's imprecise study was cited time and again as gospel. Invariably, the reporters talked about babies suffering "withdrawal." That was crazy. Cocaine, dangerous as it is, doesn't produce withdrawal. The babies may have been feeling the lack of the drug, but cocaine is a stimulant; the logical effect of sudden deprivation would be sleepiness, not the ear-piercing shrieking and trembling shown on TV. It dawned on Coles that the TV crews were either mixed up or lying.

They were filming infants suffering heroin withdrawal and calling them "cocaine babies."

Next time a reporter called, Coles challenged her. Are you going to portray this honestly? The reporter didn't call back again. Every time a reporter called, Coles would recite: cocaine isn't good for anybody, but you can't necessarily say a low-weight, jittery baby — born to an abused, badly nourished, cigarette-smoking, alcohol-drinking woman — is a "cocaine baby." Tell about the increasing numbers of women who go through pregnancy with no prenatal care, Coles would urge. Tell about the rise in infant mortality or the fact that since 1980 more than a million poor women and their children have been thrown off Medicaid.

Soon the reporters stopped calling. Instead, Coles noticed nurses at the hospital — even clerical staff and other nonmedical employees — being interviewed by news crews. The wave of "cocaine baby" stories rolled on.

~

On November 29, 1985, crack cocaine made page one of the *New York Times* for the first time. What Egil Krogh learned in Vietnam held true again. The government, putting pressure on marijuana, helped make cocaine more attractive to smuggle and sell. When the government pressed hard on cocaine, dealers found it worthwhile to boil it down into a smaller and more potent form. Users in turn found it cheaper and easier to smoke cocaine instead of snorting it.

CBS, which broke the "cocaine babies" story in September,

returned to it on December 20. Now, "cocaine babies" were "crack babies." In the first story, the reporter was a woman, the baby was white, and the story was built around a warning to pregnant women. This time, Charles Kuralt and Terry Drinkwater showed African-American babies and blamed their mothers for creating "victims who aren't even old enough to know better." Zooming in on an eighteen-month-old girl destined to become "a twenty-one-year-old with an IQ of perhaps 50, barely able to dress herself, and probably unable to live alone," Drinkwater snarled, "the mother told authorities she was just a *recreational* user."

~

Even after the first wave of "crack baby" stories and making page one of the *New York Times,* crack wasn't yet a household word. TV news reported on it, the newspapers followed along, but the drug hadn't yet captured the public's horrified imagination. Just as it took Nancy Reagan to add the "just" to the Ad Council's "say no" in order for the phrase to clang in the public's ear, it took a quote in the spring of 1986 for crack truly to shimmer into a recognizable apparition.

The quote came from Arnold Washton, director of the 1-800-COCAINE hotline. Although the hotline had been revealed three years earlier as a marketing ploy, Washton, as reporters say, gave good quote. When *Newsweek* called him for its March 17, 1986, cover story, "Kids and Cocaine: An Epidemic Strikes Middle America," Washton didn't disappoint.

"*There is no such thing* as recreational use of crack," Washton said (emphasis in the original). "It is almost instantaneous addiction." From then on, crack was rarely referred to without a reminder that it was "instantly addictive." A sidebar to the *Newsweek* story profiled teenagers ruined by drugs, including one who "went from preppy to punk in seven months." "Crack, in short, may well be the nightmare drug that proves the Cassandras right," the magazine wrapped up, and "may yet cost a generation the joys of growing up."

"Crack is the most addictive drug known to man right now," Washton told *Newsweek.* Technically, this was untrue. Cocaine does not create a physical need the way heroin does. Cocaine is, however, powerfully *reinforcing.* In other words, a cocaine high makes the user want more. In about a sixth of the people who use cocaine regularly this desire is so strong that it is a kind of psychological addiction. Crack, bypassing the narrow blood vessels of the nose by being smoked, is said to be even more reinforcing than cocaine. It may be one of the most reinforcing of all known drugs.

But if crack is "instantly addictive," then everybody who tried it once would be in trouble, and that is far from the truth. Among high school seniors in 1987 (the first year they were asked about cocaine), 4.1 percent had used crack in the past year. Less than a third of those had used it in the past month, and a fortieth of those who had tried it were using it every day. (The proportions have remained about the same since then as overall crack use has declined.) The numbers actually indicate that nicotine is more reinforcing than crack. In 1987, fully 65 percent of the high school seniors who smoked cigarettes at least once a month smoked them every day, in most cases half a pack or more.

Washton, the government, and the press didn't have the 1987 numbers when they were issuing their dire warnings. They did, however, have the 1984 statistics from the Drug Abuse Warning Network, or DAWN. Emergency rooms nationwide report incidents of overdose and other drug-related emergencies to DAWN. The numbers are notoriously inaccurate because if cocaine is found in the body of a heroin addict who overdoses or a drunk who passes out and never wakes up, the incident may be recorded as a "cocaine death." Such reporting anomalies tend to overstate rather than understate the cocaine problem. But even so, the 1984 DAWN figures showed cocaine killing fewer people than either aspirin or the flu. Cocaine was "mentioned" in 604 deaths in 1984. That doesn't mean cocaine killed that many people, just that the drug was present in the bodies of 604 people who died suddenly from substance abuse. It was a threefold increase from 1981, but hardly the biggest health crisis facing the country; five times as many Americans died choking on food and ten times as many died from ulcers. To say nothing of stroke, heart disease, auto wrecks, handguns, and other causes of preventable death.

"There is simply no question," *Newsweek* wrote in "Kids and Cocaine," "that cocaine in all its forms is seeping into the nation's schools." In truth, however, only one senior in eight had tried cocaine by 1987. Fewer than half of those were using it every month, and only about 1/26 of them — or 0.4 percent of all high school seniors — were using it daily. Cocaine deaths among children were almost nonexistent. The total number of Americans under eighteen who died from cocaine in 1984 was eight.

That issue of *Newsweek,* with a cover photo of a teenager snorting coke on a suburban home's carpeted stairway, sold 15 percent more copies than that year's average. Recognizing a good thing when he saw it, editor-in-chief Richard M. Smith put crack on the cover again three months later. "An epidemic is abroad in America," he wrote in a signed editorial, "as pervasive and dangerous in its way as the plagues of medieval times." Thus was cocaine, which killed 1/400,000 of the population that year, compared with the Black Death, which wiped out a third of Europe.

~

William Bennett moved from the NEH to the Education Department without altering his fundamental mission: to promote what he called "values." Bennett still believed himself engaged in a "cultural war." Bilingual education, multiculturalism, and chasing God from the classroom have ruined schooling, he said, and it was time to return to a curriculum that could fairly be characterized as white-guys-plus-Martin. The fundamental lessons of life were worth learning, in Bennett's view, only from the Bible, Rome, Greece, and Europe. The only exceptions were "the public" Martin Luther King's "Letter from Birmingham Jail" and "I Have a Dream" speech.

As to the "drug crisis" in schools, Bennett refused to consider any other explanation than the bad conduct of rotten kids. Drug use is *wrong*, Bennett argued. Kids caught using drugs a second time should be kicked out of school. No counseling: counseling smacked of "moral relativism." No exploration of why the kid is using drugs: that would be too much like Ramsey Clark's root causes. Drugs must equal expulsion, Bennett told Congress, "right now, no ifs, ands or buts. . . . [send] a clear message to all kids that if you're using drugs, you're out of school."

When Congressman Benjamin Gilman, a conservative Republican, suggested that expulsion "isn't really solving the problem," Bennett snapped back, "I'm sorry. I believe that *is* education. I think it's a very effective form of education." Damn the downstream consequences. The point was to make a point.

Bennett brought with him from the NEH a young political science instructor named John Walters, who took charge of drug policy in the Department of Education. Walters, a cheerful, humorous man who looks a little like the actor Richard Dreyfuss, shared Bennett's view that the "fight against drugs" is a convenient arena in which to promote an agenda stressing individual rather than social responsibility. He wrote a seventy-five-page booklet called *What Works: Schools Without Drugs* for distribution nationwide.

Many of the suggestions in Walters's book are common sense and constructive. Parents should try harder to talk to their kids and should set good examples, it advised. But the book is mostly a call to replace reasoned discussion about drugs with platitudes and fear, and to replace counseling and openness with surveillance and punishment. And by all means, close the debate. "Look for 'warning flag' phrases and concepts" in drug-education materials, Walters's booklet warns. " 'Mood-altering' is a deceptive euphemism for mind-altering . . . 'There are no good or bad drugs, just improper use' . . . is a popular semantic camouflage in pro-drug literature." To be certain that materials conform to current orthodoxy, "check the date of publication. Material published before 1980 may be outdated."

As a service to principals, Walters included in *Schools Without Drugs* an analysis of the Supreme Court case from New Jersey with pages of suggestions on how to take advantage of it. Parents and schools should not hesitate to search students and then notify police. Offenders should be suspended or moved to another school. Most of all, schools and parents should be "tough." They should set tough standards, mete out tough punishments, hire tough security guards, demand tough enforcement by local police, and encourage kids to be tough on each other.

At the time *Schools Without Drugs* was published, high school drug use had been declining for seven years. But in the booklet's introduction Bennett flatly stated: "Use of some of the most harmful drugs is increasing." An unwarranted air of crisis pervades the book. "Because of drugs, children are failing, suffering and dying," Bennett concluded. "We have to get tough, and we have to do it now."

At the height of the crack epidemic, 96 percent of high school seniors had never tried it. The news about teenage drug use in 1986 was actually pretty good. Neither the government nor the press, however, had much to gain by saying so.

~

The media at the end of 1985 radically changed the way they portrayed the "cocaine problem." Until now, the typical coke user had been white, rich, attractive, and ultimately tragic. Now, almost all of those shown snorting or smoking cocaine were either black or Hispanic. Cocaine users were no longer tragic, but menacing, and their neighborhoods were "like a domestic Vietnam." No dispatch from "the front lines of the Drug War" was complete without a picture of a white cop arresting a dark-skinned crackhead. The switch may have been one of simple opportunity; it's easier to film black people doing drugs on the street than white people doing drugs in their homes. Two University of Michigan researchers tallied the coke users portrayed on television and found that, beginning in December 1985, the depiction of white cocaine users fell by as much as two-thirds while that of black users rose by the same amount. "These numbers support our view," the researchers concluded, "that, during the Reagan era, the cocaine problem as defined by the network news became increasingly associated with people of color."

At right around the same time, a Democratic polling company surveyed working-class Democrats in suburban Detroit who had recently become Republicans. "These white Democratic defectors express a profound distaste for blacks," the study found. Quality of life was measured in this group by distance from blacks; "not being black is what constitutes being middle class; not living with blacks is what makes a neighborhood a decent place to live."

~

Just as the image of young black men was turning uglier, the public was captivated by sports-page news from the University of Maryland. But then, Len Bias — six feet eight inches tall "with a gunpowder leap and a velvet jump shot" — was the highest scorer ever at Maryland and a veritable ballerina on the court. Dazzling on the sports pages, he was a darling of the "people" pages, too. Squeaky clean, surrounded by a tight-knit, religious family, and sporting a smiley, frank attitude, Bias was a welcome antidote to the slouchy, cap-on-sideways, rap-booming, crack-dealing black man who was becoming daily television fare. On June 17, 1986, Bias became Cinderella: the Boston Celtics, champions of the NBA, made Bias their number one draft pick for the coming season. Reebok signed him the same day to a ten-year, multimillion-dollar contract.

"It's a dream come true," Bias said, blinking tearfully into the bright lights.

~

- Amount saved by California from 1976 to 1985 by reducing marijuana possession to a finable offense: $958,305,499.
- Percentage increase in California marijuana use during that time: 0.

15

Sarajevo on the Potomac
1986

The people like us are We,
And everyone else is They.

— *Rudyard Kipling*

THE NATIONAL PASTIME notwithstanding, the Congress of the United States has long been more devoted to basketball than to any other sport. Maybe it's because there's a basketball court in the House gym, and members throw the ball around to unwind. Maybe it's because every school in America has a gym and every backyard a hoop. Maybe it's because both Georgetown and the nearby University of Maryland have exciting teams, whereas the capital's baseball team, the Washington Senators, had been the American League's laughingstock for years before packing up for Texas in 1971. For whatever reason, Congress loves basketball like no other game.

This was especially true in 1986, when the NBA championship was held by the Celtics, home team of the formidable House Speaker, Tip O'Neill.

On his way to work one swampy June morning that year, Eric Sterling noticed in the paper that Len Bias had died the night before. Strange, Sterling thought; Bias was so young. But not being a sports fan, Sterling wasn't much interested in the story.

Until he arrived at work.

It was like Pearl Harbor had just been bombed; nobody in the Longworth House Office Building was talking about anything but Bias.

Apparently, upon returning to his University of Maryland home after the Celtics signing ceremony in Boston, Bias had celebrated hard with some friends. Late on the night of June 18, he suddenly said he didn't feel well and went to lie down. He never got up.

His heart had failed, and it was the opinion of the Maryland medical examiner that cocaine poisoning had killed him. Because his stardom had hinged in part on a squeaky-clean image, the assumption was that the dose of cocaine that killed him had been his first. The press and public, primed to the idea of "instantaneous addiction," assumed that first taste was crack. (It never was established what type of cocaine Bias took, or whether it was his first time.)

Congress's hometown basketball hero, the nation's model for healthy young black manhood, had been cheated out of his contract with the Speaker's championship hometown team, and the culprit was the most terrifying drug on the street. It isn't just a match in a tank of gasoline, Sterling thought, it's a blowtorch in a tank of nitroglycerin.

Immediately upon returning from the July 4 recess, Tip O'Neill called an emergency meeting of the crime-related committee chairmen. Write me some goddamn legislation, he thundered. All anybody up in Boston is talking about is Len Bias. The papers are screaming for blood. We need to get out front on this now. This week. Today. The Republicans beat us to it in 1984 and I don't want that to happen again. I want dramatic new initiatives for dealing with crack and other drugs. If we can do this fast enough, he said to the Democratic leadership arrayed around him, we can take the issue away from the White House.

In life, Len Bias was a terrific basketball player. In death, he would become the Archduke Ferdinand of the Total War on Drugs. What came before had been only skirmishing; the real Drug War had yet to begin. Within weeks the country would be marching, bayonets fixed.

The same week Len Bias died, coincidentally, William Rehnquist was nominated to replace Warren Burger as chief justice of the United States Supreme Court.

~

It was a hot summer evening in the mostly black Washington Heights section of Manhattan, barely a month after Bias died. The streets were alive: children jumped rope, rap blared from open windows, curbside mechanics burrowed under the hoods of gypsy cabs, prostitutes tottered on pointy heels toward the entrance ramps of the George

Washington Bridge. And all up and down 240th Street, young men in baseball caps hawked their wares: 'ludes, smoke, crystal, and crack. A typical evening, except for the unmarked van parked nearby, with a huge TV antenna mounted on its roof.

Down the street came two unlikely looking white guys: a paunchy UPS delivery man and an unusually well-groomed Hell's Angel with an intense, jaw-clenching stare. They paused before a street dealer, positioned him for the best camera angle, and nervously did business. That evening, millions of TV viewers watched a street dealer sell crack to Senator Alphonse D'Amato and the U.S. attorney for the Southern District of New York, Rudolph Giuliani.

~

Crack was a congressional member's dream: an issue on which there was no real disagreement, only a question of who could prove himself more committed to the cause. Eric Sterling couldn't tell whether Congress was leading television or vice versa. In the month following Bias's death, the networks aired seventy-four evening news segments about crack and cocaine, often erroneously interchanging the two substances and blithely asserting it was crack that killed Bias. The advertising industry donated a billion dollars' worth of ads and TV time to the antidrug cause. "We're on the verge," Bill Rhatican of the Ad Council told *U.S. News & World Report.* "On this issue, we're ready to go over the top!"

On July 28, a second black athlete, the Cleveland Browns' Don Rogers, dropped dead from cocaine poisoning. Though it wasn't clear how often Rogers had used cocaine before, the lessons of Bias's death were repeated in the press: cocaine can kill the strongest and most disciplined among us, even when used a single time. The same day, ABC News introduced a type of TV report that hadn't yet been seen in the Drug War but would become a network standard: raid footage. The network sent a news crew on a crack-house raid and aired breathless, hand-held footage that put the viewer right there with the police as they smashed a door and charged in.

Police and DEA loved such reports because they helped the viewing public identify with the raiders. And it was easy to enlist news crews to come along. Crack, said the head of the New York DEA office, "is the hottest combat-reporting story to come along since the end of the Vietnam War." After ABC's report, raid clips became part of the networks' image bank and snippets of raids appeared in about a quarter of all Drug War reports during the next two years, continually reinforcing the public's identification with the well-armed guys in ski masks bashing in the door.

In his seven years working for Congress, Sterling had never seen such a frenzy grip the Capitol. Usually, committees would hold hearings on a bill, refine points of law, and finally bring the bill into a markup session to polish the language. Now, though, members were having staff draw up hardline proposals and rushing them straight into markup sessions — without benefit of hearings. Sterling found himself in one such session, in which members of the Crime Subcommittee found themselves, by the seat of their pants, writing laws to put the drug defendants' attorneys in prison.

It's not enough to seize their fees, Congressman Clay Shaw of Florida argued. "The only way we will get at this [drug] problem is to let the whole community, the whole population, know that [defense attorneys] are part of the problem and they could very well be convicted if they knowingly take these funds." Congressman Dan Lungren of California, an attorney, wanted to exempt lawyers but nobody else who deals with a drug pusher. Make it illegal for a dry cleaner or a grocery store to take money from a drug dealer, he argued, and if they do, seize the business. Put the merchant in jail. "The whole Len Bias story, it seems to me, suggests we have been far too lenient," Lungren said. Romano Mazzoli of Kentucky agreed but added, "I don't really think lawyers ought to be given a preference here, some sort of special status. . . . We are trying to fight this conspiracy of violence, a conspiracy of action in which unfortunately some lawyers have been involved."

Chairman Bill Hughes, the former prosecutor, urged everybody to cool off. To do their jobs properly, he said, defense attorneys have to learn as much as possible about their client's affairs. Make it a crime for a lawyer to take fees from somebody he knows is guilty, Hughes said, "and the more he finds out, the more he possibly is exposing himself to criminal prosecution." Hughes was able to table the discussion.

A few days later, the subcommittee met again without holding hearings to "do something" permanent about such "designer drugs" as MDMA (Ecstasy). Dan Lungren waved around the source of his knowledge on the subject: "Now I got the most recent article or the most recent issue of *Discovery* magazine, August," he said, "and its article is 'Beyond Crack: The Growing Peril of Designer Drugs.' " On the basis of *Discovery*'s article, Lungren wanted the definition of a designer drug broadened to read, "a substance which has a stimulant, depressant, or hallucinogenic effect on the central nervous system." Sterling, taking notes, stifled a groan. That would include coffee, alcohol, and a long list of legal pharmaceuticals, he thought. But protocol required Sterling speak only if answering a member's question, and nobody was asking any questions.

~

Where the 1986 drug law really departed from tradition was in its adoption of heavy mandatory minimum sentences. In most cases where federal law speaks to a sentence, it is to set maximum limits. But mandatory minimums do have a long history in federal law; the first were passed by Congress in 1790 to punish the most dreaded criminals of the time — pirates. Federal mandatories over the years reveal the ebb and flow of crimes considered most egregious in their day.* In nearly two hundred years, Congress had passed only fifty-eight mandatory minimum sentences.

In the aftermath of Len Bias's death, Congress added another twenty-nine mandatory minimums — a 50 percent increase in four months. What set the 1986 mandatories apart was not only their number, but that they applied to crimes — unlike practicing pharmacy in China — that great numbers of people commit. Of the twenty-nine new mandatories, twenty-six involved drugs. By the time Congress was finished, first-offense small-quantity street dealing could result in a mandatory minimum sentence of ten paroleless years in a federal prison.

Carlton Turner approved heartily. "If we have mandatories for a first offense," he said, "we won't have people back out on the streets committing crime."

On July 31, Hughes opened the bidding with a mandatory penalty of five years for possession "with intent to sell" of 20 grams of crack or 500 grams of cocaine. "Not plea bargainable, no probation or parole," he said. William McCollum, Republican of Florida, urged Hughes higher. "I don't think we ought to be embarrassed," he said. "It would be embarrassing if we came in and wound up being less tough when we put a bill out this fall."

George Gekas, Republican of Pennsylvania, wanted to cut to the chase. "I do intend to pursue the death penalty in narrowly circumscribed cases in drug abuse," he said. "I mean, drug trafficking."

* In 1915, Congress passed a mandatory sentence for "the practice of pharmacy and sale of poisons in China." In the gangster era of the 1930s, mandatory sentences were established for murder of a federal agent or murder during a bank robbery. "Treason and sedition" were added in the red-scare days after World War II, and skyjacking was added in the 1970s.

Hughes rolled his eyes. He knew Judiciary Committee chair Peter Rodino would kill any bill that contained it. After the 1982 disaster, he'd had enough of crafting legislation that went nowhere. But Gekas kept talking death penalty. Finally, Hughes held up a hand.

"We are all inclined to really sock it to people," he said. "Everybody wants to be tough on criminals. . . . But I think that we have to make sure what we do makes sense."

Hughes, with his no-plea-bargaining stance, knew he was courting chaos. The biggest experiment with drug mandatories in recent history was New York's 1973 "Rockefeller laws." Heavy sentences and no plea bargaining gave defendants nothing to lose by going to trial. Predictably, the percentage of cases tried by jury more than doubled. So the time it took to dispose of the average drug case also doubled. Despite a big expansion of New York's court system, a 2,600-case backlog developed in the first eighteen months.

And neither the crime nor addiction rates in New York improved.

Likewise, there was *federal* experience with mandatory minimums to draw upon. In 1956 Congress enacted mandatory sentences for various drug crimes, but repealed them in 1970 because they "had not shown the expected overall reduction in drug law violations."

Hughes's subcommittee might have known all this had it held hearings on the wisdom and efficacy of mandatory sentences. It didn't, though. With crack leading the morning paper and the evening news every day that summer, there was "no time." Similarly, the subcommittee didn't learn about a new federal survey suggesting that tough law enforcement doesn't discourage drug abuse. Rather, fully three-fifths of the drug-using prison inmates surveyed had not tried drugs until after their first arrest.

~

Eric Sterling had once seen a film shot in Tanzania; a million wildebeest grazing peacefully, until one of them started running. Assuming danger, a few more joined in, and in no time the whole herd was stampeding wildly, trampling the sick and the slow, laying waste to flora and fauna alike in a senseless headlong panic. Those images kept occurring to him as he watched Congress in the weeks following Len Bias's death.

"I don't see how it is possible to make some decisions until we find out exactly what we are talking about," Hughes said. His subcommittee was back at it, talking about criminalizing cornstarch.

Hughes summoned Frank Shults, the DEA's liaison to Congress, and asked: when the law says 1,000 grams of cocaine, does that mean pure cocaine?

"I don't believe it is pure, no," Shults said.

"Does Roger, does Justice know?" Hughes asked, turning to the Justice Department's Roger Pauley.

"I believe Mr. Shults is correct, that it is, uh, mixture."

Leave the law the way it is, McCollum urged, "because if we try to get any more technical we are going to screw up the court proceedings, the proof, and everything." Lungren agreed.

"My recommendation," Larry Smith of Florida said, "is that we don't worry ourselves about dosage units. We don't worry about anything. . . . What difference does it make how many dosage units are in it? They shouldn't have any of the substance in their possession. And if somebody has got 400 parts of cornstarch and one part of cocaine, it is obvious that they are intending to kill somebody."

"I think," Hughes mumbled, "we ought to have one conversation at a time."

No hearings, Sterling thought, perched in the corner. I held *days* of hearings on that piddly pharmacy-robbery bill, and these guys are changing the entire structure of federal sentencing *without holding a single hearing*.

⁓

On August 9, President Reagan peed in a bottle and then issued a press release about it. Two days later, Vice President Bush did likewise, demonstrating, in the words of one columnist, that "he has neither a conscience nor a mind of his own." During their reelection campaign, the governor and first lady of Arkansas, Bill and Hillary Clinton, likewise had themselves urine-tested and touched off a short-lived fashion among campaigners nationwide.

The figure most often quoted to justify workplace urine testing came from the prestigious Research Triangle Institute, which surveyed households around the country under federal contract in 1982 and concluded that drug abuse cost the country $47 billion a year. Here's how RTI reached that figure:

It called 3,700 households and learned that adults who had *ever* smoked marijuana daily for a month earned an average 28 percent less money than those who hadn't. Calling the difference "reduced productivity due to daily marijuana use," RTI extrapolated from those 3,700 phone calls to arrive at $26 billion. Then it added on another $21 billion for drug-related crime, accidents, and medical care.

Although the lives of poor people differ greatly from those of the rich in terms of nutrition, stress, environment, and access to care, RTI elected to examine only marijuana use and conclude that a month of daily pot smoking some time in the past *caused* the lower incomes.

RTI also glossed over its own data on what it called *current* drug use — at least once in the past thirty days. When current use was placed beside income, no differences could be demonstrated. RTI, in other words, was saying that a single month-long pot binge sometime in a person's past causes lower income, while regular drug use has no effect on productivity whatsoever. Somehow, these conclusions were said to support widespread workplace drug testing.

~

Congress, meanwhile, continued throwing together what it hoped would be the biggest, baddest drug bill in history. With no time for hearings, legislators informed themselves from television, magazines, constituents' letters, and each other's increasingly florid statements to the TV cameras. Clay Shaw of Florida declared drugs "the biggest threat that we have ever had to our national security." House majority leader Jim Wright of Texas upstaged him by calling drugs "a menace draining away our economy of some $230 billion this year, slowly rotting away the fabric of our society and seducing and killing our young." The $230 billion figure — roughly equal to the Social Security budget — apparently was plucked from thin air.

The bills flew fast and furious. No more probation for druggies! No more suspended sentences! Death penalty for kingpins! A billion dollars for new prisons! A billion for state and local narcotics squads! Repeal the exclusionary rule! Elevate the drug czar to cabinet status! Urine-test all federal employees!

"In football there's a thing called piling on," said Patricia Schroeder, Democrat of Colorado. "I think we're seeing political piling on right before the election."

Drugs are "a threat worse than any nuclear warfare or any chemical warfare waged on any battlefield," South Carolina Republican Thomas Hartnett said, sponsoring a measure to force the president to stop all drug smuggling within forty-five days. Senator Sam Nunn of Georgia called it "the equivalent of passing a law saying the president shall, by Thanksgiving, devise a cure for the common cold."

It passed anyway.

The drug bill's absurdity and political utility were plain for all to see. It's "out of control," David McCurdy of Oklahoma told *Newsweek,* "but of course I'm for it." The junior senator from Indiana was equally unabashed.

"You want to get on top of the wave when it's cresting," Dan Quayle told *U.S. News & World Report.*

~

On September 2, fifteen million people watched the CBS News documentary "48 Hours on Crack Street." It was the biggest news audience in six years. NBC followed three days later with "Cocaine Country." And not to be outdone, Geraldo Rivera ran a special of his own, "The Doping of a Nation," that argued for expanded drug treatment while showing almost nothing but raid footage and other thrilling scenes of drug enforcement.

The new Drug War is "urgent and necessary," *Time* reported in its news pages. *Time* acknowledged that "drugs kill, but not nearly so often as the family car." It conceded that "the current cocaine epidemic has already peaked and the use of other drugs is declining." But it put cocaine on its cover five times that year, as did *Newsweek.* Other national newspapers and magazines published about a thousand stories about crack in 1986. So enthusiastically did the press jump on crack, and with such unanimity, that the curator of the Nieman Foundation, which trains journalists in ethics, publicly lamented the decline of traditional pro-and-con exchanges on controversial subjects. "Now all you get is the con," curator Howard Simons said. "Drugs are bad. Period."

Deserters from the war were figuratively taken out and shot. At the height of the summer hype, Paula Hawkins, Republican of Florida, rose on the House floor to accuse the *Washington Post* of treason in the War on Drugs. She cited the *Post*'s "sustained attack" on the administration's Drug War, its "extensive coverage of the ACLU's opposition to drug testing," the "bad press" it gave "the tough but successful drug treatment program operated by Straight Inc.," and its habit of letting "long-time advocates of illicit drug use" publish essays on the op-ed page. The real problem, she implied, is the First Amendment. "It is indeed unfortunate that newspapers and journalists, unlike judicial nominees, have so little scrutiny over their prior public record," Hawkins said, "let alone their personal behavior and their comments made in private."

As Richard Nixon had noticed almost two decades earlier, Americans were more willing to believe television than their own experience.

Three-quarters of Americans polled that summer said they believed drugs a terrible problem "for the country." And yet barely a third of the same people said drugs were a problem in their own community.

~

The United States of America quietly passed a milestone in 1986. Eighty-four percent white and 12 percent black, the nation now held more black than white people in prison.

~

The week of August 18 was an odd one. First, William Rehnquist owned up to having been hooked on the sleeping pill Placidyl for nine years. Then, thirteen-year-old Deanna Young turned in her parents' marijuana stash to police after listening to an antidrug lecture at the Peace Lutheran Church in Orange County, California. For her trouble, Deanna was placed in foster care as a ward of the state while her parents faced three years in prison.

"Every action Deanna took," said Bob Theemling, director of a county foster-care facility, "was to make things better at home and to have a good thing happen to her parents. [It was] a genuine act of love."

~

Ronald Reagan went on television on September 14. And this time, he brought Nancy with him to urge Americans to adopt "outspoken intolerance."

In an unusual joint address from their private quarters in the White House, the Reagans summoned Americans to a crusade they compared to World War II, in which everybody, "not just the boys flying the planes and driving the tanks," took part. Americans, the president said, "have never been morally neutral against any form of tyranny."

"There's no moral middle ground," Nancy said. "Indifference is not an option."

The lofty tone recalled FDR on poverty, Kennedy on the space program, and Lyndon Johnson on civil rights. This time, though, the cause was drugs. "We want you to help us create an outspoken intolerance for drug use," Nancy said. "For the sake of our children, I implore each of you to be unyielding and inflexible in your opposition to drugs."

Drugs are a "cancer," the Reagans said, and drug dealers "work every day to plot a new and better way to steal our children's lives — just as they've done by developing this new drug, crack."

"So," the First Lady wound up, "won't you join us in this great new national crusade?"

~

Next morning, Reagan signed Executive Order #12564, titled Drug Free Workplace, ordering all federal agencies to plan to urine-test all workers in jobs requiring "a high degree of trust and confidence." The order didn't specify how many of the government's 2.8 million civilian employees fit that description. The contents of one's bladder would now be the boss's business. The Pee House of the August Moon was coming home.

First-time offenders would be counseled. In a cabinet meeting prior to issuing the order, White House counsel Peter Wallison suggested that firing federal workers who failed their second drug test would be "punitive." "It's meant to be punitive," retorted Education Secretary William Bennett. He waved his booklet *Schools Without Drugs*, which recommends expelling second-time users, and asked, "How can you be harder on kids than you are on tax-supported federal workers?" Bennett's view became policy.

Despite all the talk about drug-impaired workers, impairment clearly was not the issue. If it were, urine testing wouldn't be necessary; work impaired by drugs is evidenced by bad work. Urine testing — even if it happens to be accurate — detects only drug residue in the body, not impairment. One of the most-repeated arguments of Carlton Turner, the parents' advocates, and other marijuana prohibitionists was the drug's fat solubility, that it remains in the body's fatty tissues for weeks after the smoker felt the effects. Now the Drug Warriors wanted it both ways; marijuana is bad because it's present in your body even when you're not stoned, and urine testing, which detects that marijuana residue, is good because it prevents people being "stoned" at work.

"Federal employees who use illegal drugs, on or off duty, tend to be less productive, less reliable and prone to greater absenteeism than their fellow employees who do not use illegal drugs," read Reagan's executive order. Same could be said of insomniacs, alcoholics, the clinically depressed, and anyone going through a divorce or caring for a sick child. Ameliorating any such condition might be a compassionate and prudent goal for an employer to attempt. If the worker is a user of particular drugs, though, dismissal was recommended — followed, presumably, by a visit from the police.

"The results are in and you've done it again!" White House chief of staff Don Regan wrote in a memo to the writer of the Reagans' joint speech. The White House pollster's analysis, Regan wrote, "indicates that never have reactions to one of the president's speeches been so favorable!"

~

Three weeks later, Congress delivered the baby. In passing the long list of mandatory sentences, Congress seemed to have forgotten that two years earlier it had created a commission to write sentencing guidelines. Those guidelines were scheduled to go into effect in 1987. Nobody on the Hill foresaw what would happen when the two contradictory sentencing systems — mandatories and guidelines — became law at the same time and parole was simultaneously abolished. The federal prison system already was at 150 percent of capacity, a condition that would soon be looked back upon with nostalgia.

"The drug thing has just caught flame; it is *the* issue!" exulted Congressman Trent Lott, Republican of Mississippi, when the vote was over.

Opponents saw it differently.

"I'm afraid this bill is the legislative equivalent of crack," Congressman Barney Frank of Massachusetts said. "It yields a short-term high but does long-term damage to the system. And it's expensive to boot."

House Judiciary Committee chairman Peter Rodino was less playful. "We have been fighting the War on Drugs," he said, "but now it seems to me the attack is on the Constitution of the United States."

~

Right around then, the DEA issued a report on the "distortion of the public perception of the extent of crack use." It generally isn't available outside New York and Los Angeles, the DEA said, and is almost nonexistent in the suburbs.

But this was one crack story the media hardly touched. Neither CBS nor ABC reported it, the *New York Times* ignored it altogether, and the *Washington Post* buried a small item on page 18.

~

Once the November elections were over, Reagan quietly cut a billion dollars from the $4 billion Drug War bill he'd spent most of the year mobilizing, including the entire treatment budget and all grants to state and local police. The Pentagon also pulled the plug on the operations against drug labs in Bolivia it had launched earlier in the year with great fanfare. Some 200 U.S. troops had spent four months raiding cocaine labs, but the whole adventure was compromised by corruption, ineptitude, and a general sense of hopelessness.

U.S. News & World Report — usually a staunchly conservative ally of Ronald Reagan — was candid about what all the drug panic of 1986 really meant:

> Easily the most prominent beneficiary of the drug furor is Ronald Reagan. Just weeks ago, the President seemed trapped in a thicket of thorny problems. . . .
>
> For now, at least, all that has changed. Other issues have not gone away, but they have been pushed to the back burner, providing Reagan with much needed breathing room and a chance to do what he does best — rouse the troops in a campaign summoning the traditional American values so key to his popularity.

16

Times of War
1987

If it's a dope case, I won't even read the petition. I ain't giving no break to no drug dealer.

— *Justice Thurgood Marshall, to* Life *magazine, 1987*

AMTRAK'S *Colonial,* with 616 passengers aboard, was traveling at 105 miles an hour when it piled into a string of Conrail freight engines heading toward Harrisburg, Pennsylvania. Fifteen people were killed and another 176 injured — the worst accident in Amtrak's history.

Federal investigators said they were focusing on two possible reasons why the trains ended up on the same track: a warning whistle was disabled, and a bulb was missing from a critical signal light in the *Colonial*'s cab.

Within days, though, Dr. Delbert J. Lacefield, chief of the Federal Aviation Administration's forensic toxicology unit working under contract to the Federal Railroad Association, announced that he had found THC in the blood of two members of the freight train's crew. THC is fat-soluble and stored in the body for weeks, so a urine test cannot measure marijuana impairment. Nevertheless, the news that railroad employees had at some point smoked pot sparked an outcry for wider urine testing in the transportation industries.

The Senate Commerce Committee overwhelmingly approved a bill to require random drug tests on airline pilots. An alarming figure was cited: the number of midair near misses had more than doubled since 1981. That happened to have been the year Ronald Reagan fired — on a single day — almost every qualified air-traffic controller in the country for participating in a strike. Five years later, the corps of controllers still wasn't up to strength and little more than half of those working were fully qualified. To top it off, the administration admitted that in 1986 it had looted an $8 billion air-safety fund from the Transportation Department. There may have been many causes for the rise in near misses, but once again the blame was falling on drug takers.

The Reagan administration, insisting that improved testing was 98 percent accurate, released a final plan to urine-test a quarter of its 4 million civilian employees. If 98 percent accurate, urine testing a million people still placed the careers of 20,000 innocents at risk. The National Treasury Employees Union filed suit immediately. And with old-fashioned entrepreneurial flair, a mail-order company began offering guaranteed drug-free urine for $49.95 a sample.

~

After visiting drug-treatment centers and finding that "roughly 40 percent" of patients under eighteen had engaged in homosexual activity, Carlton Turner told a *Newsweek* reporter that homosexuality "seems to be something that follows along from their marijuana use."

"Weren't these men maybe gay first?" the reporter asked.

"Oh no," Turner answered. "The drug came first."

Newsweek headlined the story REAGAN AIDE: POT CAN MAKE YOU GAY, inciting a gale of vituperation from both the gay community and drug-treatment providers.

Now that crack and cocaine were replacing marijuana as chief public bugaboo, Carlton Turner's place in the drug-policy firmament was murky. Shortly after the new year he resigned. Dr. Ian Macdonald, the Florida pediatrician elevated to head ADAMHA, took over Turner's job as drug czar. It didn't take him long to realize he was largely a figurehead.

Meese took the word "Enforcement" out of his Drug Enforcement Policy Board, telegraphing his intention to take over the whole ball game. Meese's board convened monthly to set drug policy. The meetings were painful for Macdonald. Everybody got excited about side-looking radar on the Aerostats, or the F-18A's look-down-shoot-down capabilities, or tapes of NORAD's real-time satellite intelligence of the border. Slides glowed on the wall, grainy high-altitude photos stamped TOP SECRET circulated, recordings of intercepted phone calls trilled, a war-room atmosphere prevailed.

In the midst of such talk, Macdonald ventured ideas about twelve-step techniques for addicts or a new series of drug-education films. All heads would swivel toward him with the bored look of penned cattle.

At one meeting, Customs Commissioner William Von Raab argued forcefully that the air force should be allowed to shoot down suspected drug-smuggling planes that didn't respond to warnings. If we down just one, he said, people will take us seriously. The room flew into an uproar. Even for Ed Meese, the idea was too much, maybe even unconstitutional. A single voice rose in defense of Von Raab's idea. Actually, Assistant Attorney General William Weld said calmly, the Supreme Court has ruled it legal for police to shoot a felon who's about to commit a violent felony. Given the level of violence and death caused by drugs, Weld said, shooting down drug smugglers is constitutional. Weld, fair-haired and mild-mannered, almost swayed the board. Ultimately it wasn't the Constitution but the specter of a lawsuit that quashed the idea. What if we shoot down four vacationing doctors with a bum radio? someone asked, and that was that.

As they left the meeting, Coast Guard Commandant Paul Yost sidled up to Von Raab and put a hand on his shoulder. Jesus, Willie, he said with a nervous chuckle, lay off this talk about shooting down planes. My people have been firing on smuggling boats for months. They're supposed to aim at the rudders, but every now and then they kill somebody. You keep talking about planes and somebody will notice what we've been doing about the boats. It'll raise a hell of a stink.

~

An invitation to the trough: that's how many corporations viewed the White House request for donors to support drug treatment.

Nancy Reagan's chief of staff, Jack Courtemanche, invited Procter & Gamble executives to lunch at the White House and gave them exclusive rights to use the Just Say No slogan. He also let them use Nancy's face in their promotions for Downy fabric softener and White Cloud toilet paper. P&G was willing to spend $40 million on the campaign but only under certain conditions. "Our relationship *must be exclusive* in the packaged goods industry," P. H. Goldman of P&G wrote to William Adams of the Just Say No Foundation, which arranged the deal with the White House (emphasis in original). "We remind you that our primary objective is to build the business."

Jaycees Clubs and other civic organizations had been unsuccessful in getting Nancy Reagan's endorsements for antidrug campaigns. "White House policy precludes the use of the first lady's name," Courtemanche wrote again and again. Yet for Procter & Gamble, Mrs. Reagan agreed to pose for the cameras with sacks of P&G coupons for Folger's Coffee, Puritan Oil, and other fine P&G products. The coupons, emblazoned with Just Say No pledges and attached to a signed message from the First Lady, were mailed to 48 million households.

With so much emotion and prestige invested in Just Say No, it is not surprising that charlatans hustled to capitalize on it, too. In the spring of 1987, the White House threatened Colonial Corp. of Culver City, California, with legal action for pressuring people on the phone to buy two and three hundred dollars' worth of Just Say No bumper stickers. "Think of all those kids dying," the Colonial telemarketers urged. "Isn't this worth it for them?" Likewise, Amstar Distributing Corp. of Bellflower, California, called people with the good news that they'd won "a prize." All they had to do to collect was buy $399 worth of Just Say No bumper stickers.

~

It bothered Ian Macdonald that the country was getting het up about crack and cocaine while losing interest in the illegal drug that most often sidetracked young people: marijuana. By now, the antidrug campaign was so completely severed from reality that as drug czar Macdonald was pushing outright falsehoods. When the publishers of the Just Say No Club Members' Handbook asked him to review a copy, Macdonald sent back this suggestion: "Change the last sentence to read, 'Marijuana also is a drug you can get addicted to.' "

~

The Federal Aviation Administration quietly announced in April the "temporary reassignment" of Dr. Delbert J. Lacefield. A month later, Lacefield pleaded guilty in federal court to falsifying blood test results not only in the Amtrak-Conrail crash but others as well. The Federal Railroad Association said Lacefield "was unable or unwilling to do the tedious and complicated job of preparing blood plasma extracts for analysis." As a result, the association said, he was reporting that railroad personnel were using drugs as little as six hours before accidents "when no testing had been done to confirm that."

≈

A full 83 percent of Americans in a 1987 opinion poll approved of reporting drug-using family members to the police. It was in this atmosphere that the U.S. Supreme Court decided that drug defendants — even nonviolent ones — are inherently dangerous and can be denied their Eighth Amendment right of reasonable bail.

"We have repeatedly held that the government's regulatory interest can, in appropriate circumstances, outweigh an individual's liberty interest," the Court ruled. "For example, in times of war or insurrection . . . the government may detain individuals whom the government deems to be dangerous." Thus was the War on Drugs anointed a real war by the Supreme Court.

≈

The DEA man faced a roomful of blank faces. You can help us, he told the assembled brass of the North Carolina Highway Patrol. Let us train your troopers to spot drug couriers and search vehicles.

Nobody seemed very excited. That's not our mission, one of the North Carolinians said. We're highway police, not drug enforcers.

Well, the DEA man said, there will be plenty of seized assets to share.

Now the DEA was talking. As a Highway Patrol official later told Congress, "Everybody's eyes lit up."

Indeed they did. From a standing start in 1984, the value of assets seized by law enforcement nationwide zoomed to half a billion dollars in three years and kept growing. For policemen like North Carolina's, there was money to me made. Serious money.

North Carolina law required assets confiscated from drug dealers to be sold and all the proceeds deposited in the state school fund — none for police. If, however, a case was taken federal, the North Carolina police would get a cut under the federal asset-sharing program. That arrangement also could shower money on police in such states as Montana, Indiana, and Missouri, which required all seized assets to be paid into the state's general fund.

California was nicer to its police; it allowed 65 percent of assets seized in state or local drug busts to be paid to the participating police, with the rest going for mental health, district attorneys, and informants. But the lawmen of the Golden Bear State still preferred to go federal. They perfected the art of presenting 100 percent complete cases to the U.S. attorney for "adoption," paying the U.S. Justice Department a 10 percent processing fee and keeping a full 90 percent of the seized assets. "That is, we receive a case which is in every respect a local case . . . and we put our cover on it," U.S. attorney Joseph Whitely told Congress. "This is a very useful tool in California." It was so useful, in fact, that in the first few years of the asset-sharing program California received as much in shared assets as all other participating states combined. When Congressman Larry Smith suggested that the scheme was making the federal government a partner in "subverting" California laws, Whitely could only agree.

~

DEA agents continued using "drug courier profiles" — characteristics of "typical" drug couriers — to detain and frisk travelers in airports. First-class travelers, for example, might be suspect for wearing sloppy or ill-fitting clothes. "We do see some real slimeballs," DEA agent Paul Markonni, the "father" of drug courier profiles, told a Florida judge. "You know, some real dirt bags, that obviously could not afford — unless they were doing something — to fly first class."

By 1987, so many such cases had piled up that the *North Carolina Law Review* published a list of 155 "suspicious" characteristics the DEA had recently used. They included:

"Round-trip ticket, one-way ticket . . .

"Non-stop flight to and from source city (such as Los Angeles or Miami), taking connecting flights to or from source city, direct flight to and from source city, taking circuitous route to and from source city . . .

"Walking slowly, walking quickly, being very tense, calm demeanor, appearing "cool" . . .

"Carrying no luggage, carrying medium-size bag, carrying two apparently heavy suitcases, carrying American Tourister luggage, carrying leather briefcase . . .

"Individual traveling alone, two or more people traveling together . . .

"Black male, female, black female, Hispanic, youth, sloppily dressed, casual dress, smartly dressed . . .

"First to deplane, last to deplane, deplaning from the middle . . .

"Placing long distance call immediately after deplaning, placing local call immediately after deplaning . . .

"Attempting to leave the airport immediately by taxi, attempting to use public transportation to leave airport, using limousine to leave airport, using hotel courtesy van, attempting to leave airport in private vehicle . . ."

In other words, the DEA felt justified in searching everybody.

~

On July 7, the Kentucky State Police kicked off Drug Awareness Month by raiding the ninety-acre farm of James Burton, a thirty-nine-year-old glaucoma patient. Burton said he was growing a few marijuana plants to keep from going blind and hadn't tried to hide his crop. The jury believed his medical-necessity claim and found him guilty only of simple possession — not the more serious charge of manufacturing or intent to sell. He was sentenced to a year in federal prison without parole. In addition, U.S. District Judge Ronald Meredith ordered Burton's entire farm confiscated and gave the Burtons ten days to clear out of their home of eighteen years. Burton wasn't allowed to testify on his own behalf and no witnesses were called during the confiscation hearing. Explained Judge Meredith, "There is no defense to forfeiture."

~

William Von Raab was frustrated. He'd been able to wrest a large measure of drug-investigation power from the DEA and had talked Congress into quadrupling his corps of Customs investigators. The Customs Service was now a full-fledged police force in the War on Drugs. But Von Raab felt impatient as he watched the drug trade roll on, with smugglers importing ever-bigger quantities and pushing cocaine prices to new lows. Lots of people were being arrested, and prosecutors too often dropped charges for fear of clogging the courts and prisons. This was no way to run a War on Drugs, Von Raab thought. It reminded him of something Chou En-lai once said: "China has no law it doesn't enforce." If the War on Drugs was the law of the land, it was time to enforce it, by God. It was time for a new approach.

A memo landed on Von Raab's desk concerning the technique used by Pete Nunez, the U.S. attorney in San Diego. Nunez was prosecuting everybody, no matter how small the case. He'd let defendants plead their charge down to a misdemeanor if the quantity was small enough, but everybody got some kind of punishment, whether a short jail stay, unpleasant community service, or a stinging fine. Von Raab thought Nunez was exactly right; every drug offender deserves to be punished. He decided to implement a similar policy in Customs. If an inspector found drugs — regardless of quantity — on a traveler, an airplane, or a boat, prosecution and punishment would follow. No exceptions. Von Raab talked the State Department into revoking the passport of any U.S. citizens caught with so much as a single joint and convinced the Justice Department to accept such cases for full-blown prosecution. Von Raab cast around for a name for his policy and remembered that in the Nixon White House, chief of staff Bob Haldeman had a policy he called "zero defect."

Von Raab decided to call his policy "zero tolerance."

Once Customs inspectors were homing in on tiny amounts of drugs, Von Raab's legal staff reminded him of their new powers of seizure and confiscation. Technically, the government could seize a multimillion-dollar yacht if inspectors found a single marijuana seed. That technicality became national policy — and a clarion call. As George Bush said in his nomination acceptance speech the following summer, "Zero tolerance isn't just a policy, it's an attitude. My administration will be telling the dealers: whatever we have to do, we'll do, but your day is over, you're history."

Frances Lopes was rather glad when police came to arrest her son Thomas. The poor man, wracked by mental illness since boyhood, was still living in her Hawaii home at age twenty-eight. The only time he'd leave the solitude of his bedroom was to tend his marijuana plants in the backyard. The past few months had been a nightmare. Whenever Frances asked Thomas to get rid of the plants, he threatened to kill himself.

So when a police helicopter spotted the plants, and drug agents showed up to arrest Thomas, the Lopeses mostly felt relieved. Because it was Thomas's first offense, the judge gave him probation and ordered him to see a psychologist. Finally, the Lopeses thought, Thomas may get the care he needs.

They wouldn't know it for another four years, but under the law their home already belonged to the government. The offspring laws of RICO, written to break criminal organizations, considered the Lopeses accomplices of their son and their home legally seizable.

~

Nathan and Lynne Raiford Carr, African-American residents of Fairfield, Connecticut, were driving on the New Jersey Turnpike near Edison when a state trooper pulled them over. Approaching with his hand on his gun, the trooper ordered the Carrs out of their car, and for thirty minutes interrogated them while searching the car for drugs he never found. He let them go without a ticket or warning, but told them to leave the turnpike at the next exit. I don't care where you're going or how you'll get there, he told them, but I want you off the turnpike.

At least they didn't spend the night in jail. To Bradley J. Ferencz, deputy state public defender in New Brunswick, it seemed an awful lot of minority drivers from out of state were being stopped and arrested by state troopers on the turnpike. Ferencz asked the state police for their arrest figures. They refused. So Ferencz convinced his superiors to hire a Rutgers University statistician to survey drivers and arrests. The survey team noted that while fewer than 5 percent of the cars on the turnpike both had out-of-state-plates and were occupied by blacks, 80 percent of those stopped and arrested for drugs were out-of-state blacks.

~

The mandatory minimum sentences passed by Congress in 1986 went into effect immediately, increasing the power of the prosecution beyond Ed Meese's fondest dreams. Mandatory minimums effectively took the power to sentence defendants away from judges and gave it to prosecutors.

Mandatories are determined entirely by the charge a defendant faces. If the charge is first-offense possession of six grams of crack, the sentence upon conviction is six years in prison. If the charge is second-offense possession with intent to distribute, the sentence is twenty years. The judge has no choice.

It's up to the prosecutor to decide the charge, and here there is much room for discretion. Did the defendant intend to distribute? How much weight exactly was he carrying? Was he close to a school? (If so, that would add another year.)

Defendants avoid charges carrying mandatories by making deals with the prosecutor — information in exchange for a reduction in charge. A kid picked up on the street with six crack rocks in his pocket typically doesn't know enough to make a worthwhile deal. So mandatories tend to reward bigger crooks who have information to trade with shorter sentences while warehousing the small fry.

Those charged with crimes carrying mandatories have no incentive to plead guilty because no leniency is allowed. So at just the moment the number of defendants was skyrocketing under "zero tolerance," federal judges found their dockets crammed with penny-ante drug cases, with no choice but to order full jury trials. The court system might have been able to handle the crush had it grown as fast as the police agencies feeding defendants into it. But in the mid-1980s police funding was rising four times as fast as court funding. The destruction of the federal court system was under way.

In 1987, a year after the mandatories went into effect, the Sentencing Commission produced the guidelines Congress had ordered up in 1984. The big difference between guideline sentences and mandatory minimums is that guidelines are designed to consider a wide range of factors: remorse, the defendant's criminal history, the level of involvement in the crime, the extent to which he or she cooperated with police, whether a firearm was involved. The mandatories, on the other hand, are hitched firmly to the quantity of drugs involved in a crime, and the conspiracy provisions invented for RICO apply. So under the mandatories, an unarmed first-time offender on the periphery of a drug sale — the guy, say, who introduced the buyer and seller — would get the same heavy penalty as the gun-toting professional dealer caught with the stash.

When the guidelines became law in November 1987, conflicts between the two sentencing systems immediately became apparent. For example, the mandatory sentence for a first offender caught dealing 5.01 or more grams of crack is five years without parole. Under the guidelines, however, the same person caught dealing 5 grams of crack could receive a *maximum* of one year in prison. Thus was a four-year difference codified for one hundredth of one gram of crack.

Judge Douglas Ginsburg appeared to be a solid choice for the U.S. Supreme Court. Learned, experienced, conservative without being an ideologue, Ginsburg seemed sure to win easy confirmation from the Senate. Until, that is, National Public Radio's Nina Totenberg revealed on the air that once as a college student in the 1960s, and then a few times in the 1970s, Ginsburg had smoked marijuana.

Reagan withdrew Ginsburg's nomination at once, even though public opinion ran three-to-one against doing so. Education Secretary William Bennett volunteered to call Ginsburg with the bad news.

Immediately, thirty-nine-year-old Senator Al Gore declared that he, too, had smoked pot during his youth. Arizona Governor Bruce Babbitt and US Senator Claiborne Pell quickly followed with similar statements of their own. Congressman Newt Gingrich jumped on the bandwagon too, owning up to smoking pot as a graduate student. Never again, the confessant legislators said, should we pillory public servants who tried a little grass in their youth.

~

Kurt Schmoke, Baltimore's chief prosecutor, became the city's mayor in December 1987. One of his first acts was to join a citywide panel looking for ways to slow the spread of AIDS. The disease was spreading fastest, he learned, in the community of intravenous drug users. They shared scarce needles, passed the virus to each other, then transmitted it sexually to spouses and sweethearts. By 1987, babies were being born infected with the virus.

It was clear to Schmoke that the city's long-standing ban on needles was doing more harm than good. The quickest way to end needle sharing was to make syringes legal and freely available. From there, it was a short leap to the bigger question that had been rumbling in the back of his mind since he had heard the tape of Marcellus Ward's murder three years earlier: does prohibition of drugs do more harm than good?

Four months after taking office he was invited to Washington, D.C., to speak to a national conference of mayors and police chiefs. Without warning his staff, Schmoke raised the question: shouldn't we mayors, whose constituents are hardest hit by both drugs and the war against them, at least debate the alternatives to drug prohibition? By the time he'd driven back to Baltimore that evening, his speech was the top story: Mayor Calls for Legalization. Next day, C-SPAN aired the speech nationally, and the fat hit the fire. This wasn't a wealthy white observer like William Buckley engaging in parlor games, but the black mayor of a largely black and drug-wracked city, a former prosecutor, calling drug prohibition a failure.

The Baltimore mayor, went the D.C. buzz, is a nice young man who once had a bright future.

~

On February 4, a federal grand jury for the first time indicted a foreign head of state. Manuel Antonio Noriega, despot of Panama, was formally charged with racketeering and drug trafficking.

To the administration's great embarrassment, the public soon learned that only nine months earlier — at the height of crack panic — DEA chief Jack Lawn had sent Noriega a letter expressing "deep appreciation for the vigorous anti-drug-trafficking policy you have adopted."

The *Miami Herald* had been reporting allegations of Noriega's drug smuggling since 1985, even while Noriega was helping Iran-Contra conspirators William Casey, Richard Secord, and Oliver North wage their secret war against Nicaragua. *The Nation* uncovered an eleven-year-old congressional memo revealing CIA deals with drug runners as far back as the early seventies. After George Bush became CIA director in January 1976, the memo said, the agency had squelched at least three big drug investigations or indictments to protect CIA operations.

In the face of such allegations, the General Accounting Office — Congress's investigative arm — tried to determine whether drug trafficking by U.S. allies influenced U.S. policy. The White House responded by banning all federal agencies from handing over any information to the GAO.

Soon after Noriega was indicted, the wind shifted in Meese's Drug Strategy Board: once again, international efforts and border interdiction were out, domestic "user accountability" was in.

~

The 1984 "bounty hunter" law and the Supreme Court's sanction of anonymous tips frequently combined to brew tragedy. On March 26, 1987, the Jeffersontown, Kentucky, police raided the home of twenty-four-year-old Jeffrey Miles because an anonymous tipster told them there was "a drug dealer" there. Miles, who had no criminal record, was killed by the raiding officers. No drugs were found in his house. A year later, San Diego police, acting on an anonymous tip, stormed the home of fifty-six-year-old Tommy Dubose, an instructor at the nearby naval air station. Dubose was shot dead by the police as he sat in his living room. No drugs were found in his home, either.

~

- Percentage of drug-trafficking defendants nationwide between 1985 and 1987 who were African-American: 99.

17

Anything and Everything

1988

There are two Americas. No other line you can draw is as trenchant as this. On one side, people of normal human appetites, for food and sex and creature comforts; on the other those who crave only the roar and crackle of their own neurons, hipped into a frenzy of synthetic euphoria. The Crack Nation. It is in our midst, but not part of us. . . .

— *Jerry Adler in* Newsweek, *November 28, 1988*

ON APRIL 9, 1988, the city of Los Angeles declared war on its poorest citizens, sending more than a thousand police officers into South Central to roust every young black man on the streets. "Tonight," a Los Angeles Police Department spokesman told reporters, "we pick 'em up for anything and everything."

More than 1,400 people — mostly young black men — were arrested and booked in mobile processing centers on charges ranging from illegal weapons to old parking tickets. Or they were picked up for violating curfews that applied only in poor black and Hispanic neighborhoods. Hundreds who weren't arrested had their names recorded in the LAPD's gang roster for further surveillance.

"This is war," Chief Daryl Gates said. "We're exceedingly angry. . . . We want to get the message out to the cowards out there — and that's what they are, rotten little cowards — we want the message to go out that we're going to come and get them."

Operation Hammer had begun.

Clearly something had to be done for South Central Los Angeles.

Between 1978 and 1982, southern California lost ten huge manufacturing plants — GM, Firestone, Goodyear, and others — and with them went 75,000 union jobs held largely by the blacks of South Central. More than 300 smaller warehouses and factories also fled South Central, many finding a new home in nearby affluent Orange County. By 1982, unemployment in South Central was half again as high as it had been in the early 1970s, and community purchasing power was down a third. The minimum wage was lower, in real terms, than it had been in the 1950s.

Then Reaganomics kicked in. The Federal Comprehensive Employment and Training Act (CETA) and the Job Corps were cut back or eliminated, putting an end to meaningful job training in South Central. A 1985 survey of public housing in the district found employed breadwinners in only a tenth of the households in some projects. Despite a southern California boom fueled by record defense spending, 40 percent of Los Angeles County's children lived below or barely above the poverty line, most of them in South Central. South Central's classrooms were more crowded than Mississippi's. Barely half of the district's children finished high school. Gangs, active since the early 1970s, claimed to have recruited a total of 50,000 members.

And then, in 1984, crack arrived.

The little rocks appeared all over LA right after Tootie Reese, the city's biggest coke dealer, got busted. Whatever order had existed in LA's cocaine trade evaporated as Reese's lieutenants each went his own way, employing the street gangs as dealers, runners, and muscle. Overnight, violence in South Central exploded through the roof. At times, not a day would go by without a gang killing. And the number of cocaine-poisoning cases in emergency rooms doubled.

The Los Angeles City Council seemed determined to make things worse. In 1987, the council changed the way it funded city parks to route more money to wealthy districts and only $30,000 to the 150 parks and rec centers in South Central. The Los Angeles Summer Job Program — a major source of black youth employment — also was eliminated. At the height of the crack wave, drug treatment wasn't a priority. No money was allocated for it in 1987, and treatment remains generally unavailable to low-income Angelenos.

Drug *dealing,* however, was a ghetto problem that Los Angeles was prepared to address. The city looked at all the problems facing the people of South Central — the plant closings, the flight of the middle class, the pinched school budgets, and more — and decided that crack was the sole source of the neighborhood's trouble. "A budget is a statement of priorities," said city council member Zev Yaroslavsky, head of the police-budget committee. "And if fighting gang violence in this city is our highest priority, it should be reflected in our budget" even though, Yaroslavsky acknowledged, "it will be at the expense of virtually anything else." Added council member Richard Alatorre, "This is the era of the police. If I were chief, I'd ask for more."

Night after night, Hammer teams roared through the neighborhoods of South Central. Any black kid seen out after dark was subject to a frisk and interrogation. "I think people believe that the only strategy we have is to put a lot of police officers on the street and harass people and make arrests for inconsequential kinds of things," Chief Gates said. "Well, that's part of the strategy, no question about it." The head of the LAPD's Hardcore Drug Squad compared South Central to Vietnam, an aptly bellicose metaphor.

In August, eighty-eight officers stormed a South Central apartment block suspected of being a gang headquarters. "This is a Class-A search," the captain in charge told his men. "That means carpets up, drywall down. Level it. Make it uninhabitable." The policemen followed orders, smashing furniture and walls with sledgehammers, ripping an outside stairway away from the building, and spray-painting "LAPD Rules" on the walls. At the stationhouse, thirty-two people captured in the raid were forced to whistle the theme song from the *Andy Griffith Show* (which LA historian Mike Davis calls "the Horst Wessel song of the LAPD") while being beaten with fists and flashlights. In the end, only two arrests were made: a couple of visiting teenagers had some dope in their pockets. No gang members, guns, or crack caches were found.

Nobody was killed in that particular raid. But by the end of 1988 LAPD officers had shot dead two unarmed citizens of South Central — a teenager suspected of being a gang member and an eighty-one-year-old retired construction worker. No disciplinary action was taken. "When you have a state of war, civil rights are suspended for the duration of the conflict," the press secretary for one state senator told reporters.

Hammer didn't rid South Central of crack and gang violence, even at the cost of civil liberties and civilian casualties. Although the LAPD had arrested, at one time or another, three-quarters of all the young black men in Los Angeles, juvenile crime was climbing 12 percent annually by the end of the decade. Crack was cheaper than ever, the gangs stronger, more violent, and better organized than before Hammer.

"Gangs are never goin' to die out," a sixteen-year-old gang member told the *Los Angeles Times* when Hammer started. "You all goin' to get us jobs?"

~

"The concept of user accountability is a fundamental theme throughout the drug strategy," Meese's 1988 National Drug Strategy report declared. "Individuals can, with proper treatment and incentive, stop using illegal drugs." The Strategy, though, was short on treatment and long on incentive. Of its twenty-four pages, ten were devoted to enforcement, interdiction, foreign operations, and "intelligence"; one was devoted to treatment. And of the four treatment objectives the only one to mention funding was number three: "Stimulate private sector involvement."

"We must do away with these previous talks of fairness and niceness," drug czar Ian MacDonald told the *Baltimore Sun*. "We've got to talk about sanctions."

~

Even in 1988 it was clear that blacks were being disproportionately targeted for drug arrest, and Meese — who hired the public relations firm Hill & Knowlton to polish the Drug War's image — was sensitive to charges that the War on Drugs was turning into a war on blacks. In March, he sent a memo to all of his U.S. attorneys encouraging selective prosecution of "middle and upper class users" in order to "send the message that there is no such thing as 'recreational' drug use." Nancy Reagan, too, swung her rhetorical guns temporarily at upper-class cokeheads. "The casual user may think when he takes a line of cocaine or smokes a joint in the privacy of his nice condo, listening to his expensive stereo, that he's somehow not bothering anyone," she said to a White House drug conference that year.

> But there is a trail of death and destruction that leads directly to his door. The casual user cannot morally escape responsibility for the action of drug traffickers and dealings. I'm saying that if you're a casual drug user you're an accomplice to murder.

Here was an argument with some potential. Anti-fur, anti-oil, anti–South Africa, anti-military, and a whole range of other activists had been making similar arguments for their causes for years. Cocaine is indeed a foul business, liberally stained with blood and corruption.

Harper's magazine had eight years earlier called on yuppies to boycott cocaine for exactly those reasons. Nancy Reagan, though, draped in fur and South African diamonds and cozy with all manner of morally questionable industries, was in no position to preach, and what might have been a valuable argument against cocaine received nothing but ridicule.

~

Admiral Paul Yost, now commandant of the Coast Guard, told Congress that "zero tolerance" meant the Coast Guard "will now, within the limits of the law, seize vessels and arrest individuals when 'personal use' quantities of illegal drugs are discovered." In April, the Coast Guard seized the $2.5 million yacht *Ark Royal* because ten marijuana seeds and two stems were found on board. The owner was able to recover the boat after paying $1,600 in fines and fees.

~

In keeping with zero tolerance, Congress introduced punishment without trial to American criminal law. It enacted a system of "civil" fines of up to $10,000 for certain drug offenses, imposed at the discretion of the attorney general and reviewable by a judge only at the defendant's expense. The law also let the government throw drug offenders and their families out of public housing and take away all of a drug offender's federal benefits, contracts, grants, student loans, mortgages, and licenses, even if the charge was only first-offense possession. Murderers, robbers, and rapists faced no such sanctions.

In two weekend-long offensives right after Washington announced its zero tolerance policy, police in Orange County, California, confiscated fifty-four cars worth a total of more than $300,000. Some of the drivers were charged only with misdemeanors because the quantities of drugs they possessed were so small, but they lost their cars anyway. Under the new federal guidelines, the police said, "Even if only a small amount of drugs is found inside . . . the law permits seized vehicles to be sold by law enforcement agencies to finance anti-drug law-enforcement programs."

~

Crack came late to Chicago. But in 1988 it hit especially hard. Ever since the 1950s, most of the city's low-income African-Americans have lived in towering, sweltering blocks of concrete rising out of treeless moonscapes built under the mantle of "urban renewal." Rent was pegged at 25 percent of family income, so anybody with a job and a salary got out, leaving only the poorest and idlest. Thousands of people live in each high-rise, jammed into tiny, airless apartments, dependent on dark and creaky elevators. A setting more similar to an urban prison than a neighborhood, it would be hard to imagine a more terrifying place for the turf wars associated with crack to break out.

Chicago's public housing was so bleak and violent that in 1988 HUD threatened to take it over. Former governor Richard Ogilvie — who twenty years earlier had recommended marijuana decriminalization to President Nixon's commission — agreed to manage the Chicago Housing Authority instead. Soon after, though, Ogilvie suffered a heart attack and died. The authority then turned to one of the most prominent black businessmen in the city, real estate developer Vincent Lane.

The elegant and mustachioed Lane agreed to try the job at $1 a year. Public housing in Chicago had always infuriated him. First the city flattens vibrant neighborhoods for suburbanites' highways, he'd say, then it crams 40,000 people into giant monoliths on the far side of those highways.

Lane held a series of meetings with project residents. He expected complaints about leaky faucets and broken appliances, but all they wanted to talk about was safety. Gunfire rattled between the buildings. Children slept in bathtubs for protection from stray bullets. Thugs charged old people a "tax" to use the elevators. After particularly violent nights, children stepped over pools of blood on their way to school.

Lane paid a visit to Chicago police superintendent Leroy Martin, a towering, coal-black, and impassive lawman. I've got to get control of my buildings, Lane told him. My residents can't take it anymore.

I don't know anything about law enforcement, Lane continued, but I watch TV. I see those movies about Pork Chop Hill: you surround the objective with enough men, you take it, you hold it. Let's do that with my buildings. Storm in, take the place, search every apartment, get the drugs and the guns, set up security guards in the lobbies, issue photo IDs to all residents. . . .

Hold on, Martin interrupted. We can't do that. It's illegal. The Chicago Police Department can't perform warrantless searches on 40,000 people. Besides, where are you going to get the money?

I'll take the money out of operations, Lane said. To hell with fixing faucets.

They haggled. Martin agreed to provide men for raids. But his men would only secure the area and stand in the halls. CHA people would have to perform the searches. Lane and Martin agreed they'd call these "inspections" — a landlord can legitimately eyeball his property. If the authority's inspectors found guns or drugs, the police would be standing right there to make the arrest.

Operation Clean Sweep was launched in September 1988. Hundreds of uniformed cops barreled into the buildings and authority officials pawed through refrigerators, drawers, and closets. They picked locks and broke latches where necessary. Without warrants, the authority inspectors merely pounded on doors and shouldered their way inside.

The real test for Lane wasn't the first high-rise hit, but the second. By then, word had gotten out. As police surrounded the building and began making their way upstairs, guns, syringes, and crack vials rained out of windows and clattered onto the pavement below.

~

Urban murders, declining for years, rose sharply as crack took hold. Paul Goldstein, the researcher who had introduced Nick Kozel to his first crack users, decided to examine the phenomenon. More than half of the 414 murders committed in New York City during eight months of 1988 were classified by the police as "drug-related," and most of those involved crack. But Goldstein, a deadpan, gravel-voiced man best known as the author of the study of addict economics *Taking Care of Business,* was an inveterate skeptic. And when he examined the circumstances of those 218 "drug-related" murders, he found only 31 of them were caused by the psychological effects of drugs. In two-thirds of those cases, moreover, the drug was alcohol. The effects of crack could be blamed for only five murders — and in two of those alcohol was also involved. In only one case could crack alone be said to have driven the killer to his deed.

Only 2 percent of the "drug-related" killings were committed by people stealing to buy drugs.

All the rest — fully three-quarters — were committed by dealers battling over territory. This was a byproduct of drug *prohibition,* Goldstein wrote, not of the drugs themselves. Alcohol, whose mood-altering effects caused twenty times more murders than crack, naturally caused no prohibition-related killings.

~

Minutes before the Senate was to vote on yet another big drug bill, Senator Jesse Helms of North Carolina introduced an amendment to create a specific mandatory minimum sentence just for possession of crack cocaine. Merely possessing five grams of crack — about one day's supply for a serious addict — would now carry a five-year sentence with no parole. Faced with the choice of approving a draconian new sentence with no debate or appearing soft on crack, Helms's colleagues voted yea. The House went along, too. "Crack is an extraordinarily dangerous drug so we must take extraordinary steps to combat it," Congressman Clay Shaw of Florida said.

Crack, though, is no more dangerous than cocaine. Crack *is* cocaine; the difference is in how it's ingested. But the new law created a huge disparity between the sentences for crack and for powder. To get the same five years, a defendant would have to possess 100 times as much powdered cocaine.

Not only is the disparity senseless, it's plainly racist. As many as 90 percent of crack dealers are black, while dealers in powder tend to be white.

~

Bob Randall and NORML scored a victory on the opposition's playing field. They amassed sufficient evidence to convince the DEA's own administrative law judge that marijuana should be rescheduled and allowed as medicine in cases of cancer, AIDS, glaucoma, and paralysis.

Although marijuana can be harmful if abused, DEA judge Francis Young wrote on September 6, 1988, "Marijuana in its natural form is one of the safest therapeutically active substances known to man."

Having read and heard the testimony of dozens of doctors, patients, and public health administrators, Young concluded that "it is clear beyond any question that many people find marijuana to have . . . accepted medical use in treatment in the United States." Moreover, "uncontroverted evidence in this record indicates that marijuana was being used therapeutically by mankind 2,000 years before the Birth of Christ."

Young declared "specious" the argument that rescheduling marijuana might "send a signal" that marijuana is okay to smoke for fun. "The fear of sending such a signal cannot be permitted to override the legitimate need, amply demonstrated in this record, of countless sufferers for the relief marijuana can provide when prescribed by a physician in a legitimate case."

Sixteen years after Randall and NORML began the push to get marijuana approved as medicine, Young recommended that DEA director Jack Lawn immediately do so. To do otherwise, Young concluded, "would be unreasonable, arbitrary, and capricious."

The antidrug orthodoxy could not accept such a recommendation. Jack Lawn held Young's recommendation for fifteen months and then rejected it. The doctors Young listened to, Lawn wrote, have "ties to NORML and [are] in favor of legalizing marijuana." As for the patients who testified before Judge Young — such as Bob Randall — "most of these individuals used marijuana recreationally prior to discovery of their illness." Their testimony, therefore, was without value.

Lawn was correct that several of the doctors who testified before Young had ties to NORML. Upon learning of the drug's medical usefulness, several had become consultants or contributors to the organization devoted to enabling its use. The most prominent of them, Dr. Lester Grinspoon of Harvard Medical School, became interested in marijuana twenty-six years earlier after finding it helped his leukemia-stricken teenage son endure chemotherapy. If the doctors had something to gain by marijuana's rescheduling, Lawn and the DEA had a great deal to lose. Medical marijuana, they felt, was the narrow edge of the legalization wedge. With marijuana a Schedule I illegal drug, the country had 45 million illegal drug users, and the DEA's budget reflected that. Were marijuana legal, the number of illegal drug users would slip to about 5 million. The "drug problem" would be reduced by some 90 percent, and the budget of the country's drug enforcement agency would likely be tailored accordingly.

A decrease in property crime might have been expected from the crackdown on drugs, on the theory that addicts steal and rob to support their habits. But when two Florida State University economists put that theory to the test, they found the opposite. In Florida, they discovered, where annual drug arrests had doubled since 1982, burglary, robbery, and auto theft all increased by as much as 65 percent. Lawmen couldn't blame higher drug prices, because the price of cocaine in Miami fell from about $30,000 to about $15,000 a kilo.

Heavy enforcement not only failed to drive up the price of drugs, it also appeared to encourage other types of crime. When police turned most of their attention to drug enforcement, they eased up on other crimes and made them easier to commit.

Skeptical of their own findings, the FSU economists looked at Illinois crime and arrest statistics for the same period. The story was similar there. Drug arrests in Illinois rose 69 percent during the decade, doubling the number of drug offenders in the state's prisons. In Illinois, it wasn't property crime but traffic enforcement that appeared to suffer. Drunk-driving arrests declined by almost a quarter during the War on Drugs, at a time traffic deaths rose more than a tenth. "Nothing less than a repeal of the laws of economics is required for the state to avoid the costs of the drug war," the FSU economists wrote. "More dangerous highways appear to be a significant consequence of Illinois's war on drugs."

Florida and Illinois were typical in their zeal to send drug offenders to prison at the expense of incarcerating other, perhaps more dangerous, criminals. The War on Drugs doubled the nation's prison population during the Reagan administration. The portion of state prisoners inside for drugs went from one in fifteen to one in three, and 85 percent of them were in for mere possession.

Thanks to the War on Drugs and the racial disparity in cocaine sentences, the country now had a higher rate of black male incarceration than South Africa; one in four young black men were either in jail, in prison, on parole, or on probation.*

Such vigorous prosecution of even minor drug offenders required the Justice Department to divert resources from other duties. According to its own figures, the duty that suffered most was enforcement of federal regulations. While drug prosecutions doubled in the last half of the Reagan administration, the prosecution of regulatory crime rose only 16 percent. Similarly, federal suspects most likely to be prosecuted were drug offenders, and those least likely to be prosecuted — barely more than a third of the time — were regulatory suspects.

As the country finished the Reagan years, county governments

* For whites, it was one in sixteen.

were spending $2 billion more on criminal justice every year than they were on education, which is remarkable considering counties don't pay for imprisonment but do finance virtually all K–12 education. Nationally, spending on education rose only 70 percent during the Reagan administration while spending on prisons and police rose almost 600 percent. This during a decade when the rate of all crimes except murder dropped or stayed flat. And dropout rates soared. And testing scores plummeted.

~

Plenty has been written about the racial element of George Bush's "Willie Horton" campaign in 1988. But his campaign rhetoric about crime and drugs was more than just fear mongering against blacks. Bush also was continuing the work begun by Don Santarelli and Richard Nixon in 1968 — discrediting the suggestion that social pressures such as poverty and racism play a role in creating crime, and promoting the notion that, like all other social problems, crime is entirely the fault of bad people making bad choices.

Liberals like Michael Dukakis, Bush said to Ohio policemen a month before the election, are "lost in the thickets of liberal sociology. Just as when it comes to foreign policy, they always 'Blame America First,' when it comes to crime and criminals, they always seem to 'Blame Society First.' "

Education Secretary William Bennett heartily agreed. Bennett had been preaching "personal responsibility" — as opposed to social responsibility — since his days at the NEH. Bush and Bennett always got along, but it was an incident during the 1988 campaign that welded the bond. On *Meet the Press* one Sunday morning, Bennett once again attacked the "liberal elite." "They have disdain for the simple and basic patriotism of most Americans," Bennett said. "They think they're smarter than everybody else. That bothers me. I think it should bother a lot of people."

Immediately after the show, Bush called to congratulate and thank Bennett. "Keep in touch after the election," the candidate told him.

Some six weeks after Bush's victory, Bennett telephoned Bush. "Mr. President," he said, "I don't know what you're planning to do about the drug job. But if you are really serious about it, and want someone to go after it for you, I'll volunteer." Bush thanked him and said he'd keep that in mind.

Bennett also called his good friend New Hampshire governor

John Sununu — Bush's chief of staff designate — and lobbied for the job. He called several times. Finally, Bennett, Bush, and Sununu met, and Bennett outlined his ideas for the drug job. At the Education Department, Bennett explained, I always wanted less money and less federal involvement. In the drug czar's job, he said, I'll want a big budget. "This is one issue, Mr. President, where I, a conservative Republican, feel comfortable advocating a strong federal role."

"Well Bill," Bush said, standing to shake his hand and offer him the drug czar's job, "so do I."

- Percentage of Michigan's budget that went to the state's prisons in 1984: 2.8.
- In 1988: 7.2.
- Percentage of Michigan's budget that went to the state's schools in 1984: 36.6.
- In 1988: 30.1.
- Number of people Florida imprisoned per month in 1985: 180.
- In 1988: 780.

18

The Hill of the Moment

1989

We must avoid the easy temptation to blame our troubles first on those chronic problems of social environment — like poverty and racism — which help to breed and spread the contagion of drug use.

— *William Bennett's first National Drug Control Strategy, 1989*

It's time to shift the primary focus from racism, the traditional enemy from without, to self-defeating patterns of behavior, the new enemy within.

— *U.S. Senator Charles Robb, Democrat of Virginia, 1989*

WHEN WILLIAM BENNETT moved across town from the Department of Education to be czar at the Office of National Drug Control Policy, he brought his people with him. All white, all male, none with law enforcement or social service experience, some had been with Bennett the entire eight years since his debut at the National Endowment for the Humanities.

Bennett's men held themselves above the mere budget cutters, tax slashers, regulation busters, and states rightsers that made up the broader executive branch. John Walters, Bennett's chief of staff at Education and author of the punitive *Schools Without Drugs,* had been to meetings of Ed Meese's Drug Policy Board and had been appalled at their inanity. Everybody was so busy jockeying for position that nobody ever ventured an honest opinion or original idea. Bennett's office, on the other hand, prided itself on being one continuous philosophy forum, with great questions of political theory and national purpose the stuff of daily conversation. Envisioning themselves a kind of ideological *Bennettista* cavalry to the Republican infantry, Bennett's crew saw their mission at the drug office as fundamentally identical to that at Education or the Endowment:

To reform America's character, by force if necessary.

It would have been okay with them to be assigned teen pregnancy, abortion, welfare — any platform from which to harangue the public about values and exact punishment for transgression. "Drugs are the hill we're fighting over at the moment, but the war is much bigger than that," Bruce Carnes, Bennett's budget director, would say. "Our fight is any issue that has a shade on character."

The "hill" they'd just been given to fight over, though, wasn't just any piece of political turf, but was the hottest hot-button issue of the decade. More than half the country believed drugs to be America's worst problem. Majorities favored mandatory drug tests for all citizens, warrantless police searches of suspected dealers' homes, and roadblocks to search cars randomly. This wasn't mere naked paintings or politically correct social studies textbooks. This was a chance to preach and kick ass on the nation's brightly lit center stage.

Even before Bennett's Senate confirmation, his men began plotting their course. The same 1988 law that created the drug czar's office also required it to produce a drug-control strategy by September, and there was no time to waste. Bennett himself wasn't around much. He'd checked himself into a $700-a-week therapeutic resort to kick his two-pack-a-day cigarette habit. But in the lofty and freewheeling style to which they'd become accustomed, Bennett's core group of advisers began laying out the assumptions on which national drug policy would hereafter be based.

At this point, the United States had been fighting its War on Drugs for twenty years. Despite the billions spent, the millions imprisoned, and the loss of liberties to both drug user and nonuser alike, drugs were cheaper, more potent, and used by younger children than when Nixon started the war. The drug cartels were wealthier and more sophisticated than ever. The number of cocaine dependents had grown. Drug violence, unheard of at the start of the Drug War, now terrorized poor neighborhoods. Drug combatants died daily; just the number of slain innocent bystanders had tripled in the two years prior to Bush's inauguration.

Rather than evaluate the efficacy of the War on Drugs and the wisdom of pursuing it, Bennett and his men merely shuffled the deck one more time. Under Nixon, heroin was the big bad drug. Halfway through Carter's reign, marijuana nudged it aside. As the public's passion to fight marijuana waned, cocaine was thrust forward to draw fire. Then crack. The Drug War front shifted endlessly too, from the border to the streets to Bolivia to the money-laundering banks to the suburbs and back to the border again.

Now it was the Bennettistas' turn, and they achieved the most radical recasting of the country's "drug problem" yet:

Drugs would no longer be discussed as a health problem.

The physical dangers of illegal drugs had always been the Drug War's *causa belli.* Even the "zero tolerance" policy of the late Reagan years was couched in the rhetoric of "instantaneous addiction" and "the poisoning of our children": health terminology.

That had to stop. Because if the drug issue was going to serve the Bennettistas' decade-long crusade to police the nation's character, drug abuse needed to be placed in the same category as offensive art, multicultural teaching, and ethical relativism: a matter of *morality.*

"The simple fact is that drug use is wrong," Bennett decreed. "And the moral argument, in the end, is the most compelling argument." Terence Pell, Bennett's personal lawyer from Education and now the drug office's chief counsel, put it this way: "We have to *believe.* If you think drugs are bad, that they make people bad neighbors, horrible parents, dangerous drivers and what have you, then you think drugs are bad. There's a moral dimension."

If drugs are a health problem, then addicts are "sick," and that cast them in a sympathetic light the Bennettistas felt addicts didn't deserve. The decision to take drugs that first time, after all, is voluntary. Walters directly attacked the old approach. "The health people say 'no stigma,' " he would say, "and I'm for stigma."

The medical model of drug abuse was to Bennett's men a philosophic and practical morass. If you base prohibition on drugs' health effects, what do you say to the millions of occasional users who convincingly claim to be uninjured by the drugs they took? If you acknowledge that heavy drug users are sick, you create an expectation that the government will treat them.

The biggest problem with basing a prohibitive drug policy on the health risks, though, was the invitation to comparisons. The year the chain-smoking Bennett became drug czar, tobacco killed some 395,000 Americans — more than died in both world wars. Alcohol directly killed 23,000 and another 22,400 on the highways. The Natural Resources Defense Council in March published a report, widely praised by medical authorities, estimating that as many as 5,500 Americans would develop cancer from the pesticides they ate during their preschool years. The incidence of breast cancer in American women had more than doubled since World War II, owing largely to dioxin and other pollutants.

Cocaine, on the other hand, killed 3,618 people that year, slightly fewer than died from anterior horn cell disease. Heroin and other opiates killed 2,743. And no death from marijuana has ever been recorded.*

Drugs damage without killing, of course, but even here other preventable health problems put illegal drugs in deep shade. The General Accounting Office, Congress's nonpartisan investigative agency, estimated that some 350,000 people were using cocaine daily in 1989. While that's a big number, 15 times that many children were going to bed hungry at least once a month that year, 50 times that many Americans were sleeping on the streets, and 100 times that many had no health insurance.

Discussing drugs as a moral problem obviated such comparisons. If the case could be made that drug use is simply *wrong*, then it wouldn't matter that some people use drugs safely, that alcohol and tobacco kill more people than reefer and smack, that more American than European children know hunger.

The Bennettistas worked hard to address the inconsistencies of their approach. Their most glaring problem was the new drug czar himself. By any medical definition, Bennett was a drug addict, so dependent on nicotine after giving up the drug in its smokable form that he now carried everywhere a pack of nicotine chewing gum and was up to 40 milligrams of nicotine a day — about as much as in two packs of cigarettes.

Alcohol was another problem. Bennett's drug office had no congressional mandate to address it, his mainstream constituency enjoyed it, and the multimillion-dollar alcohol lobby wouldn't stand for further restrictions on booze. So the drug office needed somehow to place alcohol on the "moral" side of the line. No small trick. Aside from the cirrhosis and highway deaths, booze was implicated in violent crime to a much greater degree than any illegal drug. The Justice Department found that half of those convicted of homicide in 1989 were using alcohol at the time of the killing, while fewer than 6 percent said they were on drugs alone.

Bennett's men tiptoed through the minefield of alcohol and tobacco. John Walters took the position that marijuana, cocaine, and heroin "enslave people" and "prevent them from being free citizens"

* These figures are from eighty-seven medical examiners in twenty-seven metropolitan areas.

in a way that alcohol and tobacco do not. Bruce Carnes decided that drug taking was "life-denying" and "inward," but that using alcohol or tobacco was not. Illegal drugs, Bennett said in a speech that May, "obliterate morals, value, character, our relations with each other, and our relation to God." None of these conclusions was based on science, but collectively they had the effect of royal fiat.

The Bennettistas also relied on a neat bit of tautology: marijuana, heroin, and cocaine are immoral because they are illegal. Why are they illegal? Because they are immoral. Compliance, not health, was the real issue. "Now that the government has spoken to the subject that drugs are unlawful," said Paul McNulty, a Bennettista soul mate directing communications at the Justice Department, "a person who disobeys the law has made a moral choice and should be dealt with appropriately." Bennett freely admitted drug enforcement was but an instrument of a wider agenda, calling for "the reconstitution of legal and social authority through the imposition of appropriate consequences for drug dealing and drug use." "The drug crisis," he told the Washington Hebrew congregation, "is a crisis of authority, in every sense of the term, 'authority.' "

Consequently, "a massive wave of arrests is a top priority for the War on Drugs," Bennett announced. Washington, D.C., had arrested 45,000 of its citizens for drugs in the two years prior to Bennett's appointment, "without making an appreciable dent in either the drug trade or the murder rate," *Newsweek* noted. But Bennett wanted more of the same. On the day he was sworn in, he declared the city a "high intensity drug trafficking area" and unveiled a massive plan to fight drugs in the nation's capital. More than eighty federal agents would bolster the city's drug squad. A curfew would sweep the streets of minors after 11 P.M. A judge ruled the curfew unconstitutional, but the mood was infectious. Some members of Congress suggested declaring de facto martial law — placing the D.C. police under federal control and sending in the army and National Guard. Of the $100 million Bennett wanted spent in D.C., 95 percent was for law enforcement. Of that, more than half would go to a new prison, and until that could be built, Bennett proposed converting abandoned military buildings into makeshift drug prisons. As for the purpose of all this new incarceration, Bennett was characteristically blunt: "I'm not a person who says that the first purpose of punishment is rehabilitation," he told Congress. "The first purpose is moral, to exact a price for transgressing the rights of others."

~

Pregnant women would pay the highest price "for transgressing the rights of others" in Bennett's War on Drugs. No other group of drug users was treated as harshly by the media, the legislatures, or the courts. No other group took as much blame for the failure of the nation at large to act with reason and compassion. Having turned its wrath variously on Negro junkies, teenage potheads, yuppie coke dabblers, and black crack dealers, the Drug War now would elevate pregnant drug users — often poor, uneducated, and unable to get treatment — to Public Enemy Number One.

The proximate roots of the "crack baby crisis" were in 1981, when federal cuts in Medicaid stripped more than a million poor mothers and their kids of access to medical care. Within a few years, half of all African-American women had access to poor prenatal care or none at all, and the effects showed up at once. By 1984, their infant mortality rate had noticeably worsened for the first time in twenty years — and this was a full year before crack appeared. The number of uninsured child-bearing women in California exploded by almost half between 1982 and 1986. And even those who qualified for public assistance weren't guaranteed access to care. Twelve of the state's fifty-eight counties had no doctors at all willing to accept Medicaid patients. Flu, infections, and pneumonia killed impoverished American babies in ever-greater numbers.

And then crack arrived on the scene.

Crack is bad news for pregnant women and their babies. Like men, women on crack binges neglect everything else — sleep, nutrition, safety, and their health in general. They tend to smoke cigarettes, drink alcohol, and use other drugs to moderate the intense highs and lows of crack.

Their babies show the effects. They are frequently premature, and on average smaller and lighter, with smaller heads. When suddenly deprived of cocaine they alternately howl and drop into deep sleep. At one Washington, D.C., hospital where the average neonatal stay was three days in 1989, babies born to crack-using mothers stayed an average forty-two days.

By 1989 scientists had had four years to study the phenomenon of "crack babies" and some were backing off from their initially alarming reports. Ira Chasnoff, the Chicago doctor whose 1985 article in the *New England Journal of Medicine* started the crack-baby panic, now cautioned that crack was only a small part of the problem for small, undernourished, and sickly babies. Pregnant women are sixteen times more likely to use alcohol than crack, he wrote, and unlike cocaine, alcohol has proven fetus-damaging effects. Chasnoff and other researchers cautioned that the lives of poor, crack-using women were bad for babies in so many ways that there was no way to isolate crack as the primary cause of their infants' health problems. Poor women have always birthed smaller and sicker babies, and the sharp increase in the number of poor, uninsured women was certain to boost the number of ailing newborns. Prenatal care — and the insurance to pay for it — was and is a better predictor of a newborn's health than whether the mother smokes crack. "In the end," Florida health officials concluded in 1985, "it is safer for a baby to be born to a drug-abusing, anemic, or a diabetic mother who visits the doctor throughout her pregnancy than to be born to a normal woman who does not." The Yerkes Primate Research Center in Atlanta tried to isolate cocaine's effects, administering a pure cocaine intravenous drip to rhesus monkeys for the entire duration of their pregnancies. Their babies were unaffected. Researchers of human "crack babies" furthermore found that the effects of cocaine wore off within a few months and that such babies who were well fed, loved, and properly stimulated could recover completely.

These were not, however, messages even the medical community wanted to hear. Research papers trumpeting the fetal dangers of cocaine were eleven times more likely to be published in professional journals than those claiming few or no harms, according to the British medical journal *The Lancet,* which analyzed all the "crack baby" studies submitted to the Society of Pediatric Research during the eighties. Moreover, the "negative" studies were better, controlling more effectively for other fetus-damaging factors and taking more care to verify cocaine use, *The Lancet* found.

Yet the myth of the "crack baby" grew ever larger. Syndicated columnist Charles Krauthammer dismissed "crack babies" in 1988 as a "biologic underclass whose biological inferiority is stamped at birth." Boston University president John Silber criticized "spending immense amounts on crack babies who won't ever achieve the intellectual development to have consciousness of God." The *New York Times* declared "crack babies" unable to "make friends, know right from wrong, control their impulses, gain insight, concentrate on tasks, and feel and return love." Even *Rolling Stone* condemned "crack babies" as "like no others, brain damaged in ways yet unknown, oblivious to any affection."

Reporters sent out to write "crack baby" stories sometimes got their facts right without knowing it. After forty-odd inches of horror stories of low-income women giving birth to "crack babies," the *Wall Street Journal,* in a typical July 1989 front-page article, let drop that "their mothers aren't all low income. Linda, an impeccably dressed

34-year-old, now looks more like the accountant she once was than a recovering addict who once had a $2,000-a-week crack habit." Turns out, the *Journal* reported, "her son was born healthy." No explanation was offered as to why a woman smoking $2,000 worth of crack a week can give birth to a healthy baby. And no connection was made to the fact that, unlike every other mother in the article, Linda is an impeccably dressed accountant who likely had health insurance and proper care.

Getting poor women to stop using drugs during pregnancy wouldn't have guaranteed healthy babies, but it certainly would have helped. Even if the effects of drug exposure *in utero* are relatively short-lived, the home of a crack addict is no place for a baby to grow up. Infants of crack users frequently show up in the hospital again, dehydrated, underfed, filthy, and sometimes injured. If only for the sake of babies after they are born, getting pregnant women off drugs would have been not only humane, but a genuine bargain. The cost of caring for babies neglected and abandoned by crack-using parents was estimated in 1989 in the hundreds of millions of dollars a year.

Yet the federal government refused to pay for residential drug treatment for the poor because it classified drug abuse as a mental illness, and under Medicaid rules that was a state responsibility. The states were similarly unwilling or unable to provide care. Of the various drug-treatment programs in New York City in 1989, 54 percent refused pregnant women, 67 percent refused pregnant women on Medicaid, and 87 percent specifically denied treatment to Medicaid women dependent on crack. Only one hospital in the entire Chicago metropolitan area had a residential treatment program for pregnant addicts, and the program had only two beds. The state of Indiana had only sixteen beds for the treatment of pregnant addicts. Nearly a third of the women living in California had no prenatal care at all, let alone treatment for prenatal drug abuse. "We seem more willing to place the kid in a neonatal intensive care unit for $1,500 or $2,000 a day, rather than put $1,500 into better prenatal care," one psychiatrist complained to *Time*.

Jennifer Johnson, a black twenty-three-year-old mother of three living in Seminole County, Florida, tried several times during her fourth pregnancy to get treated for her cocaine addiction. "I thought that . . . if I tell them I use drugs they would send me to a drug place or something," she later testified. Alas, there was no "drug place" for her in Seminole County. What there was instead was jail, and the confiscation of her newborn.

When she delivered her baby on January 23, 1989, the attending doctor recorded that the baby "looked and acted as we would expect a baby to look and act." But Johnson told the doctor she had used cocaine during the pregnancy, and urine tests on mother and child bore that out. The hospital reported the birth of a "crack baby" to a state child-protection agency, which in turn called the local sheriff, who ordered Johnson's arrest.

Assistant state's attorney Jeff Deen had been waiting for just such a case to test a new prosecution tactic. Deen was fed up with seeing pregnant women get away with abusing their unborn children by using drugs. When Deen heard about Jennifer Johnson, he decided to charge her with delivering cocaine to a minor. Courts throughout the country had held to the legal doctrine — which lies at the heart of abortion rights — that a fetus is not a person in the eyes of the law. But Deen had a new argument: In the sixty seconds between the baby's birth and the cutting of her umbilical cord, Johnson had "delivered" cocaine to her baby through the cord.

Judge O. H. Eaton Jr. of the Seminole County Circuit Court declared himself "convinced" and convicted Johnson, sentencing her to a year of house arrest and fourteen years probation. Jennifer Johnson thus became the first woman to be convicted of the special crime of using drugs while pregnant. The Court of Appeals for the Fifth District affirmed her conviction.

Given Johnson's repeated attempts to find treatment for her drug abuse, Eaton's decision seems particularly cruel. "Pregnant addicts . . . have a responsibility to seek treatment," he ruled. The same judicial reasoning applied in the 1988 prosecution of a heroin addict in Butte County, California, who was convicted of birthing a drug-tainted baby after making Herculean efforts to get treatment. For months, she traveled 130 miles round-trip to a private methadone clinic that charged $200 a month. When her car broke down, she hitchhiked. When her money ran out, the clinic stopped treating her, even knowing she was seven months gone. Visibly pregnant, she asked several doctors and clinics in her area to help her, but none would do so. Twenty-four hours after giving birth, the district attorney confiscated her baby and charged her. "I don't see people making a choice unless you force them," he explained.

As has often been the case in the War on Drugs, the drug warriors wanted it both ways. Drugs are immoral, Bennett's drug office was saying at the time, because they "enslave" people and "take away their ability to function as free citizens." Yet when people fall into the "slavery" of drug use, they are prosecuted for making a bad "choice."

It is no accident that the first woman prosecuted for prenatal drug abuse was black. During a single month in 1989, Ira Chasnoff and his colleagues collected urine samples from every pregnant woman who visited a public health clinic or private obstetrician in Pinellas County, which contains St. Petersburg and is the fourth most populous county in Florida. They found that equal percentages of both black and white women — about 15 percent — used drugs during pregnancy. But the black women were ten times more likely than the whites to be reported to authorities for drug use. And the poorest women — with incomes of less than $12,000 — were seven times more likely to be reported than those earning more than $25,000. Private hospitals and obstetricians weren't about to intrude on their paying customers' privacy with a drug test, but public hospitals often were required to do so. Typical was South Carolina, where one characteristic used by public hospitals to identify "probable drug users" for testing was "no prenatal care or late prenatal care (24 weeks)." In South Carolina, Medicaid doesn't cover prenatal care before nineteen weeks.

"If these mothers were walking away from treatment, I might feel differently," said the director of Family and Children's Services in San Francisco. "But they are not walking away from treatment. They are walking away from waiting lists."

With drugs at the top of every pollster's list, the country walked away from treating pregnant users. In one national poll, almost half thought prenatal drug abuse should be a criminal offense. Which perhaps isn't surprising, given such headlines as (in the *Washington Post*) CRACK BABIES: THE WORST THREAT IS MOM HERSELF and SHE SMOKED CRACK, THEN KILLED HER CHILDREN. Senator Pete Wilson of California in 1990 asked Congress to give treatment funding only to states that make it a crime to give birth to a drug-tainted baby, a classic Catch-22: few pregnant women would seek drug treatment in a state where doing so invited jail and loss of the baby. In Florida, where such a law was already on the books, doctors complained to the *St. Petersburg Times* that pregnant women withheld important information about their drug use "because word had gotten around that the police will have to be notified." San Francisco deputy city attorney Lori Giorgi began noticing an increase in "toilet-bowl babies" — born at home or in secret. "They're afraid their babies will be taken away," she concluded.

If they birth them at all. In one Washington, D.C., case, a woman "miscarried" days before appearing before a judge who'd threatened to jail her because he thought she was using drugs while pregnant. Researchers reported being told often about such abortions. This is particularly ironic, since the movement to prosecute drug-using mothers gets much of its steam from the anti-abortion movement. Such prosecutions create a legal division between mother and fetus that doesn't exist elsewhere in the law. If a woman can be prosecuted for drugging her unborn baby, why not for killing it?

~

We're not writing some technical document here, Bennett told his staff as they brainstormed their *Drug Control Strategy.* We don't have time. The strategy is about who we are as a nation and what we *believe.*

Bennett lounged back in his desk chair, feet up, jacket off, obsessively shelling and masticating sunflower seeds to take his mind off cigarettes. Papery shells covered the carpet. Carnes and the others took to calling Bennett's office "the aviary."

David Tell sat across from Bennett, legal pad on lap, jotting notes. Tell had abandoned the Democratic Party only three years earlier — at age twenty-six — to work as Bennett's speechwriter. He liked to wear high-top Converse basketball sneakers with his shirt and tie, which, with his high forehead, wild red hair, and glasses, gave him the air of a boy physicist. Sitting near him was his twin wunderkind from Bennett's Education Department, Dan Casse. A year younger than Tell, Casse looked instead like a boy investment banker — strict buttoned-down clothes, perfect hair, and an affected severity; when he spoke, his lips barely moved. Canadian by birth, Casse had managed *The Public Interest* magazine before a year at Harvard's Kennedy School of Government and joining Bennett.

Like Dick Williams a decade earlier, Bennett was uninterested in hard-core addicts. They're lost already, he said, and they're too small a group. We want to reach everyone.

User accountability, said Tell.

Right, Bennett said. There is no such thing as innocent drug use, and those who have even the barest contact with drugs should be punished a lot more severely.

Casse spoke up. I studied under James Q. Wilson at the Kennedy School, he said. He posits a contagion model. It isn't hard-core users that spread drug abuse, because everyone can see they're a mess and nobody wants to be like them. Instead, it's the casual user, the one whose life hasn't fallen apart, that is the vector for drug abuse, because he makes it look like you can use drugs and not pay a price.

I like it, Bennett said.

When Casse and Tell sat down to write Bennett's *Drug Strategy,* they leaned hard on Wilson's "contagion" theory. The typical cocaine user, the *Strategy* asserts, is likely to be "white, male, a high-school graduate, employed full time. . . ." This type must be singled out for punishment, Casse and Tell wrote, because he is "likely to have a still-intact family, social and work life. He is likely still to 'enjoy' his drug for the pleasure it offers." That drugs are dangerous isn't the issue; it's that they're illegal — and that their use is defiance of authority — that matters. In the fourteen-page introduction to the *Strategy,* the health consequences of drug abuse got one paragraph.

The National Institute on Drug Abuse threw Bennett a curve ball in July 1989, just two months before the *Strategy* was due, by reporting dramatic reductions, since 1985, in drug abuse among the nonaddicted public. With the exception of daily cokeheads, every age, geographical, and ethnic group was reporting less drug use — in some cases as much as 48 percent less than five years earlier.

So much for the contagion theory.

Casse and Tell dismissed the NIDA report in two paragraphs, calling it "very good news" but "difficult to square with commonsense perceptions . . . a wealth of other, up-to-date evidence suggests that our drug problem is getting worse, not better."

The first piece of evidence they cited was "fear." "Fear of drugs and attendant crime is at an all-time high," they reported. Upon that fear the Bennettistas based their drug-control policy.

Bennett's *Strategy* got in its licks at crack-using mothers, too. "Young women are one of the fastest growing crack-user groups," it reads. On page 2, the *Strategy* claims they give birth to 200,000 tainted babies a year. By page 44, that number is down to 100,000. Whatever. No federal treatment dollars for pregnant women would be forthcoming, but rather "states would be encouraged to make outreach efforts."

While Bennett did ask Congress to boost the federal treatment budget an impressive 52 percent, he wanted drug enforcement spending more than doubled, creating a three-to-one ratio in spending on the "hard" and "soft" sides of drug policy. The single biggest item in his proposed drug budget was a breathtaking 130 percent increase for new federal prisons. For the first time in history, prisons would cost as much as the entire judicial branch of government.

~

On paper Michael Quinlan was the big winner in Bennett's *Drug Strategy*. But he wasn't a happy man.

Quinlan, a mild, sandy-haired man of forty-six, had chosen a career in corrections after hearing a single lecture about it as a student at George Washington Law School. The idea of turning criminals into law-abiding citizens combined psychology, ethics, and the law in a way that intrigued him. Right out of law school in 1971, Quinlan joined the Federal Bureau of Prisons. In 1989 he was its director.

The public passion for "turning criminals into law-abiding citizens," Quinlan believed, had mutated into a desire simply to warehouse them. In the old days, members of Congress liked to tour the federal prison at Butner, North Carolina, the most humane and cleverly managed in the system. Now when members of Congress wanted to see — and be photographed at — a federal prison, it was always the one at Marion, Illinois. Marion was the toughest prison in the system, a hard, brutal place whose only goal was keeping bad guys from escaping. The change in high-level interest saddened Quinlan.

His budget had doubled in the past year, and it stood to double again in the coming year. He was glad for that, certainly. But Congress could double his budget again the year after next and then again, and he wouldn't have enough money to incarcerate humanely all the people Congress wanted sent to prison. Everybody from the White House to the Hill wanted more drug crimes federalized, more drug cases swept into federal court, longer sentences, and reductions in plea bargaining, parole, and probation. The whole process was out of control.

Nobody was talking to Quinlan. Members of Congress would invite him up to testify, but eyes glazed over when he described what happened to the masses of people sentenced under ever-tougher drug laws. Congress just wanted to "look tough." It was even talking about cutting the amount of time a prisoner could get off for good behavior from 180 days per sentenced year to 54. That would deal corrections a double blow — reducing prisoners' incentive to behave themselves while further jamming the institutions. A disaster! Quinlan sent memo after memo to Deputy Attorney General Don Aire: please include me in your planning sessions. Let's create a working group for both the federal law-enforcement agencies and the Bureau of Prisons. We must all understand the ramifications of policy.

No response.

~

- Percentage of the nation's sixteen- to thirty-five-year-old black men arrested during 1989: 35.
- Percentage of black men who said in 1980 they could earn "more on the street doing something illegal than on a straight job": 44.
- Percentage who said the same thing in 1989: 66.
- Federal funds paid to drug informants in 1987: $35 million.
- In 1989: $63 million.
- Percentage increase, between 1986 and 1991, in the number of women in state prisons: 75.
- Percentage of them convicted of drug offenses: 55.
- Percentage of women prisoners in 1991 who had children under eighteen: 67.
- Number of children this represents: 56,000.
- Chances that a state prison inmate has had an immediate family member precede him or her in prison: 37.
- Percentage of women in federal prison in 1990 who were either pregnant or had just given birth: 25.
- Number of full-time OB-GYNs employed by the federal prison system in 1990: 0.

19

Our Most Serious Problem

1989

It's a funny war when the "enemy" is entitled to due process of law and a fair trial. By the way, I'm in favor of due process. But that kind of slows things down.

— *William Bennett to* Fortune *magazine, March 12, 1990*

USERS ARE BUMS," declared the *Reader's Digest* in an article with that title in June 1989, "whether they are doorway junkies, trendy weekend consumers or once a month dabblers." A month later, America's biggest-selling magazine was back with another drug article, saying that because attacking "the supply side of the drug crisis has failed miserably . . . let's get tough with drug users!"

Police in Hudson, New Hampshire, got tough with a drug user on August 3. Bruce Lavoie was William Bennett's worst nightmare, an occasional smoker of marijuana with a job, an intact marriage, three small children, and no criminal record. On a tip that Lavoie was dealing drugs, the Hudson Police conducted a "no-knock" surprise search at five o'clock in the morning with guns drawn. Sergeant Stephen Burke was so excited kicking in the door that his pistol went off in his hand.

The shot and the sound of doors and windows exploding inward jolted the family out of bed. They rushed into the hall, and Sergeant Burke fired his gun again, killing the thirty-four-year-old Lavoie as his wife and children looked on. Then the police had their search, which turned up no weapons and only a few joints' worth of marijuana.

~

With politicians, polls, the press, and the Office of National Drug Control Policy braying in unison, police everywhere got "tough on users." Arizona's state police imported nine tons of marijuana in 1989 to sell so they could get tough on users by selling it to them and then clapping on the handcuffs. In the course of the operation, seven tons of it disappeared into the streets. "That's no small change," a U.S. Customs Service spokeswoman told the *Arizona Republic*. "That's a major organization." The DEA paid a handsome informant $73,000 to seduce innocent women into drug deals so they could be busted. Eighteen women, most with no criminal record, were tricked into prison after the informant promised them love and marriage in return for "one little favor." Kalamazoo, Michigan; Alexandria, Virginia; and Washington, D.C, got tough on users by making it a crime to "loiter" in a "recognized drug-trafficking area." Such areas were "recognized" only in African-American parts of town, so the effect was to make it illegal for black people to hang out in their own neighborhoods.

In Boston any "known drug dealers or gang members who in any way cause fear in the community" — which was limited to three nonwhite districts — would be summarily searched on sight. One judge called the policy "a proclamation of martial law . . . for a narrow class of people — young blacks." Three weeks later, a Boston patrolman pointed his pistol at thirty-year-old Rolando Carr as he walked with some friends to a corner store in the black neighborhood of Dorchester. The officer ordered Carr to put his hands on a nearby wall, and as Carr did so the officer shot him in the lower back. "Get up," the officer told him. Carr couldn't, and as he lay bleeding the officer frisked him, finding no weapon, no drugs, no evidence of criminal activity.

Bennett chalked up such excesses to "the overriding spirit and energy of our front-line drug enforcement officers — which we should be extremely reluctant to restrict within formal and arbitrary lines." FBI director William Sessions agreed that drugs are such "awesome threats" that the nation must "strike a new balance between order and individual liberties." Admiral William Crowe, chairman of the Joint Chiefs of Staff, told the *Atlanta Constitution* that to pursue the War on Drugs, "you're probably going to have to infringe some human rights."

The public was willing. Sixty-two percent of those polled in 1989 said they would "give up some freedoms" to fight drug abuse.

On the first day of spring that year, the Supreme Court did its best to oblige. In two separate urine-testing cases — one of them the lawsuit filed by Customs agents against Commissioner Von Raab — the Court upheld the government's right to demand random urine tests from workers in "sensitive" positions. Without testing, the government argued, Customs agents might bungle cases, be subject to blackmail, even shoot each other. So it needed the right to demand "an excretory function traditionally shielded by great privacy" while "a monitor of the same sex . . . remains close at hand to listen for the normal sounds." Justices Thurgood Marshall and William Brennan disagreed. "There is no drug exception to the Constitution," they wrote.

This time they were joined by Justice Antonin Scalia, usually a law-and-order stalwart. As Scalia pointed out, the government failed to cite "*even a single instance* in which any of the speculated horribles actually occurred" (emphasis in the original). Rather, Scalia noted the memo implementing the drug-testing program, in which Von Raab said that it "would set an important example in our country's struggle with this most serious threat to our national health and security."

"The impairment of civil liberties," Scalia responded, "cannot be the means of making a point." Scalia, Marshall, and Brennan, however, were in the minority.

In yet another drug case that year, the Court — with Scalia back in the majority — approved of police descending in a helicopter to within 400 feet of a citizen's house to peer through the windows. On the basis of such spying, the Court ruled, police may obtain a search warrant.

This was the last straw for William Brennan. Back in 1984, when the Court created the "good faith exception" to the exclusionary rule, Brennan declared that "the Court's victory over the Fourth Amendment is complete." But that was before the Court allowed the warrantless search of schoolchildren, let police rummage warrantless through citizens' garbage in search of evidence, and let Customs force travelers to defecate on command. Now, six years later, Brennan despairingly referred to 1984, but not the year of the Court's dark "victory." The 1984 he referenced was George Orwell's. Dissenting in the helicopter case, Brennan quoted:

> "The black-mustachio'd face gazed down from every commanding corner. There was one on the house front immediately opposite. BIG BROTHER IS WATCHING YOU, the caption said. . . . In the far distance a helicopter skimmed down between the roofs, hovered for an instant like a bluebottle, and darted away again with a curving flight. It was the police patrol, snooping into people's windows."

"Who can read this passage without a shudder," Brennan asked, "and without the instinctive reaction that it depicts life in some country other than ours?" A month later Brennan resigned, effective immediately. President Bush nominated New Hampshire judge David Souter to replace him.

~

One person on Bennett's senior staff had some real-world experience of drug abuse and crime. Reggie Walton worked as a public defender in Philadelphia, where he learned firsthand of the problems of drugs and crime. At forty, when he met Bennett, he had been a Washington, D.C., criminal judge for eight years, processing hundreds of drug offenders each year through the justice system. Built like a wrestler, Walton was known for meting out heavy sentences along with fire-and-brimstone lectures. He was a friend of William Bennett's brother Bob, who invited him to dinner to meet the new drug czar.

Walton believed the drug fight was important and was encouraged because Bennett had just told the *Wall Street Journal* that he was "committed to fighting the [drug] problem . . . over a long period of time." As an African-American who'd had some breaks and considerable hard-earned success, it pained him to see so many young black men paraded before him on their way to prison.

At the dinner, Walton was impressed by Bennett's intelligence and earnest manner. He listens well, Walton thought. When Bennett offered him a job, though, Walton had a tough decision: a $10,000 pay cut was involved at precisely the time Walton's wife was quitting her $35,000-a-year job to enter a medical school costing $25,000 a year. Walton also was in line to become presiding judge of the criminal court and was starting to handle bigger, more interesting cases.

But he agreed to take the job Bennett offered: conveying federal drug policy to state and local governments and getting them to comply.

Get out there on the stump, Bennett told him. Be visible.

But a friend warned him: Watch your back over there. Don't travel too much. Be sure you get an office as physically close to Bennett's as you can. Otherwise you'll get cut out.

Don't be infantile, Walton retorted, and accepted an office one floor down from Bennett's.

It didn't take long for Walton to realize his friend had been right, though office geography may have had little to do with it. Walton was the only person of color with any seniority in the entire drug office. That amazed him, because while more whites used drugs, drugs were obviously a bigger problem for minority communities. What's more, none of the white guys surrounding Bennett seemed able or willing to discuss race. Walton would raise the racial implications of drug policy and they'd respond with platitudes about "color-blindness" and "merit."

Walton got along well with Bennett personally, but rarely got to see him. Both traveled a lot, making speeches. When they were in town, Walton couldn't seem to get past the palace guard of Walters, Carnes, Casse, and Tell — the core Bennettistas who had been with Bennett since before the drug office. That little clique often lunched together with Bennett, lunches in which Walton was never included. They'd come back with policy decided. They liked talking on a high-handed plane of morality and theory, but had never gone out and talked to local police or county drug-treatment providers, the way Walton did every week. None had ever sentenced a nineteen-year-old to twenty years in prison. And most of all, none had seen case after case of constitutional rights trampled by cops overeager to make a bust. Walton worried that the Drug War was ratcheting up police excesses and was appalled that the core Bennettistas ignored that concern.

~

Bennett would eventually become a millionaire proselytizing such virtues as Friendship, Courage, and Loyalty. In May 1989, he was working out his definitions of those terms. Children should inform school authorities about their friends' drug use, he said, and schools should then expel the offenders. Turning in one's friends, Bennett said, is "an act of true loyalty — of true friendship."

~

Bennett's *Drug Strategy* cited a "doubling" of frequent cocaine use in the past five years as "terrible proof that our current drug epidemic has far from run its course."

Stirring words, but total nonsense.

The percentage of households reporting any cocaine use had fallen by almost half since 1985. Within that reduced number of households, the portion using coke regularly seemed to have risen by a third, not doubled. "To put it another way," a *New York Times* op-ed piece said, "a man's arms will constitute a greater proportion of his total body if you cut off his legs, but that doesn't mean his arms have grown."

The "drug crisis" — never statistically large — was in truth abating. But a drug strategy calling for massive increases in police power, prison construction, and restriction of defendants' rights wouldn't make much sense if that were acknowledged. Instead, the *Strategy* warned of the nation's "intensifying drug-related chaos" and "appalling, deepening crisis." Drugs, it said, are the "gravest present threat to our national well-being."

~

Benjamin H. Renshaw III was an exceedingly correct man. Compact of build, he made up in posture what he lacked in height. Having been a boxer in college he went to work each day with shoulders squared and chin tucked. A large gold collar pin anchored his shirt to his throat so firmly he rhythmically thrust his chin forward, turtle-like, for relief.

Renshaw was a numbers man, a compiler of criminal justice statistics since being hired by D.C. mayor Walter Washington in 1973. Joining the federal government after Nixon resigned, Renshaw moved up the ranks of those who assemble data on crime and drugs for a string of alphabet-soup agencies.

One warm spring day in 1989, Renshaw took the metro to the Drug Enforcement Administration's forbidding twin black office towers overlooking the Pentagon. The DEA library held one of the government's best collections of data on drugs, and signing himself in, Renshaw began looking for figures on the relationship between drugs and crime. Surely they must exist, he thought. The country had been fighting a War on Drugs for two decades out of terror of the drug/crime nexus. Somewhere in here, he thought, I'll find the facts and figures that underpin that effort.

But try as he might, he couldn't find them.

Just about every branch of government had at one time or another generated statistics on some aspect of drug abuse or crime. Usually, they were buried and ignored, but one copy was always filed in the DEA library. Renshaw began stacking them up on a carrel desk. He built a small mountain of computer printouts, monographs, and government reports unopened since their printing. He piled up statistics gathered by police, hospitals, treatment providers, and the courts. All were full of numbers that, properly crunched, could yield a wealth of information about how drugs affect — or don't affect — crime.

Amazingly, nobody had done that work. Renshaw sank into a chair, dumbfounded. The country was spending billions of dollars, locking up hundreds of thousands of its citizens, and tearing up its own Constitution, without knowing if the effort made sense. Worse, the raw data existed. It had just never been assembled.

Slowly, it dawned on him that there was only one explanation: the government didn't have the numbers because the government didn't want the numbers.

Data are risky, Renshaw thought. What if they demonstrate a reality counter to the one the government wants to project?

After several days at the DEA, Renshaw went to see Richard Weatherbee, Attorney General Richard Thornburgh's drug-enforcement deputy. I want to assemble all the data on drugs and crime and produce one big, easy-to-read report, he said. Give me a decent staff, and I can have it done in two years. Thornburgh says 45 percent of Justice's budget goes to the Drug War. If the department really wants to know about the drug problem it's doing so much to combat, Renshaw said, this is what we have to do.

Weatherbee shrugged. Nice idea, Ben, he said, but let's wait a bit. Bennett's shop is going to produce its Drug Strategy any day now, and we don't want to steal their thunder. But hey, keep in touch.

⁓

By 1989 the practice of confiscating citizens' property was openly defended as a law-enforcement cash cow. The man who supervised Arizona's disastrous marijuana-selling sting operation told reporters it was worth letting seven tons of pot hit the streets to net $3 million in seized assets. The operation was, in his words, "a success from a cost-benefit standpoint." The Justice Department, which had just been given 175 additional prosecutors to work on nothing but forfeiture cases, crowed in a public handout that "a natural byproduct is revenue which is pumped back into law enforcement so that forfeitures beget more forfeitures like a snowball rolling downhill."

Assets seized annually in concert with federal agents had increased twentyfold in just four years, to more than $600 million. Ninety-five percent of that was plowed back into law enforcement, with almost half going to build more prisons.

The advantages to local police of taking a case federal were enormous. Federal sentences were longer. The rules in federal court were heavily weighted in favor of the prosecution — e.g., requiring the defense to be ready for trial in seventy days* and the right of the prosecutor to appeal a sentence. And above all, it was easier and more

* "They call it the Speedy Trial Act, but really it's the Speedy Conviction Act," says Louisiana defense attorney Thomas Lorenzi. "The government takes five years to prepare its case and bam! You're arraigned today, motions due in 15 days, trial in six weeks."

lucrative to seize assets under federal law. Standards of proof were usually lower, the process was more streamlined, and more of the money ended up in the coffers of the state and local police.

That, however, was scheduled to change. Congressman Larry Smith was still seething over his exchange with U.S. attorney Joseph Whitely in 1987 on the way California police were circumventing state law by taking their drug cases federal. Smith wrote an amendment that tightened the rules. Buried in the big 1988 drug law was Section 6077, which required the attorney general to assure that federal forfeitures don't violate state laws. Section 6077 was scheduled to go into effect on October 1, 1989.

Police organizations from every corner of the country lobbied feverishly to avert the change. The most impassioned — and honest — plea came from Joseph Dean of the North Carolina Department of Crime Control and Public Safety:

> If you take the profit out it, you'll do away with it. This is the thing that takes the profit out of it. . . .
>
> If this financial sharing stops, we will kill the goose that laid the golden egg.

Police and pro-police legislators had long argued that the primary goal of confiscating drug dealers' assets is law enforcement, not to make money for police. But in the heat of trying to get Section 6077 repealed, one U.S. attorney told Congress that if it failed to restore easy asset sharing, "drug agents would have much less incentive to follow through on the asset potentially held by drug traffickers . . . and would concentrate their time and resources on the criminal prosecution."

The police groups won the day; Section 6077 never went into effect. Congress secreted its repeal in a huge defense appropriations bill. Asset sharing, and the circumvention of state law, continued as before.

~

The Florida Department of Health and Rehabilitative Services (HRS) was getting ready to pull the plug on Straight Inc., the cult-like drug-rehab corporation that had brutalized Karen Norton six years earlier. A jury had been so convinced of Norton's story it had awarded her almost three-quarters of a million dollars in damages. Other lawsuits were pending. Complaints were stacking up at HRS.

But George Bush had been elected president with substantial

help from Straight's founders, Mel Sembler and Joseph Zappalla. Each had contributed $100,000 to Bush's campaign, and each was in line for an ambassadorship. Attempts to investigate and even close Straight kept falling apart. Fred Gravius, an agent in the HRS inspector-general's office, set out to investigate whether high-powered influence had helped Straight keep its license.

The supervisor of one of HRS's alcohol, drug abuse, and mental health district offices told Gravius he'd received "phone calls from state senators inquiring about the Straight program and letting it be known that they strongly supported the program," according to Gravius's memo to his boss.

But more to the point, an HRS team was visiting Straight on August 22, 1989, when a phone call arrived. Team member Susan Heavner took the call, and the voice on the other end told her that "no matter what they found Straight would receive their license." By the time she told her story to Gravius, Heavner had forgotten who made the call.

Another HRS official remembered a meeting with several staff members working on Straight's case and their boss, Dr. Ivor Groves. When one of the staff members mentioned the allegations of abuse against Straight, Groves told her that "if you do anything other than what I tell you to do on this issue, I will fire you on the spot." Later in the same meeting, Groves told them "there was a lot of pressure to get this thing resolved." Yet another HRS official remembers telling Groves about her reservations about Straight, only to have him respond that he "wanted Straight to get their license." Groves denied to Gravius pressuring staff members to approve Straight's license or threatening to fire them if they didn't.

In his memo, Gravius noted that "it cannot be unequivocally corroborated" that outside influence helped Straight retain its license. But "there were indications that outside influence was involved with this licensing issue. It appears that pressure may have been generated by Ambassador Sembler and other state senators."

Straight operated in Florida for another four years.

~

For years, Congress had done all it could to funnel drug cases into federal court. In addition to encouraging state and local police to take their drug cases federal, Congress allocated big budget increases to the DEA and the FBI and doubled the number of federal prosecutors just in the past three years.

What Congress didn't do was increase the number of federal judges, which stood in 1989 exactly where it was in 1985, before the great crack panic.

Predictably, drug cases began pushing other cases to the bottom of judges' dockets. Three years after being filed, for example, the biggest groundwater contamination case in Florida's history still hadn't been heard by a federal judge. None had the time. Not when three-quarters of the federal caseload was drug cases, each demanding a speedy trial.

Even in the hinterland, drugs were taking over the federal courts. In the court of appeals for Missouri, Minnesota, Iowa, Nebraska, Arkansas, and the Dakotas, drug cases had more than tripled since 1980 to a quarter of the court's caseload. In the western district of Texas, the number of federal drug defendants had increased 80 percent in one year.

Not that state courts had it any easier. Three-quarters of all criminal cases in Los Angeles in 1989 were for drugs. In Chicago the number of felony drug cases almost quadrupled from 1984 to 1988.

Tom Fitzgerald, Chicago's presiding criminal courts judge, knew he had to do something drastic. The pending caseload for each judge was more than double that recommended by the Bar Association. With the Chicago Housing Authority running Operation Clean Sweep in the projects and the Chicago Police fielding a newly expanded narcotics squad, the situation was unbearable.

Fitzgerald, a wry, florid man in his forties, knew Cook County wasn't going to build him another courthouse. And he knew the Chicago Police weren't going to arrest fewer people for drug offenses, which constituted half of the criminal courts' cases.

Florida's state's attorney, Janet Reno, was just beginning an experiment with something called a "drug court" in Miami, which diverted first-time possession offenders into treatment with a promise of a clean record if they successfully completed the program. Treatment cost $700 a year as opposed to $17,000 a year for a jail cell, and for those who finished, the re-arrest rate was about a ninth that of those who went to jail. Moreover, Miami's drug court took small-time possession cases out of the mainstream criminal court.

Fitzgerald liked the idea. He wheedled about $2 million out of the county commission — a pittance compared with building a new courthouse — and started running five special drug courts at night. He pressed traffic court judges into service to hear drug cases from four in the afternoon until midnight. An informal drill was established: if the quantity of drugs in question was small and if the defendant was a first-timer, he could plead guilty, get probation, and be out on the street the same night.*

The public defender's office objected to the night courts from the start. Private defense lawyers won't work nights, chief public defender Randolph Stone said, which means you've restricted defendants' choice of counsel. Segregated drug cases will lead to canned sentences and assembly-line justice, he argued. Given who's arrested in Chicago for drug possession and street dealing, the night court judges are going to see only young black men before them. The judges will lose perspective.

Yes, yes, Fitzgerald said. You're right. It isn't a perfect plan. But trust me. We'll only have to do this for a few years. It's a stopgap.

~

When David Tell and Dan Casse had drafted a Drug Control Strategy, Tell leaked a copy to the *New York Times*. "At last," the editorial page enthused, "a drug policy." Bennett's drug office had a hit on its hands.

George Bush had been president six months and had yet to deliver a televised speech. He didn't know in which direction to jump. The polls were all over the place, with no single issue deemed "the country's most important" by more than 9 percent of the population. Also, it wasn't easy to succeed the Great Communicator. Bush was trying to fashion a fresh media image. Rather than keep the press at arm's length — shouting over the roar of helicopter engines — and then deliver theatrical speeches, Bush was cultivating relationships with individual reporters. He played tennis regularly with ABC-TV White House correspondent Brit Hume. He frequently showed up unannounced in the White House press room to field questions. He had small groups of reporters into the Oval Office for informal briefings.

By midsummer, though, things were falling into place for a presidential address on drugs. After sloshing this way and that, the polls had gelled: a solid majority of Americans believed drugs were the country's biggest problem. Eighty-three percent approved of turning in family members to the police. Bennett's Drug Strategy was boffo with the *New York Times*. "The risk of ignoring this issue is one hundred times worse than the risk of trying to do something in a credible way," pollster Richard Wirthlin told Bush.

On August 11, "drug speech 9/5" showed up on the president's

* If it was a possession case and he needed treatment, he was usually out of luck. Unlike Miami, Cook County was prepared to treat but a small fraction of the 13,000 drug offenders who shuffled through its courts in 1989.

speech schedule, the speechwriting staff's first indication that a major address on the topic was due less than a month away. Mark Davis, who'd spent the Reagan years writing political speeches for the Republican Party, was handed the job, along with a memo from Bennett's office outlining the points the speech should make.

Two things struck Davis. First, he had very little time. Under Reagan, major addresses were planned months in advance. Even more troubling, though, was the vagueness of the assignment. The memo from the drug office was watery gruel. The big questions weren't answered: What exactly is the administration doing and why? What is so important about the drug issue that we need a televised presidential address? In conversations with the Bennettistas, Davis divined that they wanted the drug issue presented as a moral issue. They wanted drugs stigmatized so the country would make a cultural shift away from drug abuse. And the way to achieve that stigmatization was to enforce the law.

That's fine as far as it goes, Davis thought, as he looked at his sparse notes. But it isn't much on which to hang a major Oval Office speech.

It figures, Davis thought. Were this a foreign policy speech I'd have met with the president already and the National Security Council would have buried me in briefing books. Domestic issues make this president nod off. To make this speech work I'm going to have to pull a large rhetorical rabbit out of a very small hat.

Chriss Winston, the deputy director of White House communications, sat down with him to work on the speech and had an idea. We keep talking about crack cocaine, she said, but nobody knows what it looks like. As a parent, I know I'd like to know what it looks like. Why don't we have the president hold a bag of it up to the camera?

Very good, Davis said. It will give the president something to do with his hands, which might be comforting during his first big speech.

But they agreed it was risky. The crack would have to come from a cache already seized. If the DEA went out to score some especially for the speech and somebody got hurt, it would be a public relations disaster. Winston and Davis went to see White House communications director David Demerest and pleaded with him to make these concerns clear to the DEA. It doesn't really matter where the crack was seized, Davis said, as long as it was somewhere in the nation's capital. The DEA must have plenty on hand that they've confiscated. Demerest asked cabinet secretary David Bates to call the Justice Department about borrowing some crack, but to order the DEA specifically not to make a special arrest for it.

The request filtered down from the attorney general's office to Jack Millford, assistant to the DEA chief. Millford then called the number two man in the DEA's D.C. field office, William McMullan.

"Do you have anything going on around the White House?" Millford asked.

"I don't know," McMullan said. Maybe "four or five blocks away."

"Any possibility of you moving it down to the White House?" Milford asked. "Evidently the president wants to show it could be bought anywhere."

On August 31, McMullan walked up to one of his agents, a stocky, spiky-haired undercover man named Sam Gaye. "Can you make a drug buy around 1600 Pennsylvania Avenue?" McMullan asked.

For four months, Gaye had been buying small amounts of crack from an eighteen-year-old high school student named Keith Jackson. Two of the buys had been within a thousand feet of the school that had in June been certified "drug free" in a White House ceremony. Gaye had been hoping to coax Jackson into selling him a big amount before busting him, but the rush was on. He called Jackson and asked him to meet him that night in Lafayette Park. Jackson had never heard of it.

"It's across the street from the White House," Gaye said.

"Where the fuck is the White House?" Jackson responded.

Gaye explained. "Oh yeah!" Jackson finally said. "Where Reagan lives!" But Jackson didn't show up. The next day, Gaye called Jackson again, and to make sure he arrived sent a DEA informant to drive him there.

Gaye wore a hidden tape recorder to meet Jackson, but the microphone went dead. He handed Jackson $2,400 in cash and took the bag of crack. When an agent nearby tried to videotape the buy and bust, a homeless woman reared up and attacked him, shouting, "Don't take my picture! Don't take my picture!"

None of this was known to Davis, Winston, or anybody else in the White House. On September 5, an agent brought the crack to the White House, insisting it never leave his sight. Although the Oval Office is barely large enough for the president and the TV cameras, the agent insisted on squeezing in too, to preserve what he called "the chain of evidence." The lights came on, and Bush told the nation, "Our most serious problem today is cocaine and, in particular, crack."

Bush picked up the bag. "This — this is crack cocaine," he said, "seized a few days ago by Drug Enforcement agents in a park just across the street from the White House."

Bush outlined Bennett's drug strategy, with its heavy emphasis on law enforcement. "We won't have safe neighborhoods unless we're tough on drug criminals — much tougher than we are now," he said. He invoked the specter of crack babies and "four-year-olds [playing] in playgrounds strewn with discarded hypodermic needles." He promised the death penalty for drug kingpins and "appropriate use of the armed forces" to stop drug smugglers. "All of us agree," Bush said, "that the gravest domestic threat facing our nation is drugs."

At the time, the General Accounting Office estimated, some 350,000 Americans were using cocaine daily — about half as many as were hurt in construction accidents that year.

"Who's responsible?" Bush asked. "Let me tell you straight out. Everyone who uses drugs. Everyone who sells drugs. And everyone who looks the other way."

At a reception in the cabinet room immediately after the speech, Mark Davis shook the president's hand. Thank you for your work, Bush told him. You did an excellent job.

Then the president turned to shake hands with a stocky fellow with an odd, spiky haircut. This, an aide said to the president, is the agent who seized the crack you displayed. Davis's heart skipped a beat. Relax, he told himself. It may just be the agent who seized the drugs Bush happened to use.

But no. Seventeen days later the *Washington Post* had the story on page one: DRUG BUY SET UP FOR BUSH SPEECH: DEA LURED SELLER TO LAFAYETTE PARK. "We had to manipulate him to get him down there," McMullan said. "It wasn't easy." Confronted with the story by a reporter, Bush shrugged it aside. "I don't understand," he said. "I mean, has somebody got some advocates here for this drug guy?"

Three months later, Jackson went before a federal jury on four charges of selling cocaine. Because two of the alleged sales happened near a school, he faced a ten-year sentence with no possibility of parole. After four days, the jurors declared themselves deadlocked at eleven-to-one for acquittal and the judge called a mistrial.

"The majority of the jurors felt it was a setup," the jury foreman told reporters. "People felt as though because it was the president saying, 'get me something to show on TV,' the government was pressured to go out and say, 'get anybody.' "

The DEA was unrepentant. "My only regret, very frankly, is that a dope peddler is still out on the street," spokesman Mario Perez said. "I'm sure that we can live with what we did. Hopefully, [the jury] in their own consciences can live with what they did."

~

- Percentage of wiretap applications submitted to state and federal judges in 1990 that were for drug cases: 60.
- Percentage of those approved: 100.
- Percentage increase, from 1980 to 1989, in the number of Americans arrested for the sale or manufacture of cocaine or heroin: 800.
- 1990 Justice Department budget for the "McGruff" Take a Bite Out of Crime ads: $2.7 million.
- 1990 Justice Department budget for drug treatment in jails: 0.
- Percentage of Americans needing drug treatment in 1990 who were getting it: 13.
- Estimated number of incidents, between January and April 1990, in which drug police killed black civilians: 15.

20

"Are We Winning?"
1989–1990

[The drug problem] comes from this tradition of freedom and liberty, which gets distorted into license and "do your own thing" and the gospel of the sixties.

— *William Bennett to* U.S. News & World Report

WILLIAM TAYLOR never imagined he'd miss Ed Meese. Taylor, a red-haired and red-bearded defense lawyer, was a member of the American Bar Association's team trying to keep the Justice Department from tilting the playing field too far in favor of the prosecution. From a defendant's point of view, the Meese years had been grim. It was Meese who called the American Civil Liberties Union a "criminals' lobby." It was Meese who said anyone indicted is "probably guilty." It was Meese who told defense lawyers that in the War on Drugs "there are no bystanders, not even the lawyers." And it was Meese who accused lawyers of using constitutional freedoms as a "screen" to protect defendants who engage in "the evils of drugs." Meese's Justice Department had been the first to issue administrative subpoenas against defense lawyers — compelling them to inform on their clients. His had been the first to confiscate the money drug defendants might use to hire a lawyer. And Meese applauded a 1984 law requiring everybody to report cash transactions of $10,000 or more and even to write down how much was paid in $100 bills. Defense lawyers argued that put them in the position of effectively informing on their clients.

Bad as Meese was, at least he listened and was cordial. Taylor and other ABA officials met regularly with Meese and his assistant, William Weld, to scope potential conflicts between Justice and the defense bar. Weld took notes at the meetings and at the end would fairly summarize the ABA positions. Ultimately, little would change. You've got to understand, Weld told them, forfeiture is here to stay and the public won't tolerate lawyers getting huge fees from drug dealers. But at least Meese and Weld paid attention. Meese's Justice Department, for example, honored the ABA's ethics rule — adopted by courts in all fifty states — that prevented a prosecutor from contacting a defendant without the defense lawyer present.

But after Meese left, the Justice Department slipped into a cold war against the defense bar. The change was noticeable as soon as Pennsylvania governor Richard Thornburgh replaced Meese as attorney general in 1988 and stayed on when Bush took the White House. Thornburgh, renowned for his tough law-and-order administration in Pennsylvania, came into office with guns blazing for drug traffickers and money launderers. He shared Meese's passion to expand federal law enforcement. Other Justice Department issues, such as busing, affirmative action, and discrimination, were noticeably absent from Thornburgh's public rhetoric, and his critics suspected him of holding to "safe" issues in case he wanted to return to elective office later. Despite ample statistics from his own department, Thornburgh didn't believe the prisons were filling with nonviolent, small-time drug offenders. "Even a low-level person can make a deal with somebody," he'd say, pressing thumb to ring finger, "and talk their way out of prison like that": *snap*. Whenever drug treatment came up, he'd flap a hand. "The attorney general is not the secretary of HHS," he'd say.

Thornburgh particularly disliked the ABA. The organization was in the thrall of the defense bar, Thornburgh believed, and he had a prosecutor's disdain for defense attorneys. They would use any kind of technicality or subterfuge, he believed, to set dangerous criminals free. The ABA ethics rule barring prosecutors from contacting people without their lawyers present was a good example of the ABA's kowtowing to defense attorneys. It was a flagrant assault on prosecutorial authority, Thornburgh believed. Why, a prosecutor could end up disbarred for doing his job!

As soon as Thornburgh took over as attorney general, the ABA suddenly found itself unwelcome at the Justice Department. Thornburgh wouldn't see ABA officials and referred them to underlings who didn't return phone calls.

On June 8, 1989, the cold war between Thornburgh and the defense bar turned hot. Thornburgh sent a long memo to all of his prosecutors telling them to ignore the ABA ethics rule against making contact with the clients of defense attorneys if it will help them make cases. Thornburgh's spokeswoman said the rule was "a distraction" from the department's mission of "getting the bad guys." The Justice Department, said the federal prosecutor in New York City, is "charged with the enforcement of federal law and nobody — emphasize nobody — can interfere with that duty."

The U.S. Supreme Court weighed in against defense attorneys and their clients, too. In two separate decisions on June 22, the Court upheld the practice of confiscating legal fees and the money defendants plan to use to pay their lawyers. As usual in drug cases, eloquence in defense of civil liberties was only politely noted. "It is unseemly and unjust," Justice Harry Blackmun wrote in his dissent, "for the Government to beggar those it prosecutes in order to disable their defense at trial."

Then the Internal Revenue Service climbed on board. Soon after Bush's drug speech, the IRS wrote to nearly a thousand defense attorneys threatening them with jail or fines if they didn't send in proper cash-reporting forms. The lawyers had been sending in forms, but leaving blank the space for the client's name. If the IRS wants to track the flow of cash and assure taxes were paid, the lawyers argued, then it doesn't need clients' names. Hidden in the big 1988 drug bill was a provision bumping failure to report from a misdemeanor to a felony, and now the IRS — the biggest federal law enforcement agency, with a budget more than five times that of the FBI and DEA combined — had become a drug buster with equal contempt for the ABA. "My job is enforcement of the law," one IRS agent told the *National Law Journal*. "We don't have anything to do with the ethical rules of the bar."

The antidrug orthodoxy already had made enemies of harmless and unaffected drug users, critical journalists, and the terminally ill. By 1989 the orthodoxy had grown so huge it couldn't tolerate defense attorneys anymore. Some gave up and announced they would no longer take drug cases. It's too dangerous to represent an accused drug dealer, attorney Joel Hirschhorn of Miami told reporters, but "it's OK to represent a murderer. Everybody approves of that."

~

William Bennett liked to tell a story:

One of his teachers at Gonzaga High School in Washington, D.C., once held up a rubber ball and asked the adolescent Bennett if he'd be willing to bet a dollar that the ball would return to earth if he threw it up in the air. Young Bennett responded: Of course. The teacher lofted the ball, and sure enough it fell back down. Now, said the teacher, would you be willing to bet me a thousand dollars it will fall to earth? Certainly, Bennett told him, and he won that bet, too.

Now, Mr. Smart Guy, the teacher said, would you bet me *your immortal soul* the ball will come back down?

And, as Bennett liked to tell it around the drug office, he didn't take the bet.

~

Six weeks after Bush's drug speech, Joseph Hoberman was in his greenhouse tending his orchids when four unmarked cars pulled up outside his Raleigh, North Carolina, home. He could see through the glass that the six men and one woman who climbed out were cops from the way they acted, glancing this way and that, pulling their jackets closed. Hoberman, an outdoorsman, occasionally taught Raleigh police recruits how to navigate the dense forests of the area and he figured this delegation had come to ask him to teach another course.

But these weren't Raleigh police. They were state drug agents, and they wanted to search the greenhouse.

"For what?" Hoberman asked.

"Marijuana plants," one of the agents said. "And if you say no, we'll come back with a warrant and we won't be in a great mood."

Hoberman let them in.

They looked at the orchids, shrugged, and started to leave. Hoberman asked why they were searching someone who didn't use drugs and had no criminal record, and the agents told him he'd received not one but three shipments from a store that advertised in *High Times* magazine.

"It was a light meter for my orchids!" he exclaimed. "There were three shipments because the first two meters were defective." He said he didn't know the store had advertised in *High Times;* he'd gotten its name from the American Orchid Society. The agents left.

The following day, the DEA conducted raids in forty-six states on retailers selling the kind of indoor-gardening equipment that could be used to grow marijuana — or orchids. The DEA selected the stores because they'd advertised in *High Times.*

High Times, whose circulation floated around a quarter million, advertised drug paraphernalia. It ran a monthly "Trans-High Market Quotation," to track pot prices in various cities. Its photo spreads featured loving full-color photos of marijuana buds bursting with THC.

These facts constituted "an open invitation to violate the drug laws," in the DEA view. *High Times* also was a leading satirist of the War on Drugs, making fun of the DEA, drug policy in general, and William Bennett personally. The magazine called him the "Drug Bizarre" and ridiculed his cigarette addiction. WHAT JERKS! ran one typical headline. BENNETT BLASTS POT WHILE AIDE HAS NICOTINE FIT!

As word got out about the raids, *High Times* lost two-thirds of its advertisers. Though the DEA claimed it wasn't exercising unlawful prior restraint on *High Times*'s First Amendment rights to publish, harassing its customers was having the same effect.

~

George Bush's first year in office ended with a rapid-fire series of explosive "drug" stories. Five days before Christmas, the United States invaded Panama and captured the onetime CIA asset and current Drug Enemy Number One, Manuel Noriega. The citizens of Kansas City, Missouri, running against a national tide of tax cutting, voted to boost their sales tax by 0.25 percent to beef up drug enforcement. Keith Jackson was finally convicted of selling crack to the DEA for President Bush to use as his speech prop. And the FBI paid a former girlfriend of D.C. mayor Marion Barry to lure him into a hotel bedroom and — over his repeated and fully recorded demurrals — offer him a crack pipe until he accepted. The grainy footage of the mayor smoking crack aired everywhere, an example, some pundits said, of the scope of this national tragedy.

But others were dubious. "If Mayor Barry was a crackhead," the *New Republic* asked, "the kids may be forgiven for wondering how come he was able to give speeches and hold press conferences and do a superficially passable job of running a big city?" *Newsweek*, which had first printed Arnold Washton's "instantaneous addiction" quote, ran a short piece titled "A Dirty Little Secret" that conceded "crack isn't instantly addictive . . . 2.4 million Americans have tried crack, less than half a million now use it once a month or more."

Newsweek was beginning to break ranks with the other big newsweeklies. On Christmas Day 1989, it published "Taking on the Legalizers," about as balanced and sober a discussion of the legalization debate as had appeared anywhere in the mainstream press. Four months later, it became the first newsweekly to devote an entire article — "Uncivil Liberties?" — to the dark side of the War on Drugs. "America is beginning to confront the true cost, in terms of civil liberties and the rights of the individual, of the nationwide war against drugs," it said. Except for one short report in July on "Good News in the Drug War: Prices Up, Purity Down," *Newsweek* never again gave the War on Drugs the kind of laudatory coverage that it had in the past — and that its competitors would continue.

≈

Ben Renshaw at the Bureau of Justice Statistics couldn't exactly say he was prevented from assembling clear data on the scope of the country's drugs-and-crime problem. Nobody ever ordered him to stop. But there always seemed to be some other project his bosses wanted done first. And prying even secretarial help out of the personnel office was murder. Clearly, nobody high up at Justice had much interest in gathering into one place a true picture of drug abuse in America and its effect on crime.

Bennett's *Drug Strategy* was a joke, Renshaw thought. Nothing but pontificating on values and abstractions, without a serious number in it. Renshaw did some calculations and figured that for the states to comply with everything Bennett wanted would cost them about twenty-five times more than they were receiving in federal drug-fighting funds. Absurd.

Now Weatherbee wanted Renshaw to wait until after Bennett's *second Drug Strategy*, due in the fall of 1990, before plowing ahead on his drugs-and-crime report. And Weatherbee was the Lord High Gatekeeper of drug enforcement information. Thornburgh had sent around a memo: nobody except Dick Weatherbee talks about drugs to anybody outside Justice. That means no off-the-record conversations with reporters, no friendly assistance to NIDA, no statistical support to the DEA unless it passes through Weatherbee's hands first. Renshaw asked: if Bennett's office calls me for a figure, can I give it to them? Weatherbee said no. Thornburgh had made it clear he intended to return to Pennsylvania to run for the Senate in 1992 and then for president in 1996. Bennett also was being discussed as presidential timber. Drug information was the most potent political ammunition in Washington at the moment, and Thornburgh didn't want to give Bennett an iota of advantage.

≈

Even discredited data — if dramatic enough — continue walking the earth like golems.

The Partnership for a Drug Free America had been turning out antidrug ads for three years and now was the nation's third-biggest ad campaign after those of AT&T and McDonald's. Founded in 1987 by ad agencies willing to donate creative work and networks willing to donate airtime, the Partnership kept the airwaves saturated with artfully crafted and compelling spots aimed at keeping children away from illegal drugs.

In 1990, about 17 percent of twelfth-graders were using some illicit drug every month, almost always marijuana. At the same time, almost 60 percent were drinking alcohol once a month, about half to the point of monthly drunkenness. Almost one in five high school seniors was smoking cigarettes every day (as opposed to one in fifty smoking pot daily).

But alcohol and tobacco were as absent from Partnership ads as from Bennett's Drug Strategy. When *The Nation* revealed that 3 percent of the Partnership's budget came from alcohol and tobacco companies, a Partnership spokesman said the ads don't address smoking and drinking because they're legal. Besides, he said, "how does one anti-alcohol spot compete against fifteen beer-blondes-and-beach-boobs commercials? We're a small organization. We can't fix the world's problems."

Even focusing on illegal drugs, the Partnership couldn't keep its facts straight. One ad showed the flat-lined electroencephalograph of a coma patient and called it "the brain waves of a marijuana smoker." Another claimed that in 1989 "15 million Americans used cocaine, and five million of those who survived required medical help." In fact, only about eight million Americans had used cocaine in the previous year according to NIDA. Sixty-two thousand of them had ended up in emergency rooms, and 3,300 had died. *Scientific American* magazine called drug researcher Nick Kozel at NIDA to ask where the 15 million number came from and he said, "I have no idea." So the magazine called the Partnership. The best explanation spokeswoman Theresa Grant could come up with was that the ad's creators "extrapolated from a *Newsweek* article or something."

And the Drug War rolled on. Senator Phil Gramm, Republican of Texas, and Congressman Newt Gingrich, Republican of Georgia, introduced a National Drug and Crime Emergency Act that would turn unused army bases into "detention centers" for the masses of drug offenders they expected to round up. (And for good measure, those convicted would be compelled to pay the costs of their own prosecution.) Congressman Richard Ray, Democrat of Georgia, had a better idea: ship drug offenders to penal colonies on the "extremely remote Pacific islands" of Midway and Wake. Ray convinced the House Armed

Services Committee to approve the plan. "There's not much chance they're going to get anything but rehabilitated on two small islands like these," said Ray. "You can't go anywhere. . . . You won't be interrupted by families to come visiting every weekend."

Ray first tested the idea, he told reporters, on a group of sheriffs and police chiefs. "I got a standing ovation," he said. "They thought it was a great idea."

In light of other proposals from high quarters, penal colonies for drug offenders was quite mild. The nation's most famous and dynamic police officer, Los Angeles Police Chief Darryl Gates, offered this suggestion to a Senate committee: "Casual drug users should be taken out and shot." Even casual drug use, he said, "is treason." His remark might have been dismissed as the flamboyant musings of a known law-and-order extremist had not the nation's drug czar floated a similar proposal. On *Larry King Live,* William Bennett let drop that he believed beheading drug dealers was "morally plausible" if "legally difficult." When King pressed him on it, Bennett said it again. "Yeah. Morally I don't have any problem with it."

This wasn't just rhetoric. Both houses of Congress were preparing to impose a federal death penalty on "drug kingpins," whether or not a murder could be pinned on them. "The death penalty debate is over," Deputy Attorney General William Barr told a House subcommittee convened to hold precisely that debate. The House Judiciary Committee — the traditionally liberal graveyard for death-penalty legislation — not only approved the idea, but added more capital offenses than President Bush originally wanted. Only a last-ditch effort by opponents was able to stall it in committee long enough for Congress to recess without a vote on it.

As he picked up his honorary white quill pen off the counsel's table in the U.S. Supreme Court, James Reilley couldn't believe he was back here again. Outwardly, little had changed in the eight years since he'd argued *Illinois v. Gates.* The massive marble columns still radiated their somber coolness, the gold-leaf friezes and heavy drapes lent the massive courtroom the air of a temple. But now William Rehnquist sat in the chief justice's chair where Warren Burger sat last time. And in Rehnquist's old chair was the man Don Santarelli had plucked from obscurity nineteen years earlier, Antonin Scalia.

It was amazing to Reilley that this case had made it this far. When

Edward Rodriguez had phoned him from Chicago's central jail in 1985 to say police had busted him after his girlfriend let them into his apartment, Reilley had hardly given it a thought. As Reilley expected, the trial judge threw the case out of court because the girlfriend had no authority to let the police into Rodriguez's house. The Illinois Appellate Court agreed the search was illegal, and the Illinois Supreme Court wouldn't even hear the case.

And yet, as he prepared to argue the case before the highest court in the land, Reilley felt a cold dread. When he'd argued *Gates* he was confident he'd win. This time he was sure he'd lose.

~

Ade Adedokian had been cooped up in a 747 for eighteen hours and wanted nothing more than to go home, take a hot bath, and go to sleep.

A Nigerian pharmacist living as a legal U.S. resident in Houston, Adedokian was returning from a family gathering in Lagos. He picked up his suitcases and headed for what he expected would be a quick pass through Customs.

But the agent at Houston International Airport was full of questions. Why were you in Nigeria? In which hotel did you stay in Lagos? What did you eat for dinner? *Why* were you in Nigeria? *Which* hotel? Unsatisfied with Adedokian's answers, the agent led him to a windowless room and searched him thoroughly. "They told me to spread my legs," Adedokian said later. "They fondled my private parts." They did not, however, find the slightest evidence of wrongdoing.

But Adedokian fit a profile — the same one Rosa Montoya de Hernandez fit in 1984 — that of a "body packer," one who smuggles drugs in condoms inside his own digestive tract. The agents told Adedokian he had two choices: consent to an X-ray or stay in this room until he defecated into a wastebasket in the presence of a drug agent. Exhausted and furious, Adedokian agreed to be taken in handcuffs to a hospital twenty minutes away, where, after a three-hour wait, an X-ray proved his innocence. Eight hours after landing, he was free to go home.

Nationwide, the Customs Service put one innocent person through the same ordeal for every "body packer" it caught. The Houston team, however, was particularly unskilled; for every body packer it caught, fifteen innocents were forcibly X-rayed. Eighty-six percent of those subjected to the alimentary inspection were Nigerian.

"An agent," one DEA spokesman told the *New York Times,* "can spot a drug dealer the way a woman can spot a deal at the supermarket."

~

The Justice Department in May asked a federal grand jury to determine whether *High Times*'s ads for a catalogue of marijuana seeds sold in Holland — where marijuana is legal — constituted a "continuing criminal enterprise" subject to RICO penalties and forfeiture. DEA agents appeared in the magazine's New York office with a subpoena, demanding the names and address of all current and former employees of *High Times.* Long-standing sensitivity to First Amendment issues had led the Justice Department to implement rules demanding prosecutors get the attorney general's permission before investigating a publication. In this case, though, the requirement was waived. *High Times* already was down $100,000 a month in lost ad revenue, and this latest attack threatened to put the most prominent Drug War critic out of business altogether.

Investigating *High Times* was too much even for the conservative editors of the *Washington Times,* who opined that harassing *High Times* "fulfills our worst fears about [Bennett's drug] strategy. . . . The purchase of horticultural equipment, even through *High Times* magazine, doesn't seem to meet the requirements of probable cause. Nor does it seem terribly efficient to exhaust taxpayer dollars tracking down people who purchase wares advertised in such magazines."

~

Saturday morning, while parents sleep late, is national cartoon time on American television. On April 21, 1990, kids watching NBC were treated to a half-hour commercial-free Disney cartoon: *Cartoon All Stars to the Rescue.* In it, Bugs Bunny, Garfield, Winnie the Pooh, and the Smurfs come to life to help convince teenaged Michael to stop smoking pot and hanging out with friends who do. Kids who found the show scary, irrelevant, or boring and changed the channel to CBS found . . . *Cartoon All Stars to the Rescue.* On ABC: *Cartoon All Stars to the Rescue.* On Fox, the Disney Channel, USA, and Nickelodeon: *Cartoon All Stars to the Rescue.* Nearly a thousand stations coast to coast broadcast the antidrug cartoon simultaneously. Traditionally, only State of the Union addresses got such treatment; no other entertainment show had ever monopolized the airwaves. Just about the only way to escape *Cartoon All Stars to the Rescue* that morning was to take refuge in C-SPAN or American Movie Classics. Or turn off the TV. McDonald's Corp., which paid $2 million to produce and air the cartoon, figured it reached three-quarters of all American kids under twelve.

In the cartoon, Michael — all scowls and bloodshot eyes —steals from his little sister's piggy bank to buy a joint, the smoke from which turns into a death's head speaking with George C. Scott's voice. "Being weird is part of being a teenager," Dad says as Mom puts a plate of cookies on the table. "He'll get over it." Michael, though, is hanging out with a "bad crowd." The climax is a genuinely trippy roller-coaster ride through the human brain and a "bad trip" sequence in which Michael runs up to a "see your future" carnival booth — manned by Daffy Duck — and sees himself wrinkled and green. At which point, he puts his arm around his sister's shoulder and says, "C'mon sis, let's talk to Mom and Dad." The cartoon chorus breaks into a rousing melody, "Your life begins the day you learn to say no," as the credits roll.

When critics pointed out the cartoon focused on a white, middle-class, suburban family with no other apparent dysfunction, executive producer Roy Disney shot back, "We are not all things to all people, and we are not going to solve the drug problem with a 30-minute TV show." When reviewers criticized the show for not mentioning alcohol, producer Buzz Potemkin said it would have been too complicated to explain to children that they can drink some things but not others. "If you use drugs, it is completely different from the normal action pattern for children," he explained to the *Los Angeles Times*. "On the other hand, they drink every day of their lives. They drink orange juice, they drink water, they drink milk."

To reach those kids who missed the film that day, videotape copies were sent to 72,000 schools, 16,000 public libraries, and video stores everywhere to lend free to their customers.

~

The first day of summer 1990 was a big news day. Ten thousand people died in an earthquake in northern Iran. Nelson Mandela, resplendent in a Yankee cap and jacket, walked into Yankee Stadium and told a wildly cheering crowd that America's freedom had been his inspiration through more than a quarter century's imprisonment. A constitutional amendment against flag burning died in the Senate. Marion Barry's spectacular trial was yielding juicy tidbits by the hour. And *Robocop II* opened. "He's back," the marquees declared, "to protect the innocent."

So the papers didn't have much space to devote to *Illinois v. Rodriguez*. Antonin Scalia, who had uncharacteristically asked not a single question during oral arguments, wrote the opinion allowing police to search a home on the say-so of a visitor. Justices Marshall, Brennan, and Stevens wrote in their dissent that "the majority has taken away some of the liberty that the Fourth Amendment was designed to protect," but that was hardly newsworthy after *Gates, Leon, Montoya de Hernandez*, and the other Fourth Amendment drug-war cases of the eighties. The *New York Times* gave *Rodriguez* three paragraphs. The *Washington Post* gave it one paragraph in a box titled "In other action yesterday."

~

Bennett was lumbering around the corridors of the drug office in his shirtsleeves, poking his head into staff members' offices, pumping his fist and asking, "Are we winning? Are we winning?" and admonishing them in a football coach's voice that "you're either on offense or defense. There's no in between and no time out. Got it?"

Memo from Judge Walton, Bennett's secretary said, handing it to him. Bennett read it and gathered his core group into his seed-strewn office — David Tell, Dan Casse, John Walters, Bruce Carnes, and congressional liaison Joe McHugh.

Walton wants the drug office to prepare a report on the root causes of drug abuse, Bennett explained, on the theory that drugs are part of a larger problem involving the hopelessness of poverty, bad education, and so forth.

There was an embarrassed silence, which Bennett finally broke.

We have a drug problem, he growled. We don't have the time or authority to fix the housing or jobs or poverty problems.

The others concurred in chorus. Looking at root causes would only dilute the focus on drugs, said one. The drug office has a mandate to stop drug abuse, nothing more, said another. We aren't the department of social welfare, said a third.

~

As though zero tolerance and user accountability weren't pouring enough drug defendants into federal court and prisons, the Justice Department set out to imprison again people already punished on the state level.

Life was a roller coaster for Donny Clark. For a while, he was the biggest sod farmer in Florida, a business he sold for more than a million dollars. But money management wasn't his strong suit. Now, at forty-nine, he was farming watermelons and doing all right in the swampy lowlands near Tampa.

The thought of those swamps made him shudder. In 1985, Clark had concocted a scheme to grow marijuana in floating pots and set them adrift in nearby state wetlands. Quickly apprehended, Clark was sentenced to a year of probation, which he promptly violated by keeping hunting guns on his farm. That led to six months on a road crew.

But that was four years in the past, over and done. Or so he thought.

For more than three years the federal prosecutor in Tampa had been building a drug case against Clark. Police in Clark's area had stumbled upon a ring of young marijuana growers that included two of Clark's sons and his ex-brother-in-law. An informant in the case said it was Clark who had taught some of them how to grow pot in 1981, four years before he was convicted on the state charge. There was no evidence or testimony that Clark had had anything to do with marijuana since getting caught in 1985.

But when a thirty-nine-count indictment was handed up by a federal grand jury in Tampa in February 1990, Donny Clark was listed as one of twenty-eight people involved in the conspiracy. On July 20, just as the watermelons were ripening on the vines, federal agents arrested him on his farm.

All twenty-eight defendants were held without bond. Gradually, all pleaded guilty and were sentenced to, at most, six years in prison. Except Clark. Knowing he had committed no crime other than the one for which he'd already served time, he refused to plead. He alone was bound over for trial.

On August 2, an event took place halfway around the world that had nothing to do with drugs but which radically altered the course of the War on Drugs. Only the sudden death of Len Bias had as big an effect on the public's perception of the "drug problem" as the invasion of Kuwait by Saddam Hussein's Iraq.

The scope of the drug problem didn't change a whit with the invasion of Kuwait, of course. White middle-class use, and use by teenagers, continued falling at about the same rate it had been falling since before Bennett took over. The violence surrounding the drug trade worsened, as before. So did the terrifying spread of AIDS among drug users.

But from the moment Saddam's tanks crossed the border, what had been the nation's "number one problem" vaporized. Press coverage of the drug issue and the Drug War fell off a cliff. In 1989, 244 stories about the country's drug problems appeared in mainstream magazines. In 1990, 219 were written. In 1991, 138, and in 1992, 111.

~

Having been told by Bennett to "get out there on the stump," Reggie Walton found himself criticized within the drug office for traveling too much. It made Walton furious: those supercilious know-nothings surrounding Bennett harped constantly that he was spending too much of the agency's money on air tickets. Walton's wife was going through a difficult pregnancy for much of the time he was at ONDCP and he longed to be with her. But his mandate was clear: carry the antidrug gospel to the state and local level. It didn't take long for Walton to realize it wasn't only the number of trips he was taking that annoyed the Bennettistas, but also their destinations. He visited Indian reservations and barrios. He palavered with the People's Coalition in Chicago, a low-income community group that was one of Bennett's biggest critics when he was secretary of education. "These people are Americans and they deserve to be heard," Walton argued. "I'm not just going to visit governors and police chiefs."

A couple of weeks after Iraq invaded Kuwait, Walton told Bennett that a judgeship was opening again on the D.C. criminal court and he wanted to resign to take it. Please don't, Bennett said. Between us: I'm going to quit soon and I'd like you to be in position to be my successor. Walton was angry — he wouldn't have left the bench in the first place had he known Bennett was going to quit so soon — but he agreed to stay on for a shot at the czar's job.

~

One of the main arguments in favor of letting prosecutors confiscate a drug defendant's potential lawyer fees was that defendants can always rely on public defenders. "Under the Constitution, defendants are entitled to legal advice, not to high-priced advice," one federal prosecutor explained at the time the law was first proposed.

But now even low-priced advice was becoming unavailable. The number of drug cases filed in DeKalb County, Georgia — suburban

Atlanta — increased 1,000 percent from 1985 to 1990. Then, Bennett's Drug War budget sent almost $18 million to Georgia's police and prosecutors to help catch and convict more drug offenders, but gave not a penny to the state's public defenders. As a result, the public defender in DeKalb County had about ten minutes to spare for each client before pleading him through to sentencing. "That's not justice," he said. In the city of Atlanta, one public defender refused to take any more drug cases. She had handled 600 in ten months, she told a judge, about four times the number the ABA considered appropriate.

The situation was similar elsewhere. Anywhere from 70 to 90 percent of drug defendants nationwide were indigent. State legislatures and county commissions were reluctant to pony up money to help what was widely seen as "the enemy" in the Drug War and tended to agree with one Georgia lawman who said his profession viewed "indigent defense as a proxy for evil."

~

"Don't be silly, Jack," said Laurie Robinson, cradling the phone between ear and shoulder. "We'll go ahead without you."

Robinson, chief of the criminal division of the American Bar Association, had worked hard to arrange a meeting of ABA officials with Deputy Attorney General William Barr and didn't want to have to reschedule. Matters were too far out of hand. First, the attorney general had written his famous memo instructing prosecutors to ignore ABA ethics rules to jail drug dealers. Then, after months of frosty memos and snide innuendoes, Thornburgh threw a verbal grenade at the ABA. Speaking to the group's annual meeting in August, Thornburgh accused defense lawyers of "hindering the War on Drugs" by vigorously defending drug offenders. Robinson objected immediately, writing to request a meeting with Thornburgh. Thornburgh assigned the task of receiving the ABA to Barr.

Jack Curtain, a Boston lawyer serving as president of the ABA, was rushed to surgery for lung cancer just ten days before the scheduled October 9 meeting. "You're not going ahead without me," he told Robinson from his hospital bed. "Keep the appointment." Gaunt and pale, he hobbled into Barr's office leaning on Robinson's arm the day of the scheduled meeting.

Seated behind his desk, Barr didn't rise to greet them. He held his round, boyish face downward, studying a single piece of paper on his vast desktop. The ABA lawyers stood while a group of Barr aides filed into the room and took places around the long oak table. Finally, Barr looked up and waved the ABA group to chairs.

Robinson spoke first. The ABA and the Justice Department have had their differences, she said, but nobody is served by having us at each other's throats. The rhetoric is getting too hostile and we need to address that.

Barr cut Robinson off. Listen, he said, drumming a fingertip on the tabletop. We all know the ABA is playing a shell game with the rules. We have a national crisis on our hands and this Justice Department is doing all it can to combat it. As far as I'm concerned, the defense bar, and the ABA, are nothing but fellow travelers of the drug dealers.

Robinson looked at her colleagues and then across the table at the Justice lawyers. Nobody said a word. The room was so tense and quiet she could hear twenty watches ticking.

"Well," she said, sliding her papers into her briefcase. "Thank you for your time." She stood up, helping Curtain to his feet. Ten minutes after arriving at Barr's office, the group from the ABA was riding the elevator back down to the street. "I think," Robinson said, "the Justice Department told the defense bar to go fuck itself."

~

The War on Drugs made the criminal justice system one of the top growth industries during the eighties and nineties. Police jobs at all levels of government swelled by 36 percent and prison jobs by 86 percent during the Reagan years alone, while overall government employment rose by only 16 percent. Dick Thornburgh doubled the corps of federal prosecutors during his two-year reign under Bush. For those in the enforcement trades, the War on Drugs was boom time.

For everybody else, the period was marked by a commensurate increase in police intrusion. There are rarely victims or witnesses in drug crimes. Drug use usually takes place in private, and drug dealing occurs between a willing seller and a willing buyer. So to wage the Drug War an expanding army of police had to use ever more wiretaps, dog sniffs, snitches, warrantless searches, surveillance, and undercover operations. The administration elected on a promise to remove government from people's lives had turned the country — in one law professor's phrase — into "a society of suspects."

Police and federal drug agents also had plenty of civilian proxies.

So many employers were urine-testing their workers by 1990 that testing was a $300 million industry. The Omaha Police Department launched Operation Hotel-Motel, training chambermaids, bellhops, and desk clerks in fifty area hostelries how to spot drug dealers by watching for people carrying beepers or cellular phones, paying cash, extending a stay day by day, refusing maid service, or making or receiving lots of calls. The DEA began training airline ticket clerks in ways to spot likely drug dealers — such as those traveling to or from Los Angeles, Miami, Denver, or Kansas City, and as incentive offered a piece of whatever assets drug agents subsequently seized. Government use of paid confidential informants mushroomed; Washington paid $63 million for snitches in 1989, which was half again as much as it did to operate the Office of Management and Budget. A lot of this money went to small-time crooks. Some of it went to big-time crooks. In one legendary case, a convicted drug dealer who was flat broke upon his release from prison in 1984 became a multimillionaire by 1990 — all on government snitch payments. "That's the sad part of protecting society," the chief federal drug prosecutor in Miami told the local *Herald*. "Sometimes you have to deal with people you detest."

Sometimes, too, you have to deal with people you love. Shertest Corp. of New York began offering parents snitch-in-a-can, a $50 aerosol called Drug Alert that when sprayed on children's clothes, belongings, desktops, and doorknobs turns color in the presence of drug residue. "We do not test people," the company's general manager told reporters. "We test objects."

~

In October 1990, top newspaper editors and publishers from around the United States and Canada gathered in Reston, Virginia, to talk about their role in the War on Drugs. Katherine Graham, publisher of the *Washington Post*, argued forcefully that newspapers had no special role in the Drug War, that they should do what they always do — cover the issue as thoroughly as possible.

But she was in the minority. "This is not a normal story," said Thomas Greer, executive editor of the *Cleveland Plain Dealer*. "We're losing the War on Drugs. . . . We have to take an unusual posture. [The media] have not solved anything with [their] traditional role." The managing editor of the *Philadelphia Daily News* said that "any story you do is not enough to help the drug problem" and that her reporters were dissatisfied because after all their work, there were still drugs in

Philadelphia. The editor of the *Atlanta Constitution* said he believed that "newspapers ought to look for the opportunity to step in where others are not doing anything."

The panelists heard about a newspaper in California that joined with a local cable station to produce a forty-eight-hour antidrug telethon. Then there was a paper in Tennessee that donated $350,000 in free ad space to antidrug messages.

"We may not have all the answers, but it's our duty to get involved," said the editor from the *Clinton (Iowa) Herald*. "I suggest it's time to quit polishing our halo of detachment."

~

Less than a year after taking office, Bennett began claiming victory. "It seems to me it is very likely that one can say we're at least at the end of the beginning," he told *U.S. News* in February. In March, he told *Newsweek*, "The healing has started and will continue. A year from now it will be better yet. We are starting to win."

Barely a month later, Bennett was forced to concede the drug-enforcement showcase in Washington, D.C., was a failure. Crack and cocaine remained as available as ever and the violence surrounding them continued to grow ferociously. The drug problem in D.C. "remains as bad as it is anywhere in the country," he said. "A bitter disappointment to all concerned."

But after that brief brush with reality, Bennett was back to answering publicly his own incessant question — are we winning? — with a resounding yes. A brief upturn in price and downturn in purity of cocaine was celebrated as divine absolution by the drug czar, even though FBI crime statistics showed that violence increased more rapidly as cocaine supplies dwindled.*

"I think this vindicates the notion that counterpressure against the traffickers will work," Bennett said. President Bush agreed, declaring, "We're on the road to victory." In November, Bennett claimed his War on Drugs was succeeding "beyond my wildest dreams."

That said, Bennett announced he was bailing out. After eighteen months, he was leaving the job he'd committed to keeping for "a long period of time."

Bennett didn't gather his staff to break the news; he let it dribble out. Joe McHugh, Bennett's congressional liaison, was sitting beside

* In the first six months of 1990, violent crime increased 10 percent, assault increased 10 percent, and murder increased 8 percent, according to the FBI.

Bennett on a plane, heading for one of Bennett's many speaking gigs, when Bennett shifted in his seat and grunted.

"Excuse me?" McHugh asked.

"Leaving," Bennett said as the plane started up the runway.

"What?"

"I'm leaving. You've been great. It's been great. We've been great. But, leaving."

Bennett hadn't been around much lately, anyway. He'd spent much of the past few months in North Carolina, helping Senator Jesse Helms defend his seat against a serious black challenger, Harvey Gantt, and stumping in Alaska for a referendum to recriminalize marijuana possession.*

Maybe it was the midterm election on November 7 that inspired Bennett to quit. The Republicans got shellacked. Maybe it was that the public lost interest in the drug issue after Saddam invaded Kuwait. Maybe it was the lack of meaningful results. One administration official told the *New York Times* Bennett had simply "run out of gas." His deputy for demand reduction, Dr. Herbert Kleber of Columbia University Medical School, said later that Bennett's departure, while sudden, did not surprise him "as a psychiatrist."

Also, Bennett's $99,500 drug czar salary wasn't covering his expenses. He was in debt. Bennett could well remember more lucrative days. In the four months between leaving the Education Department and taking the drug czar's job, he'd racked up $240,000 in speaking fees. He'd signed two book contracts with Simon & Schuster, collecting a total of $187,500 in advances, but that money was gone. It was time to deliver those two books and maybe collect some royalties and speech fees.

So he did what critics had urged the United States to do in Vietnam: he declared victory and walked away. Congressman Charles Rangel of Harlem, chair of the House Select Committee on Narcotics Abuse and Control, called Bennett's tenure "a colossal failure."

"I don't understand this idea about declaring victory and quitting," Rangel continued. "He must be smoking cigarettes without printing if he thinks he can lead me to any city, town, or village and find anybody who will say, 'Thank you, Bill Bennett, there's light at the end of the tunnel.' "

* Alaska, one of the first states to decriminalize personal possession of marijuana in the 1970s, voted 53 to 46 percent to reimpose criminal penalties. So many people voted in that referendum, and so few did in the contest that made Walter Hickel governor, that bumper stickers rightly claimed, "Pot Got More Votes Than Hickel."

"Mr. Rangel," Bennett retorted at his final press conference as drug czar, "is a gasbag."

Leaving the drug office, Bennett accepted the chairmanship of the Republican National Committee. But RNC lawyers told him he couldn't write books and keep his for-profit speaking schedule. So, two weeks after accepting the $125,000-a-year job, he quit that too.

"I didn't take a vow of poverty," he told reporters. The Age of Czar Bennett was over.

- Number of Americans arrested in 1990: 1.1 million.
- Number arrested for marijuana possession: 264,000.
- Percentage of high school seniors who said cocaine is "easy or very easy" to get in 1980: 48.
- Percentage who said the same thing in 1990: 59.
- Percentage change, from 1989 to 1990, in states' spending on primary and secondary education: +7.3.
- On corrections: +29.
- Percentage change, from 1989 to 1990, in states' capital expenditures for colleges and universities: +46.
- For prisons: +150.6.

21

Apologies to None
1991–1992

If you want to use that "War on Drugs" analogy, then forfeiture is like giving the troops permission to loot.

— *defense attorney Thomas Lorenzi*

RANDY BROWN was working in his Sacramento, California, metal shop on Washington's Birthday, 1991, when a storm of shotgun and pistol fire blew the locks off his front door. Forty police officers rushed in wearing ski masks, handcuffed Brown to a chair, and started rifling his shop. "I get this," one officer said, picking up a drill. "I'll take this," said another, affixing a tag to a vise. One officer planted himself in front of the Model A Ford Brown was renovating, smacked a hand on the hood, and told him, "I have a friend who'll be thrilled to get this." A coffee can holding $4,600 in cash went into a police evidence bag, along with Brown's business records and $313 from his wallet.

The reason for the raid: a box of legal chemicals that could, if mixed with other compounds, be used to make methamphetamine. No illegal drugs were found either at the shop or at Brown's house. Brown had no criminal record, for drugs or anything else. A month later, the district attorney dropped all criminal charges.

The DA's forfeiture unit returned Brown's equipment, but refused to give back his money or business records. They insisted Brown prove the cash was legitimate. Furious, Brown dug up receipts and got customers to sign affidavits accounting for $7,200 — far more than was seized. When Brown brought the paperwork to Deputy District Attorney Esther Jackson, she waved him away.

"You're just trying to get your money back," she said.

"Yeah," Brown said. "That's the general idea."

After two years, Brown and the DA's office struck a deal. He could have $2,000 back — leaving more than $2,900 with the prosecutor's office — but only if he signed an agreement that police had good reason to seize the money in the first place.

⁓

With the departure of William Bennett and the start of the War on Iraq, the War on Drugs switched to auto-pilot. President Bush left the drug czar's post vacant for four months, and finally nominated not Reggie Walton but former Florida governor Bob Martinez, a former schoolteacher and mayor of Tampa. Martinez, an old family friend of the Bushes, had lost to Democrat Lawton Chiles in November despite Bush's many appearances for him.

Bob Martinez was by all accounts a decent administrator, but he brought no passion to the drug czar's job. He preached more of the same — heavy funding for enforcement and interdiction, lip service to treatment and education. He brought with him eleven senior staff members, none of whom had worked for any of the lead agencies in the Drug War.

The Office of National Drug Control Policy is essentially symbolic and needs a master of the bully pulpit like Bennett to give it presence. With the air war in full fury over Iraq and the quiet, colorless Bob Martinez in the drug czar's seat, the drug office all but disappeared from the nation's political radar. No new initiative was launched, no precedent-breaking law was promoted or passed.

But while the cockpit was empty, the Drug War roared on.

⁓

Bureau of Prisons director Michael Quinlan sat down at his desk, picked up the *Washington Post,* and gasped. There, on page one, the U.S. attorney in Philadelphia was announcing his intention — as part of his "get tough" program against drugs — to take over forty drug cases a month from the state prosecutor. Quinlan scribbled some quick calculations on his desk blotter. The prosecutor's plan would end up costing the Bureau of Prisons $1.2 billion over the next ten years, and this was only one of ninety-four U.S. attorneys! Already the Bureau of

Prisons was the fastest-growing agency in government, with enough new prisons under construction to increase capacity by half. If every federal prosecutor followed Philadelphia's lead, the Bureau of Prisons would have to become as big as the Defense Department. Quinlan fired off yet another memo to Deputy Attorney General Don Aire, pleading, as he had for two years, for a meeting of the heads of federal law enforcement agencies to coordinate prosecutions and punishment. As usual, he received no response.

~

One Thursday morning soon after taking office, drug czar Martinez called Reggie Walton into his office and fired him.

You've missed too many staff meetings, Martinez said.

Because I've been doing my job, Walton retorted.

Be out of here by tomorrow afternoon, Martinez said, and that was that.

Embarrassed, the White House created a position for Walton on its staff. He spent the next seven months twiddling his thumbs at a desk in the Old Executive Office Building until another judgeship opened up.

~

A detective on the Hawaiian island of Maui sat thumbing through old drug cases, trolling for assets to seize.

Open on his desk was the case of Thomas Lopes, an emotionally disturbed youth busted in 1987 for growing marijuana in the yard of his parents' Maui home. Lopes's parents knew their son was growing marijuana, the file noted, and in fact had been glad for the arrest because they figured he might then get the counseling he needed. But the detective saw the Lopeses in a different light: they knew about the crime and that made them accomplices. The house was legally seizable. Though the case was four years old, it was inside the five-year limit for asset forfeiture. The detective picked up the phone and called the Maui DEA office.

Frances Lopes, Thomas's mother, was in her carport when the police car and a van pulled up. A man got out and flashed a badge. "Let's go into the house, and we will explain things to you," he said. The men ushered her to a chair and explained, "We're taking the house." For the rest of the day, Frances and Joseph Lopes followed the agents around as they videotaped what used to be the Lopeses' property. Leave everything exactly as it is, the agents warned as they returned to their vehicles.

"Take care of the yard," one called to Frances from his car. "We'll be back."

~

In the spring of 1991, Harvard University researchers surveyed a third of the country's oncologists, and of the thousand who responded about half said they would prescribe marijuana if it was legal. Of those, almost all said they'd done so anyway, telling at least one patient that, though illegal, marijuana can fight the debilitating nausea of chemotherapy. The survey, published in May, seemed to discredit the DEA's contention that marijuana has "no accepted medical use." Even before the Harvard researchers published their findings, the U.S. Court of Appeals for the Third Circuit ordered the DEA in April to reconsider its long-standing ban on the medical use of marijuana.

By 1991 the community of AIDS sufferers was organized and noisy, demanding access to marijuana to block the nauseating effects of AZT and other drugs, and to stimulate appetite to control "wasting syndrome." In addition to Bob Randall, only nine people in the country had experimental permits to smoke pot, receiving tins of 300 government-issue marijuana cigarettes every month. But between the court decision, the oncologists, and the AIDS patients, the government was starting to receive a stream of new applications to its Compassionate Investigative New Drug (IND) program and was expecting a tidal wave of them.

So the government killed the program. On June 21, Dr. James O. Mason, chief of the Public Health Service, announced the government would no longer make marijuana available to desperately sick people — even on an experimental basis. Those who were getting the drug would continue to do so, but everybody else — including the thirty-odd patients who'd been accepted for the program but hadn't yet started receiving their tins — would be shut out. In his press conference, Mason acknowledged the decision was based on politics, not health. "If it's perceived that the Public Health Service is going around giving marijuana to folks," he said, "there would be a perception that this stuff can't be so bad."

The public, which until now had generally cheered each escalation of the War on Drugs, finally balked. Massachusetts quickly became the thirty-sixth state to pass a resolution recognizing marijuana's medical value; governors and legislators from every corner of the country went on the air to denounce Mason's decision, and most major medical associations dealing with AIDS, glaucoma, cancer, or paralysis weighed in against the decision. Editorial pages as far afield as the British magazine *The Economist* and the Marquette, Michigan, *Mining Journal* blistered the government's insensitivity. Even Bob Martinez's Office of National Drug Control Policy declared the end of the IND program "unconscionable." "We've had a lot of dying people calling and asking us for help," a Martinez spokesman told the *Washington Post*. "It's sad."

The Public Health Service, however, wouldn't budge. "The government has a responsibility to see to it people receive appropriate treatment," said Mark Barnes, the highest-ranking drug-abuse official at the Department of Health and Human Services, which houses the Health Service. "It doesn't have a responsibility to put them into a state of euphoria."

~

AIDS was harassing the drug warriors on another front as well.

Intravenous drug users were the biggest victims of AIDS. Needles were illegal drug paraphernalia, so addicts hoarded and shared them, and the virus went along for the ride. Since Bush's inauguration, the number of drug-related AIDS cases had jumped from 12,000 to 16,000. A third of all the country's AIDS cases were believed to have originated with a dirty needle.

The obvious solution was clean needles, and several cities experimented by either legalizing their sale and possession, distributing them free, or handing out clean ones for every dirty one returned. The latter was the most politically promising. Pharmacists didn't want junkies coming into their stores to buy needles. Parks and sanitation workers didn't want to handle discarded and potentially lethal syringes. Requiring addicts to bring their needles back provided an opportunity for counseling, health care, even addiction treatment.

New Haven launched the country's biggest needle exchange program in 1990. Rather than requiring addicts to come to a central distribution point, the city funded a roving van to travel to the addicts. Police were ordered not to hassle addicts coming to meet the van. Every needle was assigned a number, and every addict a fictitious name. For every used needle an addict turned in, he or she got a clean one.

In the program's first months, about two needles in ten came back to the van, and about 68 percent of them tested positive for the

AIDS virus. Two years later, some seven in ten were coming back, and the percentage of those testing positive was down to 44. Moreover, one of every six addicts participating had gone into drug treatment, and all were given the chance to get flu shots, checkups, and other basic care previously unavailable. While far from a panacea, needle exchange seemed to be doing considerable good — and cheaply. Moreover, clean needles didn't attract people to the junkie lifestyle; the rate of intravenous drug abuse didn't rise. The mayors of New York and Washington, D.C., launched similar pilot programs.

For an administration bent on "zero tolerance," however, needle exchange was intolerable. Within Martinez's drug office, discussion of needle exchange was forbidden. "We [cannot] allow our concern for AIDS to undermine our determination to win the War on Drugs," he said. He exhorted Congress not to legalize needles or fund nationwide needle exchange, and in this he was partly successful. Congress kept in place the ban on using federal funds for needle exchange, but allowed states to use federal funds to give bleach to addicts to disinfect their needles. Ultimately, Congress placed the decision whether to fund needle exchange in the hands of the surgeon general. If Antonia Novello (or her successors) wanted to fund needle exchange, they could lift the ban with the stroke of a pen. Novello declined the option.*

In the midst of the congressional wrangling, Tim Westmoreland lost his temper. Westmoreland, slight and boyish with a mustache the size of a croissant, was the member of Congressman Henry Waxman's staff in charge of AIDS policy. He'd been fighting with conservatives over AIDS policy for more than a decade, and to him resistance to needle exchange was one more example of their ideological insensitivity. In one particularly contentious meeting with a group of Republican staff members, Westmoreland threw up his hands. "Why don't we just hand out needles tipped with strychnine to kill drug users outright?" he snapped. "That would be cheaper and quicker!"

The room got very quiet, and Westmoreland couldn't quite tell how his colleagues took that.

~

Willie Jones, owner of a Nashville, Tennessee, landscaping business, was on his way to Houston to buy shrubbery. Jones was used to car-

* At the last minute, Senator Jesse Helms tried to insert an amendment not only banning the use of federal funds for needle exchange, but also the use of *state* funds. The Helms amendment would have withdrawn all HHS funds — including Headstart and Medicaid — from any state that failed to prosecute needle swappers.

rying large amounts of cash, because his growers preferred it: for this trip he'd withdrawn $9,600, plus enough for his flight. At the American Airlines counter, Jones pulled out a wad of bills.

Big mistake. An African-American male paying cash, Jones fit a drug courier profile. The ticket agent, who stood to gain 10 percent of any assets she helped seize, excused herself for a few minutes. Next thing Jones knew, DEA agents had him against a wall. Jones was terrified: his only previous brush with the law was a ticket, fifteen years earlier, for drag racing.

The drug agents didn't arrest Jones. They just took the money. His DEA receipt reads, "unspecified amount of US currency." The DEA said a dog had sniffed drugs on the cash, but Jones never saw a dog. The loss nearly put him out of business. The DEA finally agreed to give his money back if he paid $900. When he filed an application to get the money without paying $900, the DEA said simply his application was "deficient."

"I didn't know," Jones said, "that it was against the law for a forty-two-year-old black man to have money in his pocket."

Police annually seize thousands of dollars from people on tips from dogs. Trained dogs sniff cash, and if they bark, that's taken to mean the money is contaminated with drugs and is therefore "drug money" and seizable. The *Pittsburgh Press* found in 1991 that virtually all currency in the United States is tainted with enough cocaine to trigger a dog's response. Two different private labs tested currency from banks in eleven cities and found as much as 96 percent of it showing traces of coke. Clean money put in the same drawer as "dirty" money will later make a dog bark.

Police and federal agents don't clean or destroy drug-tainted cash they seize. They deposit it in the bank, to be put into circulation — perhaps to be seized — again.

~

Thomas Kline was arrested because he wrote a pro-legalization letter to his local paper.

Kline spent most of his adult life working in Nevada's casinos before moving in 1986 to the tiny hamlet of Post Falls, Idaho, "to be left alone." He married in Post Falls, had a daughter, and lived off odd jobs and reselling what he called "low-end classic cars." He wore a gray ponytail, kept a Jim Morrison poster on his living room wall, and considered himself something of a political activist, trying without success to organize a Post Falls chapter of NORML. In August 1990, he wrote a mild letter to the editor of the nearby Spokane *Spokesman Review*, advocating the legalization of marijuana and hemp as medicine, fiber, and fuel, and the decriminalization of "personal use" of marijuana. Two months later, he sent the same letter to the editor of the other big newspaper in his region, the *Coeur d'Aleñe Press*.

Walt Richard, an agent of the Idaho Department of Law Enforcement (IDLE), read the letter in the Coeur d'Alene paper and took it as a tip. The U.S. Supreme Court ruled in 1988 that police may search the garbage outside a private home without a warrant, so Richard hopped into an unmarked pickup, drove to Kline's house, and collected two bags of trash that were sitting on a curb. He found nothing illegal among the eggshells and coffee grounds, but he did find some NORML literature. So a week later he went back, and this time found three-tenths of a gram of marijuana stems, which he brought before a judge, who signed a search warrant. In Kline's house, police found one-ninth of an ounce of marijuana.

When asked why IDLE went to such lengths to arrest Thomas Kline, Richard's boss, Wayne Longo, said, "It's not that often that we see people writing in saying they're using dope."

~

Every day during Donny Clark's six-week marijuana-conspiracy trial, Judge Elizabeth Kovachevich reminded Clark that the maximum sentence for the crime of which he was accused was life without parole. More than a thousand marijuana plants were involved in the conspiracy. When the other alleged conspirators were arrested, they possessed firearms. Clark himself had a drug record, had not helped the police, and had shown no remorse. Under the sentencing guidelines, that added up to life. Did he want to change his plea?

Your honor, Clark would say, I do not want to change my plea. I gave no help to the police and show no remorse because I'm not guilty. I was involved with marijuana in the early eighties, but I have since paid my debt to society for it.

Clark's lawyer repeatedly pointed out that not even the prosecutor alleged that Clark had committed any crime since the one for which he'd already served a state sentence. He was being tried again for the same crime.

We've been through that, Judge Kovachevich said. The state of Florida and the United States are different sovereigns. Double jeopardy does not apply.

It took the jury four and a half days to find Clark guilty. On

November 5, 1991, Judge Kovachevich ordered Clark taken to federal prison for the rest of his life, with no possibility of parole. He is there today.

Shortly after sentence, the Justice Department institutionalized the practice of sending people to federal prison for crimes for which they'd already served time in state prison. Under Operation Triggerlock federal prosecutors were instructed to comb closed state cases for people who had, in the course of the same crime, violated federal gun or drug laws. Such people would be rearrested by federal agents, as they walked out the door of the state prison if necessary. As in Donny Clark's case, the Fifth Amendment protection against double jeopardy didn't apply.

"The intent," a Justice Department spokesman said, "is to get the bad guys off the street with apologies to none."

~

Gary Spencer thought he'd found a bad guy. Despite repeated evidence to the contrary, the Los Angeles County drug detective became convinced that a half-blind, sixty-one-year-old millionaire named Donald Scott was growing 3,000 marijuana plants on his Malibu ranch. On October 2, 1992, Spencer burst into Scott's house, armed with a warrant and a 9-mm Beretta, and shot him dead. Then he searched the place, finding no marijuana plants. The Ventura County district attorney concluded, in a seventy-page report, that the L.A. County Sheriff's Department "was motivated, at least in part, by a desire to seize and forfeit the [$5 million] ranch for the government." The report pieced the story together this way:

Spencer had been unable to shake his obsession with a tip about Scott's ranch, despite discouragement from other agencies. The DEA had examined Scott's phone records as part of a drug investigation in 1980 and had found no evidence with which to charge him. Scott's Trail's End Ranch adjoined a national recreation area, and when Spencer called the National Park Service for maps the ranger was equally discouraging. Funny you should call, he told Spencer. I was on that ranch three weeks ago. Scott and I walked all across the ranch, and I didn't see any sign of marijuana. He was real friendly. He invited me back.

Still, Spencer asked the Air National Guard to fly over the ranch and take pictures. He took the photos to DEA agent Charles Stowell, the local commander for the CAMP marijuana eradication program and a self-described expert at spotting marijuana from the air. "Marijuana," Stowell liked to say, "has a color not found anywhere else in nature."

Stowell looked at the Air Guard photos and though he didn't see any plants, he identified an unconcealed water tank near the ranch buildings as an "illegal water system." Stowell himself then flew over the ranch, and on his third pass recorded seeing "50 marijuana plants." Although he had a camera with him, he took no pictures, a departure from standard DEA procedure. He didn't use his binoculars either, because, he later said, they make him feel sick.

Now the U.S. Forest Service and the Park Service got involved. The Trail's End Ranch was on a list of property surrounding the national recreation area that the Park Service wanted some day to acquire. Spencer told Park Ranger Tim Simonds that if the ranch was seized, Los Angeles County might give it to the Park Service.

At a meeting with Spencer and Stowell, a Forest Ranger got the idea of sending the Border Patrol onto the Trail's End Ranch to look around. The Border Patrol has authority to conduct warrantless searches for illegal immigrants on or near the border. Although Malibu is more than 160 miles from the border, the Border Patrol authorized the search because the Forest Service suggested illegals might be living on the ranch to harvest the pot. Twice during the night of September 24, Border Patrol agents, equipped with climbing gear, cameras, and weapons, roamed throughout the rugged ranch terrain while Scott slept unawares. They found no illegal aliens and no marijuana.

Spencer's search warrant request was full of falsehoods. He said that he'd verified the location of the "50 plants" from the ground; that Stowell had used binoculars on his flight; that Stowell had "noticed" the plants during a routine reconnaissance flight. The warrant request failed to mention that Stowell was a thousand feet high during his naked-eye inspection; that Stowell saw nothing the first two times he flew over the ranch; that both the Park Service and the Border Patrol had visited the ranch and seen no marijuana. The judge, misled, granted the search warrant, which, as the Ventura County district attorney put it, "became Donald Scott's death warrant."

Spencer organized a guns-drawn raid on the farm with thirteen deputies, two state drug agents, two DEA agents, four LAPD officers, and two agents from the Forest Service. Conspicuously absent, given that Scott's house sat within Ventura County, were any Ventura authorities; investigators later speculated that "Los Angeles County did not want to split the forfeiture proceeds with that agency."

The team hit the ranch at 8:30 A.M. Roused from sleep by shouting and the sound of his door being battered, Scott walked into the hallway with a pistol in his hand. He'd been up late drinking and was still drunk. He didn't drop his gun quickly enough and, according to Spencer, while lowering it pointed it in Spencer's direction. Spencer fired twice, and Scott became what the deputies called on the radio a "927D": a dead man. The search team went over every inch of the ranch and found no marijuana plants and no evidence that any had ever been there.

Because the killing took place across the county line from Los Angeles, Ventura DA Michael Bradbury investigated. He acknowledged Spencer's "bad faith" in preparing the warrant but cleared Spencer of homicide or manslaughter charges.

Bradbury also noted the Trail's End Ranch was worth millions of dollars and concluded, "This case involves numerous individual agencies and is fertile ground for speculation as to the motivations of each of them."

- Value of assets seized by the Justice Department from 1986 through 1990: $1.5 billion.
- Value of assets seized by the Justice Department in 1991 alone: $500 million.
- Percentage of people who had property confiscated by police in 1991 who were never charged with a crime: 80.
- Percentage of travelers who had money confiscated in 1991 without ever being charged who were black, Hispanic, or Asian: 77.
- Percentage of the flying public that is black: 4.
- Average number of prisoners, per prison guard, nationwide: 3.
- Average number of pupils, per public school teacher, nationwide: 30.

22

Just Say No

1992

Weed & Seed works this way: First, we join federal, state, and local forces to "weed out" the gang leaders, the violent criminals, and the drug dealers who plague our neighborhoods. [Then] we follow up with part two: we "seed" those neighborhoods with expanded educational opportunities and social services.

— *President George Bush, January 27, 1992*

Weed & Seed works this way: First, it imposes a federal police presence in inner city, low-income neighborhoods that violates the civil rights and civil liberties of community residents. Then, it commandeers existing federal social service programs and places them under the authority of the Department of Justice, the FBI, and the Immigration and Naturalization Service.

— *Labor/Community Strategy Center of Los Angeles, September 1992*

THE WAR ON DRUGS has always had its critics, but in the second half of the Bush years the first glimmers of serious resistance began to appear.

The Sentencing Project, a tiny liberal nonprofit organization, had been tracking big increases in incarceration since 1981, issuing a series of reports that quickly disappeared into obscurity. By 1990, a mounting number of Drug War horror stories had shown up in the press, and that year, the Sentencing Project stumbled upon wording that, like "Just Say No" and "instantaneous addiction," had a resonance the public could hear. "America has more black men in prison than in college," it wrote. "One in four are under control of the criminal justice system — jail, prison, probation or parole."*

As though a boil had been lanced, the country began talking about the racial implications of its War on Drugs. Newspapers in Dayton, Philadelphia, Topeka, Dallas, San Jose, and other cities began looking at statistics in their areas. In city after city, front pages shouted that blacks were arrested more often, offered fewer opportunities for bail, and sentenced to longer stretches than whites. In each case, drug sentences punishing small-time drug possessors with years of hard time were at the heart of the disparity. Then *USA Today* did a national story, DRUG WAR FOCUSED ON BLACKS, that led off: "Urban blacks are being detained in numbers far exceeding their involvement" in the drug trade.

Never was Bennett's absence more noticeable. Not a peep of response emanated from the drug office.

Local Bar Associations — notably in Boston and Rochester, New York — issued thick reports on the waste, racial disparities, injustice, and futility of the Drug War. Even the National Association of Counties, as staid an organization as any in Washington, passed a resolution demanding Congress end the War on Drugs and replace it with a fully funded drug-treatment program.

With the issue of injustice and the Drug War on the table, judges began speaking out as well. Carol Berkman, a New York City criminal judge, blasted the city's police for the courier-profile program it ran in Port Authority Bus Terminal. "I arraign approximately one third of the felony cases in New York County and have no recollection of any defendant in a Port Authority Police Department drug interdiction case who was not either black or Hispanic," she said. "Minorities did not fight their way up from the back of the bus just to be routinely stopped and interrogated on the way through the terminal." In Minnesota, which had adopted a version of the 1988 federal law imposing heavier penalties for crack than for powdered cocaine, a judge dismissed crack charges against five black men. The only difference between crack and powder, she wrote, is that one is favored by blacks and one by whites. Therefore, she ruled, Minnesota's sentencing law is discriminatory. The state supreme court agreed.

Norman Lanford, a criminal-courts judge in Houston, considered himself a conservative, law-and-order Republican. It wasn't racial outrage or pity for the drug offenders paraded before him that got

* By 1995, it would be one in three.

him thinking, but the sheer number of paltry cases he saw. Buying one rock of cocaine. Buying two rocks of cocaine. Selling one rock of cocaine. The third time a person got caught with a single crack rock he could be sentenced to twenty-five years in prison. Lanford decided to begin keeping track. What he learned about his own court in 1991 amazed him.

Almost a third of those convicted in his court were drug offenders, almost all of them minor possession cases. More than 2,500 people from the county had been sent to prison in 1991 for holding less than a gram of cocaine. Most drug convicts held half that much. Three-quarters of them were black, even though blacks constituted less than a fifth of the county's population.

Average sentence for a minor drug possessor in Houston that year: eight and a half years. Lanford figured it cost Houston's taxpayers almost $22 million in 1991 to imprison all the people convicted of holding less than half a gram. He identified 2,113 people imprisoned in Houston that year for possessing — among them — seven ounces of cocaine.

Lanford spoke out: "We're occupying a 25-year space in prison for a guy [about whom] all we can prove in his entire criminal career is ownership of $40 worth of crack." The comment cost Lanford his judgeship. When he came up for reelection in early 1991, an assistant district attorney hammered him for being "soft on drugs" and knocked him out of the primary.

~

Kurt Schmoke, however, dodged the bullet.

Written off politically in 1988 for suggesting the legalization of drugs, Mayor Schmoke approached his first reelection campaign in 1991 with trepidation. But every time one of his opponents in either the primary or the general election tried to blast him with the "legalizer" attack, the shot went wild and it never became an issue. Having won office in 1987 with 51 percent of the vote, "Legalizer Schmoke" won reelection with 58 percent.

~

For Reggie Walton, it was wonderful getting back to the real world of D.C. criminal court in December 1991. But in the two years he'd been gone, juries had begun acting strangely. He noticed it one afternoon when, after a case he thought clearly proved the guilt of a young crack dealer, the jury returned a verdict of not guilty. Then it happened again.

And again. Typical cases, which in the old days would have resulted in a quick guilty verdict, were tumbling to acquittal. Or juries would end up deadlocked because a single juror refused to convict. After observing this for a few months, Walton finally asked a jury foreman, an imposing black woman, about their verdict to acquit.

"We decided we aren't sending any more young black men to prison," she said.

The next time it happened, he asked the foreman again. Same answer. "No more black men to prison." A believer in the War on Drugs, Walton was frightened for the first time. If the people lose faith in their justice system, he wondered, what then?

It was a good time to ask. On March 3, 1992, George Holliday pointed a video camera out his window and recorded Los Angeles Police officers beating Rodney King.

~

James Gray was not black, not the product of the Philadelphia projects, not given to ruminating about root causes. Trim, youthful, and preppy, he had spent the past fifteen years as a vigorous soldier in the War on Drugs, first as a navy prosecutor, then as an assistant U.S. attorney, and now as a tough-sentencing state judge in Santa Ana, California. He considered himself conservative even by the standards of Orange County, among the most staunchly Republican enclaves in the country.

Although his fundamental politics hadn't changed, Gray was about to break ranks with his party, his ideological soul mates, and the Republican governor who appointed him. In a series of speeches and op-ed pieces, Judge Gray defected from the drug warriors and became a full-bore advocate for the legalization of all drugs.

"We couldn't design a system worse than the one we've got," he'd say. "The courts are doing a good job, as is the DEA and everybody else. But we're farther away from a resolution than when I started on the bench."

He laid out an alternative: sell controlled doses of drugs in plainwrapped packages with a sterile needle and information about both the dangers of drugs and where help is available. Ban their advertising and their sale to minors. Maintain the price low enough so a black market doesn't coalesce. Put the money saved on drug enforcement into treating the likely — but not certain — increase in drug casualties.

Gray braced for a storm of public ire, with the most vicious attack expected from the editors of the *Orange County Register.* But they too had had enough of a policy that only wasted money and eroded the public's respect for the law. "Clearly, prohibition isn't working," they wrote. "We cannot fail to consider that war may be inappropriate as a domestic policy."

On July 28, 1992, the biggest of journalistic guns swiveled on the Drug War. The *New York Times* put the failure of the War on Drugs on page one for the first time: SOME THINK THE 'WAR ON DRUGS' IS BEING WAGED ON THE WRONG FRONT. As part of a series on George Bush's record as president, reporter Joseph Treaster wrote that "Mr. Bush has poured more and more money into tactics that over the last 20 years have repeatedly failed to change the course of the campaign against drugs" — interdiction, enforcement, and ever-longer sentences. Treaster gave the first word in the piece to Eric Sterling, now a full-time activist for legalization. "Enforcement has had little effect on the supply or the use of drugs," Sterling said, a comment Treaster called "the common wisdom in the field." The story began above the fold and ran to an entire inside page, but its hardest blow was in the headline: the quotation marks around "War on Drugs."

~

After this series of individual acts of resistance to the War on Drugs, a whole segment of a major city's population rose up to reject the Drug War's latest incarnation. Remarkably, the people who did so were among the most powerless anywhere — the impoverished blacks and Hispanics of South Central and East Los Angeles.

When the officers accused of beating Rodney King were acquitted by an all-white jury and Los Angeles exploded in days of rebellion, President Bush made a highly publicized visit to the city. What now? reporters asked. What is Washington's plan for this city now?

We're bringing to Los Angeles a dramatic new Justice Department program, the president said, to weed out the drug dealers, gang members, and violent criminals from these communities and seed them with opportunity-creating funding. We call it "Weed & Seed."

All over East and South Central Los Angeles, community leaders looked at each other in alarm. The "seed" part sounded good. The "weed" part scared them. They looked into it, and found the plan called for a massive series of drug sweeps. Then all social spending was to be routed through the Justice Department, with the local U.S. attorney coordinating housing, nutrition, job training, and other social programs. A few weeks after Bush's visit, the LA City Council approved two pilot Weed & Seed programs, both in minority communities in South Central and Koreatown.

Joe Hicks, stocky and egg-bald, had been a civil rights activist in Los Angeles since the 1965 Watts riots and now was running the local office of the Southern Christian Leadership Conference. In his view, all the talk of drugs and guns was nothing but code for the criminalization of poverty. He called around the country and learned that Weed & Seed had been operating in Chicago and Seattle, where community activists weren't happy about it. The brunt of the "weed" portion had been predictably borne by young black men. Worse, the "seed" part came tangled in strings. The Justice Department had told Seattle, for example, that it couldn't use its "seed" money for the teen health clinic, drug treatment center, or youth counseling it wanted; it could go only to "programs with a law-enforcement component." In Kansas City, Trenton, and Philadelphia, community activists likewise said the only visible portion of Weed & Seed was more drug sweeps and tougher penalties for those caught in them.

Not only that, Weed & Seed was actually taking money away from social programs Hicks and the SCLC believed had already been starved to death. Of the $500 million Bush budgeted for Weed & Seed, only $280 million was new money. The rest was funds already earmarked for the Job Corps, Aid to Families with Dependent Children, Community Development Block Grants, and other crucial inner-city programs.

What alarmed Hicks and the SCLC most of all was the precedent of giving the Justice Department authority over social programs. Weed & Seed would turn U.S. attorneys into viceroys of the colonial power back in Washington — and a hostile colonial power at that.

The name was awful, too. The idea that any members of the community were "weeds" was patently offensive. Hicks saw that not as a problem, however, but an opportunity — something to make people mad.

He picked up the phone. Los Angeles teems with labor organizations, police-watchdog groups, immigrant-rights offices, and other community groups, many of which were as alarmed about Weed & Seed as Hicks. They began holding meetings and rallies, which culminated in a big one at Greater Bethany Community Church in South Central in October 1990. More than 200 people turned out to tell members of the LA City Council and assistant U.S. attorney Terree Bowers they wanted no part of the new federal plan. Of the $18 million earmarked for LA, only $1 million was specifically for the police, but even that was too much for the assembled crowd. "Am I a weed?" one young man asked Bowers over and over. "Tell me, am I a weed?"

At any other time, a coalition of minority groups opposed to Weed & Seed probably wouldn't have had a chance against the combined might of the LAPD, the city council, and the Justice Department. But the ashes of the rebellion were still warm, and groups were as active and motivated as they'd ever been. Also, the city council had created an Ad Hoc Recovery Committee whose chair, Mark Ridley-Thomas, represented one of the districts targeted for Weed & Seed. The committee held a hearing in a downtown hotel, at which it got an earful of opposition. "Two and a half years ago I was what the Justice Department would have labeled a weed," said one recovering addict now working as an addiction counselor. "If the Weed & Seed program had been working then, I would now be serving time in prison and would be no use to the community at all."

Nine days after George Bush lost the election to Bill Clinton, Ridley-Thomas led the Ad Hoc Recovery Committee to reject the $1 million "weed" portion of Weed & Seed. "[It] has been imposed on communities of color with the purpose of incarceration and not rehabilitation," Ridley-Thomas said.

The lame-duck White House was incensed. The chief of Bush's Presidential Task Force on Los Angeles Recovery said if Ridley-Thomas didn't want the $19 million, "I'll recommend to the White House we spend the money in one of the several communities throughout this nation that desperately want the program." Added Bowers, "You can't buy this meal à la carte. It's a full-course meal or nothing." If Los Angeles wanted the social spending, it had to take the police money, too. In an editorial, the *Los Angeles Times* pleaded with the council to "take the money and run with it."

In the end, Mayor Tom Bradley, the city council, and the Justice Department struck a deal. Los Angeles got the $19 million. But the $1 million law-enforcement portion was placed entirely in the hands of the LA City Council to spend as it wished without Justice Department strings. Ridley-Thomas said it would go toward bicycle patrols, Spanish lessons for city police officers, and other "community policing" projects, not drug sweeps. "The heavy-handed approach" used elsewhere, he said, "is history."

As was the name. Weed & Seed became CPR — Community Project for Restoration.

Epilogue: Night and Day
1993–1994

The definition of insanity is doing the same old thing over and over again and expecting a different result.

— *candidate Bill Clinton, July 1992*

ALL ALONG K STREET, Washington's political-memorabilia stores were dusting off the donkey. Twelve-year-old displays of Alf Landon and Wendell Wilkie were giving way to windows full of FDR and Jimmy Carter. Vendors sold souvenirs on every corner — toy saxophones, framed photos of the new First Couple and their frizzy-haired teenager, coffee mugs bearing the boyish likenesses of the president- and vice president–elect. A 300-pound Latina in a Styrofoam skimmer held out a commemorative button the size of a saucer: the incoming chief executive in sunglasses, wailing on the sax: "Inhale to the Chief." But George Bush was still president — for another eight days, anyway — and since I was headed for his Drug Policy Office I declined the button.

A guard behind bulletproof glass buzzed me into a windowless waiting room at the Office of National Drug Control Policy. Facing the couch were the recruitment posters of the War on Drugs: a fried egg in a pan, a girl with a pistol up her nose, a tagged toe. The wall behind me was covered with pictures of William Bennett shaking hands. With the president of Colombia. With camouflaged soldiers. With a class of schoolchildren. With Antonin Scalia. With Chuck Norris. Bennett had been gone from this office for more than two years, but clearly those were the days to remember.

The press secretary appeared at the bulletproof window and opened the door to me by punching 3989 — Bennett's Senate confirmation date — into the electronic lock. Ben Banta was built like a bouncer, with dark, deep-set eyes. Though it was Tuesday, he was wearing Saturday clothes — chinos and a flannel shirt. As I followed him down a long silent hallway, I realized why. He was alone in the office. No phones rang, I heard not even the whir of a photocopier. Doors stood open to rooms with empty desks. Portraits of George Bush and Bob Martinez sat stacked on the floor. Once, this had been the most happening office in Washington, but now it felt like a military post being abandoned to the enemy. I half expected to see panicked officers burning documents in the wastebasket.

THIS IS HUMPTY DUMPTY ON DRUGS said the poster on Banta's door, with the ovoid character sizzling in a frypan. I asked Banta if he'd smoked pot in college.

"Of course," he said. I asked him for a copy of the half-finished *Drug Strategy* never released during Bush's last year in office, and he handed me a stack of typewritten pages, with X's every place a number was expected to go. I asked what he'd done before fronting for the drug office.

"Worked on the Miller Lite campaign," he said. I smiled. "Hey," he shrugged. "Then I sold drugs. Now I unsell drugs." Then Banta looked at his watch and shooed me out: he was off to meet a headhunter.

~

Bleachers for the inauguration parade were going up along Pennsylvania Avenue as I walked down to the Justice Department. Unseasonably radiant sunshine sparkled off the monuments and a lively breeze fluttered the bunting. Washington felt like Oz after the Wicked Witch had melted. It was more than just a party shift; it was a generational coup d'état. Before my eyes the culture of the Depression and World War II was giving way to its mirror image — that of the Great Society and Vietnam. Rock and roll blared everywhere; I must have heard Martha and the Vandellas singing "Dancin' in the Streets" fifteen times that day. Every man in town seemed to have grown a ponytail overnight. And the desk guard at Justice — a legendarily uptight lady — had her hair in dreadlocks.

Upstairs, Ben Renshaw lit up when he saw I had Bush's unpublished Drug Strategy under my arm.

"That came to me at one point," he said. "I remember one sentence: 'The number of women requiring drug treatment has declined X since X.' " Renshaw threw up his hands and laughed. "They typed the X's and expected us to fill in the blanks! There is absolutely no empirical evidence that the number of women requiring treatment has declined at all!"

I noticed on Renshaw's lapel something I'd seen in government offices all week: a little gold pin in the shape of a saxophone. Like the sign of the fish in pre-Augustan Rome, the saxophones identified Democrats to each other now that it was safe to do so.

"We never did publish my drugs-and-crime report," Renshaw said. "It could never happen under Bush, and you know why? Statistically, you can't demonstrate that drug abuse causes crime. The drug trade, drug *prohibition*, sure. But not drug abuse." He settled back in his chair and swiveled happily left and right. "The switch to Clinton is like night and day," Renshaw said. "I feel real change coming."

I left Renshaw to his numbers and stopped in at the offices of NORML, which had been fighting for that "real change" longer than any other organization. As usual, most of the staff was on the phone, advising callers how to fool urine tests. "Drink lots of water," they said over and over.

Allen St. Pierre, NORML's assistant national director, was feverishly feeding press releases to the fax machine. "The guy Clinton has in mind to head the Public Health Service is on record supporting medical marijuana for cancer and AIDS patients," he told me, running a hand through his damp hair. "Now we hear Clinton is going to name Joycelyn Elders surgeon general. She's a known advocate of a gentler drug policy and she's invincible; you can't argue with a black woman doctor over what's best for inner-city children."

Lying on a table was the issue of *Rolling Stone* with Bill Clinton on the cover. More than anything, it was having a baby boomer in the White House that seemed to hold out hope that a humane drug policy would replace the War on Drugs. Bill Clinton, after all, grew up on rock and roll and went to college in the sixties. He'd marched against the Vietnam War. Even if he'd never inhaled, he's a member of the drug-taking generation and his own brother was a user. No yawning cultural chasm separates Clinton from the 70 million Americans who have smoked pot. Clinton might have thought marijuana is unhealthy. He might even have thought it a gateway drug. But surely he understood that marijuana isn't an instrument of the Antichrist, that pot smokers, however misguided, aren't "immoral."

The prospect of even a slight softening on marijuana was tantalizing, because if anything is clear from the past twenty-five years of drug warfare, it is that marijuana — not crack, cocaine, or heroin — is politically the most important illegal drug. Precisely because it doesn't kill people who use it, spawn gun battles in city streets, enrich foreign drug lords, or inspire women to abandon their babies, marijuana separates drug policy for public welfare from drug policy for public relations. Without the marijuana ban, the country's "drug problem" would be tiny. There wouldn't be 11 million regular* users of illegal drugs in the United States, there would be 2 million. Of those, about 350,000 use cocaine every day. Along with the country's half million heroin addicts, these hard-core users are our real "drug problem": tragic, resistant to solutions, but statistically minuscule.

Heroin and cocaine are the scary drugs that keep the Drug War's home fires burning, but vastly more people are touched personally by a war on marijuana that yields few benefits. Lives aren't saved. Violent criminal organizations aren't disrupted. Instead, a lot of harmless potheads — and the generally peaceful growers who supply them — go to prison at enormous expense to the taxpayer. Diverting resources from that war to the treatment of our small but desperate population of drug dependents would be an act of medical logic and fiscal genius. In the golden sunlight of inauguration week, this was the promise the presidency of Bill Clinton held out.

"It wouldn't even take an immediate change in the law," St. Pierre said, reaching for a ringing phone. "Just a quiet change in budget priorities." He asked the caller to hold a moment and pushed the hold button. "I hesitate to be so optimistic," he told me, "but we could be seeing the beginning of the end of the War on Drugs."

A heady day all around. But that evening I opened a thick critique of Bush's drug policy issued just prior to the election by Democratic senator Joe Biden's Judiciary Committee. "The President's Drug Strategy: Has it Worked?" Biden asked in the title. No, Biden answered, but only because Bush didn't spend *enough* money on law enforcement, wasn't tough *enough* on those addicted to drugs, didn't give the military *enough* power and money to fight illegal drugs. In 194 pages, the report never once used the words "racism," "AIDS," "poverty," "tobacco," or "civil liberties." As much as Republicans, I reminded myself, Democrats like their Drug War rhetoric served hot.

~

* The government defines "regular" use as monthly.

May 1994.

I'm inching forward in low gear, careful not to kill somebody. A chilly rain falls through the dismal Chicago twilight, but the streets are full of people all walking in the same direction. Some gather briefly around fires in trash cans. Snack trucks do a lively business. But mostly the people stream along the pavement. Despite the wind and drizzle, the atmosphere is almost festive. Between that, and the uniformly black faces, I might be headed to a championship soccer game in Zimbabwe.

The crowd is not flowing toward a stadium, though. It's converging on a forbidding building that towers over this battered neighborhood of liquor stores and check cashers. COOK COVNTY CRIMINAL COVRTHOVSE declares the building's facade: multi-hafted Roman axes are etched into it and Julius Caesar's standard, SPQR, glowers from every corner. The base of the building teems with people. This, I learn, is nothing special — just another Friday at Night Drug Court.

After fifteen minutes waiting to pass through metal detectors I find a bulletin board listing the evening's cases. A small crowd presses against it. The board can't hold all the cases, and computer lists tacked there dangle to the floor.

The elevators are hot and slow, so I walk up to the second floor. Here, too, the wide hallways are alive with black people. Children doze on benches and fuss in strollers. The air is heavy with cigarettes, hair oil, floor disinfectant, and lollipops. A young woman holding a wriggling toddler leans into the pay phone: "They done give him six years. I don't know. Honey, hush. I don't know. Round ten o'clock. Pizza, I guess."

When I called to request an appointment with the man who created Night Drug Court, presiding judge Tom Fitzgerald, he said, "Go witness it first. I'll be interested to know if you think it's terrible or just bad."

Selecting a courtroom at random, I pull open the door to number 208.

~

The optimistic sunshine of inauguration day feels like it must have shone on another planet. Clinton, neck fully extended for another cause of the cultural left — gays in the military — backed quickly away from drug policy reform. CAMP helicopters descended upon northern California that summer with undiminished zeal. The DEA continued shadowing Grateful Dead concerts, determined to bust deadheads for LSD until, in the words of the agent in charge, "this whole thing turns around." A seventy-five-year-old Boston pastor was frightened into a fatal heart attack when ninja-suited drug agents crashed through his windows on a mistaken tip. Clinton's first drug budget duplicated precisely Bush's heavy emphasis on law enforcement. As for drug treatment, Clinton promised to launch it with his titanic reform of health care. In the meantime, he offered to add 140,000 new treatment slots a year, which, given the 2.5 million users he said could benefit from treatment, would achieve his promised "treatment on demand" two years after the end of the second Gore administration.

On Pearl Harbor Day 1993, Joycelyn Elders gave an hour-long speech to the National Press Club about AIDS, teen pregnancy, and other matters of public health, concluding that the country faced many difficult choices. During questions, legalization activist Eric Sterling asked if legalization isn't "one of the difficult choices we must face to fight violence."

"I do feel that we would markedly reduce our crime rate if drugs were legalized," Elders answered. "But I don't know all the ramifications of this. I do feel that we need to do some studies."

The White House sided with Elders's many critics. "The president is against legalizing drugs," press secretary Dee Dee Myers said, "and he's not interested in studying the issue." For good measure, a New York congressman introduced a bill "to prohibit federally sponsored research pertaining to the legalization of drugs."

Eight days after Elders's comment, Arkansas police arrested Elders's son Kevin for his role in a two-gram cocaine deal they'd known about for seven months. Though it was his first offense, he faced a ten-year mandatory sentence without parole. Still, the surgeon general came back in early January saying she'd studied up on legalization and now "realized I probably made a more honest, aboveboard statement than I knew I had made."*

But the War on Drugs raged on as ever. Amid the hysteria following the murder of California teenager Polly Klaas, Clinton pushed a crime bill that included the death penalty for drug kingpins, "three strikes and you're out" life sentencing, and ever more money for prisons and the DEA. The chief of the Public Health Service, for whom cancer, AIDS, and glaucoma patients had such high hopes, announced

* Clinton ultimately would fire Elders that December, five days after the newly elected House Speaker, former pot smoker Newt Gingrich, accused the White House staff of being riddled with pot-smoking "counterculture people." William Bennett, quoted in the *Los Angeles Times*, would write Elders's political epitaph: "I would call this the first personnel decision of the new Republican majority."

he wouldn't reopen the experimental marijuana program summarily closed by Bush's Public Health chief. And Janet Reno, who once derided boasts of arrests and drug seizures as a "body count mentality," now bragged about arrests and seizures, especially those of her many Weed & Seed programs around the country.

~

Behind the door of Courtroom 208 is a thick Plexiglas wall with a door in it. On my side of the wall are three rows of seats. On the other side is a round, windowless chamber with raised judge's bench, a few tables, and a small jury box. There is no jury in it. A young black man stands before the judge wearing lightweight tan pants and pullover, both stenciled D.O.C. A white woman hugging a pile of papers stands beside him. The judge, white and white-haired, is talking to the young black man without looking at him. He's moving papers around on his desk, signing things and handing them to his clerks, churning out the paperwork while reciting his litany. A scratchy and intermittent speaker relays his words.

"By agreeing to a 402 conference you are waiving your right to a jury trial," says the judge. "Do you understand what a jury trial is, Mr. Wilson?"

"Uh huh."

"In answering questions, Mr. Wilson, do not shake or nod your head and do not use such expressions as 'uh huh' and 'mmm-mmm.' Do you understand what a jury trial is?"

"Yes sir."

"If you choose to plead guilty, you will waive the right to contest the legality of evidence gathered against you. In short you will waive the right to a trial of any kind. Do you understand these facts as I have explained them to you, Mr. Wilson?"

"Yes sir."

Darius Wilson is twenty-five years old and charged with a class-four felony, in this case possession of three bags of cocaine. On the streets of Chicago, a "bag" contains a tenth of a gram. Darius Wilson is before the judge this evening for possession of a third as much white powder as in a Sweet 'n Low packet. The judge and Wilson's public defender start to haggle, a year in jail or eighteen months? Says the judge, "To quibble about the difference between a year and eighteen months is to quibble about the difference of ninety days." In Illinois, a prisoner can cut his sentence in half by good behavior.

Wilson speaks. "Your honor, sir, ninety days may not seem like a lot to you, but it is to me. I am HIV positive."

The judge looks up. "Since when?"

"Since the thirteenth of December, your honor."

"Apparently it didn't affect your ability to commit crimes. Okay, I'm saying fifteen months now if he wants to take it. You'll be out in seven months." Wilson takes the deal and is led away.

The clerk calls a name, and beside me a black man lifts his small daughter off his lap, sets her on the seat beside him, and tiredly walks through the Plexiglas door. The girl, dressed as for church in green velvet dress and shiny black shoes, curls up in her seat and goes to sleep. As the clerk cues up her father's case, I open the late edition of the *Chicago Tribune:* NATION'S PRISON POPULATION TOPS ONE MILLION: More than 1,500 people a week were sent to prison in the first six months of 1994 alone, the biggest increase ever reported.

A hand settles on my shoulder.

"Dan? Phil Mullane." A mountain of a man stands over me, balding, rumpled, and gray with fatigue. "Let me show you around."

Mullane is one of Cook County's small army of public defenders. We weave through the crowded hallway toward the elevator. I mention to Mullane that the only white faces I've seen all night are his, the judge's, and that of Wilson's lawyer.

"That didn't take you long to figure out," he says with a tired grin. "What we do here is process young black men for prison. It works like this." He began counting off fingers. "A kid gets picked up in a sweep. After a few hours in jail, he goes before the judge and gets a choice: plead guilty and walk tonight with probation, or ask for a trial and sit in jail for three months waiting for it. The kid may not have done anything illegal, but he wants to be on the street, especially if he's got a drug problem. So he takes probation and walks. Now," Mullane says as the elevator doors open, "now he's got a record."

We start up. "The kid's been stamped with the mark of Cain," Mullane says. "The next time he's picked up they don't even have to try him. Probation violation. Straight to prison. So he's gone through the system into prison without ever having a trial, maybe without having done anything wrong." The elevator stops and in walk two beefy men in creaky leather jackets, police radios murmuring softly. Mullane ignores them.

"We do maybe four hundred a night, five nights a week," Mullane continues. "Day judges would throw out the bullshit little cases we handle, but at night in the special court, two grams is a big deal."

We reach the top floor and Mullane walks me to a window. We're looking down on the back side of the neighborhood, a kind of garishly lit industrial park that stretches to a distant highway and, beyond that, the blackness of Lake Michigan. Directly below is a windowless building topped with twinkling concertina wire. "That's Cook County Jail," Mullane says.

"What are all those buildings around it?" I ask.

"You misunderstand," he says. "That's *all* Cook County Jail. All the buildings you see between here and the highway. We have six times more people locked up than in the biggest prison in the United States. Twelve thousand. Aside from a few serving short sentences, all of them are waiting for trial and presumed innocent."

We're both silent for a minute, gazing down upon Chicago's penal neighborhood. "This is American justice at the end of the twentieth century," Mullane says. "I'll bet you feel safer already."

Afterword to the Paperback Edition

The War on Drugs made headlines again during the presidential campaign of 1996. Lloyd Johnston's annual survey of high school seniors, published in the spring, found a doubling of teenage marijuana smoking in the past five years and Bob Dole tried to pin it on President Clinton. It had been, after all, exactly five years since Clinton said he "didn't inhale." But the issue never quite caught fire and Dole dropped it by Labor Day. Either the public had grown tired of the drug issue or not even Drug War rhetoric could revive Dole's campaign. That summer, it wasn't clear which.

But on election day, the country got a clue. The voters of California and Arizona unambiguously rejected central tenets of the War on Drugs, passing by wide margins the most radical drug law reform since the wave of marijuana decriminalizations in the seventies. California effectively legalized marijuana for medical use, allowing physicians to recommend marijuana for certain conditions — AIDS, glaucoma, and nausea brought on by chemotherapy — and permitting marijuana defendants to cite such recommendations in their trials. The vote was 56 to 44 percent. Arizona went further, forbidding the imprisonment of first- or second-time nonviolent drug possessors (requiring mandatory probation and treatment instead), permitting the medical use of marijuana, and opening the door to medical use of heroin and LSD as well. The vote there — in an overwhelmingly Republican state — was 65 to 35 percent.

The Drug War establishment reacted with horror; Drug Czar Barry McCaffrey said he was ready to send the DEA to California and Arizona to make marijuana arrests those states wouldn't. But considering how the public might react to televised images of federal agents hauling skeletal patients off to prison, the drug czar had to switch tactics. Doctors, not patients, would be the enemy, he said; the DEA would revoke the prescription license of any doctor who recommended marijuana.

Then the *New England Journal of Medicine* blasted the Clinton administration for resisting the will of the people of California and Arizona. Federal recalcitrance, wrote the journal's editor, is "misguided, heavy-handed, and inhumane," thus signaling that doctors weren't willing to have their authority curtailed in the name of the Drug War and would put up a bruising fight. Columnists and commentators praised the initiatives, and legislators from Texas to Maine said they would try to get similar laws passed in their states. "We can't let this go without a response," huffed Senate Judiciary Committee Chairman Orrin Hatch of Utah. But as 1997 began, McCaffrey, Congress, and the White House seemed to recognize they had no comfortable options. Being the only legal source of marijuana in the country, the federal government could either provide pot to patients, turn a blind eye, or resist the initiatives with force. Force was dangerous in an era when devolving power to the states was held a virtue and Beltway hegemony a vice. But either supplying marijuana or allowing the initiatives to stand unchallenged would slay the central myth of the War on Drugs: that marijuana is a lethal, addictive destroyer of souls with no medical value. For if marijuana is such evil, how could our government make peace with it? And if it is not, then how do we justify confiscating pot smokers' houses and sending nonmedical users to prison for five years? For the first time in twenty years the martial trumpet of the War on Drugs was giving an uncertain sound.

McCaffrey appeared everywhere on television, warning that the initiatives in California and Arizona were the narrow edge of the legalization wedge. It may turn out he was right. The California and Arizona campaigns provide new models for reform activists. In California, a broad-based coalition was slowly and noisily built during five years, with local initiatives in San Francisco and Santa Cruz preceding the statewide fight. Twice the legislature passed medical-marijuana bills only to have them vetoed by Gov. Pete Wilson. By the time the initiative reached the ballot, the issue was familiar to California voters and had widespread grassroots support. Arizona's campaign was the mirror image of California's. A small cadre of elites — retired Sen. Barry

Goldwater among them — organized themselves privately and then pounced with a huge media blitz that introduced voters to the issue as it sought to sway them.

In both campaigns, out-of-state billionaires provided unprecedented bottomless pockets that may not be offered again. The drug-policy reform movement has a long history of shooting itself in the foot. And the initiatives galvanized powerful prohibition interests — parents' groups, treatment corporations, law enforcement — who will resist future reforms. Inauguration day passed, the 105th Congress was sworn in, and the laws changed in California and Arizona, but it was by no means clear whether what happened in two states could ever be repeated elsewhere. As always, the lessons of the moment were available to everyone on all sides of the question, to profit from as they may.

Notes

The sources for each subchapter are described below in separate paragraphs.

INTRODUCTION

The comparison of spending on the Drug War to spending on private health insurance is pieced together from several sources: *The World Almanac and Book of Facts* 1990, page 74; *The World Almanac and Book of Facts* 1995, page 128; and an interview with Peter Reuter of the RAND Corp., who estimates the $120 billion figure. The comparison of Drug War spending and the budgets of various federal departments and programs is from *The World Almanac and Book of Facts* 1995, page 107. The comparison of the federal prison population in 1980 with the current federal drug-offender prison population is from *Sourcebook of Criminal Justice Statistics,* 1990 and 1992, U.S. Justice Department. The criminalization of a third of the nation's young black men is from "Young Black Men in the Criminal Justice System: Five Years Later" by Marc Mauer, The Sentencing Project, 1995.

". . . more than the character of the pitiful few . . ." etc. is from *Crime in America* by LBJ's attorney general, Ramsey Clark. The characterization of William Bennett's viewpoint is taken from his *The De-Valuing of America: The Fight for Our Culture and Our Children,* page 254.

PROLOGUE: LAW AND ORDER

The recollections of Don Santarelli and insight into the Republican mind-set of 1967 come from two long breakfast interviews at Santarelli's home on January 28, 1993, and April 11, 1994, as well as several telephone conversations. The Katzenbach Commission quotes come from *The Challenge of Crime in a Free Society, A Report by the President's Commission on Law Enforcement and the Administration of Justice,* February 1967, Nicholas deB. Katzenbach, chair, page 6. The Ramsey Clark quotes are from his book, *Crime in America,* page 17.

The Gallup poll on marijuana and demonstrators was published in *U.S. News & World Report,* June 2, 1969. The quote from President's Commission on Campus Unrest (Scranton Commission) was printed in *Time* on October 10, 1970. J. Edgar Hoover's memo was quoted in *High in America: The True Story Behind* NORML *and the Politics of Marijuana* by Patrick Anderson, page 54.

"It is 'incontrovertibly clear.' . . ." comes from *Newsweek,* April 21, 1969. The poll showing Americans willing to turn in their own drug-using children was cited in *The Facts About Drug Abuse,* issued by the Drug Abuse Council, page 126.

Richard Nixon's remarks about the "forgotten Americans" were in a speech delivered in Anaheim, California, on September 16, 1968, a transcript of which was provided by the Nixon Library. Nixon's letter to Dwight Eisenhower was quoted in *Nixon: The Triumph of a Politician* (vol. 2) by Stephen Ambrose, page 145.

Nixon's comments about drugs are from his September 16, 1968, Anaheim speech.

1: A PRACTICAL MATTER

Nixon's observations about blacks in the epigraph are from *The Haldeman Diaries: Inside the Nixon White House* by H. R. Haldeman, page 53.

The account of the meeting in Roman Hruska's office comes from a four-hour interview with Egil Krogh on July 27, 1994.

The meeting with John Mitchell about building up federal drug enforcement was recounted in *Agency of Fear* by Edward J. Epstein, page 64, and elaborated on in the interviews with Don Santarelli and Egil Krogh.

The account of the conversation between John Ehrlichman and Katherine Graham comes from several sources: an interview with John Ehrlichman on March 30, 1994, and a telephone conversation with him on July 20, 1994; a telephone interview with Katherine Graham on July 25, 1994; and the interview with Egil Krogh.

The account of the creation of the D.C. crime bill comes from the interviews with Don Santarelli and from the 1970 *Congressional Quarterly Almanac,* pages 208–219.

The Justice Department study of preventive detention is described in the 1970 *Congressional Quarterly Almanac,* pages 208–219.

The experiences of Bob DuPont, Nick Kozel, and the launching of the D.C. jail study come from several interviews: with Nick Kozel on January 11, 1993; with Bob DuPont on January 27, February 4, and March 8, 1994; and with Chris Erlewine on January 12, 1994. The quotes from the published study come from "Narcotics and Crime: A Study of Narcotic Involvement in an Offender Population" by Nick Kozel, Bob DuPont, and Barry Brown in *International Journal of the Addictions,* vol. 7, no. 3, 1972, pages 443–450.

Jeff Donfeld's recollections come from an interview with him on December 6, 1993. Egil Krogh told me of his reaction to Donfeld's views on morality in the interview with him.

Gordon Brownell's recollections come from an interview with him on December 13, 1993. The comparison between the number of Americans who choke to death or kill themselves on stairs to the number dead from illegal drugs comes from *Vital Statistics of the United States,* Volume II Mortality, Part A, U.S. Department of Health, Education and Welfare, Washington, D.C., 1971. The *Newsweek* quotes about resentment against the counterculture and "the incendiary black militant . . ." appeared, respectively, in the October 16, 1969, and October 6, 1969, issues. *The Haldeman Diaries,* pages 61–62, likewise provided insight into the political thinking inside the Nixon White House.

The account of the Timothy Leary decision comes from an interview with Michael Aldrich on December 11, 1993, and from *Marijuana Review,* vol. 1, no. 3, June–August 1969, pages 3–5.

Cheech and Chong's first comedy performance was described in an interview with Tommy Chong on October 21, 1993.

The account of Bloomquist's press conference appears in *Marijuana, the New Prohibition* by John Kaplan, page 8. The account of Bloomquist at the District Attorney's Conference appears in *Fear and Loathing in Las Vegas* by Hunter Thompson, page 139.

The story of Operation Intercept and the *New York Times*'s reporting on aerial smuggling comes from *Licit and Illicit Drugs* by Edward Brecher, pages 434–450. David Smith's quote about the lack of marijuana leading to hard drugs appeared in "Year of the Famine," *Newsweek,* September 22, 1969.

Daniel Patrick Moynihan's memo of predictions, dated October 8, 1969, is on file in the Nixon Project at the National Archives.

Brownell's plans for Art Linkletter come from the interview with him and from his memo to Harry Dent dated October 8, 1969.

A transcript of the Linkletter press conference with John Ingersoll, Sen. Roman Hruska, Robert Finch, and Ron Ziegler in the White House Roosevelt Room, October 23, 1969, is on file in the Nixon Project at the National Archives. That the authority to schedule drugs was John Mitchell's first "big win" comes from the interview with Egil Krogh.

The recollections of Lloyd Johnston are from an interview with him on May 28, 1994. The quotes from his study appear in *Drugs and American Youth* by Lloyd Johnston, pages 30, 31, and 227.

The account of Margaret Mead's appearance on *The Dick Cavett Show* is from *Marijuana Review,* vol. 1, no. 4, October to December 1969, page 6; and John Kaplan's *Marijuana, the New Prohibition,* page 13.

The account of Krogh and Donfeld's initial discussion about methadone comes from the interviews with them.

The statistics on deaths in 1969 are from *Vital Statistics of the United States,* Volume II Mortality, Part A, U.S. Department of Health, Education and Welfare, Washington, D.C.

2. THE MAGIC BULLET

Justice Black's comment in the epigraph is from his dissent in *Turner v. United States,* 396 US 398, 426 (1970), in which he went on to say that even the horrors of drugs don't justify abrogating constitutional freedoms.

The story of Bob DuPont's establishment of the Narcotics Treatment Administration comes from an interview with him on August 8, 1994.

The memos surrounding the White House meeting of television producers are on file in the Nixon Project at the National Archives. The quotes from John Ehrlichman's speech are from "Talking Points for John Ehrlichman," April 9, 1970. Also, the August 24, 1970, issue of *Broadcasting* magazine, page 35, contains an account of the White House meeting.

The story of Ralphie de Jesus is in the March 16, 1970, issue of *Time* magazine.

Keith Stroup's experiences founding NORML are from interviews with him on January 9, 1993, and April 13, 1994.

The reaction of the African-American community to the spread of heroin into white suburbs was reported in the June 1970 issue of *Ebony* magazine.

John Mitchell's speech to the D.C. Bar Association on May 1, 1970, in which he said that "Americans don't like the Constitution," was reprinted in *Vital Speeches,* June 15, 1970.

The story of the creation of RICO comes from many sources: a long interview with G. Robert Blakey on November 17, 1993; "Outgunning the Mob" by Gregory J. Wallace in the *ABA Journal,* March 1994; 1970 *Congressional Quarterly Almanac,* pages 545–569; Arthur F. Matthews, Andrew B. Weissman, and John H. Sturc, *Civil RICO Litigation;* Ellen S. Podgor, *White Collar Crime,* pages 154–173; and David Smith and Terrance Reed, *Civil RICO,* pages 10.25–10.31.

Senator Eastland's quote from the opening of his hearings on marijuana is from Patrick Anderson, *High in America,* page 129. The quote from Ed Koch is from *Marijuana Review,* 1970, page 7. That Egil Krogh had no objection to a presidential commission on marijuana comes from the interview with him.

"They aren't as radical . . ." was scrawled on the Daily News Summary for the President, July 7, 1970, on file at the National Archives' Nixon Project.

Ron Ridenhour described his experiences in Vietnam and before Congress in two telephone interviews, on March 4 and July 20, 1994. His testimony also was described in the 1970 *Congressional Quarterly Almanac,* page 541.

"The administration's position in the crime field . . ." is in a memo on file in the National Archives' Nixon Project. The creation of the LEAA is described in the 1970 *Congressional Quarterly Almanac,* page 558.

Gordon Brownell described his "mescaline conversion" in the interview with him in San Francisco.

The story of Jerome Jaffe's initial involvement with the White House and of the first recommendation to the government that methadone maintenance be adopted as public policy comes from several sources: the interviews with Jeffrey Donfeld and Egil Krogh; interviews with Jerome Jaffe on February 7 and March 15, 1994; "The Maintenance Option and the Special Action Office for Drug Abuse Prevention" by Jerome Jaffe in *Psychiatric Annals,* October 1975; and "Footnotes in the Evolution of the American National Response" by Jerome Jaffe in the *British Journal of Addictions,* no. 82, 1987, pages 587–600.

John Ingersoll's December 16, 1970, memo on "street value" is on file in the Nixon Project at the National Archives.

Egil Krogh recounted Nixon's meeting with Elvis Presley during the interview with him and also described it in great detail in his book, *The Day Elvis Met Nixon.*

The numbers of Americans who died in 1970 from various causes are from *Vital Statistics of the United States,* Volume II Mortality, Part A. The numbers of 1970 prescriptions, the amount Americans spent that year on alcohol, and the estimate of the illegal drug market in 1970 are from the National Commission on Marihuana and Drug Abuse, report to the President of March 23, 1972.

3. PEE HOUSE OF THE AUGUST MOON

"The soldier going to South Vietnam today . . ." is from the *New York Times*, May 28, 1971. "This is the kind of issue . . ." is from *Time*, June 28, 1971. The account of Krogh's meeting with the admiral is from the interview with Krogh.

The *New York Times* estimate of troops addicted to heroin is from the May 16, 1971, issue. "The specter of weapons-trained, addicted combat veterans . . ." is from *Time*, June 28, 1971. The account of Krogh's trip to Vietnam comes from the interview with Krogh. That the army created its own heroin problem by cracking down on marijuana was reported in the *New York Times Magazine*, December 5, 1971.

The account of Jaffe's summons to Washington and meeting with the Pentagon officers comes from several sources: the interviews with Jerome Jaffe; the Krogh interview; the Donfeld interview; an interview with Michael Sonnenreich on March 9, 1994; and "Footnotes in the Evolution of the American National Response" by Jaffe and "The Maintenance Option" by Jaffe.

That Keith Stroup was furious with the formation of the Marijuana Commission comes from the interview with Stroup. Material on Michael Sonnenreich comes from the interview with Sonnenreich. Sonnenreich's thoughts on "routine law enforcement rationalizations" appear in an undated memo at the National Archives' Nixon Project. The account of the back-and-forth over whether Stroup and Ramsey Clark might testify comes from the interviews with Stroup and Sonnenreich.

Nixon's fury at the big D.C. antiwar demonstration and the use of preventive detention to hold demonstrators on drug charges is documented in *The Haldeman Diaries*, pages 283–284. Nixon's statement that "I am against legalizing marijuana . . ." is from his press conference on May 1, 1974, a transcript of which is on file at the National Archives' Nixon Project. An account of Bertram Brown's firing appears in *The Haldeman Diaries*, page 288. Nixon's desire to put out a statement on marijuana "that really tears the ass out of them" is recorded on page 291 of *The Haldeman Diaries*, and his wondering "why all the Jews" are for legalizing pot appears on page 292.

The story of the army creating and then worsening its own heroin problem by cracking down on marijuana is told on pages 188–191 of Edward Brecher's *Licit and Illicit Drugs*.

The opinion survey showing 23 percent of Americans believed drugs were the country's worst problem is on file in the Handwriting Files at the National Archives' Nixon Project, as is the transcript of the press conference in which Nixon said, "I can see no social or moral justification. . . ."

The account of Jaffe's surprise appointment as drug czar comes from the interviews with Jaffe.

A transcript of Jaffe's first press conference as drug czar on June 17, 1971, is on file at the National Archives' Nixon Project.

Egil Krogh's memo warning Nixon that "even if all drug abuse were eradicated . . ." appeared in a Domestic Council Decision Paper titled "Narcotic Addiction and Drug Abuse Program," March 19, 1971, on file at the Nixon Project. Nixon's Message to Congress of June 17, 1971, is on file in the Nixon Project at the National Archives. The 1971 crime statistics are from the *Uniform Crime Report* of 1971, published by the FBI.

The story of Detroit's heroin violence appeared as "Heroin Shooting War," *Time*, June 21, 1971.

The material on the kingpin-oriented nature of federal law enforcement, Nixon's impatience with it, and Myles Ambrose's memo suggesting a street-level alternative comes from several sources: an interview with Myles Ambrose on February 2, 1994; a telephone interview with John Ingersoll on October 27, 1993; and testimony by Myles Ambrose before the Permanent Subcommittee on Investigations, Senate Government Operations Committee, August 23–26, 1976.

Nixon's recall of the ambassadors and comment that "we cannot buy good relations at the expense of temporizing" on the drug problem are in his Message to Congress of June 17, 1971. Myles Ambrose recalled the meeting with John Mitchell, Henry Kissinger, and Pat Moynihan during the interview with him.

The plan to pay Turkey $35 million not to grow opium comes from several sources: the Krogh interview; an interview with Geoffrey Sheppard on March 2, 1992; and a draft of David Gergen's "talking points for the President" from the Handwriting Files in the Nixon Project at the National Archives. Egil Krogh recalled during the interview with him how the creation of the White House Plumbers diverted his attention from drug policy.

The story of Krogh's last trip to Vietnam, and of the lessons unlearned, comes from the interviews with Krogh, Jaffe, and Donfeld.

The Roper poll and "maybe we have to demagogue it" are from *The Haldeman Diaries*, pages 327–328.

"In the past we have been guilty of a kind of overkill . . . ," other material about testimony before the Marijuana Commission, and information about disparate state sentences are from the *Congressional Record* of September 22, 1971. The Otis Lee Johnson story is from "Grass Grows More Acceptable," *Time*, September 10, 1973. That the gateway drug theory was "crap," other thoughts of Michael Sonnenreich, and the account of his meeting with John Dean are from the interview with Sonnenreich. "There's nothing the matter with this drug" is from an interview with Richard Bonnie on March 20, 1994.

The story of the selection of William Rehnquist for nomination to the Supreme Court comes from the interview with Egil Krogh.

Don Santarelli's experiences at LEAA and meeting Antonin Scalia are from the interviews with Santarelli.

4. TO THE STREETS

Nixon's selection of Myles Ambrose to be Special Consultant to the President for Drug Abuse Law Enforcement and the creation of ODALE were described in interviews with Myles Ambrose and John Ingersoll, in *Agency of Fear* by Epstein, and in Ambrose's testimony before the House Subcommittee on Investigations. The comment comparing the need to bust the occasional street dealer with Mafia dons' need to shoot each other in public was made by Geoffrey Sheppard during the interview with him.

The *New York Times Magazine*'s article on addicted newborns was titled "Heroin Babies: Going Cold Turkey at Birth," January 9, 1972. The comparison statistics are from *Vital Statistics of the United States* 1972, vols. I & II Part B.

The Hudson Institute's estimate of crime caused by addicts in New York appears in the

Drug Abuse Council's *The Facts About Drug Abuse,* page 84. "In 98 percent of the cases [the junkie] steals to pay the pusher . . ." is from a speech by George McGovern to the U.S. Senate entitled "Toward an End to Drug Abuse," given on February 15, 1972, and reported in *Vital Speeches of the Day,* March 15, 1972. Charles Percy made his estimate during Hearings on Federal Drug Enforcement before the Senate Subcommittee on Investigations, 1975 and 1976. The actual value of all crime in the U.S. is from the FBI's 1972 *Uniform Crime Report.* "Addicts spend an estimated $17 million daily on heroin . . ." was said by Myles Ambrose in "The War Against Drug Abuse: Can It Be Won?" a speech to the Town Hall Club of California, Los Angeles, on September 12, 1972, as reported in *Vital Speeches of the Day,* October 15, 1972. Bob DuPont delivered his formula for figuring the cost of addict-caused crime to the House Subcommittee on Investigations in July 1976, page 263. Richard Harkness's memo was to Treasury, ODALE, BNDD, IRS, DOD, VA, SAODAP, NIMH, Customs, and USIA, and dated May 16, 1972. It is on file at the National Archives' Nixon Project.

Egil Krogh's admission that he used to wonder if drug enforcement was counterproductive came before the House Subcommittee on Investigations in July 1976, page 779.

My summary of the Marijuana Commission's findings are drawn from *Marihuana: A Signal of Misunderstanding* issued by the National Commission on Marihuana and Drug Abuse, March 22, 1972. "Our youth cannot understand . . ." is on pages 145–146. "I read it and it did not change my mind . . ." was said by Nixon during an impromptu press conference on March 24, 1972, a transcript of which is on file in the Nixon Project at the National Archives.

"It recalls a happier day . . ." was said by Ambrose during a press conference on September 8, 1972, a transcript of which is on file in the Nixon Project at the National Archives.

Highway deaths for 1972 are from a telephone interview with Jane Hilley of the National Highway Safety Administration on September 1, 1994. Cirrhosis deaths and the lack of any recorded marijuana death are from *Vital Statistics of the United States,* Volume II Mortality, Part A, 1973.

"Total war" on "the slave traders of our time . . ." is from "The President Calls for Total War on Dangerous Drugs," *Department of State Newsletter,* October 1972. Krogh discussed his attempts to learn about CIA involvement in heroin trading during the interview with him.

The story of Gordon Brownell and the California Marijuana Initiative comes from the interviews with Brownell and Michael Aldrich, and from the *Marijuana Review,* December 1972. "I took a lot of these people at their word . . ." is from "Young Republican White House Aide Changes His Head," *Los Angeles Free Press,* May 26, 1972. Richard Cowan's article, "American Conservatives Should Revise Their Position on Marijuana," appeared in the December 8, 1972, issue of the *National Review,* as did William Buckley's pro-legalization editorial and Jeffrey Hart's assertion that the counterculture is "bad."

The figures on the growth of federal law enforcement from 1969 to 1974 are from the Hearings on Federal Drug Enforcement before the Senate Subcommittee on Investigations, 1975 and 1976, page 880.

5. TRUCE

The quote from Justice Brandeis in the epigraph is from *Olmstead v. United States,* 277 US 438, 478 (1928).

"The purpose of law . . ." is from "On Original Sin and Conservatives," by Andrew Hacker in the *New York Times Magazine,* February 25, 1973. Robert Bork wrote "No activity that society thinks is immoral . . ." in "Neutral Principles and Some First Amendment Problems," *Indiana Law Journal,* Fall 1971, page 20. Ronald Reagan's "welfare queen" anecdote is discussed in *Chain Reaction* by Thomas B. and Mary Edsall, page 148.

James Q. Wilson's article was "If Every Criminal *Knew* He Would Be Punished If Caught," *New York Times Magazine,* January 28, 1973. According to a memo to the president by John Ehrlichman dated January 23, 1973, and on file at the National Archives' Nixon Project, Nixon read the article.

The material about Bob Randall is from an interview with him on January 5, 1993.

That Jaffe credited Nixon with doing considerable good and other reflections of Jaffe's in this section come from the interviews with him. "If the trumpet give an uncertain sound . . ." is from "Footnotes in the Evolution of the American National Response: Some Little-Known Aspects of the First American Strategy for Drug Abuse and Drug Traffic Prevention" by Jerome Jaffe in *British Journal of Addiction,* no. 82, 1987, pages 687–700.

The story of Keith Stroup's travels comes from the interviews with him. The list of sentences and the material about the American Bar Association are from "Grass Grows More Acceptable," *Time,* September 10, 1973. The material about the turn toward harsher pot sentences and the so-called "Rockefeller laws" is from both *Newsweek,* January 15, 1973, and the Drug Abuse Council's *Facts About Drug Abuse.* The Rockefeller laws' counterproductivity was documented in *The Nation's Toughest Drug Law: Evaluating the New York Experience* by Association of the Bar of the City of New York (published by the Drug Abuse Council in 1977). "Crime does not go down . . ." and that two-thirds of Americans approved of the Rockefeller laws are from "Heroin Hunger May Not a Mugger Make" by James Markham, *New York Times Magazine,* March 18, 1973.

Nixon's harsh reaction to David Gergen's "namby-pamby" speech and his hard-line proposals are in a memo from Nixon to Ehrlichman dated March 6, 1973, on file at the National Archives' Nixon Project. Ehrlichman's draft of Nixon's radio address, containing the references to "freedom from fear of crime," "permissive judges," and "the line is drawn . . ." is dated March 7, 1973, and is on file in the Nixon Project at the National Archives. Ehrlichman's memo predicting the headlines is similarly on file and is dated March 8, 1973.

The description of the Collinsville raid is from *Newsweek,* May 14, 1973; "In the Name of the Law," *Time,* May 14, 1973; Hearings on Federal Drug Enforcement before the Senate Subcommittee on Investigations, 1975 and 1976; and the interview with Myles Ambrose. Ambrose's quote, "Drug people are the very vermin of humanity," is from the *Newsweek* article. "The use of DEA agents to supervise ODALE-type operations . . ." is from Hearings on Federal Drug Enforcement before the Senate Subcommittee on Investigations, 1975 and 1976, pages 14–15.

"The dinner party on Manhattan's fashionable East Side . . ." is from "Tyrannical King

Coke," *Time,* April 16, 1973. Sonnenreich's reaction to such stories is from the interview with him.

Bob Randall's experiences are drawn from the interview with him.

"We must be realistic about what can be achieved . . ." and other material from the Nixon administration's last report on drug abuse is from *White Paper on Drug Abuse: A Report to the President from the Domestic Council Drug Abuse Task Force,* September 1975. The material from the Ford-era report, including the suggestion that the government "seriously study" pot decriminalization, is from *Federal Drug Strategy: Drug Abuse Prevention,* Strategy Council on Drug Abuse, November 1976.

The view of DEA's own chief counsel is from *The Leaflet,* NORML, vol. 4, no. 1, January–April 1975, as are the quote from the *Washington Post* editorial, Gov. Hugh Carey's toying with decriminalization, and the Michigan Court of Appeals decision. The start-up of *High Times* and the size of the paraphernalia industry are from an interview with Andy Kowl on May 10, 1994. "I'm like a bottle maker during Prohibition . . ." is from "Pot Luck" by Anthony Astrachan, *New York Times Magazine,* March 21, 1976. Bob DuPont's comment that "Criminal penalties have clearly failed . . ." was reported in *The Leaflet,* NORML, vol. 4, no. 1, January–April 1975.

Ehrlichman's comment "I think there is a genuine hypocrisy in all of this . . ." came in Hearings before the Permanent Subcommittee on Investigations of the Senate Committee on Government Operations, Ninety-fourth Congress, June 9, 10, and 11, 1975.

The story of Ashley Schuchard's birthday party and of the launching of the Nosy Parents Association are from an interview with Keith Schuchard on April 5, 1994, and *Parents, Peers & Pot* by Marsha Mannatt.

The story of Bob Randall's victory is from the interview with him.

The statistics at the end of the chapter are all from Hearings before the Permanent Subcommittee on Investigations of the Senate Committee on Government Operations, Ninety-fourth Congress, June 9, 10, and 11, 1975.

6. CIVIL PUNISHMENT

Dan Quayle's quote in the epigraph was reported in "Quayle in Support of Taking a Look at Legalized Pot" by Mark Helmke, *Indianapolis Star,* March 16, 1977.

The biographical information about Peter Bourne and his attitude toward Nixon's methadone program are from two interviews with him: on the telephone on November 8, 1993, and in person on February 2, 1994. "Almost impossible to justify . . ." is from a memo from Bourne to Carter dated February 26, 1977, on file at the Jimmy Carter Presidential Library. The National Governor's Conference Survey is cited in *Facts on File,* 1977. ". . . would no longer be in contact with dealers who may offer other illicit items for sale" is from Bourne's February 26, 1977, memo. The recollections of the discussion between Bourne and Carter and the compromise they worked out are from the interview with Bourne. Stu Eizenstat's reservations are in a memo to Carter dated April 17, 1977, on file at the Carter Library. The story of the writing of Carter's message to Congress is from interviews with Griffin Smith Jr. on May 10, 1944, and with Keith Stroup on April 13, 1994. "I am very concerned about the marijuana section of this message . . ." is from a memo from Stu Eizenstat to the president, July 7, 1977, on file at the Carter Library. "Penalties against possession of a drug should not be more damaging . . ." and other quotes from Carter's message to Congress are from the Presidential message to Congress, August 2, 1977, a copy of which is on file at the Carter Library. "Polls still show that most Americans still believe that pot is addictive . . ." is from "Carter's Grass Roots Appeal," *Time*, August 15, 1977.

That the Carter White House was in easy contact with Andrew Weil is from the interview with Griffin Smith Jr. "Any drug can be used successfully . . ." is from *From Chocolate to Morphine* by Andrew Weil and Winifred Rosen, page 27. "Drugs cannot be forced out of existence . . ." is from *Federal Strategy for Drug Abuse and Drug Traffic Prevention* 1979, Strategy Council on Drug Abuse. "I am not sure we will end up making the right decisions . . ." is from a letter from Bourne to Weil dated September 10, 1977, on file at the Carter Library.

"Excessive use of . . . tobacco" is from a draft of the 1979 Carter drug strategy on file at the Carter Library.

Bourne's thoughts on Latin American countries are from a paper he delivered at a conference on federal cocaine policy held at Harvard Medical School in the fall of 1977, a copy of which is on file at the Carter Library. "Expanding legitimate uses of the leaf . . ." and "it is extraordinarily helpful . . ." are from correspondence between Andrew Weil and Peter Bourne, September 1977, from the files of the Carter Library. "There's not a great deal of evidence of major health consequences . . ." is from "The Cocaine Scene," *Newsweek*, May 30, 1977. That cocaine by year's end wasn't even on the list of eleven items to be discussed is from a memo from Bourne to his group of drug-policy advisers, dated January 30, 1978, on file at the Carter Library. "Bourne . . . believes that if cocaine were less expensive and more easily obtained . . ." is from "The Cocaine Scene," *Newsweek*, May 30, 1977.

The percentages of teenagers smoking marijuana in 1975 and 1977 are from *National Survey Results on Drug Use from the Monitoring the Future Study, 1975 to 1992* by Lloyd Johnston, Patrick O'Malley, and Jerald Bachman. That Bourne noticed the trend but placed it fourth on his written list of concerns is from his January 30, 1978, memo to his drug advisers, on file at the Carter Library. The story about Nick Kozel's trip to Bolivia and discovery of smokable cocaine is from the interview with Kozel.

Keith Schuchard's experiences and thoughts are from the interview with her. That drug experimentation by young people "is not particularly distressing" is from the Drug Abuse Council's *Facts About Drug Abuse*, page 132. Schuchard's letter to Jimmy Carter was dated February 28, 1978, and was provided to me by her. Bob DuPont's thinking on the subject of the parents' movement comes from the interviews with him.

Peter Bourne's experiences testifying before Congress, and his thinking about them, is drawn from the interview with him.

The introduction of Susan Rusche into the parents' movement, the beginning of the campaign against paraphernalia, and the story of Peter Bourne's visit to Atlanta are drawn from several sources: the interview with Keith Schuchard on April 5, 1994; interviews with Susan Rusche on March 29 and 30, 1994; the Bourne interviews; and *Parents, Peers & Pot* by Marsha Mannatt.

7. YOU DIDN'T GET THIS FROM ME

The quote from John Walters in the epigraph is from "Racism and the Drug War," a paper written by Walters in 1994.

The account of the NORML Christmas party comes from the interviews with Peter Bourne and Keith Stroup and from *High in America* by Patrick Anderson.

The account of the formation of Families in Action and of the first anti-paraphernalia laws comes from the interview with Susan Rusche.

The story of the emergence of the paraquat scare comes largely from the interviews with Keith Stroup and Peter Bourne. NIDA's report on the "tons" of paraquat-contaminated marijuana is cited in "The Case of the Poisoned Pot," *The Nation,* April 8, 1978. "If an individual smokes three to five heavily contaminated . . ." is from "Panic Over Paraquat," *Time,* May 1, 1978. The accounts of Carlton Turner's trip to Mexico City and of his early days in marijuana research are from a long interview with him on March 11, 1994. That Keith Stroup once considered recruiting him to the legalization cause is from the interviews with Stroup. The account of the growing enmity between Stroup and Bourne is from the interviews with the two men. That Stroup was using cocaine in those days, and that it "leaves you ragged on the edges . . ." is from the interviews with Stroup. That Chip Carter's Secret Service detail was uncomfortable with his alleged marijuana smoking is from the interview with Bourne. "I want you to know of the very high personal regard in which I hold you . . ." is from a letter from Bourne to Stroup on February 11, 1978, on file at the Carter Library.

The account of the meeting about THC at the National Cancer Institute and the subsequent development of Nabalone is from the interviews with Bob Randall. "There's no profit incentive to develop marijuana . . ." is from a telephone interview with Dan Spiker of the Food and Drug Administration on February 2, 1993.

The account of the push for Bourne's new forfeiture laws is from the interviews with Bourne.

The story of Bourne's writing of the Quaalude prescription for Ellen Metsky, its appearance in the newspapers, and the incident with Rona Barrett are all from the interviews with Bourne.

The account of the leaking of the Bourne-cocaine story to Gary Cohn is from the interviews with Keith Stroup. Orrin Hatch's quote that Bourne "has done more harm than any public official . . ." is from "Pot, Privacy and Power," *New Republic,* August 5, 1978.

Peter Bourne's letter of resignation, dated July 20, 1978, is on file at the Carter Library.

8. PRIDE BEFORE THE FALL

Jimmy Carter's memo to his senior staff, dated July 24, 1978, is on file at the Carter Library.

The biographical material on Lee Dogoloff, the story of his ascension to drug czar, and the insights into his thinking at the time are from interviews with him in person on January 9, 1993, and May 3, 1994, and on the phone on June 12, 1995; also, a taped "exit" interview with him was recorded by the staff of the Carter Archives on November 26, 1980, and is available at the Carter Library.

The biographical material on Buddy Gleaton and the material about his entry into the drug-prevention field are from an interview with him on March 31, 1994. The story of his meeting Keith Schuchard and their formation of PRIDE is from the interviews with Gleaton and Schuchard.

The story of Lee Dogoloff noticing the alarming 1978 high school marijuana use numbers is from the interviews with Dogoloff. The numbers themselves are from *Monitoring the Future: National Survey on Drug Use,* by Johnston, O'Malley, and Bachman.

The account of the first meeting of Buddy Gleaton and Keith Schuchard with Lee Dogoloff is taken from the interviews with Gleaton, Schuchard, and Dogoloff.

"No issue was more frustrating to me . . ." is from "Is U.S. Becoming a Drug-Ridden Society? Interview with Robert L. DuPont Jr.," *U.S. News & World Report,* August 7, 1978. That DuPont thought the experts had let the public down and the story of his granting Keith Schuchard the contract to write *Parents, Peers & Pot* are from the interviews with Bob DuPont. The quotes from the book itself are from Mannatt, *Parents, Peers & Pot.*

The material concerning Bob Blakey's RICO seminar at Cornell is from the interview with Blakey and from "Outgunning the Mob" by Gregory J. Wallace, *ABA Journal,* March 1994.

The story of Dogoloff traveling the country preaching parent power, and the quotes therein, are from the interviews with Dogoloff.

The story of Ian MacDonald's discovery by the parents' movement is from an interview with MacDonald on February 18, 1994. "It can save time and money needlessly spent . . ." is from "Marijuana Alert II: More of the Grim Story" by Peggy Mann, *Reader's Digest,* November 1980.

Keith Stroup described during the interviews with him his first encounters with the parents' movement.

The DEA's newfound interest in marijuana after Peter Bourne's resignation was described by Bourne during the interviews with him and by Peter Bensinger in an interview on November 2, 1993. "The American Cancer Society confirms . . ." and "We have no national policy . . ." are from *New Times,* November 27, 1978. Bensinger's address to the chiefs of police and his stepped-up anti-marijuana operations were described by *Politics Today,* May 1979. *Time*'s marijuana cover story was "The Colombian Connection: How a Billion Dollar Network Smuggles Pot and Coke into the US," January 19, 1979. The CDC's deflation of the paraquat scare was covered in "Paraquat: Now a Minor Risk," *Newsweek,* April 30, 1979. The Carter White House's new "war on marijuana" was covered in "White House Prepares War on Marijuana," *U.S. News & World Report,* May 21, 1979, and in the Five Year Plan written by Dogoloff in July 1979 and filed at the Carter Library. Keith Stroup's hint of DEA "blackmail" of the White House was mentioned in *Politics Today,* May 1979.

The appearance and importance of Peggy Mann to the anti-marijuana cause was described by Carlton Turner, Ian MacDonald, Susan Rusche, and Keith Schuchard in the interviews with them. A partial list of Mann's articles, from which the quotes are taken, includes: "Marijuana and Driving: The Sobering Truth," *Reader's Digest,* May 1979; "Marijuana: The Myth of Harmlessness Goes Up in Smoke," *Saturday Evening Post,* July/August 1980; "Putting a Match to the Marijuana Myth," *Saturday Evening Post,* September 1980; "The Battle Against Pot: How Parents Are Fighting to Keep Children Off Drugs," *Ladies' Home Journal,* October 1980; "Marijuana Alert II: More of the Grim Story," *Reader's Digest,* November 1980.

The story of Andy Kowl's first encounters with the anti-paraphernalia movement comes from the interview with him on May 10, 1994.

The story of H. Ross Perot's recruitment to head the Texans' War on Drugs comes from the interview with Carlton Turner on March 11, 1994.

"Does not adequately or directly address the changing social attitudes . . ." and ". . . we will not consider legalization" are from a memo from Lee Dogoloff to Stu Eizenstat dated February 8, 1980, on file at the Carter Library.

The story of Hamilton Jordan's accusation and vindication are from "Ham Jordan Gets His Vindication," *Newsweek,* June 9, 1980. "Obviously one that didn't work" is from the interview with Peter Bourne.

The first mainstream-media story about smokable cocaine seems to be "Smoking Cocaine: A Dangerous Switch" by Craig Van Dyke, *Science* magazine, December 1, 1979.

The story of Ross Perot's recruitment of Carlton Turner and their victory in the Texas legislature is from the Turner interview and *Perot: An Unauthorized Biography* by Todd Mason, pages 121–25.

The story of the spread of anti-paraphernalia laws and of Andy Kowl's appearance on the *Today Show* are from the Kowl interview, the Rusche interview, the Dogoloff interviews, and "Pot Shots and 'Head Shops,' " *Time,* April 21, 1980.

The *Washington Post* story about the eight-year-old addict, "Jimmy's World" by Janet Cooke, ran on September 28, 1980. The story of how the *Post* was taken in by Cooke comes from an interview with Milton Coleman on June 1, 1994; from "Janet's World — The Story of a Child Who Never Existed" by Bill Green, *Washington Post,* April 19, 1981; and "Dominant Ideology & Drugs in the Media" by Craig Reinarman and Ceres Duskin, *International Journal on Drug Policy,* vol. 3, 1992. "In for a dime, in for a dollar" is from the interview with Milton Coleman. The story of how the Pulitzer Prize committee was fooled comes from an interview with Roger Wilkins on May 2, 1994.

The biographical material on Dick Williams, the story of his rise through the drug-policy bureaucracy, and the insights into his thinking at the time come from three long interviews with him on January 18, January 26, and February 15, 1994. Lee Dogoloff discussed his "major adolescent drug campaign" in a memo to Gerald Rafshoon dated July 24, 1979, on file at the Carter Library. "We have neither the luxury of time nor the opportunity for esoteric debate . . ." is from a letter from Dogoloff to Mr. and Mrs. Richard Redinger of Falls Church, Virginia, dated July 30, 1979, and filed at the Carter Library. "We always talked about the three-legged problem . . ." is from the interview with Dogoloff on May 3, 1994. "We have passed from a time when the nonmedical use of any drug . . ." is from *Annual Report on the Federal Drug Program 1980,* The White House. "Let's declare drug abuse wrong and get on with it" is from the interview with Dick Williams on January 18, 1994.

9. HOUR OF THE HARD CHARGERS

The Carlton Turner quote in the epigraph is from the interview with him on March 11, 1994.

The scene in which President Reagan confirmed that "law enforcement is . . . a legitimate function of government" is taken from *The Triumph of Politics: Why the Reagan Revolution Failed* by David A. Stockman and the interview with Ed Meese on April 13, 1994.

That the criminal "has gained the upper hand over society itself" was asserted by William French Smith in a speech to the National Press Club on October 22, 1981, a copy of which is on file at the Ronald Reagan Presidential Library. "We must increase the power of the prosecutor" is from the interview with Ed Meese.

"Perhaps the interest of justice . . ." is from William French Smith's aforementioned National Press Club speech. The discussion of the exclusionary rule and the California study is drawn largely from "A Hard Look at What We Know (and Still Need to Learn) About the 'Costs' of the Exclusionary Rule: The NIJ Study and Other Studies of 'Lost' Arrests" by Thomas Davies, *American Bar Foundation Research Journal,* vol. 1983, Summer, no. 3. "Should we be surprised . . ." is from "Our Losing Battle Against Crime," *U.S. News & World Report,* October 12, 1981. "One procedure after another that glorifies the rights of the accused . . ." is from the same article. The story of the U.S. attorneys asking local prosecutors how the federal government can help is from an interview with Lowell Jensen on December 13, 1993.

The story of Nancy Reagan selecting drug abuse as an issue on which to work is from an interview with Ann Wrobleski on April 25, 1994.

The account of Pat Burch's relationship to the parents' movement is from the interviews with Buddy Gleaton, Susan Rusche, and Keith Schuchard.

"The government has simply not exercised the kind of leadership . . ." is from "Asset Forfeiture — A Seldom Used Tool in Combatting Drug Trafficking," Comptroller General to the Honorable Joseph R. Biden (General Accounting Office, 1981). Reagan's pressing the FBI into the Drug War is from "New Federal War on Drugs," *Newsweek,* May 11, 1981. "In the war on narcotics, we have met the enemy, and he is the U.S. Code" is from *Hearings before the House Select Committee on Narcotics Abuse and Control on Financial Investigation of Drug Trafficking,* 97th Congress, 1st Session 58, 1981.

Cocaine "is no more harmful than equally moderate doses of alcohol and marijuana . . ." is from "High on Cocaine: A Drug with Status — and Menace," *Time,* July 6, 1981. "After one hit of cocaine I feel like a new man . . ." is also from "High on Cocaine." "Worth at least $10 million . . ." is from "Getting off the Cocaine Express" by Anthony Haden-Guest, *New York* magazine, September 7, 1981. "These people are not the dregs of society" is from "High on Cocaine."

The decline in teenage marijuana smoking and the increase in teen disapproval of the drug are documented in the *Monitoring the Future* study. "There is less adolescent rebellion now . . ." is from "Are Kids Turning Away from Drugs?" *Newsweek,* March 2, 1981.

Dick Williams's lack of faith in statistics and his reasoning about the need for the government to focus on marijuana are derived from the interviews with him.

The cuts to various social programs are documented in *Reagan and the States* by Richard P. Nathan and Fred C. Doolittle, table 3.2. The big increases in drug-enforcement budgets are enumerated in *Sourcebook on Criminal Justice Statistics 1990,* U.S. Department of Justice. The reduction in direct federal aid to the states is illustrated in *Reagan and the States.*

The story of William Von Raab's hiring as Commissioner of Customs, his discussion with Donald Regan, and his early emphasis on drug enforcement are from a telephone interview with him on February 14, 1995. "The most important since the

French Connection" is from "Heroin Valued at $70 Million Reported Seized" by David Bird, *New York Times,* February 23, 1982.

The story of Carlton Turner's recruitment as drug czar, his conversations with Ed Meese and Michael Deaver, and his secret support of the Republican Party are all from the interview with Carlton Turner. "It is hoped by legions of hopefuls . . ." is from a letter from Roy Hart M.D. to Edwin Meese III, dated July 2, 1981, on file at the Reagan Library.

The account of Sid Lezak's disillusionment and resignation is from a telephone interview with Sid Lezak on October 17, 1994.

The biographical material on Joseph Russoniello, his conversations with Rudolph Giuliani, and his thinking about the drug problem are all from an interview with Russoniello on May 17, 1994.

"When are we going to *do* something?" is from the interview with Carlton Turner.

The quotes from Reagan's speech to the chiefs of police are from "Remarks of the President to the International Association of Chiefs of Police," Penn Hall, Rivergate Convention Center, New Orleans, September 28, 1981, transcript released by the Office of the White House Press Secretary, a copy of which is on file at the Reagan Library. During the interview with him, Carlton Turner described his experiences watching the speech.

The figures at the end of the chapter on the employment of men before and after prison are from "How the Drug War Shattered Our Cities" by Jonathan Marshall, *Washington Post,* May 17, 1992, quoting studies from the National Bureau of Economic Research and Harvard economist Richard Freeman.

10. ROTTEN BEHAVIOR

I lifted the Pliny the Elder quote from William Bennett's book *The De-Valuing of America: The Fight for Our Culture and Our Children,* page 35.

The summation of Carlton Turner's philosophy, the quotes to his staff, his barring of Bob DuPont from the White House, his skirmish with NIDA, and his feelings about methadone are all from the interview with him. Marijuana "is a cause of heroin use" is from *Science News,* October 31, 1981. "Marijuana used to be the single most serious new threat to our nation's health" is from "Marijuana Is Far from Harmless" by Bob DuPont, *Education Digest,* November 1981. "By throwing subjects into a subculture that elicits heroin use . . ." is from the *Science News* article. "A slow erosion of life," "the devastation of personality," and "another pernicious symptom" are from a series of Peggy Mann articles of 1981: "Death on the High-Way," *Saturday Evening Post,* September 1981; "Alcohol, Pot . . . and Sudden Death," *Saturday Evening Post,* October 1981; and (containing the Dr. Voth quote) "Marijuana Alert III: The Devastation of Personality," *Reader's Digest,* December 1981. "Hard-rock music, torn jeans and sexual promiscuity" is from "White House Stop-Drug-Use Program — Why the Emphasis Is on Marijuana," *Government Executive,* October 1982.

Return of the Secaucus Seven was released in 1980 and *The Big Chill* in 1983. "There has been a growing tendency among parents, particularly those with a college background . . ." and the other quotes are from *Parents, Peers & Pot: An Update.*

"If any one of those is missing, then it isn't rock and roll" is from the documentary *Hail Hail Rock and Roll* on the life of Chuck Berry. "Is your child keeping late hours?" is from *Parents, Peers & Pot: An Update.* "Is the child not doing chores, late coming home, tardy at school . . ." is from *Operation Know,* a pamphlet by the Georgia War on Drugs. Counseling "only prolonged the problems by looking for the causes in the family's behavior," the story of Phyllis and David York's experiences with their children, and "the common denominator is rotten behavior" are from *Toughlove* by David and Phyllis York and Ted Wachtel. "A dog has credibility" is from "Friendly Drug Catcher is Welcome in Schools," *Nation's Business,* October 1982.

All the information about Karen Norton's experiences with Straight Inc. are from depositions of Karen Norton; Fourth Amended Complaint by Karen Norton against Straight Inc., November 20, 1986; and telephone interview with Richard Bradbury on October 27, 1994. That Straight had centers in fourteen states is from one of the company's brochures. That the company treated more than 5,000 children is from "Drug Therapy for Abusers, but Stress for Some Families," *Insight,* December 5, 1988. The costs of putting a child into Straight is taken from an October 1988 letter from Families Against Destructive Drug Rehabs. "Peer counseling . . . which has its origins in the Twelve Steps," other promotional quotes, and "to Admit Fourteen Clients Per Month" are from "Written Plan for Professional Services," Straight Inc., March 1, 1991. "The miracle of recovery" and "the best program of its kind in the country" are taken from Straight Inc.'s brochures.

11. THE BATTLE FLAG

"The mood toward drugs is changing . . ." is from "Crackdown: The Emerging 'Drug Exception' to the Bill of Rights" by Steven Wisotsky, *Hastings Law Journal* 38 (1987), page 890.

"Alienation from the rule of law in democratic society . . ." and other material from the NAS study are from "The Hazards of Marijuana," *Newsweek,* March 8, 1982. "The report may have ignored the temper of the times" is from "The Potshot that Backfired," *Time,* July 19, 1982.

The story about the Ad Council's "Say No to Drugs" campaign is from the interviews with Dick Williams and Carlton Turner.

"All drugs are bad" and other Nancy Reagan quotes are from "Nancy Reagan: How Parents Can Help Teenage Drug Users," *U.S. News & World Report,* May 31, 1982.

That William Pollin purged reports containing the word "social" is from "Unanticipated Consequences of Criminalization" by Craig Reinarman, *Perspectives on Social Problems,* vol. 6, pages 217–232. "These publications reflect preliminary marijuana and cocaine research . . ." and the list of publications to be purged are from a letter from William Pollin to "Dear Librarian," dated July 22, 1983.

Rep. Bill Hughes's experiences during 1982 and his thinking about legislation are drawn from an interview with him on March 16, 1994. The story of the Arctic Penitentiary Act is from "Congressman Wants Criminals Iced," *Washington Post,* September 28, 1982.

"I was not present at the Battle of Verdun in World War I . . ." is from "Remarks on Signing Executive Order 12368, Concerning Federal Drug Abuse Policy Functions" by Ronald Reagan, *Public Papers of the Presidents of the United States, Ronald Reagan, January 1 to July 31, 1982,* page 813.

That Carlton Turner demanded a "drug budget" from all executive branch departments comes from the interview with him. The story of Dick Williams's phone calls to demand such numbers comes from the interviews with him. The account of Reagan demanding Drug War assistance at cabinet meetings is from the interviews with Williams and Turner and an interview with David Pickens on May 6, 1994. "I'm manipulating the damn world" is from the Turner interview.

The description of military assistance in drug enforcement before the revision of Posse Comitatus is from *Sealing the Borders: The Effects of Increased Military Participation in Drug Interdiction,* by Peter Reuter, Gordon Crawford, and Jonathan Cave, page 47. Admiral Yost's thoughts on the proper mission for the Coast Guard are from a telephone interview with him on November 8, 1995. The quotes from the military officers and Caspar Weinberger, and the woeful experience of using AWACS planes to detect smuggling, are from *The Defense Monitor,* Center for Defense Information, vol. XXI, no. 1, 1992. The accounts of the revision of Posse Comitatus and of the 196-fold jump in the Pentagon's Drug-War budget are from *Sealing the Borders.*

"There is significant evidence the crackdown is working" and "I'm afraid they're going to close the front door . . ." are from "Reagan's War on Drugs," *Newsweek,* August 9, 1982.

"In recent years this nation has been plagued by an outbreak of crime . . ." is from testimony of Rudolph W. Giuliani, associate attorney general, before the Subcommittee on Crime, U.S. House of Representatives, December 9, 1982. The 1982 crime statistics are drawn from the *Sourcebook of Criminal Justice Statistics 1990,* U.S. Department of Justice. Reagan's appointment of Judge Irving Kaufman and the editor of *Reader's Digest* to his "experts" panel is from *Steal This Urine Test: Fighting Drug Hysteria in America* by Abbie Hoffman, page 129. "At the root of this philosophy lies utopian presumptions . . ." is from Remarks Announcing Federal Initiatives Against Drug Trafficking and Organized Crime, October 14, 1982, *Public Paper of the Presidents of the United States, Ronald Reagan, August 1 to December 31, 1982,* page 1313. "Official inaction has been a major part of the problem . . ." is from Fact Sheet: President Reagan's New Program to Combat Drug Trafficking and Organized Crime, October 14, 1982, on file at the Reagan Library. "Q: Is the Carter Administration really to blame . . ." is from Q&A Material: President's Program to Combat Drug Trafficking and Organized Crime, October 14, 1982, on file at the Reagan Library.

The U.S. attorneys telling the Justice Department what laws they'd like is from the interview with Joseph Russoniello. "So that evidence is not thrown out and defendants freed . . ." is from "Suggested Legislative/Policy Changes" on file at the Reagan Library. The "wish list" of the Reagan administration, including the "permissive presumption," and the preempting of the legislation by Senators Biden and Humphrey are drawn from the Draft Statement of Jeffrey Harris before the Committee on the Judiciary, U.S. Senate, on S.2320, April 23, 1982, on file at the Reagan Library.

The transformation of Humboldt County and the experiences of the Camardas are from a telephone interview with Andrew Camarda on December 22, 1994.

The reactions of California and federal law enforcement officials to Humboldt County are drawn from an interview with John Van de Kamp on May 19, 1994, and from the Russoniello and Turner interviews. That some policemen looked upon CAMP as "summer camp" is from the Van de Kamp interview. The descriptions of life under CAMP are from the Camarda interview and a telephone interview with Ed Denson on December 19, 1994.

12. THE LEAST DANGEROUS BRANCH

The quote from Felix Frankfurter in the epigraph is from *United States v. Rabinowitz,* 339 US 56, 69 (1950).

The additional police powers listed in the opening of this chapter derive, respectively, from the following U.S. Supreme Court cases: *Texas v. Brown,* 460 US 730 (1983) and *Michigan v. Sitz,* 496 US 444 (1990); *United States v. Place,* 462 US 606, 706 (1983); *Florida v. Royer,* 460 US 491, 498 (1983), *United States v. Montoya,* 473 US 531 (1985), and *Florida v. Rodriguez,* 469 US 1, 5 (1984); *California v. Ciraolo,* 476 US 207 (1986) and *Florida v. Riley,* 488 US 445 (1989); *National Treasury Employees Union v. Von Raab,* 489 US 656, 683 (1989); *New Jersey v. T.L.O.,* 469 US 325, 333 (1985); and *Oliver v. United States,* 466 US 170 (1984). ". . . as serious and violent as the crime of felony murder" is from *Harmelin v. Michigan,* 111 S. Ct. 2680, 2706 (1991). "A loyal foot soldier" is from *California v. Acevedo,* 111 S. Ct. 1982, 2002 (1991).

The story of the unfolding of the *Gates* case is from a long interview with Charles Mader and Ken North on May 24, 1994.

James Reilley recounted his experience with *Gates* during an interview on November 16, 1993. William Hopf told me of his involvement in the case during an interview on May 26, 1994.

"The corroboration of innocent activity is insufficient . . ." is from Illinois Supreme Court Opinion, The People of the State of Illinois v. Lance Gates et al. Docket No. 53453, Agenda 6, January 1981.

Paul Biebel described his participation in the case during an interview on May 25, 1994. "Where does all this 'prong' lingo come from?" and other quotes from oral argument are from the transcript of the argument filed at the U.S. Supreme Court.

"We think the Court ought to clearly establish the role of probable cause . . ." and other quotes from the reargument of *Gates* are from the transcript filed at the U.S. Supreme Court.

"It was a classical case of one side having the facts . . ." is from a speech by William Rehnquist at the Conference on Supreme Court Advocacy, October 17, 1983. "We decide today, with apologies to all . . ." is from *Illinois v. Gates,* 462 US 213 (1983). ". . . rejected approximately 30 percent of all felony drug arrests . . ." is from footnote 13 of the decision.

13. NINETEEN EIGHTY-FOUR

The Emmanuel Goldstein quote in the epigraph is from George Orwell's 1984.

"How Drugs Sap the Nation's Strength" was the cover story of *U.S. News & World Report,* May 16, 1983. The race of drug users portrayed on television is analyzed in *Cracked Coverage: Television News, the Anti-Cocaine Crusade, and the Reagan Legacy* by Jimmie L. Reeves and Richard Campbell, page 66. The treatment ads in *Billboard* were described in "Kicking the Cocaine Habit," *Newsweek,* January 24, 1983. The growth of the treatment industry is documented in *Cracked Coverage,* page 40. The commercial nature of the 1-800-COCAINE hotline was described in "Hot Line on the Hot Seat," *Newsweek,* July 28, 1986. "Police and prosecutors know that they have no great public mandate . . ." is from "Fighting Cocaine's Grip: Millions of Users, Billions of Dollars," *Time,* April 11, 1983. "If cocaine trickles down far enough . . ." is from "Kicking the Cocaine Habit,"

Newsweek, January 24, 1983. "It's trickling down . . ." is from *Cracked Coverage*, page 126.

"The scourge of drugs . . ." is from "How Drugs Sap the Nation's Strength," *U.S. News & World Report*, May 16, 1983. "Joint by joint, line by line, pill by pill . . ." is from "Taking Drugs on the Job," *Newsweek*, August 22, 1983. Peggy Mann's "The Hidden Scourge of Drugs in the Workplace" ran in the February 1984 *Reader's Digest*. "While OSHA was created (in itself, a result, in part, of political pressure . . .)" is from "White House Stop-Drug-Use Program — Why the Emphasis Is on Marijuana," *Government Executive*, October 1982. The weakening of America's industrial capability through corporate debt is masterfully documented in *America: What Went Wrong?* by Donald L. Barlett and James B. Steele, page 18. ". . . a crisis for American business . . ." is from "Taking Drugs on the Job," *Newsweek*, August 22, 1983.

The story of William Bennett's appointment as chair of the NEH and his thoughts about "elites" and "intellectuals" are from his book *The De-Valuing of America*. His cuts of NEH funding for projects dealing with women and labor is from "Hard Right Rudder at NEH," *The Nation*, April 14, 1984. His "emergency grant" to Accuracy in Media is discussed in "The Two William Bennetts" by Michael Massing, *New York Review of Books*, March 1, 1990. "Unabashed Socialist-realist propaganda . . ." and Bennett's quotes about the "cultural war" in America are from *De-Valuing of America*.

Stephen Jacobs's experiences creating the antidrug comic books were described by him during an interview on February 14, 1994. Dick Williams and Carlton Turner described their role in selecting Jacobs for the job, and the creation of the comic books, during the interviews with them. The quotes from the comic book itself are from *Plague!* (DC Comics, New York, 1983).

The White House's reluctance to fund the parents' movement is drawn from interviews with Carlton Turner, Susan Rusche, and Keith Schuchard. Kitty Kelley describes the donation from King Fahd and the Nancy Reagan Foundation in *Nancy Reagan: The Unauthorized Biography*, page 472. Susan Rusche described her phone conversation with Carlton Turner during the interview with her.

"You'd be astonished how well the students are cooperating . . ." is from "Crackdown" by Steven Wisotsky, *Hastings Law Journal* 38 (1987), p. 918.

Bob Randall's first contacts from AIDS patients were described in the interview with him.

"We want to send the message that we will be aggressive in the War on Drugs . . ." and the actions of the Florida State Police are from "Crackdown" by Steven Wisotsky, page 916.

The upending of the Lafayette Park smoke-in is described by Peggy Mann in *Marijuana Alert: The Health Hazards, What Can Be Done*, pages 444–446.

Keith Schuchard described her revelation about construction crews and her speaking to high school classes during the interview with her.

Eric Sterling described his experiences on Capitol Hill and his thinking at the time during interviews on February 2, June 9, and December 21, 1994. The Republican crime bill of 1984 is discussed in "Major Crime Package Cleared by Congress," 1984 *Congressional Quarterly Almanac*, page 215. The disparity in federal sentences at the time is analyzed in *Special Report to the Congress: Mandatory Minimum Penalties in the Federal Criminal Justice System*, United States Sentencing Commission, August 1991.

The indictment of Roger Clinton was described during a telephone interview with Mark Webb on September 29, 1993.

The eagerness of the parent activists to see Ian MacDonald appointed head of ADAMHA was described by Keith Schuchard and Carlton Turner during the interviews with them. Ian MacDonald described his own philosophy at the time and the treatment of his son, Andy, during the February 18, 1994, interview. "You tell Madam Secretary I don't work for her . . ." is from Carlton Turner's interview.

That the Longfellow Elementary schoolchildren were assembled for Nancy Reagan's visit comes from a telephone interview with Ann Wrobleski on November 14, 1995.

"There are only two ways I could be defeated . . ." is from the interview with Eric Sterling.

Eric Sterling's secret life as a legalization activist and "the most dangerous people in America . . ." are from the interviews with Sterling.

"Cannot pay its way . . . ," ". . . unenforced honor code . . . ," and "the Court's victory over the Fourth Amendment . . ." are all from *United States v. Leon,* 468 US 897, 905 (1984).

Rep. Dan Lungren's legislative maneuvering and the contents of the 1984 crime bill are described in the *1984 Congressional Quarterly Almanac*. "The American people have shown in the latest poll . . ." is from *The Nation,* October 27, 1984. The growth of the federal forfeiture fund was described by Cary Copeland, Director of Operations, Executive Office for Asset Forfeiture, U.S. Department of Justice, during a telephone interview on November 12, 1991. Under the Constitution, defendants are entitled to legal advice . . ." is from "An Overview of the Comprehensive Crime Control Act of 1984 — The Prosecutor's Perspective," by Joseph E. DiGenova and Constance L. Belfiore, *American Criminal Law Review,* vol. 22, 1985, pages 707, 717.

The statistics at chapter's end are from *Sourcebook of Criminal Justice Statistics,* 1990, U.S. Department of Justice.

14. NO SUCH THING

"In any realistic sense . . . ," "the schoolroom is the first opportunity most citizens have . . . ," and the description of the New Jersey high-school case are from *New Jersey v. T.L.O.,* 469 US 325, 83 L Ed 2d 720, 105 S Ct 733 [No. 83-712].

The huge growth of the urine-testing industry is documented in "The Business of Drug Testing: Technological Innovation and Social Control" by Lynn Zimmer and James B. Jacobs, *Contemporary Drug Problems,* Spring 1992, page 11 (Special Reprint). "The Gold Rush of the eighties" is from *Steal This Urine Test* by Hoffman. ". . . an epidemic of [workplace] cocaine casualties every day . . ." is from "Companies are Starting to Sniff Out Drug Users," *Business Week,* February 18, 1985. The CDC/NIDA study on urine-test accuracy and "is there anybody in the audience who would submit urine . . ." are from *Steal This Urine Test,* pages 212–215.

Kurt Schmoke's experiences with the Marcellus Ward case and his thinking about it are drawn from a telephone interview with him on June 13, 1994.

"We need to put pressure on the drug user . . ." is from a transcript of the cabinet meeting of March 27, 1985, on file at the Reagan Library, as are Ian MacDonald's quotes leading up to "supply reduction works." Lloyd Johnston's reaching of the opposite conclusion and his experiences trying to get his thoughts published are from the interview with him on May 28, 1994.

Judge Aguilar's restrictions on CAMP were spelled out in Federal Rules Decisions, *NORML v. Francis M. Mullen et al.*, No. C-83-4037 RPA, U.S. District Court, Northern District of California, September 8, 1986. That CAMP ignored them is drawn from the Camarda and Denson interviews and later court documents.

The development of Marinol was described by Bob Randall during the interview with him, by Spiker of the FDA, and by Dr. Abu Alam of Unimed during a telephone interview on March 12, 1993.

"Like a year of therapy in two hours . . ." is from "Getting High on Ecstasy," *Newsweek,* April 15, 1985. "Not only did MDMA enable me to recover my sanity . . ." is from "A Crackdown on Ecstasy," *Newsweek,* June 10, 1985. ". . . is not a hallucinogen . . ." is from *Newsweek*'s April 15, 1985, article. "All of the evidence DEA has received . . ." is from *Newsweek*'s June 10, 1985, article.

Nick Kozel described his first learning about crack cocaine during the interview with him on January 11, 1993. The cuts in federal aid to the cities are documented in "The Cities Draw the Short Straw," *Newsweek,* February 25, 1985.

"I would like to suggest that there are no neutrals . . . ," "press hard on this story and connect the occasional cocaine user . . . ," and "that's exactly the role allotted . . ." are from "Meese Seeks Press Help in Drug Fight; Assist in Mobilizing Public Opinion, Journalists Urged" by Loretta Tofani, *Washington Post,* March 21, 1985. "There are no bystanders, not even the lawyers . . ." is from "Meese: Lawyers Should Be 'Suitable Role Models' in Fighting Drugs" by Merril Hartson, Associated Press, May 1, 1985. "Governmental investigations of lawyers . . ." is from *Why We Are Losing the Great Drug War and Radical Proposals That Could Make America Safe Again* by Arnold Trebach, pages 183–185.

The story of Rosa Montoya de Hernandez, "the veritable national crisis in law enforcement . . . ," "first class mail may be opened without a warrant . . . ," and "Neither the law of the land . . ." are from *United States v. Montoya De Hernandez,* 473 US 531.

The story of Gail Fischer and the arrest of Edward Rodriguez is from *Illinois v. Rodriguez,* U.S. Supreme Court, No. 88-2018. James Reilley described his experience with the case during the interview with him.

Claire Coles described her experiences with the first wave of "crack baby" coverage during an interview on April 1, 1994. The seminal "crack baby" study, containing the phrase "depression of interactive behavior," was "Cocaine Use in Pregnancy" by Ira J. Chasnoff et al., *New England Journal of Medicine,* September 12, 1985. "The message is clear. If you are pregnant . . ." is from Reeves and Campbell's *Cracked Coverage,* page 208. That a million poor women had lost Medicaid benefits since 1980 is also from *Cracked Coverage,* page 212.

The *New York Times*'s first page-one crack story was "A New, Purified Form of Cocaine Causes Alarm as Abuse Increases" by Jane Gross, November 29, 1985. "Victims who aren't even old enough to know better . . ." is from *Cracked Coverage,* pages 208–209.

"*There is no such thing* as recreational use of crack . . ." is from "Kids and Cocaine: An Epidemic Strikes Middle America," *Newsweek,* March 17, 1986. The figures on adolescent use of crack, cocaine, and tobacco in 1987 are from the *Monitoring the Future* study by Johnston, O'Malley, and Bachman. The number of cocaine-related deaths that year is from Trebach's *The Great Drug War*, page 11. The comparisons to other deaths are from *Vital Statistics of the United States*, Volume II Mortality, Part A, U.S. Department of Health, Education and Welfare, Washington, D.C. "There is simply no question . . ." is from *Newsweek*'s March 17, 1986, article. The statistics on teenage cocaine use are from the *Monitoring the Future* study. The number of child cocaine deaths is from *The Great Drug War*, page 11. That *Newsweek*'s "Kids and Cocaine" issue sold 15 percent more copies than average was reported in the *New Republic*, July 7, 1986. "An epidemic is abroad in America . . ." is from "The Plague Among Us," *Newsweek*, June 16, 1986.

William Bennett's thoughts on drugs while Secretary of Education, ". . . right now, no ifs, ands or buts . . . ," and "I'm sorry. I believe that *is* education" are all from Bennett's *The De-Valuing of America*, page 101. That John Walters believed drugs a convenient arena for the overall cultural fight is from an interview with him on June 3, 1994. "Look for 'warning flag' phrases and concepts . . ." is from *What Works: Schools Without Drugs*, U.S. Department of Education, 1986. That adolescent drug abuse had been declining for seven years in 1986, and that 96 percent of high school seniors had never tried crack, are from the *Monitoring the Future* study. "Use of some of the most harmful drugs is increasing . . ." is from *What Works*.

"These numbers support our view that during the Reagan era . . ." is from *Cracked Coverage*, page 66. "These white Democratic defectors express a profound distaste for blacks . . ." is from "Race" by Thomas B. Edsall and Mary Edsall, the *Atlantic Monthly*, May 1991.

The story of Len Bias's draft by the Celtics and "it's a dream come true" are from "The Mystery of a Star's Death," *Newsweek*, June 30, 1986.

California's savings by reducing marijuana penalties is drawn from "Savings in California Law Enforcement Costs Attributable to the Moscone Act of 1976" by Michael Aldrich and Todd Mikuriya, *Journal of Psychoactive Drugs*, vol. 20, no. 1, January–March 1988.

The zero percentage increase in marijuana use during that period is from "Are Lower Penalties a Green Light for Drug Users?" by J. Mandel, *Journal of Psychoactive Drugs*, vol. 19, no. 4, pp. 383–85.

15. SARAJEVO ON THE POTOMAC

The Rudyard Kipling quote in the epigraph is borrowed from Reeves and Campbell's *Cracked Coverage*.

The panic in Congress after Len Bias's death and Tip O'Neill's meeting with the Democratic leadership were described by Eric Sterling during the interview with him.

The sham crack buy by Alphonse D'Amato and Rudolph Giuliani is described by Abbie Hoffman in *Steal This Urine Test*, page 113.

The appearance and importance of raid footage and ". . . the hottest combat-reporting story to come along since the end of the Vietnam War . . ." are from *Cracked Coverage*, page 134. All the quotes from the conversation in the Crime Subcommittee about defense attorneys are from a transcript of the July 16, 1986, markup session on the Money Laundering Act. All the quotes from the Crime Subcommittee discussion of designer drugs are from a transcript of the July 24, 1986, markup session on H.R. 631.

The material about the history of mandatory sentences and the introduction of new ones in 1986 is from *Special Report to the Congress: Mandatory Minimum Penalties in the Federal Criminal Justice System,* United States Sentencing Commission, August 1991, Appendix A. Carlton Turner's thoughts on the subject are from the interview with him. The quotes from the Crime Subcommittee on mandatory minimums and the death penalty are from the transcript of the markup session, July 31, 1986. The poor performance of the "Rockefeller Laws" in reducing New York's "drug problem" is documented in *The Nation's Toughest Drug Law: Evaluating the New York Experience* by the Association of the Bar of the City of New York and published by the Drug Abuse Council in 1977. The results of federal drug mandatory minimums is discussed in *Special Report to the Congress,* U.S. Sentencing Commission, page 6. That most prison inmates don't use drugs until after their first arrest is from *Reckoning: Drugs, the Cities, and the American Future* by Elliott Currie, page 170.

The discussion in the Crime Subcommittee about cornstarch and mixture was on August 6, 1986, according to transcripts of the session.

The Clintons' submission to a mid-campaign urine test was reported in *Christian Century,* October 8, 1986. The flaws in the RTI urine-testing study were documented in "Your Analysis Is Faulty" by John Horgan, *New Republic,* April 2, 1990.

". . . the biggest threat that we have ever had to our national security . . ." is from "Defense Demurs," *Time,* September 29, 1986. ". . . a menace draining away our economy of some $230 billion . . ." is from *U.S. News & World Report,* September 22, 1986. "In football there's a thing called piling on . . ." and a description of the proposed 1986 drug bills are from "Congress Clears Massive Anti-Drug Measure," *Congressional Quarterly Almanac 1986,* pages 92–106. ". . . a threat worse than any nuclear warfare . . ." is from "Defense Demurs," *Time,* September 29, 1986. ". . . the equivalent of passing a law . . ." is from *Congressional Quarterly Almanac 1986.* ". . . but of course I'm for it . . ." is from "Crack in Context: Politics and Media in the Making of a Drug Scare" by Craig Reinarman and Harry Levine, *Contemporary Drug Problems,* Winter 1989, page 564. "You want to get on top of the wave when it's cresting . . ." is from *U.S. News & World Report,* September 29, 1986.

"Drugs kill, but not nearly so often as the family car . . ." is from *Time,* September 15, 1986. That a thousand articles about crack were published in 1986 is from Reinarman and Levine's "Crack in Context." "Drugs are bad. Period" was said by Howard Simon, quoted in "Drugs: Now Prime Time," *U.S. News & World Report,* August 11, 1986. ". . . extensive coverage of the ACLU's opposition to drug testing . . ." and other quotes from Rep. Paula Hawkins were reported in the *Congressional Record,* August 8, 1986. The disparity between Americans' perception of the "drug problem" and their own experience was reported in *Time,* September 22, 1986.

That the United States had more blacks than whites in prison in 1986 was reported in "Race" by Edsall and Edsall, *Atlantic Monthly,* May 1991.

William Rehnquist's Placidyl addiction and Deanna Young's betrayal of her parents were both reported in *Newsweek,* August 25, 1986.

The quotes from the Reagans' televised address are from Remarks by the President and the First Lady in a National Address on Drug Abuse and Prevention, The White House, Office of the Press Secretary, September 14, 1986, on file at the Reagan Library.

"It's meant to be punitive . . ." is from *Time,* September 22, 1986. "The results are in and you've done it again!" is from *Landslide: The Unmaking of the President 1984–1988* by Jane Mayer and Doyle McManus, page 280.

That prisons already were at 150 percent of capacity is from "Sentences by the Book," *Time,* April 27, 1987. "The drug thing has just caught flame . . ." and "I'm afraid this bill is the legislative equivalent of crack . . ." are from *Time,* September 22, 1986. "We have been fighting the War on Drugs . . ." is from the *Washington Post,* September 12, 1986, page 1.

". . . distortion of the public perception of the extent of crack use . . ." is from *Time,* October 6, 1986.

Reagan's cut of a billion dollars from his brand-new drug initiative was reported in "Drug Withdrawal," *Time,* January 19, 1987. The cancellation of the Bolivia operation was reported in *Newsweek,* November 24, 1986. "Easily the most prominent beneficiary of the drug furor is Ronald Reagan . . ." is from *U.S. News & World Report,* September 29, 1986.

16. TIMES OF WAR

The quote from Thurgood Marshall in the epigraph is taken from *Life,* vol. 10, no. 10, Fall 1987, page 109.

The discussion of the Amtrak *Colonial* crash and the call for urine testing comes from three sources: Hoffman's *Steal This Urine Test,* page 121; "Free Enterprise Rushes to Fill a Delicate Need," *U.S. News & World Report,* February 23, 1987; and "What's Behind Jar Wars" by Harry Levine and Craig Reinarman, *The Nation,* March 28, 1987.

Homosexuality "seems to be something that follows along from their marijuana use" is from "The Great Drug Debate; Reagan Aide Takes Issue with *Newsweek* Story" by Elizabeth Kastor, *Washington Post,* October 22, 1986. The nature of Ed Meese Drug Policy Board meetings was described by Ann Wrobleski, William Von Raab, and Ian MacDonald during the interviews with them. MacDonald also discussed how he felt during those meetings. Von Raab recounted William Weld's comments and those of Admiral Yost.

"Our relationship *must be exclusive* in the packaged good industry . . ." is from a letter from P. H. Goldman, promotion manager of Procter & Gamble, to William T. Adams of the Just Say No Foundation, March 23, 1987, filed at the Reagan Library. The details of the Procter & Gamble campaign are spelled out in numerous letters in the Nancy Reagan files of the Reagan Library. "Think of all those kids dying . . ." is from a letter from C. Christopher Cox, Senior Associate Counsel for the President, to David Hansen of Colonial, on November 11, 1987, and filed at the Reagan Library. "Change the last sentence to read . . ." is from a letter from Ian MacDonald to Marty Coyne, April 27, 1987, a copy of which is on file at the Reagan Library.

The reassignment of Dr. Lacefield and ". . . unable or unwilling to do the tedious and complicated job . . ." is from *Steal This Urine Test,* page 123.

The story of Scott Turow's "reprehensible" behavior is drawn from *United States v. Ronald Arthur Ofshe,* No. 86-5351, U.S. Court of Appeals, Eleventh Circuit, June 1, 1987.

That 83 percent of Americans believed in reporting drug-using family members to police is from "Crackdown" by Wisotsky, page 9. "We have repeatedly held that the government's regulatory interest . . ." is from *United States v. Salerno*, 481 US 739 (1987).

The story of the DEA's recruitment of the North Carolina Highway Patrol is told in "Should the Ranch Go Free Because the Constable Blundered?" by William Patrick Nelson, *California Law Review*, vol. 80, page 1329. The growth of the federal forfeiture program is documented in a fact sheet from the executive office for asset forfeiture, U.S. Department of Justice. The conflict between state and federal law, California's circumvention of that conflict, and "that is, we receive a case which is in every respect a local case . . ." are all from "Should the Ranch Go Free . . ."

"We do see some real slimeballs . . ." is from "Drug Agents More Likely to Stop Minorities" by Andrew Schneider and Mary Pat Flaherty in the *Pittsburgh Press*'s "Presumed Guilty" series, August 11–16, 1991. The list of "suspicious" characteristics allowing a warrantless search was published in *North Carolina Law Review*, vol. 65, 1987.

The story of James Burton and "there is no defense to forfeiture" are from "Government Seized Home of Man Who Was Going Blind," by Schneider and Flaherty, *Pittsburgh Press*'s "Presumed Guilty" series, August 11–16, 1991.

The creation of the "zero tolerance" policy is from the interview with William Von Raab. "Zero tolerance isn't just a policy . . ." is from "The Second Casualty of War: Civil Liberties and the War on Drugs" by Paul Finkelman, *Southern California Law Review*, vol. 66:1389, 1993, page 1390.

The story of the Lopes family in Hawaii is from the *Pittsburgh Press*'s "Presumed Guilty" series by Schneider and Flaherty.

The account of the Carrs' experience and the skewed search and arrest statistics on the New Jersey Turnpike are from "New Jersey Police Are Accused of Minority Arrest Campaigns" by Joseph Sullivan, *New York Times*, February 19, 1990.

That police funding was rising four times faster than court funding is from *Responding to the Problem of Drug Abuse: Strategies for the Criminal Justice System*, Report of an Ad Hoc Committee of the Criminal Justice Section of the American Bar Association, January 9, 1992, page 3.

The conflicts between guideline and mandatory sentences are copiously described in the abovementioned report and in *Special Report to the Congress: Mandatory Minimum Penalties in the Federal Criminal Justice System*, United States Sentencing Commission, August 1991.

The story of Douglas Ginsburg's withdrawal from nomination to the Supreme Court, William Bennett's role in it, and the confessions of Al Gore and Newt Gingrich are recounted in "Pot and Politics," *Newsweek*, November 16, 1987.

Kurt Schmoke discussed his decision to call for legalization during the telephone interview with him.

". . . deep appreciation for the vigorous anti-drug-trafficking policy you have adopted . . ." is from "Drugs, Money and Death: The Sordid Story of Panama's Outlaw Dictator," *Newsweek*, February 15, 1988. George Bush's CIA history with drug dealers was exposed in "George Bush's Drug Problem, and Ours," by Jefferson Morely, *The Nation*, September 3, 1988. The White House's refusal to cooperate with the GAO was detailed in "White House Just Says No to Drug Inquiry," an editorial in the *Atlanta Journal-Constitution*, August 26, 1988.

The police killings of Jeffrey Miles and Tommy Dubose are discussed in *The Dilemma of Drug Policy in the United States* by Elaine B. Sharp, page 126.

That virtually all drug-trafficking defendants in 1985, 1986, and 1987 were black was reported in "Minor Drug Players Are Paying Big Prices" by Michael Tackett, *Chicago Tribune*, October 15, 1990, quoting a RAND Corporation study.

17. ANYTHING AND EVERYTHING

For the entire first section of this chapter, I am deeply indebted to Los Angeles historian Mike Davis and his excellent *City of Quartz: Excavating the Future in Los Angeles*, and to interviews with Karen Bass, on December 7, 1993, and Joe Hicks of the SCLC, on December 8, 1993.

"The concept of user accountability is a fundamental theme throughout the drug strategy . . ." is from *Toward a Drug Free America: The National Drug Strategy and Its Implementation Plans*, Executive Summary, A Report from the National Drug Policy Board, 1988. "We must do away with these previous talks of fairness and niceness . . ." is from "Crackdown Urged on Teen Drug Users" by Mary Beth Marklein, *Baltimore Sun*, March 3, 1988, page 16A.

That Meese hired Hill & Knowlton is from "Meese Seeks Positive PR on Drug War" by Aaron Epstein, *Atlanta Journal-Constitution*, May 14, 1988. ". . . send the message that there is no such thing as 'recreational' drug use . . ." is from "A Society of Suspects: The War on Drugs and Civil Liberties" by Steven Wisotsky, *Policy Analysis*, the Cato Institute, No. 180, October 2, 1992, page 21. "The casual user may think when he takes a line of cocaine . . ." is from Elaine B. Sharp's *The Dilemma of Drug Policy in the United States*, page 56.

The Coast Guard "will now, within the limits of the law, seize vessels and arrest individuals . . ." is from *The Dilemma of Drug Policy in the United States*, page 57. The story of the *Ark Royal* is from "A Society of Suspects," page 21.

The discussion of "civil fines" is also from "A Society of Suspects," page 21.

The discussion of Orange County's car-seizure program and "even if only a small amount of drugs is found inside . . ." are from "The Second Casualty of War: Civil Liberties and the War on Drugs," by Paul Finkelman, Southern California Law Review, vol. 66, 1993, page 1439.

The experiences of Vincent Lane, his discussion with Leroy Martin, and the launching of Operation Clean Sweep are from an interview with Vincent Lane on November 17, 1994.

The study of "drug-related" New York City homicides is summarized in "Most Drug-Related Murders Result from Crack Sales, Not Use" by Paul Goldstein, Henry Brownstein, Patrick Ruam, and Patricia Bellucci, *The Drug Policy Letter*, March/April 1990.

"Marijuana in its natural form is one of the safest . . ." and other quotes through "unreasonable, arbitrary, and capricious" are from Opinion and Recommended Ruling, Findings of Fact, Conclusions of Law and Decision of DEA Administrative Law Judge Francis Young in the Matter of Marijuana Rescheduling Petition, September 6, 1988.

The studies from Florida and Illinois demonstrating how "nothing less than the repeal of the laws of economics . . ." are: "Relationship between Illicit Drug Enforcement Policy and Property Crimes" by Bruce L. Benson and David W. Rasmussen, *Contemporary Policy Issues*, October 1991; and "Illinois's War on Drugs: Some Unintended Consequences" by Bruce L. Benson and David W. Rasmussen, *A Heartland Policy Study*, April 21, 1992.

That the country's prison population doubled during the Reagan years is documented in "Hostage to the Drug War: The National Purse, the Constitution and the Black Community," by John A. Powell and Eileen B. Hershenov, 24 *University of California at Davis Law Review,* page 557. The increase in the drug-offender prison population and the numbers of people imprisoned for possession are from *The Return of the Dangerous Classes: Drug Prohibition and Policy Politics* by Diana L. Gordon, page 33, and "Hostage to the Drug War" by Powell and Hershenov. The disparity in the percentages of whites and blacks in prison is from Reeves and Campbell's *Cracked Coverage,* page 41. The shift in Justice Department priorities toward drug offenders and away from regulatory offenders is documented in *Federal Drug Case Processing, 1982–1991,* Bureau of Justice Statistics, U.S. Department of Justice, March 1994, page 1. That counties began spending more on law enforcement than education and the sharper rise in nationwide police spending over education are demonstrated in "Trading Textbooks for Prison Cells" by William J. Chambliss, National Center on Institutions and Alternatives, June 1991.

". . . lost in the thickets of liberal sociology . . ." is from "Race" by Edsall and Edsall, *Atlantic Monthly,* May 1991. The story about William Bennett's appearance on *Meet the Press* and his appointment as drug czar are from *The De-Valuing of America* by Bennett, pages 94–97.

18. THE HILL OF THE MOMENT

Charles Robb's quote in the epigraph appeared in *The Nation,* July 24/31, 1989.

The characterization of the philosophy of Bennett and his aides is derived from Bennett's *The De-Valuing of America* and from multiple sources: an interview with Terence Pell on January 12, 1993; an interview with Bruce Carnes on June 2, 1994; interviews with John Walters on January 12, 1993, and June 3, 1994; an interview with Dan Casse and David Tell on April 23, 1994. Bennett's treatment for nicotine addiction was covered in "Bennett's Big Battle," *Time,* March 13, 1989. The tripling of slain innocent bystanders was reported in "A Slaughter of Innocents," *U.S. News & World Report,* July 10, 1989. "The simple fact is that drug use is wrong . . ." is from "Should Drugs Be Legalized?" by William Bennett, *Reader's Digest,* March 1990. Tobacco deaths are enumerated in *World Almanac and Book of Facts 1995,* page 163. Alcohol deaths are from *World Almanac and Book of Facts 1991,* page 838. Alcohol-related highway death figures are from a telephone interview with Ben Langer of the National Highway Safety Administration on June 12, 1995. The NRDC report on eventual pesticide cancers was reported in *Science,* March 10, 1989. The comparison of cocaine and heroin deaths with anterior horn cell disease is from *Data from Drug Abuse Warning Network: Annual Data 1989,* Series 1, No. 9, page 53 and *Vital Statistics of the United States 1989,* Vol. II, Mortality, Part A, page 134. The vastly greater number of people high on alcohol than on illegal drugs at the time of committing a murder is from Diana L. Gordon's *Return of the Dangerous Classes,* page 107, quoting a Bureau of Justice Statistics survey. "Now that the government has spoken to the subject that drugs are unlawful . . ." is from an interview with Paul McNulty on May 10, 1994. ". . . the reconstitution of legal and social authority . . ." is from *Return of the Dangerous Classes,* page 133. "The drug crisis is a crisis of authority . . ." is from "Contradictions of Cocaine Capitalism" by Jefferson Morely, *The Nation,*

October 2, 1989. "... a massive wave of arrests is a top priority ..." is from the same *Nation* piece. The details of Bennett's plans for Washington, D.C., were reported in "DC's War on Drugs: Why Bennett is Losing" by Michael Massing, *New York Times Magazine*, September 23, 1990. "I'm not a person who says that the first purpose of punishment is rehabilitation ..." is from the *National Review*, June 16, 1989.

For an excellent discussion of the loss of medical benefits to poor women in the early 1980s, see "Medi-Cal Maternity Care and AB 3021: Crisis and Opportunity," National Health Law Program, May 1986, cited in "Memorandum of Points and Authorities in Support of Motion to Dismiss," *People of the State of California v. Pamela Rae Stewart*, February 23, 1987, page 15. The immediate physical effects of cocaine on newborns were reported soberly in "Cocaine Mothers Imperil Babies' Brains," *Science News*, April 1, 1989. Ira Chasnoff detailed his later views on "crack babies" in *NAPARE Update*, National Association for Perinatal Addiction and Research, Chicago, Illinois, June 1992. "It is safer for a baby to be born to a drug-abusing, anemic, or a diabetic mother ..." is from "When Becoming Pregnant Is a Crime" by Lynn Paltrow, *Criminal Justice Ethics*, Winter/Spring 1990. The Yerkes Primate Research Center experiment was described by Claire Coles during the interview with her. The *Lancet* study on the difficulty of getting articles published about "crack babies" counter to the prevailing wisdom was "Bias Against the Null Hypothesis: The Reproductive Hazards of Cocaine," *The Lancet*, December 16, 1989. "... biologic underclass whose biological inferiority ..." was reported in "To Help the Child, Help the Mom" by Joanne Jacobs, *San Jose Mercury News*, July 29, 1991. "... spending immense amounts on crack babies ..." was in the *Boston Globe*, April 30, 1991. "... make friends, know right from wrong ..." is from an editorial in the *New York Times*, August 19, 1990. "... like no others, brain damaged in ways yet unknown ..." is from *Rolling Stone*, October 18, 1990. "... their mothers aren't all low income ..." is from "Born to Lose," *Wall Street Journal*, July 18, 1989. The high cost of caring for "crack babies" was outlined in "How to Protect Babies from Crack," *New York Times*, March 11, 1991. Medicaid rules and the lack of treatment for New York's pregnant addicts are discussed in "When Becoming Pregnant Is a Crime" by Lynn Paltrow. Chicago's almost complete lack of treatment for pregnant addicts is outlined in "The Criminalization of Pregnant and Child-Rearing Drug Users" by Loren Siegel, *Drug Law Report*, May–June 1990. Indiana's lack was discussed in an interview with Mary Haack of the Center for Health Policy Research in Washington, D.C., on March 22, 1994. California's paucity of pregnant-addict treatment is revealed in "The Criminalization of Pregnant and Child-Rearing Drug Users" by Loren Siegel. "We seem more willing to place the kid in a neonatal intensive care ..." is from *Time*, November 8, 1990. The story of Jennifer Johnson's attempt to get treatment, her delivery, arrest, conviction, and sentence are from Siegel's "The Criminalization of Pregnant and Child-Rearing Drug Users." The discussion of prosecutor Deen's legal strategy is from "The Corruption of Motherhood" by Amy Linn, *Philadelphia Inquirer Magazine*, September 17, 1989. The story of the Butte County, California, woman arrested after seeking treatment and "I don't see people making a choice unless you force them ..." are from *Backlash: The Undeclared War on American Women* by Susan Faludi. That black women are more often tested for drugs than white was exposed in "Racial Bias Seen on Pregnant Addicts" by Gina

Kolata, *New York Times,* July 20, 1990. South Carolina's particular legal squeeze on pregnant drug users is discussed in Siegel's "The Criminalization of Pregnant and Child-Rearing Drug Users." "If these mothers were walking away from treatment . . ." is from Paltrow's "When Becoming Pregnant Is a Crime." The two *Washington Post* headlines cited appeared respectively on August 6, 1989, and January 6, 1990. Sen. Pete Wilson's crack-baby legislation is discussed in "The Criminalization of Pregnant and Child-Rearing Drug Users." ". . . because word had gotten around that the police will have to be notified . . ." is from "Angry Doctors Cut Drug Tests After Police Interview Moms," *St. Petersburg Times,* May 13, 1989. "They're afraid their babies will be taken away . . ." is from *Backlash,* page 430. The Washington, D.C., woman who "miscarried" before appearing before a judge is discussed in "When Becoming Pregnant Is a Crime."

The description of "the aviary" is from an interview with Joe McHugh on April 8, 1994. The discussion therein is re-created from the interviews with McHugh, Walters, Casse, Tell, Pell, and Carnes. Bennett's language is adapted from the wording of the 1989 *National Drug Control Strategy,* The White House, September 1989. ". . . white, male, a high-school graduate, employed full time . . ." is from the 1989 *Strategy,* page 4. ". . . likely to have a still-intact family, social and work life . . ." is from page 11 of the *Strategy.* "Fear of drugs and attendant crime is at an all-time high . . ." is from page 1 of the *Strategy.* ". . . states would be encouraged to make outreach efforts . . ." is from the *Strategy,* page 2. Bennett's proposed drug budget is laid out on pages 122–123 of the *Strategy.* The comparison with the budget for the entire judicial branch comes from the *World Almanac and Book of Facts 1991,* page 102.

Michael Quinlan's experiences and thoughts are drawn from an interview with him on January 9, 1993. The repeated doubling of the Bureau of Prisons budget is detailed in *Sourcebook of Criminal Justice Statistics 1993,* U.S. Department of Justice, page 19.

In the statistics at the end of the chapter, the percentage of young black men arrested and the changing percentages of those saying they can make money more easily committing crime than working are all from "How the Drug War Shattered Our Cities" by Jonathan Marshall, *Washington Post,* May 17, 1992, quoting studies from the National Bureau of Economic Research and Harvard economist Richard Freeman.

The ballooning federal payments to informants are from "Year of the Rat" by Cynthia Cotts, *Reason,* May 1992.

The figures on women in prison and the children they have are from *Women in Prison,* Special Report by the Bureau of Justice Statistics, U.S. Justice Department.

The chance that an inmate has a family history of prison is from *Survey of State Prison Inmates 1991,* Bureau of Justice Statistics, U.S. Justice Department.

The figures on women inmates and childbearing and the lack of OB-GYNs in the federal prison system are from *Time,* November 8, 1990.

19. OUR MOST SERIOUS PROBLEM

"Users Are Bums" by Hubert Williams appeared in *Reader's Digest,* June 1989. ". . . the supply side of the drug crisis has failed miserably . . ." is from "Let's Get Tough With Drug Users!" by Carl T. Rowan, *Reader's Digest,* July 1989. Bruce Lavoie's killing was reported in "N.H. Drug Suspect Shot by Police," UPI, August 3,

1989, and "N.H. Town to Hold Hearing on Police Shooting," UPI, September 6, 1989.

"That's no small change . . ." is from "Reports: DPS Big Drug Dealer" by Paul Brinkley-Rogers, *Arizona Republic*, December 31, 1991. The story of the DEA informant seducing innocent women into drug deals was in *Time*, April 3, 1989. The stories of the anti-loitering laws and the shooting of Rolando Carr are from "When Constitutional Rights Seem Too Extravagant to Endure," a paper by Ira Glasser and Loren Siegel of the American Civil Liberties Union. ". . . the overriding spirit and energy of our front-line drug enforcement officers . . ." is from *National Drug Control Strategy*, the White House, September 1989, page 8. ". . . strike a new balance between order and individual liberties . . ." and ". . . you're probably going to have to infringe some human rights . . ." are from "When Constitutional Rights Seem Too Extravagant to Endure." That 62 percent of Americans were willing to surrender freedoms to stamp out drugs is from *Time*, September 18, quoting a *Washington Post*–ABC poll. ". . . an excretory function traditionally shielded by great privacy . . ." is from *National Treasury Employees Union, et al. v. William Von Raab, Commissioner, United States Customs Service*, 489 US 656 L. Ed. 2d 685. "There is no drug exception to the Constitution . . ." is from *Samuel K. Skinner, Secretary of Transportation et al. v. Railway Labor Executives' Association et al.*, 489 US 602 103 L. Ed. 2d 639. " 'The black-mustachio'd face gazed down from every commanding corner . . ." is from *Florida v. Riley*, 488 US 445 (1989).

Reggie Walton's experiences prior to and during his tenure at the Office of National Drug Control Policy, his exclusion from policy decisions, and his noting Bennett's lack of concern for civil liberties are all from interviews with Walton on February 9, 1993, and June 7, 1994. ". . . committed to fighting the [drug] problem . . . over a long period of time . . ." is from the *Wall Street Journal*, September 19, 1989, quoted in *The Bush Drug War Record*, Drug Policy Foundation, September 5, 1992, page 1.

". . . an act of true loyalty — of true friendship . . ." is from "Drug Chief Urges Youths: Just Say Who" by Richard Berke, *New York Times*, May 19, 1989.

"To put it another way a man's arms will constitute a greater proportion of his total body . . ." is from "Bennett's Sham Epidemic" by Franklin E. Zimring and Gordon Hawkins, *New York Times* op-ed page, January 25, 1990. ". . . gravest present threat to our national well-being . . ." is from *National Drug Control Strategy* 1989.

The experiences and thoughts of Benjamin Renshaw are from three long interviews with him on January 25, 1993, March 16, 1994, and June 4, 1994. That Thornburgh said 45 percent of Justice's budget went to the Drug War is from "Remarks by Attorney General Dick Thornburgh to a Voice of America Drug Workshop," March 19, 1990.

". . . a success from a cost-benefit standpoint . . ." is from the "Presumed Guilty" series by Mary Pat Flaherty and Andrew Schneider, *Pittsburgh Press*, August 11–16, 1991. That Justice hired 175 prosecutors to work nothing but forfeiture cases is from *Prosecution and Defense of Forfeiture Cases* by David B. Smith. ". . . a natural byproduct is revenue which is pumped back into law enforcement . . ." and the amount of money returned to police are from *Federal Forfeiture of the Instruments and Proceeds of Crime: The Program in a Nutshell*, Executive Office of Asset Forfeiture, U.S. Department of Justice, 1990. "If you take the profit out it, you'll do away with it . . ." is from both "Police Bureaucracies, Their Incentives and the War on Drugs," a paper by Bruce Benson, David Rasmussen, and David Sollars, and "Should the Ranch Go Free Because the Constable Blundered? Gaining Compliance With Search and Seizure Standards in the Age of Asset Forfeiture" by William Patrick Nelson. ". . . drug agents would have much less incentive to follow through . . ." and the quiet repeal of Section 6077 are from "Police Bureaucracies, Their Incentives and the War on Drugs."

The story about possible interference with Florida's investigation of Straight Inc. is from Report to Lowell Clary, Acting Inspector General, Florida Dept. of Health & Rehabilitative Services, from Fred M. Gravius, Inspector Specialist, regarding Child Abuse/Neglect by Straight Inc., May 19, 1993.

The Drug War pressures on the federal court system are outlined in "Drug War Chokes Federal Courts: Assembly-Line Justice Perils Legal System" by Michael Tackett, *Chicago Tribune,* October 14, 1990. The similar pressures on superior courts in Los Angeles and Chicago are detailed in *Funding the Justice System: A Call to Action,* American Bar Association, August 1992. The story of Tom Fitzgerald and the creation of Chicago's Night Drug Court is from several sources: an interview with Tom Fitzgerald on May 23, 1994; an interview with Randolph Stone on November 19, 1993; an interview with Thomas Donnelly on November 18, 1993; and *Assessment of the Feasibility of Drug Night Courts,* Bureau of Justice Assistance Monograph, U.S. Department of Justice, June 1993. The description of Miami's Night Drug Court is from *Strategies for Courts to Cope with the Caseload Pressures of Drug Cases,* executive summary, American Bar Association, November 1991.

That the *New York Times* liked Bennett's leaked first drug strategy is from the interview with David Tell. That no more than 9 percent of the population could agree on the country's "most serious problem" is from *Marching in Place: The Status Quo Presidency of George Bush* by Michael Duffy and Dan Goodgame. That Bush tried to differentiate his style from Reagan's and held informal press briefings is from an interview with Michael Jackson, special assistant and cabinet liaison to President Bush, on May 9, 1994. That 83 percent of Americans now approved of turning in drug-using family members to police is from "A Society of Suspects" by Wisotsky. "The risk of ignoring this issue is one hundred times worse than the risk . . ." is from *U.S. News & World Report,* September 11, 1989. That Bush's drug speech appeared on the schedule less than a month before its scheduled date is from a telephone interview with Bush speechwriter Ed McNally on April 20, 1995. Mark Davis's experiences and thoughts are from a telephone interview with him on April 26, 1995. The story of coming up with the crack-bag idea is from a telephone interview with Chriss Winston on April 21, 1995. The story of the DEA creating the drug buy specifically for the speech was reported in "Drug Buy Set Up for Bush Speech; DEA Lured Seller to Lafayette Park" by Michael Isikoff, *Washington Post,* September 22, 1989. The mishaps in trying to set up and videotape the buy were reported in "Drug Purchase for Bush Speech Like Keystone Kops" by Tracy Thompson, *Washington Post,* December 15, 1989. That a DEA agent insisted on following the crack bag into the Oval Office is from the telephone interview with Ed McNally. The quotes from Bush's speech are from Address by the President on National Drug Policy, George Bush, September 5, 1989, reprinted in *Drug Prohibition and the Conscience of Nations,* Drug Policy Foundation, 1990. The number of construction accidents in 1989 is from *World*

Almanac and Book of Facts 1992, page 177. "I mean, has somebody got some advocates here for this drug guy?" is from "A Political Opiate: The War on Drugs Is a Folly and a Menace" by Lewis Lapham, *Harper's*, December 1989. The story of Keith Jackson's mistrial, and the quotes from the jury foreman and the DEA spokesman, are from "Mistrial Declared in Cocaine Arrest Near White House" by Barton Gellman, *Washington Post*, December 22, 1989.

In the statistics at chapter's end, the number of drug-related wiretap requests and the percentage approved are from "A Society of Suspects" by Wisotsky.

The percentage increase in those arrested for heroin or cocaine trafficking is from *Reckoning* by Elliott Currie, page 15.

The Justice Department's "McGruff" budget, in-jail drug treatment budget, and the percentage of those needing treatment in jail who were getting it are all from "Justice's War on Drug Treatment" by David Corn, *The Nation*, May 19, 1990, quoting the National Association of State Alcohol and Drug Abuse Directors.

The figure on police killing black civilians is from "Hostage to the Drug War" by Powell and Hershenov.

20. "ARE WE WINNING?"

"[The drug problem] comes from this tradition of freedom and liberty . . ." is from *U.S. News & World Report*, February 19, 1990.

The view of the American Bar Association and the experiences of William Taylor are from an interview with William Taylor on May 6, 1994, and an interview with Kevin Driscoll of the criminal justice section of the ABA on April 27, 1994. "Even a low-level person can make a deal with somebody . . . ," "The attorney general is not the secretary of HHS . . . ," and the thoughts of Dick Thornburgh are from an interview with Thornburgh on June 3, 1994. That Thornburgh snubbed the ABA is from the interviews with Taylor and Driscoll. ". . . a distraction" from "getting the bad guys" is from "A Society of Suspects" by Wisotsky. ". . . charged with the enforcement of federal law and nobody . . ." is from "The Second Casualty of War" by Finkelman. "It is unseemly and unjust for the Government to beggar . . ." is from *Caplin & Drysdale v. United States* 491 US 617 (1989); the companion case upholding the forfeiture of legal fees was *United States v. Monsanto* 491 US 600 (1989). The actions of the IRS against drug-defendants' lawyers are covered in "IRS Drug War Tactic Has Lawyers in Uproar; Cash Fees over $10,000 Must Be Reported" by Saundra Torry, *Washington Post*, November 15, 1989. That the IRS is the government's biggest police agency is from *World Almanac and Book of Facts 1991*, page 102, and the *DEA Fact Sheet*, published by the DEA, 1991. "My job is enforcement of the law . . ." and "it's OK to represent a murderer . . ." are from "The Second Casualty of War" by Finkelman.

Bennett's rubber-ball story is from the interview with Bruce Carnes on June 2, 1994.

The story of orchid grower Joseph Hoberman is from "Marijuana McCarthyism" by Peter Gorman, *New York Times* op-ed page, December 30, 1989. The story of the DEA's harassment of *High Times* magazine is told in "The Second Casualty of War" by Finkelman.

"If Mayor Barry was a crackhead . . ." is from the *New Republic*, February 12, 1990. "Crack isn't instantly addictive . . ." is from "A Dirty Little Secret" by Larry Martz, *Newsweek*, February 24, 1990. "Taking On the Legalizers" appeared in

Newsweek, December 25, 1989. "America is beginning to confront the true cost . . ." is from "Uncivil Liberties?" *Newsweek,* April 23, 1990.

Ben Renshaw's experiences trying to get his drugs-and-crime report authorized are from the interviews with him on January 25, 1993, March 16, 1994, and June 4, 1994.

That the Partnership for a Drug-Free America was the country's third-biggest ad campaign is from *Official Lies: How Washington Misleads Us* by James T. Bennett and Thomas J. DiLorenzo, page 241. The statistics on high-school-senior drug use are from the *Monitoring the Future Study,* page 77. "How does one anti-alcohol spot compete against fifteen . . ." is from an interview with Steve Dnistrian on October 29, 1992. The factual errors of the Partnership ads, up through "extrapolated from a *Newsweek* article or something" are from "Antidrug Message Gets Its Facts Wrong," *Scientific American,* May 1990. The Gingrich-Gramm "National Drug and Crime Emergency Act" is discussed in "When Constitutional Rights Seem Too Extravagant to Endure" by Glasser and Siegel. Rep. Richard Ray's idea to send drug offenders to Midway and Wake, "there's not much chance they're going to get anything but rehabilitated . . . ," and "they thought it was a great idea" are all from "Penal Colony for Drug Criminals Studied" by Michael Isikoff, *Washington Post,* September 30, 1990. "Casual drug users should be taken out and shot . . ." is from "Casual Drug Users Should Be Taken Out and Shot, Gates Says" by Ronald Ostrow, *Los Angeles Times,* September 6, 1990. William Bennett tells the story of his suggesting beheading drug dealers on *Larry King Live* on page 116 of his book *The De-Valuing of America.* "The death penalty debate is over . . ." and the move to institute a federal death penalty for drug kingpins are from *Return of the Dangerous Classes* by Gordon, pages 53 and 54.

The story of James Reilley's second drug case before the Supreme Court is from the interview with Reilley on November 16, 1993.

The story of Ade Adedokian and police officers' poor job at identifying "body packers" was exposed in "Airport Drug Efforts Snaring Innocents Who Fit 'Profiles' " by Lisa Belkin, *New York Times,* March 20, 1990.

The further investigation of *High Times* was reported in "Justice Department Targets High Times: Ad for Marijuana Seed Catalogue Leads to Grand Jury Probe" by Michael Isikoff, *Washington Post,* July 16, 1990. ". . . fulfills our worst fears about [Bennett's drug] strategy . . ." is from "Taking Poor Aim at Drug Users," *Washington Times,* November 13, 1989.

The story of the making, financing, and broadcast of "Cartoon All-Stars to the Rescue," "we are not all things to all people. . . ," and "If you use drugs, it is completely different . . ." are from "That's Not All Folks — Cartoons Join Drug War" by Sharon Bernstein, *Los Angeles Times*, April 20, 1990. The details of its post-broadcast circulation are from Kodak Press Release, PR Newswire, July 11, 1990.

That Scalia didn't ask any questions during the oral arguments for *Rodriguez* is from the James Reilley interview. "The majority has taken away some of the liberty that the Fourth Amendment . . ." is from the *New York Times,* June 22, 1990.

"Are we winning . . ." is from the interview with Joe McHugh, on April 8, 1994. "You're either on offense or defense . . ." is from the interview with Bruce Carnes on June 2, 1994. The reception of Reggie Walton's memo is from the interview with

Joe McHugh. The nature of the memo is from the interviews with Reggie Walton on February 9, 1993, and June 7, 1994.

The story of Donny Clark is from interviews with Tom Ostrander, Donny Clark's attorney, on November 20, 1991, and April 7, 1995; interview with U.S. Attorney Walter Terry Furr on December 3, 1991; Judgment in a Criminal Case, *United States v. Donald Clark*, November 4, 1991; Indictment — *United States of America v.* [28 defendants], February 27, 1991.

The sudden decrease in drug coverage is from a survey of the *Reader's Guide to Periodical Literature*, checking headings under "drug" such as drugs and youth, drug abuse, drugs and sports, drugs and crime, etc.

"These people are Americans and they deserve to be heard . . . ," the friction between Reggie Walton and the rest of the Drug Policy Office, and the story of Walton's near-resignation all come from the interviews with Walton.

"Under the Constitution, defendants are entitled to legal advice . . ." is from "An Overview of the Comprehensive Crime Control Act of 1984 — The Prosecutor's Perspective" by Joseph E. DiGenova and Constance L. Belfiore, *American Criminal Law Review*, vol. 22, 1985, pages 707, 717.

"That's not justice . . . ," ". . . indigent defense as a proxy for evil," and the story of the impoverishment of public defenders are all from "Drug War Draining State's Ability to Defend Poor," UPI, October 7, 1990.

The story of the meeting of the ABA officials with William Barr is from an interview with Laurie Robinson on January 15, 1993, and a telephone interview with Jack Curtain on May 3, 1994. "I think the Justice Department told the defense bar . . ." is from the Robinson interview.

The big increase in police and prison jobs is discussed in *Return of the Dangerous Classes* by Gordon, page 38. ". . . society of suspects" is from "A Society of Suspects" by Wisotsky. The big growth of the urine-testing industry is from "The Business of Drug Testing" by Zimmer and Jacobs. That Washington paid $63 million to snitches is from "Rising Use of Police 'Snitches' Questioned" by Mark Curriden, *Atlanta Constitution*, March 21, 1991. The comparison to the budget for the OMB is from *World Almanac and Book of Facts 1991*, page 102. The tale of the multimillionaire snitch is from "Rising Use of Police 'Snitches' Questioned" by Curriden. "That's the sad part of protecting society . . ." is from "Shadow World of Snitches" by Sydney Freedberg and Dexter Filkins, *Miami Herald*, July 21, 1991. "We do not test people . . ." and the write up about Drug Alert are in *Time*, September 10, 1990.

The story about the newspaper editors discussing an end to "polishing our halo of detachment" is from "Examining the Role of the Press" by Debra Gersh, *Editor & Publisher*, October 20, 1990.

"It seems to me it is very likely that one can say . . ." is from "People Are Resisting: An Interview With William Bennett," *U.S. News & World Report*, February 19, 1990. ". . . the healing has started and will continue . . ." is from *Newsweek*, March 12, 1990. "I think this vindicates the notion that counterpressure . . ." is from "Good News in the Drug War: Prices Up, Purity Down," *Newsweek*, July 2, 1990. ". . . we're on the road to victory . . ." *Time*, December 3, 1990. ". . . beyond my wildest dreams" is from *Time*, November 19, 1990. "I'm leaving. You've been great. It's been great. We've been great . . ." is from the interview with Joe McHugh. ". . . run out of gas" is from "Bennett to Resign as Chief of US Anti-Drug Effort" by Neil Lewis, *New York Times*, November 7,

1990. ". . . as a psychiatrist" is from an interview with Herbert Kleber on September 1, 1994. The quantification of Bennett's financial situation was laid out in "Bennett Walks Away from Republican Committee Job" by Richard Benedetto, *USA Today,* December 13, 1990. The vituperative exchange between Rep. Charles Rangel and Bennett, from "a colossal failure" to "Rangel is a gasbag," is from *Time,* November 19, 1990. "I didn't take a vow of poverty . . ." is from "Bennett Walks Away from Republican Committee Job" by Benedetto.

In the statistics at the end of the chapter, the total number of Americans arrested and those arrested for marijuana possession are from "A Society of Suspects" by Wisotsky.

The change in percentage of students saying cocaine is easy to obtain is from "Hawks Ascendant: The Punitive Trend in Drug Policy" by Peter Reuter of the RAND Corp., 1992, quoting the *Monitoring the Future* study.

The figures comparing spending on education and prisons is from "Trading Textbooks for Prison Cells" by William J. Chambliss, National Center on Institutions and Alternatives, June 1991.

21. APOLOGIES TO NONE

"If you want to use that 'War on Drugs' analogy . . ." is from a telephone interview with Thomas Lorenzi, then president of the National Association of Criminal Defense Lawyers, on October 5, 1993.

The entire story of Randy Brown's ordeal is from "Phone Call, Legal Chemicals Begin Man's Two-Year Battle" by Gary Webb, *San Jose Mercury News,* August 29, 1993.

That none of Bob Martinez's eleven senior aides had any Drug War experience is from "The Bad News Drug Czar," *U.S. News & World Report,* February 10, 1991.

The story of Michael Quinlan reading the news from Philadelphia and his troubles with Deputy Attorney General Don Aire are from the interview with Quinlan.

The story of Reggie Walton's firing is from the interview with Walton.

The story of the Lopeses losing their Maui home is from "Police Profit by Seizing Homes of Innocent" by Andrew Schneider and Mary Pat Flaherty, *Pittsburgh Press*'s "Presumed Guilty" series, August 11–16, 1991.

The results of the oncologists survey were written up as "Marijuana as Antiemetic Medicine: A Survey of Oncologists' Experiences and Attitudes" by Richard Doblin and Mark A. R. Kleiman. "If it's perceived that the Public Health Service is going around giving marijuana to folks . . ." is from "HHS Marijuana Program to Be Phased Out" by Michael Isikoff, *Washington Post,* June 22, 1991. "We've had a lot of dying people calling and asking us for help . . ." is from "Compassionate Marijuana Use" by Michael Isikoff, *Washington Post,* November 12, 1991. "The government has a responsibility to see to it people receive appropriate treatment . . ." is from an interview with Mark Barnes on January 12, 1993.

The number of drug-related AIDS cases is from "Drug Czar Wears Blinders When It Comes to Needle Exchange," *Drug Policy Letter,* Fall 1992. The story of New Haven's needle-exchange program, including all the statistics therein, is from an interview with Edward Kaplan, the Yale mathematician evaluating the program, on January 11, 1993. That discussion of needle exchange was forbidden in Martinez's ONDCP is from an interview with Bonnie Wilford, who worked there, on May 5, 1994. "We [cannot] allow our concern for AIDS . . ." is from

"Drug Czar Wears Blinders . . ." Sen. Jesse Helms's last-minute attempt to withhold HHS funding from needle-exchanging states was recounted during an interview with Ron Weich, aide to Sen. Ted Kennedy, on January 8, 1993. "Why don't we just hand out needles tipped with strychnine . . ." is from an interview with Tim Westmoreland, January 11, 1993.

Willie Jones's story is told in "Drug Agents More Likely to Stop Minorities" by Andrew Schneider and Mary Pat Flaherty, *Pittsburgh Press*'s "Presumed Guilty" series, August 11–16, 1991. That most currency is tainted with cocaine was exposed in "Drugs Contaminate Nearly All the Money in America" by Schneider and Flaherty, *Pittsburgh Press*'s "Presumed Guilty" series.

Thomas Kline's story is from an interview with Kline on September 13, 1994, "Intelligent Alternative to Alcohol" by Thomas Kline, Spokane *Spokesman Review*, August 27, 1991, and "US Needs to Rethink Laws on Marijuana" by Thomas Kline, *Coeur d'Alene Press*, October 18, 1991. The U.S. Supreme Court case allowing police to search garbage without a warrant was *United States v. Greenwood* 486 US 35 (1988). The account of the search itself and what it found is detailed in Memorandum Opinion and Order in re: Appeal from Magistrate's Decision on Motion to Suppress, *State of Idaho v. Thomas Kline*, August 11, 1993. "It's not that often that we see people . . ." is from a telephone interview with Agent Wayne Longo of the Idaho Department of Law Enforcement on November 21, 1991.

Again, Donny Clark's story comes from the following sources: interviews with Tom Ostrander, Donny Clark's attorney, on November 20, 1991, and April 7, 1995; interview with U.S. Attorney Walter Terry Furr on December 3, 1991; Judgment in a Criminal Case, *United States v. Donald Clark, November* 4, 1991; Indictment — *United States of America v.* [28 defendants], February 27, 1991. "The intent is to get the bad guys off the street . . ." is from a telephone interview with Justice Department spokesman Doug Tillet on November 21, 1991.

The entire story of Donald Scott's killing and the suspicions of the Ventura County District Attorney are from "Report on the Death of Donald Scott," Michael D. Bradbury, District Attorney, Office of the District Attorney, County of Ventura, State of California, March 30, 1993.

In the statistics at chapter's end, all figures regarding forfeiture, seizure, and the racial element of warrantless searches of travelers are from the "Presumed Guilty" series by Schneider and Flaherty in the *Pittsburgh Press*, August 11–16, 1991.

The figures comparing the teacher-pupil ratio with the guard-prisoner ratio are from "Hostage to the Drug War" by Powell and Hershenov.

22. JUST SAY NO

The two quotes in the epigraph are from "A Call to Reject the Federal Weed and Seed Program in Los Angeles," the Urban Strategies Group of the Labor/Community Strategy Center, 1993.

"America has more black men in prison than in college . . ." is from "Young Black Men in the Criminal Justice System" by Marc Mauer, The Sentencing Project, 1990. "Urban blacks are being detained in numbers far exceeding . . ." is from "Drug War Focused on Blacks" by Sam Vincent Meddis and Mike Snider, *USA Today*, December 20, 1990. The counties' call for an end to the Drug War was made in "The American County Platform and Resolutions 1992–1993," National Association of Counties. "I arraign approximately one third of the felony cases in New York . . ." is from "Racism and Criminal Justice" by Alan Ellis, *Los Angeles Daily Journal*, January 21, 1992. The story of Judge Norman Lanford is from "Harris Grand Jury Questions Drug Prosecutions" by Mark Ballard, *Texas Lawyer*, June 15, 1992.

The story of Kurt Schmoke's reelection is from the telephone interview with him on June 13, 1994.

"We decided we aren't sending any more young black men to prison . . ." is from the interviews with Reggie Walton.

The story of James Gray's change of heart and "we couldn't design a system worse than the one we've got . . ." are from interviews with him by telephone on October 2, 1992, and in person at the Drug Policy Foundation Conference in Washington, D.C., in November 1992. "Clearly, prohibition isn't working . . ." is from "Bush's War on Drugs Is a Bust," *Orange County Register*, as reprinted in *The Missoulian*, September 13, 1992. "Mr. Bush has poured more and more money into tactics . . ." is from "Some Think the 'War on Drugs' Is Being Waged on the Wrong Front" by Joseph Treaster, *New York Times*, July 28, 1992.

The experiences and thoughts of Joe Hicks are from an interview with him on December 8, 1993. That Weed & Seed contained a lot of previously committed money was reported in "Critics Question Bush's Urban Bottom Line" by Michael Isikoff, *Washington Post*, May 21, 1992. "Am I a weed?" is from the interview with Hicks. "Two and a half years ago I was what the Justice Department would have labeled a weed . . ." is from "Weed & Seed Project Assailed at LA Meeting" by Carla Rivera, *Los Angeles Times*, October 20, 1992. "[It] has been imposed on communities of color . . ." and "I'll recommend to the White House we spend the money . . ." are from "Panel Turns Down Riot Aid Proposal" by Carla Rivera, *Los Angeles Times*, November 13, 1992. "You can't buy this meal a la carte . . ." is from "Agreement Reached on Inner-City Aid Package" by John Schwada, *Los Angeles Times*, November 21, 1992. ". . . take the money and run . . ." is from "Take the Money and Run With It," *Los Angeles Times*, November 19, 1992. "The heavy-handed approach . . ." is from "Agreement Reached on Inner-City Aid Package." The name change from Weed & Seed to CPR is from a telephone interview with then-U.S. Attorney Terree Bowers on December 9, 1993.

EPILOGUE: NIGHT AND DAY

"The definition of insanity . . ." is from "Clinton Sets Breakneck Pace on West Coast," *Christian Science Monitor*, July 27, 1992.

The 350,000 daily cocaine users comes from "The Crack Cocaine Epidemic: Health Consequences and Treatment," General Accounting Office #HRD-91-55FS, January 1991, page 11. The full title of Biden's report was "The President's Drug Strategy: Has It Worked?" Prepared by the Majority Staffs of the Senate Judiciary Committee and the International Narcotics Control Caucus, September 1992.

The undiminished zeal of the CAMP warriors is from the Camarda interview and "Clinton and Drugs: Drug War Without End" by Alexander Cockburn, *The Nation*, November 15, 1993. ". . . this whole thing turns around" is from *Newsbriefs*, National Drug Strategy Network, January 1993. The story of the scared-to-death seventy-five-year-old pastor is from "What Killed Rev. Williams? And Is It Time to Declare Peace?" *Drug Policy Letter,* July/August 1994. Clinton's offer of 140,000 treatment slots is from *National Drug Control Strategy* 1994, The White House, pages 2 and 25. ". . . one of the difficult choices we must face to fight violence" and other quotes from the Joycelyn Elders speech to the National Press Club and Dee Dee Myers's response are from "Legalizing Drugs Would Reduce Crime Rate: Elders" by Christopher Connell, Associated Press, December 7, 1993. That it was Eric Sterling who asked the fateful question is from the interviews with Sterling. A lengthy telling of the Kevin Elders story appears as "Ten Years for a Teaspoon" by Cynthia Cotts, in *Drug Policy Letter,* Fall 1994. ". . . realized I probably made a more honest, aboveboard statement . . ." is from "Elders Again Calls for Drug-Legalization Study," Reuters, January 15, 1994. Rep. Newt Gingrich's allegations regarding White House "counterculture people" was reported in "Gingrich Spells Out His Views: On the Attack, Strong Words for Clintons, U.N.," *Bergen Record,* December 5, 1994. "I would call this the first personnel decision . . ." is from "Clinton Fires Surgeon General Over New Flap" by Paul Richter, *Los Angeles Times,* December 10, 1994. The refusal to reopen the Compassionate IND marijuana program was reported as "Clinton Administration Upholds Medicinal Marijuana Ban," in *NORML News,* July 21, 1994. Janet Reno touted her Weed & Seed programs and boasted of arrest figures during a Press Briefing by Attorney General Janet Reno, Secretary of HUD Henry Cisneros, ONDCP director Lee Brown, and Assistant Secretary of the Treasury Ron Noble, The Briefing Room, The White House, March 29, 1994, a transcript of which was made available electronically by the White House.

The passing of the one-million-prisoner mark was confirmed in "State and Federal Prison Population Tops One Million," Department of Justice release, October 27, 1994.

Bibliography

Ambrose, Stephen E. *Nixon: The Triumph of a Politician*, Vol. two. Simon & Schuster, 1989.

Anderson, Patrick. *High in America: The True Story Behind NORML and the Politics of Marijuana*. Viking Press, 1981.

Association of the Bar of the City of New York. *The Nation's Toughest Drug Law: Evaluating the New York Experience*. Drug Abuse Council, 1977.

Barlett, Donald L., and Steele, James B. *America: What Went Wrong?* Philadelphia Inquirer (Philadelphia) and Andrews & McMeel (Kansas City), 1992.

Bennett, James, and DiLorenzo, Thomas J. *Official Lies: How Washington Misleads Us*. Groom Books (Alexandria, VA), 1992.

Bennett, William J. *The De-Valuing of America: The Fight for Our Culture and Our Children*. Simon & Schuster, 1992.

Bennett, William J. *The Book of Virtues*. Simon & Schuster, 1993.

Bonnie, Richard J., and Whitebread, Charles H., II. *The Marihuana Conviction: A History of Marihuana Prohibition in the United States*. University of Virginia Press, 1974.

Bovard, James. *Lost Rights: The Destruction of American Liberty*. St. Martin's Press, 1994.

Brecher, Edward M. *Licit and Illicit Drugs*. Little, Brown & Co., 1972.

Califano, Joseph A. *Governing America: An Insider's Report from the White House and the Cabinet*. Simon & Schuster, 1981.

Clark, Ramsey. *Crime in America*. Simon & Schuster, 1970.

Crawford, Alan. *Thunder on the Right: The "New Right" and the Politics of Resentment*. Pantheon, 1980.

Currie, Elliott. *Reckoning: Drugs, the Cities, and the American Fugure*. Hill and Wang, 1993.

Davis, Mike. *City of Quartz: Excavating the Future in Los Angeles*. Vintage, 1992.

Drug Abuse Council. *The Facts About Drug Use*. Macmillan, 1980.

Duffy, Michael, and Goodgame, Dan. *Marching in Place: The Status Quo Presidency of George Bush*. Simon & Schuster, 1992.

Duke, Steven B., and Gross, Albert C. *America's Longest War*. G. P. Putnam's Sons, 1993.

Edsall, Thomas B. and Mary. *Chain Reaction*. W. W. Norton, 1991.

Epstein, Edward Jay. *Agency of Fear*. G. P. Putnam's Sons, 1977.

Esterhas, Joe. *Nark!* Straight Arrow Books (San Francisco), 1974.

Faludi, Susan. *Backlash: The Undeclared War on American Women*. Crown, 1991.

Finlator, John. *The Drugged Nation: A "Narc's" Story.* Simon & Schuster, 1973.

Gordon, Diana R. *The Return of the Dangerous Classes: Drug Prohibition and Policy Politics*. Norton, 1994.

Gould, Lewis L. *1968: The Election That Changed America*. Ivan R. Dee (Chicago), 1983.

Hacker, Andrew. *Two Nations: Black and White, Separate, Hostile, Unequal*. Ballantine, 1992.

Haldeman, H. R. *The Haldeman Diaries: Inside the Nixon White House*. G. P. Putnam's Sons, 1994.

Helmer, John. *Drugs and Minority Oppression*. Seabury Press, 1975.

Herer, Jack. *The Emperor Wears No Clothes*. Queen of Clubs Publishing Co. (Seattle), 1985.

Hoffman, Abbie. *Steal This Urine Test: Fighting Drug Hysteria in America*. Viking, 1987.

Inciardi, James A. *The War on Drugs: Heroin, Cocaine, Crime and Public Policy*. Mayfield Publishing Co. (Palo Alto), 1986.

Johns, Christina Jacqueline. *Power, Ideology and the War on Drugs: Nothing Succeeds Like Failure*. Praeger, 1992.

Johnson, Bruce D.; Goldstein, Paul J.; Preble, Edward; Schmeidler, James; Lipton, Douglas S.; Spunt, Barry; and Miller, Thomas. *Taking Care of Business: The Economics of Crime by Heroin Abusers*, Lexington Books (Lexington, MA), 1985.

Johnston, Lloyd. *Drugs and American Youth*. Institute for Social Research (Ann Arbor, MI), 1973.

Johnston, Lloyd; O'Malley, Patrick; and Bachman, Jerald. *National Survey Results on Drug Use from the Monitoring the Future Study,* 1975 to 1992. U.S. Department of Health and Human Services, Public Health Service, 1993.

Kaplan, John. *Marijuana, the New Prohibition*. World Publishing Co., 1970 (Meridian paperback edition).

Katz, Michael B. *The Undeserving Poor: From the War on Poverty to the War on Welfare*. Pantheon, 1989.

Katzenbach, Nicholas. *The Challenge of Crime in a Free Society*. President's Commission on Law Enforcement and the Administration of Justice, U.S. Government Printing Office, Washington, D.C., 1967.

Kelley, Kitty. *Nancy Reagan: The Unauthorized Biography.* Simon & Schuster, 1991.

Kleiman, Mark. *Against Excess*. Basic Books, 1992.

Krogh, Egil. *The Day Elvis Met Nixon*. Pajama Press, 1994.

Laurie, Peter. *Drugs*. Penguin (Middlesex, England), 1967.

Liddy, G. Gordon. *Will*. St. Martin's Press, 1980.

Magruder, Jeb Stuart. *An American Life*. Atheneum, 1974.

Mann, Peggy. *Marijuana Alert: The Health Hazards, What Can Be Done*. McGraw-Hill, 1985.

Mannatt, Marsha. *Parents, Peers & Pot*. National Institute on Drug Abuse (Rockville, MD), 1979.

Mason, Todd. *Perot: An Unauthorized Biography*. Dow Jones Irwin, 1990.

Mathews, Arthur F.; Weissman, Andrew B. and Sturc, John H. *Civil RICO Litigation*, 2d ed., vol. 1. Prentice Hall Law & Business, 1992.

Mayer, Jane, and McManus, Doyle. *Landslide: The Unmaking of the President 1984–1988*. Houghton Mifflin, 1988.

McGinnis, Joe. *The Selling of the President 1968*. Trident Press, 1969.

Moore, Mark Harrison. *Buy and Bust*. D.C. Heath & Co., 1977.

Muir, William Ker, Jr. *The Bully Pulpit: The Presidential Leadership of Ronald Reagan*. ICS Press (San Francisco), 1992.

Musto, David. *The American Disease*. Oxford University Press, 1973, 1987.

Nahas, Gabriel. *Keep Off the Grass*. Reader's Digest Press, 1976.

Nathan, Richard P. *The Plot That Failed*. John Wiley & Sons, 1975.

Nathan, Richard P., and Doolittle, Fred C. *Reagan and the States*. Princeton University Press, 1987.

Noonan, Peggy. *What I Saw at the Revolution: A Political Life in the Reagan Era*. Ballantine Books, 1990.

North, Douglass C., and Miller, Roger Leroy. *Abortion, Baseball & Weed: Economic Issues of Our Times*. Harper & Row, 1971.

Phillips, Kevin P. *The Emerging Republican Majority*. Arlington House (New Rochelle, NY), 1969.

Phillips, Kevin. *The Politics of Rich and Poor: Wealth and the American Electorate in the Reagan Aftermath*. HarperCollins, 1991.

Podgor, Ellen S. *White Collar Crime*. Nutshell Series. West Publishing (St. Paul), 1993, pp. 154–173.

Reeves, Jimmie L., and Campbell, Richard. *Cracked Coverage: Television News, the Anti-Cocaine Crusade, and the Reagan Legacy*. Duke University Press, 1994.

Reuter, Peter; Crawford, Gordon; and Cave, Jonathan. *Sealing the Borders: The Effects of Increased Military Participation in Drug Interdiction*. RAND Corp., 1988.

Safire, William. *Before the Fall*. Doubleday, 1975.

Sharp, Elaine B. *The Dilemma of Drug Policy in the United States*. HarperCollins College Publishers, 1994.

Shoemaker, Pamela J. *Communication Campaigns About Drugs: Government, Media, and the Public*. Lawrence Erlbaum Associates (Hillsdale, NJ), 1989.

Smith, David B. *Prosecution and Defense of Forfeiture Cases.* Matthew Bender, 1986–1993.

Smith, David, and Reed, Terrance. *Civil RICO.* Matthew Bender Press, 1994.

Stockman, David A. *The Triumph of Politics: Why the Reagan Revolution Failed.* Harper & Row, 1986.

Thompson, Hunter. *Fear and Loathing in Las Vegas.* Random House, 1971.

Trebach, Arnold S. *Why We Are Losing the Great Drug War and Radical Proposals That Could Make America Safe Again.* Macmillan, 1987.

Tully, Andrew. *The Secret War Against Dope.* Coward, McCann & Geoghegan, 1973.

Weil, Andrew, and Rosen, Winifred. *From Chocolate to Morphine.* Houghton Mifflin, 1983.

Wells, Tim, and Triplett, William. *Drug Wars: An Oral History From the Trenches.* William Morrow, 1992.

White, Theodore. *The Making of the President, 1968.* Atheneum, 1969.

Wistosky, Steven. *Beyond the War on Drugs.* Prometheus Books (Buffalo, NY), 1990.

York, Phyllis and David, and Wachtel, Ted. *Toughlove.* Doubleday, 1982.

(no author) *What Everyone Needs to Know About Drugs.* U.S. News & World Report, Washington, D.C., 1970.

(no author) *Parents, Peers & Pot: An Update.* Health Communications Inc., 1982.

(no author) *Special Report to the Congress: Mandatory Minimum Penalties in the Federal Criminal Justice System.* United States Sentencing Commission, August 1991.

(no author) *Data from Drug Abuse Warning Network: Annual Data 1989,* Series 1, No. 9. National Institute on Drug Abuse, 1990.

(no author) *Public Papers of the Presidents of the United States, Ronald Reagan, January 1 to July 31, 1982.* Office of Federal Register, National Archives and Record Service, 1983.

(no author) *Marihuana: A Signal of Misunderstanding.* National Commission on Marihuana and Drug Abuse, March 22, 1972.

Acknowledgments

MUCH AS I'D LIKE TO CLAIM CREDIT for this whole effort, I had many kinds of help. The first was financial, without which this project wouldn't have gotten started. The Fund for Constitutional Government, the Share-It-Now Foundation, Steven Markoff, Dr. Henry Jarecki, Richard Dennis, and Sherwood Shafer all wrote generous checks to keep me going while writing the proposal for this book. The Fund for Investigative Journalism helped finance the book research itself. Mead Data Central Inc. donated the use of its NEXIS/LEXIS service, which was invaluable. All have my deepest gratitude.

More than 175 people were interviewed for this book, many several times. All were patient and generous with their time, and with the sole exception of William Bennett, every important source I asked for an interview complied. Obviously, this book could not have been completed without them.

A few people deserve particular mention for assistance above and beyond the call: Marilyn Marbrook; Michael Aldrich; Allan St. Pierre; the remarkable staffs of the Nixon, Carter, and Reagan Presidential Libraries; Kevin Zeese; Mort Goren; Eric Sterling; the staffs of National Families in Action and PRIDE; the staff of Border's Books on L Street in Washington, D.C.; Linda Hall; and the faceless heroes who set up the on-line document retrieval service in the Clinton White House. Gwenyth Mapes helped with questions of biblical scholarship and Tim Bierman with matters of rock and roll.

Though you wouldn't know it from listening to the pinched mainstream drug "debate," lots of excellent thinking about drug policy is being done by some brilliant writers. A few whose writing particularly influenced me are: Craig Reinarman, Harry Levine, Jimmie L. Reeves, Richard Campbell, Steven Wisotsky, Lynn Zimmer, John Morgan, Diana Gordon, and Mike Davis.

Throughout the writing, I had the help of many fine readers who were unsparing in their criticism and suggestions. Bruce Jennings, Peter Stark, Bryan DiSalvatore, Secky Fascione, Cheri Lucas Jennings, Jim Fleischmann, Eric Johnson, Leonard Robinson, Tracy Thompson, Stephen Hering, Nathan McCall, and Tim Smith all helped tremendously. My brother, Andy Baum, dissected the manuscript with the fine eye of both a lawyer and a wordsmith and prevented me from embarrassing myself any number of times. The membership and staff of the National Writers Union (UAW/AFL-CIO) inspired and emboldened me throughout.

Roger Donald, my editor at Little, Brown and Company, illuminated the path from stack o' facts to coherent book. For a first-timer, I couldn't have been in better hands. The copyediting skills of Faith Hanson and Peggy Freudenthal were stunning. And blessings on the head of my agent, Kristine Dahl, who sold Roger on the idea to begin with.

For the past five years I've had the privilege of living alongside Bill Chaloupka, a professor of political science and environmental studies at the University of Montana. During innumerable dinners, evenings watching TV, and vituperative shouting matches, Bill has little by little provided me a splendid political education. What powers of political observation I possess, particularly regarding imagery and language, I owe largely to Bill.

Nobody, however, put more into this book than my wife, Margaret, who in addition to being my sweetheart, hunting buddy, bass player, teacher, and best friend, has been my reporting and writing partner for the past eight years. Margaret debriefed me after interviews. She spurred me to read more widely than I might have otherwise. She read and edited four drafts *before* we handed it in and two more thereafter. Often she had more energy for the project than I and was not afraid to perform a radical egoectomy on me if that's what it took to get me off my high horse and see reason. A genius at wringing exactly the proper meaning from a sentence, it was Margaret who made my unruly prose knuckle down and do its work. And she did all this while putting her own writing aside to do heroic bouts of child care. My name is on the cover, but this book is equally Margaret's.

Index